Jackson West
Lon Coley

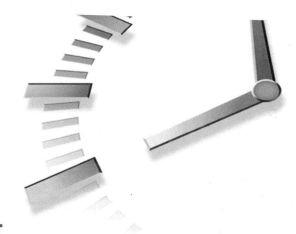

SAMS
Teach Yourself

Macromedia
Fireworks MX

in **24** Hours

SAMS

201 West 103rd Street, Indianapolis, Indiana 46290 USA

Sams Teach Yourself Macromedia Fireworks MX in 24 Hours

Copyright © 2003 by Sams Publishing

International Standard Book Number: 0-672-32405-9

Library of Congress Catalog Card Number: 2002107938

Printed in the United States of America

First Printing: December 2002

05   04   03   02   4   3   2   1

Trademarks

Warning and Disclaimer

ACQUISITIONS EDITOR
Betsy Brown

DEVELOPMENT EDITOR
Jonathan Steever

MANAGING EDITOR
Charlotte Clapp

PROJECT EDITOR
Matthew Purcell

COPY EDITOR
Publication Services, Inc.

INDEXER
Publication Services, Inc.

PROOFREADER
Publication Services, Inc.

TECHNICAL EDITOR
Robyn Ness

TEAM COORDINATOR
Amy Patton

MULTIMEDIA DEVELOPER
Dan Scherf

INTERIOR DESIGNER
Gary Adair

COVER DESIGNER
Alan Clements

PAGE LAYOUT
Publication Services, Inc.

GRAPHICS
Steve Adams
Tammy Graham
Oliver Jackson
Laura Robbins

Contents at a Glance

Contents

About the Authors

JACKSON WEST has loved computers since he was a child and has spent the majority of his life figuring out how to make them sing, dance, and look pretty. Growing up in Seattle, he was exposed to the technological revolution of the last century. Attending the Film and Television Production program at New York University's Tisch School of the Arts exposed him to the world of sight and sound, and he has had digital and analog equipment wired together ever since.

Jackson now lives in the San Francisco Bay Area, where he consults on Web programming, graphics, and multimedia applications. He has spent time at a number of top software companies, including Microsoft, Macromedia, and Sonic Solutions. He has written for CNET, McGraw-Hill, and Sams Publishing. He is always looking for ways to be cheaper and faster.

You can visit Jackson on the Web at `http://www.jacksonwest.com/`, where you can find examples of his goofy creative sensibility and sense of joy with multimedia doohickeys like "The Funky Engineer," "Random Art Generator," and "Political Action Committee Man." Jackson is a polished speaker and would be glad to speak at your next conference. Feel free to email him at `jacksonwest@onebox.com`.

Contributing Author

LON COLEY is an IT professional specializing in office and Internet applications. An experienced teacher and trainer, Lon writes and develops dedicated customized training courses for business and education. These courses cover the whole spectrum of her expertise and are always prepared with the individual client in mind. As a firm believer that anyone can work successfully with computers, given the right tools and training, Lon often works with companies and colleges who want to develop their in-house IT skills but want an expert to call on when they are struggling. She serves as a designer, trainer, and consultant through her company, Ariadne Web Design.

Dedication

This book is dedicated to my grandmothers, Janet West and Vera Deaton.
Their pioneering spirits have taught me to always keep exploring.

Acknowledgments

I'd like to take this time to acknowledge the rest of my family and friends, without whom none of this would happen. First, my mother and father, who spent their 1983 tax return on our family's first computer, an 8mhz Sanyo with 256kb of Ram and a monochrome monitor. They also showed me that it was possible to make a good living being a geek. I can't forget my brother Christopher, a talented writer and bon vivant who shared my love for good food and loud music. I will always miss him.

Robby Fahey, my live-in muse, keeps me from playing video games all day, so that I can pay my bills and continue to afford vinyl LPs. Without her and our lovely cat, Ally, the home office would be a lonely place indeed.

Garfield High School was where I got my first taste of publishing as the production coordinator for *The Messenger*. Seth Kolloen, Malia McCarthy, and Ethan Fineout endured a lot with me as the production staff, and I'm lucky to still count them as good friends (no thanks to the antiquated offset presses). Tomas Clarke, who let me in on the creative possibilities of computers, was our editor-in-chief. Pauls Toutonghi and Thor Jensen helped convince me that an artistic vocation was a realistic dream as a writer and a visual artist, respectively.

Further, I would like to acknowledge Jennifer Coleman, Timothy Jurgensen, Melissa Mecca, Raiko Alexiev, Hank Thomas, Bayete Ross-Smith, and Marcelo Perez for helping me feel at home in the Bay Area. Fellow digerati, they're a constant source of information and inspiration. Nothing makes me happier than cooking for my friends and sharing a few beers on a warm California day.

Finally, I would like to thank Macromedia for writing great software that lets me sit at home in my bathrobe and create beautiful illustrations, animations, graphics, and layouts like a real professional.

We Want to Hear from You!

As the reader of this book, *you* are our most important critic and commentator. We value your opinion and want to know what we're doing right, what we could do better, what areas you'd like to see us publish in, and any other words of wisdom you're willing to pass our way.

You can email or write me directly to let me know what you did or didn't like about this book—as well as what we can do to make our books stronger.

Please note that I cannot help you with technical problems related to the topic of this book, and that due to the high volume of mail I receive, I might not be able to reply to every message.

When you write, please be sure to include this book's title and author as well as your name and phone or email address. I will carefully review your comments and share them with the author and editors who worked on the book.

E-mail: graphics@samspublishing.com

Mail: Mark Taber
           Associate Publisher
           Sams Publishing
           201 West 103rd Street
           Indianapolis, IN 46290 USA

Reader Services

For more information about this book or others from Sams Publishing, visit our Web site at www.samspublishing.com. Type the ISBN (excluding hyphens) or the title of the book in the Search box to find the book you're looking for.

Introduction

Welcome to *Sams Teach Yourself Macromedia Fireworks MX in 24 Hours!* This book will teach you how to use Fireworks MX for graphic design, Web design, animation, and photo editing. It will also teach you how to make Fireworks MX even more powerful by working with other popular applications and creating custom tools to speed up mundane tasks. This is the book for you if you are new to working with digital images or the Fireworks MX application. If you've worked with Fireworks before, this book will help you realize the full potential of Fireworks, with clear language and examples to help you work faster and make your work look better.

You will move step-by-step through the process of creating graphics and Web pages using Fireworks MX and other popular Macromedia applications, such as Dreamweaver MX and Flash MX. Along the way you will learn good habits, tips from the pros, and how to avoid common mistakes. By the end of the book, you should be able to accomplish almost any graphic design task for the Web and should be familiar with the full breadth of Fireworks' tools and options.

Some books may approach Fireworks just as a limited part of the Macromedia Web Design Studio or as a simplified version of Adobe Photoshop. We believe that Fireworks is in fact one of the most powerful Web design tools on the market, and this book will show you how you can create many complex page elements with Fireworks MX, including drop-down menus, Flash animations, and complex interactivity. A special emphasis will be placed on professional graphic design fundamentals, such as color correction; Web design considerations, like usability; and customization tools to speed up your workflow through automation.

This book is intended as a complete course and is broken into 24 one-hour lessons. Each lesson offers instruction on using the application, graphic design, and Web design concepts; useful tips and suggestions; answers to common questions and short quizzes for you to test your new knowledge; and, of course, step-by-step tasks for you to complete. If you don't already own Fireworks MX, you can download a 30-day trial version, which will enable you to complete all the lessons in this book, from Macromedia at
http://www.macromedia.com/software/fireworks/

Who Should Read This Book

Fireworks MX has tools that almost anyone with a computer can find useful. If you're just starting out with digital imaging, this is a good primer, as many of Fireworks' tools can be found in other graphics applications, as well. Maybe you've been asked to work with graphics or Fireworks for the first time, and you just need to get something done quickly. No problem! You can review some of the beginning hours (chapters) and then jump to just what you need to know. For that matter, if you are an experienced graphic and Web designer who is looking to save time and has heard about Fireworks, you will find that almost any tool you need is covered here, along with tips on unleashing the full power of Fireworks for advanced automation, customization, and integration with other applications.

If you've ever needed to edit a digital image or design a Web page, this book is for you. You'll learn everything you need to know to make great-looking Web sites. All you need to know is how to work with Microsoft Windows XP or Macintosh OS X and browse the World Wide Web comfortably. Your computer should have Fireworks MX installed, some kind of connection to the Internet, and a pointer tool, such as a mouse, trackball, or stylus tablet. It is recommended that you have a monitor capable of displaying at 800 × 600 resolution or better.

How This Book Is Organized

The book is divided into seven parts, each focusing on a different group of tasks you can accomplish with Fireworks.

The first part, "Learning the Basics: Image File Fundamentals," will take you through the new MX interface, help you find digital images to work with, and assist you in understanding the different graphics formats.

In the second part, "Bitmap Editing: The Digital Darkroom," you will learn how to create and edit bitmap images, such as photographs, with professional editing techniques, like retouching and compositing.

Part III, "Graphic Design: Working with Art and Text," contains a wealth of techniques for designing with vector graphics and typography.

Part IV, "Creating Animations: The Power of Motion," introduces animation concepts like storyboarding and shows you how to use special tools for adding movement to your graphics. You'll also cover integrating Fireworks MX with Flash MX, Macromedia's popular animation and multimedia tool.

In Part V, "Designing Web Pages: Layout, Interactivity, and Publishing," you will learn how graphics work with HTML code to create Web pages, and you will learn how to use the Fireworks tools that make this easy. You'll also learn how to use Fireworks MX and Dreamweaver MX together, including the new Roundtrip HTML editing features.

Part VI, "Speed Up Your Workflow: Automation and Customization," contains lots of information on how to save time and work with a team on large projects.

Finally, in Part VII, "Fireworks and Friends: Working with Other Applications," you complete your course of Fireworks by learning how to work with a number of different programs that you might use as part of your work.

If you have an image file you need to get on the Web right now, you can skip to Hour 3, "Choosing Optimization Settings and Exporting Graphics." If you're a Dreamweaver MX user, you may want to skip straight to Hour 17, "Working with Dreamweaver MX." If you're experienced with JavaScript and Flash MX, take a look at Hour 20, "Harnessing the Power of Macromedia Extensions"; you'll see what we mean by "the power of Fireworks MX"!

Certain hours introduce digital imaging techniques and explain tools, concepts, and best practices for working in a professional environment. Among them is Hour 6, "Improving Photos," which discusses professional color-correction and retouching skills. Hour 10, "Tricks of the Trade," lets you in on how graphic designers use special tools to create stunning effects. Hour 24, "Microsoft Office," shows you how to use Fireworks with charts from Excel to create data-driven graphics, how to export and import graphics to and from Word, how to improve your PowerPoint graphics, and how to use Fireworks with FrontPage.

Each hour also contains a Q&A section, a few quiz questions, and optional exercises. Don't worry—these aren't tests! They should help you understand the content by anticipating your questions and reviewing what should be second nature. You should be able to answer the quiz questions in under a minute if you've worked through the entire hour; answers are provided.

Think about it: For the cost of this book and a little of your time, you can become as proficient in Fireworks as you need to be. The return on your investment can be measured in spare time. So grab a cup of coffee, stretch your mouse-clicking finger, and get ready to learn how easy it can be to create graphics for the Web through Fireworks MX.

What's on the Web Site?

Provided with the step-by-step tasks in this book are example files that contain graphics and photographs necessary to complete each exercise. These files are available from the Sams Web site at `http://www.samspublishing.com`. Simply enter the ISBN number for this book, `0672324059`, in the Search field and then click the resulting link for the book. When the book's main page loads, click the link titled `Related Materials`. You may download all the sample files for the book or simply download the files hour by hour.

Conventions Used in This Book

This book uses the following conventions:

Text and numerical values that you type appear in **boldface** font. If they can be chosen from a menu or such devices as on-screen sliders, they are in regular font.

File and folder names that you see on-screen appear in `monospace type`, as do snippets of computer code.

A **Note** presents interesting information related to the discussion.

A **Tip** offers advice or shows you an easier way to do something.

A **Caution** alerts you to a possible problem and gives you advice on how to avoid it.

Task:

The **Task** icon indicates the beginning of a task.

PART I

Learning the Basics: Image File Fundamentals

Hour

HOUR 1

Getting to Know the Fireworks MX Interface

One of the major improvements to Fireworks is the new MX interface. Macromedia has added support in other Web Design Studio MX titles for editing graphics with Fireworks, making it even easier to work with other applications. And because all the MX applications from Macromedia look almost identical, once you've learned one, it will be much easier to pick up another. Now you can move between Flash MX, FreeHand 10, Dreamweaver MX, ColdFusion MX, and Fireworks MX without missing a step!

In this hour you'll take a tour through the new interface. This material will help you get off the ground in Fireworks by explaining the MX interface. Experienced users may want to skip ahead to the "Using the Property Inspector" section, which discusses a tool that has been added to Fireworks to make settings and options for documents and objects just a click away.

In this hour you will

- Familiarize yourself with the Fireworks MX workspace
- Get acquainted with the Tools panel
- Work with the new Property Inspector
- Learn how to customize Fireworks panels
- Explore the help features and tutorials available with Fireworks

Getting Started with Fireworks MX

This section will get you started by introducing you to the Fireworks MX interface and showing you how to open an image so you can begin working. The commands shown will work in both the Microsoft Windows XP edition of Fireworks MX and the Macintosh OS X edition, as well previous versions of both operating systems. Keyboard shortcuts are shown for both editions of Fireworks MX.

Opening Fireworks MX for the First Time

To begin using Fireworks, choose Start from the Windows desktop or press the Applications button on your keyboard. Move your mouse pointer over (mouseover) All Programs, then Macromedia, and finally Macromedia Fireworks MX. The first time Fireworks loads, the screen will look something like Figure 1.1.

FIGURE 1.1

The first time you run Fireworks MX, a Welcome screen will allow you to start a tutorial.

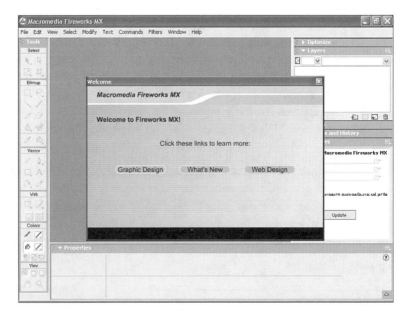

If you are using Macintosh OS X, navigate to your Applications folder by selecting Applications from the Go menu in the Finder or by pressing Option+Command+A. Expand the Macromedia Fireworks MX folder by clicking the arrow to the left. Now double-click Fireworks MX to run Fireworks. Fireworks MX will appear in Mac OS X as it does in Figure 1.2.

Figure 1.2

The same Fireworks Welcome screen appears for users running Fireworks MX for the first time on Macintosh OS X.

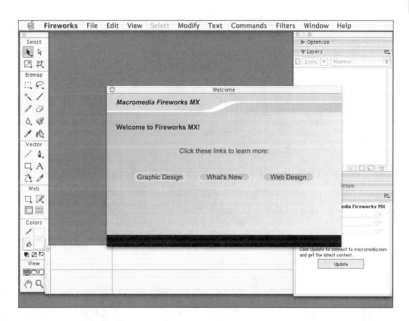

The Welcome screen in the middle will let you start one of the tutorials, *Graphic Design* or *Web Design,* or read about *What's New in Fireworks MX.* If you haven't already taken a look at the tutorials, now may be a good time. Otherwise, you can get started right now by closing the Welcome screen by clicking the red close button on the top right. The components of the workspace are menus for executing commands, panels for working with documents and objects, and a work area for document windows.

On the top is the menu. Below and to the left is the Tools panel. To the right of the Tools panel is a work area. Farther right are the docked panel groups. The Layers and Answers panels are both expanded. Below the docked panels is the Property Inspector panel. The Property Inspector may be familiar to Dreamweaver users. Its options change depending on what you're working on. Right now you haven't started working yet, so it is blank. You'll cover the Property Inspector in more detail in a few moments.

The menu includes the File, Edit, View, Select, Modify, Text, Commands, Filters, Windows, and Help menus. You'll go over each one in more detail. For now, open an image file from your hard drive. Click File, Open, from the drop-down menu. You can also use the keyboard shortcut Ctrl+O. The Open dialog window, shown in Figure 1.3, will appear and will open to your My Pictures folder. If you are using Macintosh OS X, the file will open to your Pictures folder.

FIGURE 1.3
The Open dialog defaults to the My Pictures *directory, allowing you to view thumbnails of your images.*

Double-click the Sample Pictures folder that came with Windows to open it. If you're a Macintosh OS X user, you can find an image in the Desktop Pictures folder under the Library folder on your startup drive. We recommend Snowy Hills from the Nature folder for Macintosh OS X users and Blue Hills for Windows XP users. Select an image by clicking it, and then click Open or press Return. The photo will appear in your workspace, like in Figure 1.4.

FIGURE 1.4
Now you're ready to start working on the photo of your choice.

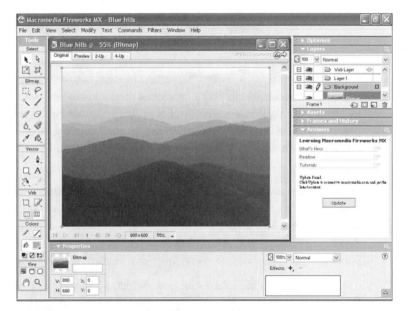

File Menu

The File menu contains the basic file operation commands you're already familiar with, such as Open, Open Recent, Close, Save, Save As, Page Setup, Print, and Quit. The File menu is also where you'll go to Import and Export graphics, Update or Preview HTML, and Batch Process a number of files automatically. (On Mac OS X, Quit can be found under the Fireworks menu.)

Edit Menu

The Edit menu is where you'll find the Cut, Copy, and Paste commands as well as a number of special graphics functions, such as Duplicate, Paste Attributes, and Crop. The Find and Replace function is common to word-processing programs, but Fireworks lets you use Find and Replace for graphics, as well as text. This is also where you can make changes to your Preferences or add and change Fireworks Keyboard Shortcuts. (On Mac OS X, Preferences and Keyboard Shortcuts can be found under the Fireworks menu.)

View Menu

The View options include controls such as Zoom In, Zoom Out, Magnification, and Fit to Window. Other options let you set up Rulers, a Grid, or Guides and allow you to show and hide Fireworks interface elements, such as edges, panels, and the status bar.

Select Menu

With the Select menu options, you can modify what's selected in a number of ways. The Select All command selects all the pixels in a bitmap or all the elements on the Canvas. Feather Selection allows you to create a gradual transition around your selection. Marquee options give you the ultimate control over complex selections, which you can then save using Save Bitmap Selection.

Modify Menu

Modify includes many of the most common image operations. You can resize the Canvas, Transform an object, Arrange it in front of or behind other objects, Group them, and then use Flatten Selection to create a single bitmap image from a number of objects.

Text Menu

The Text menu options include the familiar Font, Size, Style, and Align attributes. Fireworks lets you edit text directly in the image, but if you're a user of a previous version, you may still want to use the Text Editor. You can even check your text with Check Spelling without having to leave Fireworks!

Commands Menu

The Commands menu allows you to Manage Saved Commands, Manage Extensions, and Run Scripts. A number of commands come with Fireworks, including the Data-driven Graphics Wizard and Web commands like Create Shared Palette. You can download Macromedia Extensions or create your own custom scripts and add them to the Commands menu quickly and easily.

Filters Menu

Filters are graphics tools that allow you to make complex changes to an image or selection, such as Blur, Sharpen, or Adjust Color. Included are some of the more creative Eye Candy filters by Alien Skin Software, and more filters can be added if you run out of interesting effects.

Window Menu

The Window menu allows you to access a panel quickly if it has been closed. You can also Cascade or Tile images to make them easier to find and work with, or select an image file to bring to the front.

Help Menu

The Help menu will be there whenever you need it. You can begin one of the tutorials by opening the Welcome screen, browse the *Using Fireworks* PDF, visit the Support Center, or interact with other Fireworks users in the Macromedia Online Forums.

Finding Your Tools

Fireworks MX has both added new tools and reorganized the Tools panel. Tools are grouped according to what they are used for—Select, Bitmap, Vector, Web, Colors, and View. Clicking a tool icon selects that tool. Related tools can be found by clicking the dark gray triangle underneath a tool icon. If you get confused, hold your mouse over a tool icon for a tooltip that names the tool and shows you the keyboard shortcut.

If you are an experienced graphic designer, this list should lead you right to the tools you need to get started working on your own. If you are a new user, some of these terms and tools might seem strange and useless. Don't despair! You will learn to use all of them in due time. For now, it's adequate to acquaint yourself with the names of the tools and be able to find them on the Tools panel.

Select Tools

The Select tools are used to choose objects on the Canvas to work with, including bitmap, vector, text, and group objects. They are shown in Figure 1.5.

FIGURE 1.5

The Select group includes the Pointer, Subselection, Free Transform, and Crop tools.

— Select Group

Pointer and Select Behind

The Pointer tool is used to select objects on the Canvas. The Select Behind tool is used to select an object arranged behind another object. Press V or the number 0 to select the tool and toggle between the Pointer and Select Behind tools.

Subselection

The Subselection tool is used with groups and paths to choose only part of an object. Press A or 1 to choose the Subselection tool.

Scale, Skew, and Distort

The Scale tool is used to change the size or aspect ratio of an object. The Skew tool can shift two sides of an object diagonally. The Distort tool stretches any corner of an object. Select an object and press Q one or more times to select the Scale, Skew, or Distort tools.

Crop, Export Area

The Crop tool allows you to choose an area of the Canvas to preserve and then discards the rest. The Export Area tool allows you to export any portion of the Canvas quickly. Toggle between the Crop and Export Area tools by pressing C.

Bitmap Tools

The Bitmap tools, shown in Figure 1.6, are used for creating or editing bitmap objects.

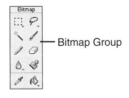

FIGURE 1.6

The Fireworks MX Bitmap tools include the new Darkroom tools, such as Dodge, Burn, Blur, Sharpen, and Smudge.

— Bitmap Group

Marquee and Oval Marquee

The Marquee tool selects a rectangular group of pixels in a bitmap object. The Oval Marquee tool selects an oval or round group of pixels in a bitmap. To toggle between the Marquee tool and the Oval Marquee tool, press M.

Lasso and Polygon Lasso

The Lasso tool allows you to select any group of pixels by drawing a shape around the pixels you would like to select. The Polygon Lasso is similar, except that instead of drawing a single line, you choose only points that are connected by straight lines. To cycle through the Lasso and Polygon Lasso tools, press L.

Magic Wand

The Magic Wand tool selects surrounding pixels with color values similar to the original pixel you selected. This is good for selecting areas of solid or shaded color. To use the Magic Wand tool, press W.

Brush

The Brush is used for painting pixels. All sorts of interesting digital painting effects are possible with the Brush. To start using the Brush tool, press B. If the Pencil tool is selected, press B again.

Pencil

The Pencil is very similar to the Brush, except that it is more often used for editing individual pixels than for broad strokes. To use the Pencil tool, press B. If the Brush tool is selected, press B again.

Eraser

The Eraser tool is used to remove portions of the bitmap. You can switch to the Eraser tool by pressing E.

Blur, Sharpen, Dodge, Burn, and Smudge

These tools are for fine photo retouching. The Blur tool blurs an area of the bitmap. The Sharpen tool does the opposite. Dodge makes a portion of the bitmap lighter, whereas Burn makes it darker. The Smudge tool is used to smudge pixels together like a finger smudging a wet painting. Press R to cycle through these tools.

Rubber Stamp

The Rubber Stamp tool can copy one area of pixels to another. It can remove facial blemishes, repair dusty or scratched images, and do all sorts of other neat things. To choose the Rubber Stamp tool, press S.

Eyedropper

The Eyedropper tool is used to sample a color from the Canvas. Sampled colors can then be used in other parts of the image or added to the Swatch panel. Press I to select the Eyedropper tool.

Paint Bucket and Gradient

The Paint Bucket is used to fill an area of the bitmap with a new color. The Gradient tool is used to create a gradual transition between colors in a filled area. Press G to toggle between the Paint Bucket and Gradient tools.

Vector Tools

The Vector tools are used to create and edit vector objects, such as lines, shapes, and text. The Vector tool group is shown in Figure 1.7.

FIGURE 1.7

The Vector group includes the Path tools and the improved Text tool.

Line

The Line tool is used to create a straight path between two points. Press N to choose the Line tool.

Pen, Vector Path, and Redraw Path

The Pen tool is used to create and edit precise paths. The Vector Path tool is used to draw a path freehand; it determines points and curves automatically. You can use Redraw Path to alter a portion of a vector path. Press P to cycle through these tools.

Rectangle, Rounded Rectangle, Ellipse, and Polygon

These tools create simple filled shapes. The Rectangle tool creates rectangles and squares, Round Rectangle creates rectangles with beveled edges, Ellipse creates circles and ovals, and Polygon creates a regular, multisided shape. Press U to choose a Vector shape tool.

Text

The Text tool allows you to enter text directly on the Canvas. To start typing, press T and click an area of the Canvas.

Freeform, Reshape Path, and Path Scrubber

Freeform allows you to grab points and lines on the path to edit them by eye; you simply click and drag a point to change a section. Reshape Path is another method for altering an area of the path instead of a point or line segment. The Path Scrubber tool gives you access to speed and pressure settings for path strokes, allowing you to vary settings such as stroke width, color density, and edge softness as though you were working with a real brush. Cycle between these tools by pressing O.

Knife

The Knife tool slices a continuous path into segments. The Knife tool is available only when you have selected one or more ungrouped path objects. To choose the Knife tool, press Y when you have a path object selected.

Web Tools

The Web tools, shown in Figure 1.8, are used for laying out HTML tables and adding interactivity to your graphics.

FIGURE **1.8**

The Web group of tools includes the Slice tool for creating HTML table slices on the Web layer.

 — Web Group

Rectangle, Circle, and Polygon Hotspot

These tools allow you to create links within an image or slice. They create an image map that is exported as HTML. To cycle between the Hotspot tools, press J.

Slice and Polygon Slice

Fireworks creates HTML table layouts for your image from slices that you draw with the Slice and Polygon Slice tools. Press K to begin slicing your image.

Hide and Show Slices and Hotspots

The last two Web tools allow you to show or hide your slices and hotspots quickly, making the transition from graphic design to Web design instantaneous. To toggle Slice and Hotspot visibility, press 2.

Color Tools

The Color tools, shown in Figure 1.9, can be used to choose the colors for the bitmap painting tools or to change the stroke and fill settings for vector paths.

FIGURE 1.9

The stroke and fill colors can be set, reset, turned off, or swapped with the tools in the Color group.

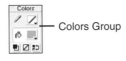 — Colors Group

Stroke Color

When drawing with the Brush, Pencil, or any of the Vector tools, you can specify a stroke color, which is the color of the line the path defines. Click the pencil to choose Stroke color, and then click the triangle underneath the current color to bring up a standard palette or your custom swatches.

Fill Color

When using the paint bucket or drawing with any of the Vector tools, you must specify the color inside the shape in the Fill color palette. You can also change the Stroke and Fill colors with the Eyedropper.

Default Stroke and Fill

Resets the stroke and fill color defaults set in the Fireworks preferences (initially a black stroke and white fill). When a path object or group is selected, you can press D to change the strokes and fills to back the default. Click the button on the Tools panel to reset the stroke and fill when you have no objects selected.

No Stroke or Fill

Select the Stroke or Fill setting and click this button to turn off the stroke or fill color. This will make the Stroke or Fill disappear.

Swap Stroke and Fill Colors

This changes the stroke color to the fill color, and vice versa. Press X to Swap Stroke and Fill Colors when one or more path objects are selected.

View Tools

The View controls allow you to maximize screen space or change the magnification and position of your canvas in the workspace. They are shown in Figure 1.10.

FIGURE 1.10
*The View tools include
the Screen Mode,
Hand, and Zoom tools.*

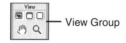 — View Group

Standard Screen, Full Screen with Menus, and Full Screen Mode

These modes allow you to maximize your workspace. The default is Standard Screen, which displays the Canvas in its own window and displays the Menu at the top. Full Screen with Menus removes a good portion of the Canvas window, freeing up more space for working on the image. Full Screen mode removes everything but the panels, for maximum workspace. Press F to cycle through the different Modes.

Hand

The Hand tool is used to navigate an image that may be larger than the screen or Canvas window. By clicking and dragging, you can move the image around as though it were a slide under a microscope. Press H to select the Hand tool.

Zoom

The Zoom tool is pretty straightforward. Press Z to activate the Zoom tool. Click an area of the Canvas to Zoom in.

Task: Navigate an Image with the View Tools

▼TASK

Okay, now that you have an image open in your workspace and an idea of where to find your tools, you can begin with some basic image-navigation techniques. As you work on an image, you'll often want to zoom in to work on a detail and then quickly zoom out to evaluate your work. This can all be done with the View tools and their equivalent keyboard shortcuts.

The *Canvas* in Fireworks is where you will spend most of your time working. Each image file lies on a Canvas, but the Canvas does not carry any image information itself except for dimensions and a background color. Objects such as bitmap images, vector graphics, and text are arranged on the Canvas to create the final image, the same way you might create a collage from picture and text clippings.

With a document window open in the work area, select the Zoom tool from the Tools panel by clicking its magnifying glass icon. Move your cursor over the Canvas. The cursor will change to a magnifying glass with a plus sign in the middle. Click your mouse button. This will zoom in on your image. Now hold down Control (Windows) or Option (Macintosh).

The plus sign will change to a minus sign. While still holding down the Control/Option key, click the Canvas again. Your image will zoom out to its original view.

You can also zoom in and out by holding Control (Option on the Mac) and pressing the minus (hyphen) key or the plus (equals) key. To quickly zoom to where the entire Canvas can be seen, press Control (or Option) and the number 0. You can also access all these commands through the View menu. Adjust the magnification by clicking View, Magnification, 100%. This will show the image at its native, or original, resolution. Here you can see each individual pixel that goes into composing the image (Figure 1.11).

FIGURE 1.11
100% magnification will show you the image with true pixel accuracy.

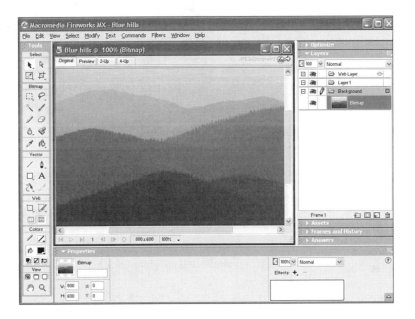

Zooming in on the Canvas can sometimes make large portions of the image invisible because they can't fit in the workspace. To view portions of an image that won't fit completely on your screen, use the Hand tool to move the image relative to the view window. To select the Hand tool, click it or press H. When you move the cursor over the Canvas, it will become a hand icon. Now click and drag the hand to the left. You'll notice as you move the hand that the visible portion of the Canvas in the workspace changes.

Task: Explore the Various Screen Modes

Now that you're familiar with some of the tools and with all the View controls, go ahead and switch screen modes. This can be initially disorienting for a new user, but you should be well prepared to take the plunge. By learning the keyboard shortcuts and View controls, you can get rid of all the panels and use the whole screen for working with your image!

To switch screen modes, do the following:

1. Click the Full Screen with Menus Mode button under View on the Tools panel. Alternatively, you may press F to cycle to this setting. (See Figure 1.12.)

FIGURE 1.12

Full Screen with Menus mode gives you more room to work.

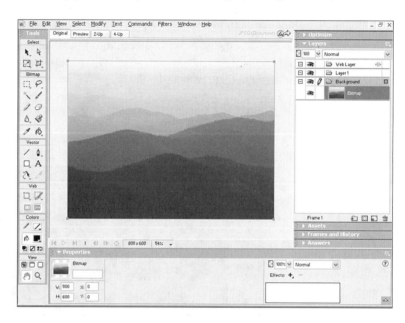

2. Press the Tab key. Voila! All your panels have disappeared. Don't worry—you still have the Menu up above. (See Figure 1.13.)

FIGURE 1.13

The Tab key toggles panels on and off, clearing out the clutter.

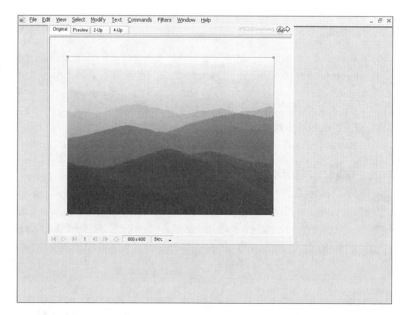

3. Press F to cycle to Full Screen Mode. Now you can work with image on your entire screen. (See Figure 1.14.)

FIGURE 1.14
Full Screen Mode allows you to use the entire monitor you've paid for.

4. Press Z to activate the Zoom tool, and click the Canvas to zoom in. Do it one more time.
5. Press H to select the Hand tool. Click and drag the Canvas to inspect it in its entirety.
6. Press Ctrl+0 (Windows) or Command+0 (Macintosh) to zoom out and center the image so that it fits the screen.
7. Press the Tab key to bring the panels back.
8. Press F to cycle back to Standard Screen Mode.

To fit a particular area of the screen into the window, use the Zoom tool and click-drag a rectangular area of the Canvas. That area will now fill the workspace.

Now that you're familiar with the tools and comfortable with the View tools, you can move on to the rest of the panels that you'll be using while you work.

Using the Property Inspector

The Property Inspector is a new tool in Fireworks MX. It is a contextual panel, which means that the menu options change, depending on what context you're working in. If a bitmap object is selected on the Canvas, the Property Inspector will allow you to view and change the settings for that bitmap object. If you then select the Brush to paint on the Canvas, the Property Inspector would show the Brush tool options. Whatever you're working with or working on, all the features and settings are only one click away. The Property Inspector is shown in Figure 1.15. (Although called Property Inspector, the panel itself reads simply "Properties.")

Properties Inspector Panel

FIGURE 1.15

The Property Inspector is where you specify settings for tools and objects.

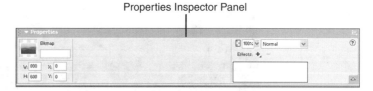

With the example photo open in the workspace, choose the Pointer tool (by pressing V or 0) from the Tool panel and click the image of rolling hills. It will be surrounded by a thin border with square handles at the corners, as in Figure 1.15.

You'll also notice in Figure 1.15 that the Property Inspector now shows a small thumbnail and reads "Bitmap" on the left. This is to let you know that it is a Bitmap object, and the thumbnail shows you the entire object (in case it's masked or obscured by other objects). On the bottom right of the Property Inspector is an arrow. This toggles the Property Inspector from simple to advanced options. If the arrow is pointing down, click it to reveal the entire Property Inspector.

Below "Bitmap" is a form field where you can name the object. Naming objects can be useful when you are trying to keep track of lots of objects; for advanced techniques, such as scripting; and just as a good habit. Below that are the dimensions and location of the image. W is the width of the image in pixels. H is the height. X is the horizontal position of the bitmap object's top left corner.

The position is measured in pixels and is relative to the top left corner of the Canvas. Y is the vertical position. Positions on the Canvas are always measured from the top left corner, and negative X or Y values will place the image off the Canvas to the left and above, respectively.

On the right of the Property Inspector are the transparency settings for the object. 100% means completely opaque, whereas 0% means completely transparent. There are different types of transparency rendering available from the drop-down menu to the right. Below that the Property Inspector lists the Effects that have been applied to the object.

These topics merit much more discussion, but you'll skip them for now. Knowing where to find them is all you need until you learn more about them in Hour 5, "Editing Bitmap Graphics."

With the bitmap object selected, click the Brush tool icon or press B. The Property Inspector will now show the Brush tool icon and name in the upper left corner. To the right will be the Brush settings, including the stroke color, brush size, brush style, edge softness, texture, and texture density. Click another tool and examine the changes in the Property Inspector. This is a great way to get to know your tools.

Before you move on to the other panels, take a moment to examine the Canvas properties. Zoom out until there is a gray area around the image. Now click the gray area with the Pointer tool selected. The Property Inspector will now show a thumbnail of your entire image, the file name, and the Canvas settings. You can now change the Canvas background color, Canvas size, Image size, and Compression preset.

Laying Out Panels

Fireworks uses an ingenious, if sometimes misunderstood, method of presenting options to the user. These are the Macromedia panels, which can be manipulated in any number of ways. They can be grouped, hidden, renamed, docked, collapsed; you can even create your own custom panels! Additionally, when you're done putting the finishing touches on your ultimate customized interface, you can save the layout and take it with you wherever you go. Figure 1.16 shows a group of panels that are docked together.

FIGURE 1.16

Panel groups can be docked together by clicking the gripper and dragging them together.

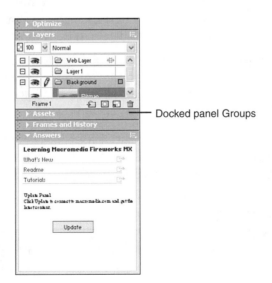

Docked panel Groups

Now you'll take a look at the Fireworks MX panels, and then you'll play around with them a bit. You'll go over each panel briefly and learn the keyboard shortcut so that you can always find it quickly. All the panels can be opened individually from the Window menu.

Tools—You've already gone over the Tools panel a little. To toggle the Tools panel on and off, press Ctrl+F2 (Windows) or Command+F2 (Macintosh).

Property Inspector—The Property Inspector is also a panel. To show or hide the Property Inspector, press Ctrl+F3 (Windows) or Command+F3 (Macintosh).

Answers—The Answers panel is where you can go for help and the latest tips and extensions. Use Alt+F1 (Windows) or Option+F1 (Macintosh).

Optimize—This panel contains compression and export settings. F6 (Windows and Macintosh).

Layers—To help you manage your Canvas, the Layers panel contains many useful features. F2 (Windows and Macintosh).

Frames—Frames are used in animations and other tasks. Shift+F2 (Windows and Macintosh).

History—The History panel keeps track of everything you do so you can undo it or repeat it. Shift+F10 (Windows and Macintosh).

Styles—Styles are custom stroke, fill, and effect settings you can use to quickly apply your signature look. Shift+F11 (Windows and Macintosh).

Library—The Library is where you can organize symbols and graphics for easy access. F11 (Windows and Macintosh).

URL—The URL panel lets you specify the location for a Hotspot or Button link. Alt+Shift+F10 (Windows) or Option+Shift+F10 (Macintosh).

Color Mixer—The Color Mixer gives you complete control over choosing your colors. Shift+F9 (Windows and Macintosh).

Swatches—Swatches are palettes of colors you can save and share with others. Ctrl+F9 (Windows) or Command+F9 (Macintosh).

Info—The Info panel gives you stats about cursor location and the color value of the pixel underneath. Alt+Shift+F12 (Windows) or Option+Shift+F12 (Macintosh).

Behaviors—Behaviors are special interactive features used with Button Symbols and Hotspots. Shift+F3 (Windows and Macintosh).

Find and Replace—The Find and Replace panel will let you make quick changes to documents with no hassle. Ctrl+F (Windows) or Command+F (Macintosh).

Project Log—The Project Log shows you the results of batch processing and find and replace operations. You can assign your own keyboard shortcut to be used with this panel.

Align—The Align panel helps you align objects on the Canvas for a more professional look. You can assign your own keyboard shortcut to be used with this panel.

Sitespring—Sitespring is a Macromedia program for helping teams work together more efficiently. You can assign your own keyboard shortcut to be used with this panel.

Docking and Grouping Panels

When you first start Fireworks MX, all the visible panels are docked, which means they are snuggly fitted against the edges of the screen. The Tools panel is docked on the left, the Property Inspector is docked at the bottom, and the panel groups are docked to the right. Panel groups are a number of panels put together. For instance, the Colors panel group has both the Color Mixer and Swatches panels.

Each panel and panel group can be undocked by clicking the panel gripper found in the upper left, next to the panel name. While still holding down the mouse button, drag the panel away from the edge of the screen until a clear box appears around your cursor. Release the mouse button. Now your panel has been undocked, and you can reposition it wherever you'd like. To close the panel, click the red button in the upper left corner of the panel. To dock it, click the top window bar of the panel and drag the panel toward the edge of the screen. It should snap into place when it can be docked.

Panel groups also have an arrow that allows you to expand or collapse them. Choose a panel group on the right-hand side with the arrow pointing to the right. Now click the arrow. The panel group will expand to show you the panel options. If there are more than one panel in the panel group, they can be chosen from the panel tabs underneath the panel group name. To undock one of these panels, click the tab and drag it away from the panel group until the cursor is surround by a clear box. Release the button to place your panel on the screen.

In the top right corner of each expanded panel is a drop-down menu with more actions and options for that particular panel. This is the panel Options menu. You can find more options for each specific panel, or you can use this menu for general panel management, like help or rearrange panel group. If you want to group one panel with another, choose Group With from the panel's Options menu. Select New Panel Group to create a group with just the selected panel, or choose an existing panel group from the list.

Task: Saving Your Panel Configuration

If you feel like all this user interface customization is overly complicated and a big waste of time, don't worry, because once you're happy with your workspace, you can just save it and return to it at any time, no matter what document you're working with. Take a moment to organize and dock the panels you think you'll be using most. If you're a graphic designer, you might want just the Layers, Colors, and Assets panel groups, the Property Inspector set at half-height for minimal options, and the Tools panel undocked so that it can be moved to where you're working. A Web designer might want just the Optimize, Behaviors, and URL panels, with the Property Inspector at full height and the Tools panel docked to the right. Choose whatever configuration is most comfortable for you to use.

To save and restore your custom panel layout,

1. Click the Command Menu and choose Panel Layout Sets, Save Panel Layout.

2. Give your new Panel Layout Set a name and press Return.

3. Return to the Command Menu and Choose Panel Layout Sets, 800 × 600 (or a more appropriate setting for your screen dimensions). Note how all the panels have reverted to their default dimensions.

4. Click the Command Menu one more time and choose Panel Layout Sets, then [*Your Panel Layout*], where the bracketed text is whatever you named your Panel Layout Set in Step 2.

5. Voila! Your custom panel layout is fully restored!

Looking for More Help?

If you ever need help, it's rarely more than a click away. Whether you are online or offline, you can always find a Fireworks Help resource handy. Before you continue, take a look at your options for finding out what you need to know.

To access Fireworks Help at any time, just press F1 (Windows) or Command+? (Macintosh). This will open the *Using Fireworks* documentation, shown in Figure 1.17. You can also open *Using Fireworks* from the Help Menu. The Help Menu is where you'll also find links to the Macromedia Fireworks Support Web site, with TechNotes and a searchable knowledge base. The Macromedia Online Forums are a great place to talk shop and swap files with other Macromedia Fireworks MX users.

FIGURE **1.17**

The Using Fireworks *guide is just a click away from the keyboard Help menu, Help button, or Answers panel.*

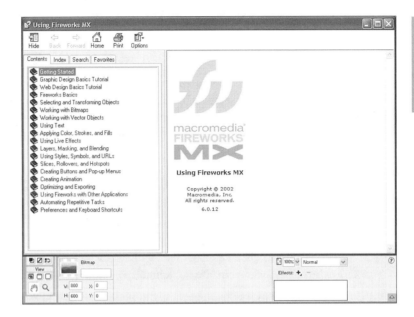

Help is also available for panels via the Help button, a question mark icon. This can usually be found in the upper right of any panel. This will take you to the appropriate section of the *Using Fireworks* guide for whichever panel you're having trouble with. If you need help with a tool or an object, select it with the pointer and click the Help button in the Property Inspector. This will bring up help about that particular tool or type of object.

The Answers panel gives you immediate access to the latest information from Macromedia regarding Fireworks. The drop-down menu at the top lets you choose between Getting Started, TechNotes, Extensions, and Settings. Getting Started lets you quickly access What's New, the Fireworks MX Readme file (which contains release notes for your particular version), and the Tutorials. TechNotes are where to go for the latest technical help. Extensions lets you know when new custom application extras become available. Choose Settings and click Update to download the latest info from Macromedia while you're connected to the Internet.

You can also access or print the documentation from the Adobe Acrobat PDF files that were installed along with Fireworks. To view the print documentation, you must download and install the Adobe Acrobat Viewer if you don't already have it (http://www.adobe.com/acrobat). Three titles are available with Fireworks MX—*Getting Started, Using Fireworks,* and *Extending Fireworks. Using Fireworks* is also accessible from the Help menu or by pressing F1

(Windows) or Command+? (Macintosh). *Extending Fireworks* is for advanced users and contains everything you need to know to write your own custom panels and extensions. The *Getting Started* guide has helpful installation tips and both the graphic design and Web design tutorials.

If you feel like you need some more hands-on experience with Fireworks before you get started working on the examples, it is suggested that you take the time to go through at least the graphic design tutorial. You can come back to the Web design tutorial when you're more comfortable with some of the concepts behind good Web design, which will be discussed later.

Summary

With a brand-new look and a more familiar feel, the Fireworks MX interface is better than ever. So far you should know how to use the menus, be familiar with some of the tools, know how to open and examine an image, and even be able to save your own custom layout to make your life less cluttered.

Although you didn't do much designing in this hour, you learned your way around, and in coming hours it should be much easier to find what you need, which is generally half the problem. If some features of the Fireworks interface still seem confusing, don't worry. You'll examine elements in detail throughout the rest of the book.

Workshop

The Quiz following Q&A will ask some questions about the topics covered in this chapter. In case you can't recall an answer quickly, simply refer to the quiz answers afterward for an explanation.

Q&A

Q When I open Fireworks, I can't find anything you're talking about. Where are the tools, panels, and Property Inspector?

A If you aren't running Fireworks for the first time, you or someone else may have made changes to the panel layout. To quickly return to the default, click the Commands menu and then choose Panel Layout Sets, 800 × 600. To bring up the Welcome screen, expand the Answers panel, choose Getting Started from the drop-down menu, and click on What's New or Tutorials to access the content from the Welcome screen.

Q All my panels have disappeared completely! What's going on?

A Pressing the Tab key quickly hides all of your panels. Pressing it again brings them back. If all of your panels have been undocked and closed, you can find them in

1

the Window menu at any time. If you can't even find the menus, press F to cycle through the Screen Modes until the menus are visible at the top of the screen.

Q **I can't find the Sample Pictures or Desktop Pictures folder on my hard drive. What happened?**

A You or someone else may have deleted these folders to make more room on the hard drive. For the purposes of this hour, any image file will do. If you can't find any, open your favorite Web browser, find a picture you like on the Web, and save it by right-clicking (Windows) or click-and-holding (Macintosh) on the image and selecting Save As from the pop-up menu. Save the image to your My Pictures (Windows) or Pictures (Macintosh) folder and repeat the steps covered earlier to open a file from within Fireworks.

Quiz

1. Where can you find a tool's name and keyboard shortcut?

    a. From the Tools menu

    b. By mousing over the tool icon for a tooltip

    c. From the Extending Fireworks PDF

2. Which keyboard shortcut selects the Zoom tool?

    a. M

    b. G

    c. Z

3. Where can you grab a panel to dock or undock it?

    a. The *gripper* in the upper left

    b. The *docker* in the lower right

    c. The *border* around the panel

Quiz Answers

1. b.—You can quickly find out a tool's name and keyboard shortcut by holding your mouse over the tool's icon for a tooltip.

2. c.—Z is the keyboard shortcut for the Zoom tool. Zoom out by Ctrl-clicking (Windows) or Option-clicking (Macintosh) with the Zoom tool cursor on the Canvas. Zoom in by clicking with the Zoom tool cursor.

3. a.—The panel gripper is what you click and drag to dock and undock panels and panel groups.

Hour 2

Image Collection and Management

The first step in any graphics project is to assemble the images that you're going to be working with. Next, you must cull the images you need from all the images you have available. This can be an important part of the creative process. You can store thousands of images on a compact disk, but you'll likely use only a few dozen in a Web site. Choosing just the right images can be critical, and being able to find them later is always a plus.

Today you'll be working with a few different applications available with your operating system. All the applications you'll cover are either bundled with your system software or are freely available on the Web. Some steps require special hardware, such as a scanner, that may come with its own software. Consult the hardware documentation on how to connect your hardware, install necessary drivers, and use any bundled applications.

In this hour you will

- Learn how to create working images to protect source graphics
- Import almost any image into Fireworks' native format

- Use different hardware and applications to collect images from almost anywhere
- Preview and organize groups of images by using thumbnails
- Back up your work so that all will never be lost

Creating Fireworks Native Images (PNG)

Though Fireworks can open and import almost any type of image file, it has its own file format that supports all of Fireworks' special features. This is the preferred format for creating working copies of all your source images. Fireworks will save an image only in its native format; to create other formats from Fireworks, you will use Export.

It's always good to make a second copy of your image; the first is your *data source,* and the second your *working image.* From your image source, you'll export the *final output.* You'll not want to edit your data source directly; it's a good idea to leave it completely intact in case you need it later. The working image, in Fireworks' native PNG format, will be where you do your editing. When you are done working, you will create your final output.

The PNG format is very flexible and features a full set of options, including broad support in other applications, non-lossy compression, and full, three-channel-plus-alpha RGB color space. Fireworks MX can also use the PNG format to store information about layers, text and fonts, vectors, Web slicing, and other features you'll learn to use later. In the following task you'll create a blank PNG image and save it to your hard disk.

Task: Create a Blank Source Image

In this task you will create a new document with a blank Canvas and save it to your hard drive. This will create a Fireworks source PNG that will support the full range of Fireworks features.

1. Open Fireworks MX.
2. Choose New from the File menu or press Control+N (Windows) or Command+N (Macintosh). You will be asked to choose the Canvas settings for your new document, as in Figure 2.1.

FIGURE 2.1

These are the Canvas settings for the new file. The default unit of measurement for Web graphics is pixels.

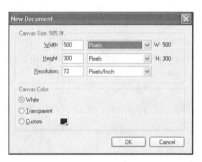

3. Make sure the Width is set to 500 by pressing Tab to select the Width field and then typing **500**. Next, select the Height field and enter **300**. The resolution setting is what determines the output size of the image when printed—for now, leave it at 72. Click on the radio button corresponding to the White setting for Canvas Color. Click OK to create the new document.

4. The new document will now appear in your workspace as a blank white Canvas.

5. The name of the image appears on the workspace window's title bar—in this case Untitled-1.png. The number after the @ symbol is your current view magnification. Fireworks defaults to the Fit to Window view when opening or creating new images. To change the name and save the file to your hard drive, choose Save from the File menu or press Control+S (Windows) or Command+S (Macintosh). You will be presented with the Save As dialog in Figure 2.2.

FIGURE 2.2

The Save As dialog will allow you to save files only in Fireworks' native PNG format.

6. Once in the Save As dialog window, click the Create New Folder icon (Windows) or the New Directory button (Macintosh). Name the new folder Fireworks Examples. This folder, shown in Figure 2.3, is where you will be storing all of the files that you will work on with this book.

FIGURE 2.3

The new folder, Fireworks Examples, *has been created in the* My Pictures *folder.*

7. While still in the Save As dialog, navigate to your `Fireworks Examples` folder. Select the File name field and type **blank_layout**. Click Save or press Return to save your image and return to Fireworks. The window will now be named `blank_layout.png`, as shown in Figure 2.4.

FIGURE 2.4

The Canvas window now reads `blank_layout.png`, *and the file is saved on your hard drive.*

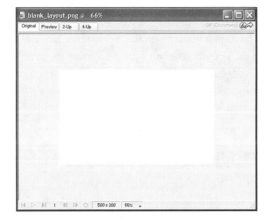

If you have image information stored in your system clipboard with the Copy command, the New dialog will default to the dimensions of the clipboard contents. This can be used to create new images from selections you've copied in Fireworks or almost any other application that supports your system clipboard. Simply create a new document with the clipboard dimensions intact and Paste in your copy to save it in the Fireworks PNG format.

Using Supported Formats

Fireworks supports almost any image file format you might encounter. These formats include bitmap and vector graphics, Adobe Photoshop files, GIF and JPEG images, and system-specific formats like BMP and PICT. In most cases Fireworks will also interpret a format's special features, such as editable text, layers, masks, and more. The following list details the types of files you can import and work with in Fireworks:

Fireworks (`.png`)—Of course, you can import Fireworks graphics from this or earlier versions. You can also import PNG files created by other applications.

FreeHand (.fh, .fh7, .fh8, .fh9, .fh10)—Used to import Macromedia FreeHand drawings, including text and vectors as well as bitmaps, masks, and layers. This works great if you're more comfortable creating graphics in FreeHand but want to use Fireworks to optimize them for the Web.

GIF (.gif)—CompuServe's GIF is one of the most common image formats for Web graphics. It uses a limited 8-bit adaptive palette and non-lossy compression to create very small image files. GIFs can also be animated by containing multiple frames.

JPEG (.jpg)—The Joint Photo Experts Group format was developed for photographs and other materials that required a full palette. Lossy compression, which trades image detail for file size, is used to create very small image files. JPEG is probably the most popular single-image format used today.

Photoshop PSD (.psd)—Fireworks can open documents saved in Photoshop's native format, PSD, that were created in Photoshop 6 or earlier. Fireworks supports a large range of the Photoshop format's features, including editable text, layers, masks, saved paths, and more.

CorelDRAW (.cdr)—Fireworks can import many of the file features of the CorelDRAW file format. Fireworks cannot interpret compressed CorelDRAW files and does not support many text and paragraph features, so the imported pages may not appear correctly.

WBMP (.wbmp, .wbm)—The wireless bitmap format is used for browser systems designed to run on hand-held devices, such as cellular phones and PDAs. It is a one-bit format—each pixel is either on (white) or off (black), keeping image files tiny and display requirements minimal.

TIFF (.tif, .tiff)—The TIFF format is an industry standard for print images and is a high-quality format for working with images from other applications, such as 3D graphics applications, scanners, professional digital photo equipment, or any other imaging environment where no loss in quality is acceptable. This means TIFF files can be relatively large unless some compression is employed.

Targa (.tga)—Targa is often used by applications that generate bitmaps from other art, such as 3D modeling programs. Targa is similar to TIFF in that it can support a number of bit depths, including alpha channels, plus different kinds of compression.

BMP (.bmp, .dib, .rle)—This is the most common format for Windows applications. It is very similar to the TIFF standard. It can use bit depths up to 24-bit color and does not usually employ compression, making high-resolution image files much larger than in some formats.

Adobe Illustrator (.ai, .art)—Fireworks imports Illustrator files like FreeHand files, with full vector capabilities and support for layers, masks, and placed bitmaps. Fireworks MX supports Illustrator files up to version 9.

EPS (.eps)—Fireworks can read the encapsulated post script Level 1 files produced by many popular programs, such as Quark XPress, Adobe Acrobat, and even engineering applications. EPS files can contain images, vector art, and text like FreeHand, CorelDRAW, and Illustrator files, but they don't include advanced features such as layers and gradient fills.

> If you know that a file is an image file but it doesn't show up in the Import window when you're in the proper directory, choose All Files (Windows) or All Available Files (Macintosh) from the file type drop-down menu. This will force Fireworks to display all the files in the directory. Now double-click the file, and Fireworks will open it if it is a valid image file in one of the supported formats.

Task: Import Additional Graphics

Go ahead and select some graphics to import into your blank layout. First you'll use a Web browser to visit the Sams Web site and download the files you will need to complete all of the examples in this book. You will be creating a Web site for a vacation rental property in Hawaii, and you'll start with an under-construction page. For that, you'll use some vector graphics and photos to assemble your temporary home page.

1. Open your Web browser.

2. Go to the Sams Publishing Web site by pressing Ctrl+L (Windows) or Command+L (Macintosh) and typing **http://www.samspublishing.com**. Press Return to load the Sams Publishing home page.

3. In the Search field in the upper left, enter this book's ISBN number: **0672324059**. Click Search (to the right) or press Return to continue.

4. Choose Sams Teach Yourself Macromedia Fireworks MX in 24 Hours from the search results page by clicking its title.

5. Choose Downloads, which is located below the cover shot of the book.

6. Here you may choose to download the entire set of example files or download the example files for each hour as you work on them. Some example files will be used in multiple hours, so make sure you download each set up to the one you're working on. The files are ZIP archives and can be uncompressed directly in Windows XP with a ZIP utility, such as WinZip, or by using Aladdin StuffIt Expander with Macintosh OS X.

7. To download a set of examples, click the link and follow your browser's instructions. It should automatically unzip the file for you. If not, you will want to locate

the downloaded zip file and double-click to extract the contents. You will want to copy any files in the ZIP archive into the Fireworks Examples directory you created earlier in this hour.

The files for each hour are in folders named Hour 02 through Hour 24. Open the Hour 02 folder. You will see two files: under_construction and honokaa_home. You can easily import these into your blank_layout file to lay out your temporary home page.

1. Open Fireworks MX.

2. Choose Import from the File Menu or press Control+R (Windows) or Command+R (Macintosh).

3. From the Import dialog, shown in Figure 2.5, navigate to the Hour 02 folder under My Pictures, Fireworks Examples.

FIGURE 2.5

The Import dialog lets you preview and import files from a location on your computer, such as the Fireworks Examples *folder on your hard drive.*

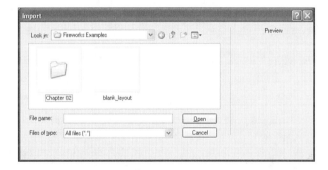

4. Choose honokaa_home by double-clicking it. Your cursor will change into a right-angle bracket, like an upside-down L. This represents the top left corner of the imported image.

5. Choose a place for the image corner above and to the left of the center of the Canvas so that the image fills the bottom right corner, as in Figure 2.6, and click the mouse button to place the bitmap object there.

FIGURE 2.6

When you import an image into Fireworks, you can place it wherever you'd like.

> If you placed the image so that some of it runs off the Canvas, don't worry.
> The bitmap or vector object is still intact; the Canvas is simply a way of com-
> posing objects within a viewable area. Anything that runs outside the Canvas
> will be preserved.

6. Choose Import again and double-click `under_construction`.

7. The `under_construction` file is an Adobe Illustrator graphic, so you will be
   shown the Vector File Options dialog, as in Figure 2.7. This is where you can specify how Fireworks handles dimensions, layers, anti-aliasing, and bitmap rendering.
   For now, just leave the default settings intact and click OK or press Return.

FIGURE 2.7

*The Vector File
Options dialog is
where you can specify
how Fireworks handles
a vector file.*

8. Using the angle bracket, click to place the imported graphic in the top left corner,
   as in Figure 2.8.

FIGURE 2.8

*Now you have placed
the necessary elements
for your page on the
Canvas.*

9. If you're not happy with how the images are arranged, select an object by clicking
   with the Pointer tool (press 0 or V to choose the Pointer tool), and while holding
   down the mouse button, drag it to where you would rather have it placed. Release

the mouse button to stop moving the object. Use the same operation to move the other objects, if necessary.

> You can nudge objects using the cursor (arrow) keys on your keyboard while that object is selected. Nudging an object moves it 1 pixel in whichever direction you choose—left, right, up, or down. Holding down the Shift key while pressing a cursor key moves the object 10 pixels.

2

10. Choose Save As from the File Menu or press Control+Shift+S (Windows) or Command+Shift+S (Macintosh) to save `blank_layout` as `temp_layout` in the `Fireworks Examples` folder.

Now you have a temporary home page graphic for the example Web site. The remainder of this hour will cover other ways you can find images to work with in Fireworks. You will return to this layout in the next hour, "Choosing Optimization Settings and Exporting Graphics."

Collecting Graphics

Now you'll go over the different ways you might collect graphics for a project using Fireworks. In the following how-to sections, you'll go over screen shots and images on the Web, disk, scanners, digital cameras, and video clips. You'll go over how to do everything on both Windows XP and Macintosh OS X. Some hardware requires its own drivers or software; consult the documentation that came with the product on how to install and use it.

How to Collect Images from the Web

You can use any popular Web browser to save images from Web sites. This is a great way to look for images to stand in for graphics that you don't have yet, use water-marked *comp* images from stock image libraries, or share images for other image editors to work with.

Task: Collect Images from the Web

To collect images from the Web, follow these steps:

1. Open your favorite Web browser, such as Internet Explorer, Netscape Navigator, or Opera. It doesn't matter what operating system you are running.

2. Navigate to a Web page with an image you would like to save and work with.

3. With your mouse, right-click (Windows) or Control-click (Macintosh) the image you would like to save. A pop-up menu will appear.

4. Choose Copy Image to copy the image to your clipboard, and then choose Save (or Download Image) to save the image in its own format to your hard drive. For now, select Copy Image by clicking it.

5. Open or select Fireworks MX.

6. Choose New from the File menu or press Control+N (Windows) or Command+N (Macintosh) to create a blank Canvas. The Canvas dimensions will automatically be set to those of the Clipboard content.

7. Click OK or press Return to continue.

8. Select Paste from the Edit menu or press Control+V (Windows) or Command+V (Macintosh) to paste the image object to your Canvas.

9. Choose Save from the File menu or press Control+S (Windows) or Command+S (Macintosh).

10. Select a folder, type a name, and click OK or press Return to save the image as a Fireworks PNG image.

How to Browse a Removable Disk for Images

Many images may be delivered to you on CDs or other removable media. Most photo labs can deliver your developed negatives on CD instead of paper prints, you can buy CDs of license-free stock images from many companies, and you or your client may want to burn your own CDs of digital images to ship or back up lots of images.

The important thing to remember is that you can't actually edit the images directly on a CD because they are read-only media. You will have to create a copy on your hard disk if you need to make any changes. Removable magnetic media, such as floppy and ZIP disks, do allow you to both read and write to a file, allowing you to make changes directly to the image on such disks.

Task: Work with Images on a Removable Disk

This task will get you started collecting files from CD-ROM, floppy, and ZIP drives, among other removable media options.

1. Insert the disk into the appropriate drive.

2. From the Start menu (click Start or press the Applications key on your keyboard), select My Computer.

3. From the list of drives, select the disk you just inserted.

4. Navigate the disk to find the image files you are looking for.

5. Select them with the cursor by clicking the file icon. Select multiple files with Control-click.

6. Choose Copy from the Edit menu or press Control+C to copy the selected files.

7. Navigate back up to My Computer and then select the drive and folder where you would like to copy the files.

8. While in the destination folder, choose Paste from the Edit menu or press Control+V to begin copying the files from the removable disk to your hard disk.

How to Scan a Photograph

Fireworks can communicate directly with scanners using the TWAIN protocol (Windows) or the Photoshop Acquire Plug-in (Macintosh). Check the documentation included with your device to determine whether the appropriate drivers are supplied and how to install them correctly. You may also check the manufacturer's Web site for updated drivers.

> For Macintosh OS X users, the Scan option on the File menu will not be available until a Photoshop Acquire Plug-in has been located. To locate a Photoshop Acquire Plug-in, choose Preferences from the Fireworks menu. From the Preferences dialog, choose Folders from the drop-down menu at the top. Click Browse (next to Photoshop Plug-ins) to browse your hard drive for the folder with your Photoshop Acquire Plug-in (either in your scanner's software folder or your Adobe Photoshop Plug-ins folder). You can also copy the scanner's Photoshop Acquire Plug-in directly to the Plug-ins folder in your Macromedia Fireworks MX folder to make it available to Fireworks MX.

Task: Scan an Image Using Fireworks

Here's how to scan an image with Fireworks:

1. Choose Scan from the File Menu and then choose your scanner from the submenu.

2. Your scanner's TWAIN or Plug-in interface will now appear. Consult the device documentation on how to use your scanner's software. You will likely be given options including color depth, resolution, color and contrast correction, and scaling.

3. When you've completed your scan, it will appear as a new image file in your workspace.

4. Save the new image to your hard drive as a Fireworks PNG image.

If your device doesn't support TWAIN or Photoshop Acquire, it may have its own program that you can use to scan images. Use the program to scan your photographs or artwork, and save the scans as file types that you can open using Fireworks.

How to Import an Image from a Digital Camera

Many digital cameras also support TWAIN modules or the Photoshop Acquire Plug-ins, much like a scanner. In this case, the software is used to choose from a number of images that might be stored in the camera's memory. Check the documentation that came with your digital camera to see whether the correct drivers are supplied. Updates may also be available on the manufacturer's Web site.

Task: Import an Image from a Digital Camera

To import an image from a digital camera into Fireworks, follow these steps:

1. Choose Scan from the File Menu, and then choose the digital camera from the submenu. Your camera's TWAIN interface will now appear. Most interfaces will present a series of thumbnails and the option to view file information, such as dimensions and the time the picture was taken.
2. Choose an image and continue as directed.
3. The chosen image will now open as a new document in Fireworks.
4. Choose Save to save your image as a Fireworks PNG file.

Many digital cameras also come with their own software for saving your photographs to disk. Consult the documentation included with your digital camera to learn how to use the software provided by the manufacturer.

How to Import a Still from a Video Clip

You may want to import an image from a video clip that you've digitized. You can digitize video clips if you have some video device, such as a VCR or video camera, and video digitization hardware installed in your machine. Many digital video devices can be connected directly to your computer via FireWire. WebCams and TV Tuners can also be used. With Mac OS X you might use iMovie or QuickTime Pro to capture media and export a still image. In the following section, you'll use Movie Maker with Windows XP to create a still image from a FireWire input.

Task: Capture a Still Using Movie Maker with Windows XP

To use Movie Maker to capture a video still from a FireWire device, follow these steps:

1. From the Start menu, choose Movie Maker, shown in Figure 2.9.

Movie Maker is normally installed with Windows XP. Use Add/Remove Windows Components from the Add or Remove Programs control panel in Windows XP to add it, if it was not initially installed.

FIGURE 2.9
Windows Movie Maker lets you work with your video capture or digital video equipment.

2

2. Choose a Collection for your still photos.

3. With your FireWire device connected, choose Record from the File menu or press Control+R. The Record dialog will appear.

4. If you have multiple devices installed, select your FireWire device by clicking the Change Device button.

5. Using the Movie Maker playback controls or the controls on your FireWire device, shuttle to the frame you would like to capture.

6. Once you have selected a frame, press the Take a Photo button (the camera icon below the preview window).

7. Choose a name for your still image. Clicking OK will save your image as a JPEG image file.

8. Close the Record dialog by clicking Cancel.

9. Open or switch to Fireworks MX.

10. You may now use Open or Import from the File menu to begin working with the image in Fireworks.

Organizing and Sharing Graphics

One of the most important aspects of dealing with large numbers of graphics is being able to organize them. Maybe you've had a roll of film developed and the negatives scanned so that you received the images on CD rather than as paper prints. When you put such a disk in your drive, you're faced with a couple dozen files, not necessarily in the order you took the pictures. Maybe some of the pictures were taken outside and some inside, or some vertical and some horizontal, some with people and some without. How can you quickly sift through the image files to rename them and organize them into folders?

Windows XP uses the `My Pictures` folder to let you preview and organize large groups of images because it uses Thumbnails view by default. Thumbnails view lets you preview each image in the current folder. To preview images in any Windows XP folder, choose Thumbnails from the Views menu when exploring a folder. Macintosh OS X uses iPhoto to show thumbnail views of images you would like to preview and organize. This book will use the Windows XP `Sample Pictures` folder, under the `My Pictures` folder, for the images in this example.

Task: Manage Multiple Images Within the `My Pictures` Folder

To use the `My Pictures` folder to preview image files, follow these steps:

1. Bring up the Start menu and choose the `My Pictures` folder. Note that each folder shown in the `My Pictures` folder contains up to four miniature previews of the files within, just like the `Sample Pictures` folder shown in Figure 2.10. These help you preview the contents of a folder.

2. Double-click the `Sample Pictures` folder to open it. In the `Sample Pictures` folder, each image file will be represented as a thumbnail. This way you can preview the contents quickly.

FIGURE 2.10

In the `My Pictures` *folder, large icons display miniature thumbnails of the images in the folder.*

Sample Pictures

3. Mouseover to bring up some of the image properties—dimensions, format, and file size—as shown in Figure 2.11.

FIGURE 2.11

Individual image files show a larger thumbnail preview. Mouseover the files to display their image properties.

2

4. To preview the image, double-click it to open the Windows Picture and Fax viewer, as shown in Figure 2.12. Click the red button with the white X at the top right or press Alt+F4 to close the viewer and return to the `Sample Pictures` folder.

FIGURE 2.12

The Windows Picture and Fax Viewer allows you to quickly preview many images.

5. Right-click to bring up a pop-up menu. Here you can choose to Edit with Fireworks, copy, delete, or rename the file, as well as bring up the file properties, as shown in Figure 2.13.

FIGURE 2.13

You can choose instead to open the image in Fireworks with only two clicks—right-click to open the pop-up menu and then Edit with Fireworks to open the image in Fireworks.

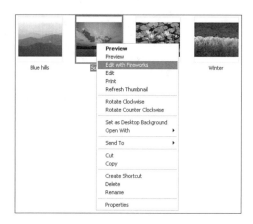

6. To create a new folder at any time, choose New, Folder, from the File menu. New folders created under the My Pictures folder will display folder preview thumbnails and image file thumbnails.

Creating Backups of Source Images

One of the most important steps in any project after you've assembled all your images is to back them up so that you can refer back to them later. The cheapest, fastest, and most reliable way to back up your images is with a CD-R or CD-RW drive. You can buy an external USB CD burner for less than $200. Media can cost less than one dollar for 650 megabytes of storage. If the disks are properly taken care of, the data on them will persist indefinitely; you can come back to perfect copies in 50 or 100 years.

Other backup methods include using other types of removable media, including ZIP and JAZ drives, tape backup drives, and DVD-RAM and DVD-R drives. There are also network backup services where you post files to a network account, where they are then backed up by the service provider.

There are a number of software utilities available to help you organize and complete a backup session. These include compression programs such as Aladdin DropStuff and WinZip, backup scheduling and management software such as Retrospect, and CD burning software such as Toast or EasyCD.

Legal Considerations

With the advent of the Internet, intellectual property law entered a completely new frontier. Regardless of how some laws are eventually applied and new laws are enacted, there are a number of classic taboos that it's important to remember when working with any images. There are copyright laws, which deal with who owns the rights to an image, phrase, or sound. There are trademark laws, which deal with how an individual or group identifies its business and product. There are patent laws, which involve a useful application of a new tool or procedure. And finally, there are privacy and publicity laws, which guarantee an individual's right to ownership of his or her life and likeness.

The suggestions in this book are based on the legal statutes and precedents of the United States of America. Remember, however, that anything you post on the Web can be accessed by a global audience. If you are reading this book in the United States, your work on the Web is still subject to the laws in any other country. And no matter what country you're in, your work may be subject to the laws of the United States. It pays to be conscientious; lawsuits are expensive, even if you win.

2

Copyright

Copyright laws can seem subjective, but if you follow a few basic rules, you shouldn't make any terrible mistakes. Copyright law applies to any creative practice you could possibly imagine— writing, painting, drawing, photography, motion pictures, theater performance, songwriting, audio recording. Copyrights are valid for 50 to 100 years after the creation of the copyright material, depending on when the material was created. Material with an expired copyright is said to be in the public domain. These include plays by Shakespeare, paintings by Michelangelo, scores by Mozart, and books by Dante.

You cannot use any portion of copyrighted content without the consent of the copyright holder. Not a single sentence from a written passage, a character from a font, a small piece of a photograph, a second-long sample of audio, or a single frame from a motion picture. Copyrights include distribution and modification rights, which means by modifying a piece of copyrighted material and publishing it, you are actually breaking the law on two counts: The copyright holder could sue you for unauthorized modification of the material and for unauthorized distribution of the modified material.

There is a provision for using copyrighted material upheld by the Supreme Court called *fair use*. Fair use includes cited passages of text, images, sounds, footage, or other areas where copyrighted material is being commented upon, such as critical analysis or parody. Fair use is limited as a defense of the use of copyrighted material except in very specific cases. You should never assume that you will be legally protected by the fair use provisions of the copyright law and should look for ways to reference the copyrighted material without actually using it.

Since 1989, there has been no requirement to include a copyright statement when publishing original material. This means that anyone who posts a snapshot to his home page holds a copyright to that image. If you are working for a company producing original content, you may have signed over your right to the material in your contract. On the other hand, a contractor or freelancer hired to provide material for your company may hold the copyright. In the case of a Web site, one person may hold the copyright to the design of the site, a second to the text copy, a third to the logo graphic, and a fourth to the photographs.

To use copyrighted material, you must normally obtain a *license* from the copyright holder. Licenses allow you to use the material in a specific context and often involve a license fee. Alternatively, some material is sold as *license free*. This means the copyright holder has signed a blanket license agreement, allowing the material to be used in almost any context. There is also the *general public license,* where the copyright holder has ceded free public use of the material as long as it's properly credited.

Trademark

A *trademark* is how an individual or organization identifies itself and its products. You cannot apply another company's trademark to your own product—hence the criminality involved in fake Rolex watches. You also cannot use a trademark that could possibly deceive a consumer into believing that they are buying another product. It would be difficult to defend your use of a "Wave" that looks like a Nike Swoosh if it's being put on athletic shoes.

This also means that you must ask permission to display trademarks in a copyrighted work if they are to be the focus of your content. For instance, in a photograph of New York's Times Square, there are hundreds of trademarks, but no one trademark is the focus of the image. If you were to crop the image to remove everything but a Sony trademark, the context would be removed, and therefore the same image (though cropped) would now be seen as an application of Sony's trademark to your work and therefore against the law.

Patent

It is unlikely as a Fireworks user that you will infringe on anybody's patent, but you may feel that you've created a uniquely useful script or Web site and therefore want to patent it. Generally, the requirements for patenting a new technology are pretty stringent.

- You cannot simply patent an improvement on an existing product.
- You cannot patent common trade practices.
- You cannot patent a technology that's been described in the local or foreign press.

As with copyright law, if you develop a new technology while on contract with an employer, the employer may hold the patent rights.

Privacy and Publicity

Everyone has the right to control his or her own image. This means that you can't use images of people in private situations or benefit commercially from someone's likeness. You must always obtain a written release from subjects in a motion picture, sound recording, or photograph—and if you are the distributor, demand this of the director, producer, or photographer to minimize your liability.

The right to privacy guarantees that you will not be publicly humiliated by published images of your private life. This includes recorded speech. The most effective defense against being accused of invading people's privacy is to provide a release form for the subjects to sign to ensure that they know they are being recorded and agree not to hold you accountable for their appearance or behavior.

The right to publicity is meant to make sure that you receive some portion of any profits made from your likeness. This means that no one can use any image or recording of you that contributes commercially to their work without your permission. Although the right of privacy is generally considered to expire upon death, this is not the case with the right to publicity. The estate of the deceased retains the right to publicity.

> Intellectual property laws are not meant to hinder the creative process; instead, they are meant to protect creative professionals from being cheated. As an author, designer, or developer, you are in a unique position to understand, appreciate, and respect the time and effort that goes into creative work. It is only right that you be allowed to demand credit and remuneration for your work. If you need to use copyrighted material, simply ask permission and make sure you get it in writing. If you can't afford the licensing fees, try something new and different. It could be worth your while.

Summary

Today you learned how to create PNG files, how to import other types of image files, where to find image files on your system, methods for organizing your images, and some of the legal issues related to graphic and Web page design. You should now be completely prepared to begin working on an extended project.

Fireworks may seem confusing in the way it handles opening and saving files, but it's built to protect you from yourself; by forcing you to treat originals as your data source, create working images in the PNG format, and then export your final output, Fireworks keeps you from destroying your originals, preserves your editing decisions for further revision, and lets you output your work through any number of different formats and versions.

Workshop

The following questions will test your knowledge of image formats, document settings, and other topics discussed in this hour. Answers are provided for your reference.

Q&A

Q I opened a JPEG image, so why couldn't I save it as a `.jpg` file?

A The Fireworks Save, Save As, and Save a Copy commands will save your work only in the Fireworks PNG format. When you opened the JPEG image, Fireworks created a new, unsaved PNG image. This way the JPEG data source is left untouched. Saving creates a working image, and if you're working in Fireworks, this will be a PNG image. You have to export your PNG image to create a JPEG image as your final output.

Q My scanner is connected to my computer, but I can't use Scan on the File menu. What's wrong?

A Fireworks can use only scanners that support the TWAIN protocol. There are hundreds of different scanners from dozens of manufacturers, and each may be installed on different types of hardware with drivers for different operating systems. Check with your scanner manufacturer to find the necessary drivers for your system. If you cannot configure TWAIN support for your scanner, you may be able to use the manufacturer's scanning software to scan images and save them to your hard drive outside of Fireworks.

Q I grabbed a still of Jimi Hendrix from a documentary, added a lot of crazy effects, and turned it into a tiny logo. Is that illegal?

A You've broken a lot of laws here. Every frame of the documentary is protected by modification and distribution copyrights, as well as by the reuse rights of any talent or crew who participated in the production. Jimi Hendrix's estate has the right of publicity to protect his likeness from unauthorized commercial use. By using this image as a logo, you are creating an illegal trademark that implies the production or endorsement of your products by Jimi Hendrix. Needless to say, you'll be lucky if you reach a settlement.

Quiz

1. How do you save an image from a Web page with your browser?

    a. Choose Save As from the browser's File menu.

    b. Right-click (Windows) or Control-click (Macintosh) the image and select Save Image.

    c. Press Control+S (Windows) or Command+S (Macintosh) and choose JPEG as the file type.

2. How do you create a new file with the same dimensions as your Clipboard?

    a. With no canvas in the workspace, choose Paste from the Edit menu.

    b. In your My Pictures (Windows) or Pictures (Macintosh) folder, choose Paste from the Edit menu.

    c. Choose New from the Fireworks' File menu, accept the dimensions, and paste the Clipboard contents.

3. How does one establish the copyright to an image?

    a. By publishing the image to the Web, in print, or on screen.

    b. By paying a fee to the national copyright office.

    c. By adding a copyright symbol or statement to the image.

Quiz Answers

1. b.—The other two options would save the HTML document, not just the image.

2. c.—Fireworks automatically sets the dimensions in the New dialog to match the contents of the clipboard.

3. a.—It is no longer necessary to add a copyright notice to your work. Publishing images in any form grants full legal protection.

HOUR 3

Choosing Optimization Settings and Exporting Graphics

Where Fireworks really shines is in enabling you to export graphics into many different formats quickly and easily, with fine control over every detail, including colors, transparency, and compression. In the previous hour, "Image Collection and Management," it was pointed out that the Fireworks Save command saves your work as a Fireworks PNG source graphic. To create other kinds of graphics in many different formats, using the Export command will be discussed here.

In this hour you will

- Learn about the different export formats
- Preview and compare different export options
- Change settings to optimize quality or file size

- Save custom settings to make output more consistent
- Create a simple placeholder Web page graphic

Working with Different Output Formats

There are a number of different graphics formats that Fireworks can export, each with its own strengths and weaknesses. For instance, exporting as TIFF might create a file even bigger than the Fireworks source PNG. JPEG is particularly bad as a format for images with lots of text, like a screenshot or button. The following is a list of different file formats that can be optimized and exported with Fireworks:

GIF—GIF images are one of the most widely supported formats for computers and the Web. Images with lots of text or line art and a limited palette work best as GIF images. GIF images have a palette of no more than 8 bits but can create very small files. GIF images can also contain a transparency mask.

Animated GIF—Animated GIF export creates files of the same format as regular GIF files, but they can contain multiple frames and display them at intervals to create moving images. Animated GIFs can become very large unless special steps are taken to optimize them.

JPEG—Another widely used format for the Web is JPEG, which is best for photos and other images with a full range of colors. With JPEG you can vary the level of compression by trading image detail for file size—the smaller the file size in bytes, the less detail the image will contain.

PNG—PNG export is for creating PNG graphics without Fireworks' special features. Most Web browsers and graphic applications do not support all of Fireworks' special PNG features but do support the more basic format features. The basic PNG format uses non-lossy compression like GIF but saves more detailed color and transparency information.

WBMP—The wireless bitmap format is used for creating graphics for tiny, monochrome displays common on wireless devices, such as cell phones and PDAs. These images are naturally very small because each pixel must be either black or white and the dimensions must be similarly restrained. Non-lossy compression, such as GIF compression, is employed to make the files even smaller.

TIFF—This format is often used in the print industry and for moving images between graphics applications. Many Web browsers do not support this format. TIFF files exported from Fireworks employ non-lossy compression and can contain the full RGB palette plus an 8-bit alpha channel.

> When your image-processing software, in order to reduce the file size, removes information that is more or less redundant to the human eye, this is known as *lossy compression*. The advantage of lossy compression is that it gives a very high degree of compression, often 5 to 30 times. The disadvantage is that the quality of the image is reduced as the compression increases.
>
> When you use a *non-lossy compression* format, all original information will be saved in the image. The disadvantage is that the compression ratio is much lower, leading to larger file sizes.

PICT—Used almost exclusively on the Apple Macintosh platform, this format does not use compression; files can be made smaller only by restricting the palette or dimensions. PICT image files are rarely used in Web pages. They are used mostly in production as a backup or transfer format.

BMP—This is the basic image format for Microsoft Windows. Like PICT, it can use the full RGB palette but does not use compression—but this can also create very large files. For this reason this format is also less common on the Web.

Comparing Compression

Fireworks makes it easy to choose between different compression formats. Open the file `temp_layout`, which was created in Hour 2, so that you can see how different compression formats affect image quality and file size. (If you have not yet completed Hour 2, you will need to jump backwards to create the file and folder now.) Choose Open from the File Menu or press Ctrl+O (Windows) or Command+O (Macintosh). Select the file `temp_layout` from the `Fireworks Examples` folder.

With the Canvas open in your workspace, look up to find the tabs Original, Preview, 2-Up, and 4-Up above the Canvas and below the menus, as shown in Figure 3.1. These tabs let you switch between editing the original and previewing the export output. When you want to view or edit the source graphic, choose the Original tab (default). To preview how the output file will appear when exported into a different format, click on the Preview tab. The 2-Up and 4-Up tabs let you compare different types of compression at the same time. Click the Preview tab now to view the optimized output.

FIGURE 3.1

The view mode tabs include Original, Preview, 2-Up, and 4-Up.

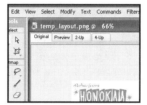

To change the optimization settings, you can use the Optimize panel, as shown in Figure 3.2. Expand the Optimize panel in the dock by clicking the arrow next to its name. If the Optimize panel isn't visible, choose Optimize from the Window menu or press F6.

FIGURE 3.2

The Optimize panel lets you fine-tune format settings.

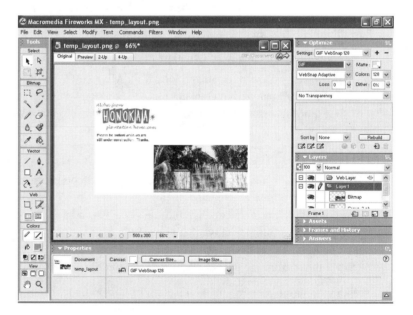

At the top of the Optimize panel is a drop-down menu named Settings. This menu is where optimization presets are stored. The default setting is GIF WebSnap 128. If this isn't the current setting, select it now. Now change the setting to JPEG—Smaller File (see Figure 3.3). Click the 2-up preview tab; then notice how the image preview on the right changes. Also, underneath the two previews is the file size and an estimate of how long it will take to download over a 56Kbps modem.

FIGURE 3.3

Heavy JPEG compression can blur image detail.

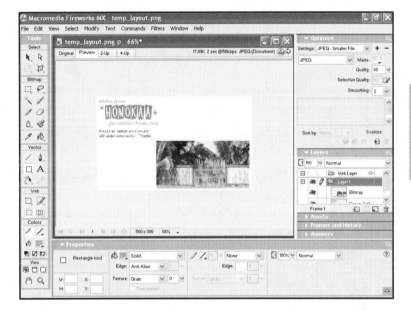

To compare the current setting to the original images, choose the 2-Up tab. The workspace will split into two—the left will represent how the original document appears; the right will preview the optimized file. To compare the original to different compression options, choose the 4-Up tab. The workspace will split into four windows, with the original image in the top left, as in Figure 3.4. Click a quadrant to change the optimization settings for that preview. This way you can preview a number of different compression settings at once, with the original as a reference.

FIGURE 3.4

The 4-Up preview mode allows you to compare and contrast optimization settings by eye.

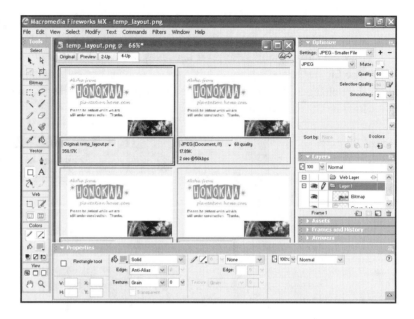

Working with the Optimization Panel

With the workspace in 4-Up preview mode, get to know how to use the optimization settings by previewing the image and adjusting the settings for the best possible output with the smallest file size.

Task: Preview Different Compression Settings

▲ TASK

In this task you will look at how different rates of compression and different file types affect an original image. Using this system of previewing and checking will ensure that your exported files are of the size and quality you require.

1. Click the upper right preview pane to select it.

2. On the Optimize panel, select GIF Web 216. Figure 3.5 shows the optimization settings for the upper right pane. This preset specifies GIF format, with the palette composed of the 216 colors that comprise the standard Web palette.

FIGURE 3.5

Selecting a pane allows you to choose optimization settings to preview in that pane.

3. Click the lower left preview pane.

4. On the Optimize panel, select GIF Adaptive 256. This preset specifies GIF format also, but the palette is chosen of colors that may change (adapt), depending on the available system palette.

5. Click the lower right preview pane.

6. On the optimize panel, select JPEG—Better Quality File. JPEG uses a fully accurate 24-bit palette, but detail in high-contrast and high-detail areas, like outlines, can be lost as part of the compression.

7. To examine the previews in detail, you can use the Zoom tool (press Z) to change the view magnification to 100% or more. This does not actually edit the image; it merely changes the way you see the file during the preview. Use the Hand tool (H) to change the view of the canvas and pan a particular area into view. Note how the different types of compression affect the temp_layout file differently. The line art will look jagged with GIF Web 216, and the photograph will be dithered, which means it loses detail. The photo will improve with the GIF Adaptive 256 setting, but the color of the line art may shift slightly because the adaptive palette will be skewed to the colors from the photograph. The colors will look most natural with JPEG, but the text and line art will seem slightly blurred, as shown in Figure 3.6, which shows temp_layout at a magnification of 300%.

FIGURE 3.6

You'll notice the effects of different compression rates when you zoom in on the preview panes. Different elements of the image react differently to the compression settings.

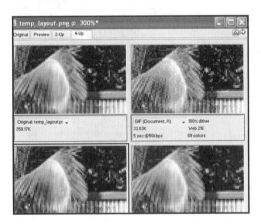

8. Now compare the file sizes. This will be below the preview frame, listed in kilo-bytes, like in Figure 3.7, which shows a detail of the previous figure. The first GIF will be around 45 kilobytes. The next GIF will be around 51KB—it is larger because there are more colors in the palette. The JPEG will be about 37KB. The image should be around 30KB, and JPEG offers the best color depth and most control over compression, so you'll select the lower right quadrant to work with.

FIGURE 3.7

Below the visual preview is a data preview detailing the export output file size and transfer time.

9. Click the 2-up tab above the canvas (see Figure 3.8). Since the JPEG frame had been selected in 4-up mode, it will now be the export preview choice on the right.

FIGURE 3.8

2-Up preview compares the selected optimization settings for a closer comparison.

10. On the Optimize panel, notice the Quality value (80). For JPEG this represents the ratio of size to image quality—0 means the smallest size and worst quality; 100 means largest file and best quality. To the right is a down arrow. Click this to bring up the Quality slider. Using the slider, change the value to 70, as shown in Figure 3.9. The exported image preview and file size will update, and you should be well under 30KB.

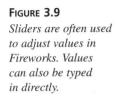

FIGURE 3.9
Sliders are often used to adjust values in Fireworks. Values can also be typed in directly.

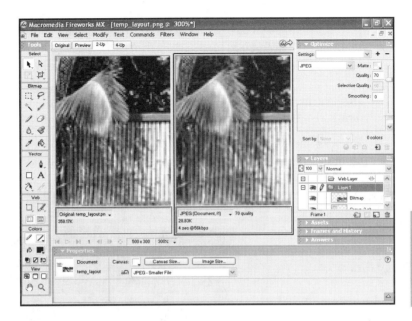

In this situation you are exporting the entire image as a single file, so you can use only one form of compression. Fireworks helps optimize by letting you slice an image into multiple parts and apply a different format and optimization setting to each part—such as GIF compression for the line art and JPEG compression for the photograph. Slicing images will be discussed in more detail in Hour 14, "Slicing Layouts."

Advanced Compression Settings

Now take a closer look at the two most common compression formats you'll be using, GIF and JPEG. Since they approach file size compression completely differently from each other and also handle colors and other information differently, they should be used for distinct purposes. If you're ever confused as to which one to apply, use the Preview tabs in the workspace to compare and contrast.

GIF Compression

Compuserve created the GIF standard when 256 colors were all that most computers were capable of displaying. Over the years the format developed into the 89a version, which is still in use today. GIF was very popular for line art and text scanning and early multimedia applications, but for photographic purposes it is very limited. With photographs the limited palette means dithering and posterization must be added to approximate the original color. This can be considered an artifact of the compression, because it artificially compromises image detail.

Still, for the vast majority of uses on the Web, GIF is a fine tool for designers. GIF images are used for typographic effects, icons, buttons, and all sorts of elemental design graphics. Incredibly small GIFs, when tiled, can create very interesting effects. The GIF format also supports multi-frame, or animated, images.

To access the GIF format directly on the Optimize panel, simply select it from the drop-down menu at the top right, underneath the Settings menu, as shown in Figure 3.10.

FIGURE 3.10

The GIF format forces you into an 8-bit palette but creates small files and gives you ultimate control.

Palette

The GIF palette is limited to 256 total colors, or 8 bits. However, the palette can consist of as few as 2 colors, or 1 bit. The following is a list of the palette settings and tools available on the Optimize panel with the GIF format. When the GIF format is chosen, the palette presets will be available from the drop-down menu directly beneath the format menu. Many of these palette and optimization settings are also available for other 8-bit formats including PNG, PICT, BMP, and TIF.

Adaptive—An adaptive palette chooses colors based on the colors in the original image, approximating similar colors to reduce the total number of colors. This means slight gradations will flatten into a single color (posterize) and some important colors may be changed slightly.

WebSnap Adaptive—This is similar to the adaptive setting except that it favors colors within the Websafe palette. This is important when you've chosen to use Websafe colors but don't want to lose them to approximation by a regular adaptive palette.

Web 216—The Web 216, or Websafe, palette consists of colors that can be assumed to look the same on both Macintosh and Windows systems. Because of gamma, however, colors generally appear darker on a Windows system and brighter on a Macintosh system. To preview the Web 216 palette at a different gamma setting, select Macintosh Gamma or Windows Gamma from the View menu.

Exact—This can be used only when the source graphic already contains an 8-bit palette, as do imported GIFs and some Bitmap and TIFF images. This preserves the original palette colors.

Macintosh—This is the Macintosh system palette. These colors will always appear correct on Macintosh systems.

Windows—This is the Windows system palette. These colors will always appear correct on Windows systems.

Grayscale—The grayscale palette consists entirely of gray (neutral) colors. This will remove any color information from the output but will most reliably maintain subtle gradations of light and dark.

Black and White—Black and White is a 1-bit format that contains only two colors: black and white. This is usually used for line art and transparency masks.

Uniform—Uniform preserves the gradation of the palette itself, disregarding the original color information. The uniform palette is based on pixel values from the RGB Color Model.

Custom—Custom palettes can be imported from ACT palette files and from other GIF images. This is especially useful because it means you can apply a preexisting palette to new output, ensuring consistency throughout a project. After you choose the custom setting, Fireworks will prompt you with a dialog to open the ACT or GIF file.

When you change the palette setting, the results will be reflected in the palette view below. These swatches represent each of the colors that will be used in the final output. The following sections list a number of advanced controls for editing the palette.

Color Depth

To reduce the size of a GIF image quickly, use the Colors setting to reduce the number of colors. This setting determines the total number of colors available for the palette. This figure can be anywhere from 2 to 256. Halving the number of colors will generally halve the size of the image. Of course, this makes fewer colors available to the image output and could compromise quality.

You may use the dithering to approximate lost colors. Dithering arranges the available colors to simulate gradations in shading. Dithering can compromise quality when used with anti-aliasing or transparency, and dithering can carry a penalty in output file size. Setting Dither to 0 forces no dithering, whereas setting it to 100 will dither any colors outside the palette. Loss can also be used to offset the size of a full-palette or dithered GIF but carries a penalty in detail similar to JPEG compression. A setting of 0 ensures pixel accuracy; 100 fully compromises detail for file size.

Transparency

GIF images support transparency. Transparent pixels allow any color information under them, such as a Web page background color or another image layered underneath, to show through. Use the Matte setting to choose the intended background color, if different from the Canvas background color. Directly above the palette is a drop-down menu that allows you to choose between No Transparency (the default), Index Transparency, and Alpha Transparency. GIFs support only Index Transparency—pixels are either on or off, so there can be no gradation to the transparency, which often conflicts with anti-alias shading (much more on this later in the book, but see the following tip for now). Alpha transparency allows transparency shading but is only supported by the PNG format. To pick a color for transparency, choose the Select transparent color eyedropper at the bottom of the Optimize panel. To add more colors as transparent, choose Add Color to Transparency; to remove them, choose Remove Color from Transparency. Transparency will appear in the palette as a swatch of gray-and-white grid.

> *Aliasing* is the jagged edging of curved and diagonal lines in a bitmap image. Enlarging a bitmap image accentuates the effect of aliasing. *Anti-aliasing* is the process of smoothing out those edges. Anti-aliasing is often also referred to as *font smoothing*. Font-smoothing software anti-aliases on-screen type. Graphics software programs have options to anti-alias text and graphics.

Swatches

There are more tools for managing the different colors, or swatches, in the palette. Directly below the palette display is the Sort menu, which allows you to sort the colors by Luminance or Popularity. Luminance sorts from light to dark; Popularity sorts pixels based on how often they appear in the output. Below this, and next to the transparency tools, are tools for managing individual swatches. Select a swatch and choose Edit color to choose a new value from the system color picker. Choose Snap to Web Safe to change the color to the nearest value in the Web 216 palette. The Lock color button allows you to lock the color value from further changes. To the right Add color and Delete color let you add or remove specific colors.

There are a few options for optimizing GIFs that are available only through the Optimize panel Options menu. As shown in Figure 3.11, this menu is located in the upper right corner of the Optimize panel.

FIGURE 3.11

The Optimize panel Options menu offers more options for optimizing images, based on your current selection. Here you see the Options menu when GIF format is selected.

Interlaced

Interlacing allows the pixels in an image to be written in alternating order, so that as the image downloads, it can seem to appear full size more quickly. Every other line loads first, and these are all doubled to display an approximation of the original. Then the remaining lines are loaded in place of the doubles, clearing up the image to full detail. This is commonly used to make images appear more quickly when loading on Web pages because it carries only a small file-size penalty.

Remove Unused Colors

The default for GIF optimization, this allows you to trim down the palette quickly by removing any colors that aren't used in the output (generally because they aren't in the original, either). Remove Unused Colors will not affect locked colors in the palette. Turn this off if you want to work with a full palette and delete colors yourself.

Save Palette

This will save the palette as an ACT palette file for use with Fireworks or other applications. The Load Palette command can also be accessed from the Optimize panel menu, but this is identical to choosing a Custom palette from the palette settings in the panel itself.

JPEG Compression

Because of the limitations GIF posed to photographers, the Joint Photo Experts Group commissioned a standard that came to be known as JPEG. JPEG uses variable lossy compression, which trades quality for file size by approximating the original pixels with an algorithm. The more compression applied, the less original data available for the image, a fact which makes the image appear blurry. This blurriness is another artifact because the approximations won't always be correct, especially at high compression ratios.

JPEGs are now a standard for sharing detailed images in high resolutions. As with GIF images, the Optimize panel offers choices specific to JPEG images, as is seen in Figure 3.12.

FIGURE 3.12
The JPEG format is deceptively simple but can offer incredible compression ratios with acceptable loss.

Matte

The Matte setting is not relevant when woring with JPEG images. It is used to match anti-aliased images to the background color of the target Web page. Matching the matte color to the background removes the blurry edges caused by previous anti-aliasing.

Quality

This is the setting for the level of lossy compression. A value of 100 is indistinguishable from the original, whereas 0 creates the absolutely smallest files. In terms of file size, the change is most noticeable between 100 and 80; a setting in this range will dramatically decrease file size with a minimum of detail loss. A setting of 60 or below gives a very small file, but detail is very noticeably compromised.

Selective Quality

One of the great features of the JPEG format is the ability to use selective compression. With this process important details can be compressed at one level, while background information is compressed at another. You'll go over selective quality in more detail in Chapter 6, "Improving Photos."

Smoothing

JPEG compression breaks an image into a grid and then uses a mathematical algorithm to approximate the content of the grid. The more compression that is applied, the more noticeable the grid and the approximations become. To help alleviate the problem, smoothing can be applied to blur these artifacts. Smoothing is a compromise, however, as it does not improve image detail and can make images appear blurry or out of focus.

Two more important JPEG settings are available from the drop-down menu in the upper right corner of the Optimize panel. Progressive JPEG, which is similar to the GIF Interlaced setting, allows for faster image displays for the Web. Sharpen Color Edges can improve text and line art detail compressed in the JPEG format.

Saving Compression Presets

Once you've worked with the Optimize panel and the preview window to examine the different qualities of GIF and JPEG compression, you may want to save them for use later. Saved setting presets are available in the Settings menu on the Optimize panel, so they're easy to find later, and as a file on your hard disk, so you can share them with others.

To save a custom setting, simply make your optimization choices and press the plus icon next to the settings drop-down. You will be prompted for a name for your preset. Enter one and press OK to continue. The preset will now be available in the settings drop-down menu. To remove a setting from the menu, choose it and then press the minus icon. You will be asked to confirm the deletion. You may also save your custom preset with the Optimize panel drop-down menu by choosing Save Settings.

Another great tool available for GIF, JPEG, and PNG compression is Optimize to Size, which you will find in the Optimize panel's drop-down menu. You will be prompted to enter a size in kilobytes, and the format settings will be automatically changed to fit the image under that value.

Exporting from Fireworks

Now it's time to export your image for use on the Web. You'll have to glance over some basic Web publishing and HTML page topics while you're getting started. You will also be introduced to the Export Preview dialog, where you can fine-tune your optimization settings before exporting and finish a simple placeholder page for your Web site.

Task: Export Image as Page for Web

You have had a chance to look through the most commonly used optimization settings. Now you will take an image file and work through the process of exporting it for Web usage.

1. Choose Export Preview from the File menu or press Ctrl+Shift+X (Windows) or Command+Shift+X (Macintosh).

2. The Export Preview dialog will appear, as shown in Figure 3.13. On the left is where you specify format options, as well as file and animation settings, which are available as tabs in the upper left. On the right is the preview area, which gives you file size feedback, the Settings drop-down menu, and an area to preview the image output.

FIGURE 3.13

The Export Preview dialog lets you focus on the export output settings.

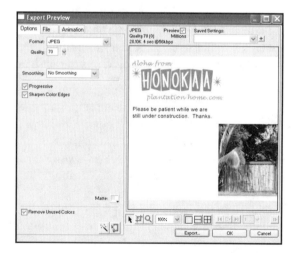

3. From the Format drop-down menu on the Options tab, make sure JPEG is selected and that the Quality setting is at 70.

4. Check the box to select Progressive to create a progressive JPEG. This should also help reduce the file size, which should be less than 30KB.

5. Check the box to select Sharpen Color Edges. Zoom in on the text and graphic with the magnifying glass to see how this affects text and line art—there should be a subtle improvement.

6. In the lower right are the dialog options. Export will begin the process of exporting your graphics. OK will save the current export settings and change the Optimize panel settings to reflect your decisions. Cancel will disregard any changes and return to where you left off. Click Export to continue exporting your image.

7. The Export dialog is where you will save images for use on the Web and other applications. Navigate to the `Fireworks Examples` folder on your hard disk. For the file name go ahead and type **index,** as in Figure 3.14. This will export the image as a file named `index.jpg`.

FIGURE 3.14
The Export dialog allows you to save images in an optimized format and automatically create HTML code.

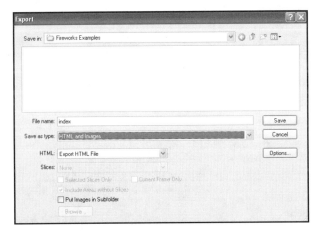

8. For the Save as Type menu, choose HTML and Images. This will export code generated automatically by Fireworks along with the image.

9. The HTML drop-down menu should now be active. Make sure Export to File is selected. This will create a file named `index.htm`. Copy to Clipboard would copy the HTML source code to the clipboard for use in another application, such as a text editor.

> On a Web server the `index.htm` file is often the default file displayed when the parent directory is accessed. Your Web host or network administrator will tell you what your file needs to be called. Other common names are `index.html`, `default.htm`, and `default.html`.

10. Now you may go ahead and click Save or press Return to export your image and Web page.

11. Launch your favorite browser and choose Open from the File menu. Browse to the `Fireworks Examples` folder and select the file `index.htm`. The Web page will now open in your browser and display the image `index.jpg`, as in Figure 3.15.

Figure 3.15
The JPEG image `index.jpg` *is now referenced by the HTML file* `index.htm` *to create a Web page.*

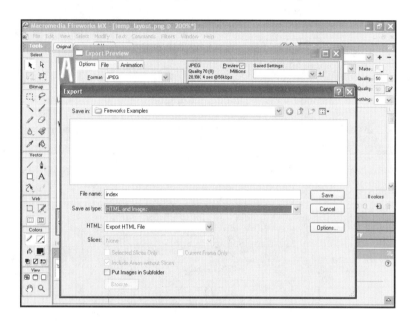

Great! You've started a Web site. You're not quite qualified to start advertising your services as a Web designer, but you should easily be able to get any image into a format ready for the Web. To actually publish your work on the Web, you'll need a World Wide Web host server, which is discussed in the "Using Dreamweaver's Web Publishing Tools" section of Hour 17, "Working with Dreamweaver MX."

Summary

In this hour you covered the basics of export formats and compression techniques, including available export file formats, GIF and JPEG optimization with the Optimize panel, previewing export output, and finally, using Export to save your output to your hard drive along with a simple HTML file so that you can post the image to the Web. In upcoming hours, now that you're prepared to find, create, and finish graphics for the Web, you will be delving more deeply into Fireworks tools and developing your graphic design techniques.

Workshop

In this hour you have covered a lot of ground regarding how to get the best from the Optimize options in Fireworks. Use the following questions and quiz not only to test your memory but also to check that you have understood the concepts involved in image optimization. At the very end are some optional exercises designed to give you ideas on where these techniques can be used.

Q&A

Q What's the best kind of compression?

A There is no universally "best" kind of compression. Different kinds of compression are suited to different kinds of material. Non-lossy compression is better for images where detail is critical. Lossy compression is better for images with many colors or gradients (like photographs) or large dimensions, where detail can be sacrificed for file size.

Q Why would I ever use BMP or PICT files?

A BMP and PICT files do not employ compression and therefore are reliable ways to move images between applications or as backup formats. BMP and PICT files can also be used for system images, such as icons and desktop wallpaper. BMP is the Windows system format; PICT is the Macintosh system format.

Q What on earth is HTML, and why should I care?

A HTML, or Hypertext Markup Language, is the most common method used to compose Web pages. It was developed in the early days of the Internet to format and describe documents for display. HTML files are text files that contain tags to describe the layout. To add an image to a Web page, you insert an HTML image tag that tells the browser where to find the image and where to place it on the page—the HTML file does not actually contain any image files. Fireworks does most of the work for you, but if you're completely unfamiliar with HTML, you may want to pick up a primer, such as *Sams Teach Yourself HTML and XHTML in 24 Hours* by Dick Oliver.

Quiz

1. What export format supports 8-bit alpha transparency?

    a. GIF

    b. JPEG

    c. PNG

2. How does the JPEG format make files smaller?

    a. By approximating image data through lossy compression

    b. By changing the image dimensions to reduce the number of pixels

    c. By employing a 256-color palette to limit color depth

3. What is the Web 216 palette?

    a. The maximum number of colors displayed on a Web page

    b. The colors considered safe on most systems

    c. The only colors available with the GIF format

Quiz Answers

1. c.—GIF images support only index transparency. Alpha transparency allows for transparency shading, or graduated levels of opacity, and is available only in the PNG format. JPEG does not allow for transparency.

2. b.—JPEG uses an algorithm to approximate the original image with less actual data. The accuracy of the approximation, or ratio of compression, determines how much detail is traded for the reduction in file size.

3. b.—The colors in the Web 216, or Websafe, palette will appear reasonably similar on almost any computer system. These colors should be the starting point when considering colors to be used on the Web and are intended to help foster color accuracy for creative and commercial images and artwork.

Exercises

1. Locate a selection of files in different formats. You should find quite a few on your hard drive, or you could download some from the Internet. Use the Optimize panel in Fireworks to see in more detail how the different settings can cause major changes. This is best seen over a number of images.

2. If you are not confident about optimizing your own images at this point, then experiment with the Export Wizard. Not only can you choose between different file types, but you can still make changes to the settings from within the panel.

3. Get used to optimizing your images in a sensible order. Start by using the preview panes to choose the best option for your image. Then choose options specific to your chosen format, before finally adjusting colors as required. Using this 1-2-3 approach should produce consistent results.

PART II

Bitmap Editing:
The Digital Darkroom

Hour

Hour 4

Working with Bitmap Images

In this hour you will begin working with bitmap images, which are the foundation of computer graphics. First you'll learn how to work with the Canvas, layers, and colors, and then you'll try out the bitmap drawing and painting tools. The next two hours in this part, "Editing Bitmap Graphics" and "Improving Photos," will introduce you to bitmap editing and advanced creative techniques.

In this hour you will

- Learn what makes up a bitmap object
- Change the Canvas color and size settings
- Become acquainted with the Layers panel
- Work with the Color Mixer and swatches
- Use the drawing and painting tools to create bitmap graphics

What Is a Bitmap?

A bitmap image is a two-dimensional grid of units called pixels. The two dimensions are width and height. The resolution of a bitmap is measured in dots or points per inch (DPI or PPI). A higher DPI generally means a more detailed image. As you increase the magnification of a bitmap image using the Zoom tool, the individual pixels become larger and larger, until you can see each individual area of color.

Each pixel carries a number that determines what color it is. This number is a series of bits, or 1's and 0's. The more bits assigned to each pixel, the greater the color depth. A 1-bit pixel is usually either black or white. Eight bits can create up to 256 (2 to the power of 8) colors. Fireworks supports 24-bit RGB color, which is the standard color space for computer monitors. The Fireworks native format is 32-bit, which supports both RGB color and an 8-bit alpha channel for transparency masking.

Bitmaps are limited in two ways: Extreme resizing can degrade image detail, and as image size or resolution is doubled, the file size increases fourfold. In particular, if an image is made very small, most of the detail will be lost. If a small image is made bigger, on the other hand, artifacts called jaggies occur. Such situations are improved somewhat by a resampling algorithm, but large changes still degrade the final image. And as color depth or pixel dimensions increase, file size begins to increase exponentially. A 24-bit scan at 300 DPI of an $8\frac{1}{2}$-by-11-inch drawing, for example, is over 24 megabytes if not compressed. Doubling the resolution to 600 DPI quadruples the file size to nearly 100 megabytes!

Changing the Canvas

On the Web images are rarely more than a few hundred pixels wide or tall, and by using GIF or JPEG compression, you can keep almost any image under 100 kilobytes without sacrificing too much detail. Using the Property Inspector, it's easy to quickly resample a bitmap image or change the size of the Canvas to cut a bitmap down to size.

 Sometimes you will want to rotate both the image and the dimensions of the Canvas. To do this, choose Rotate 180, Rotate 90 CW, or Rotate 90 CCW from the Canvas commands on the Modify menu. This will rotate the Canvas and all the objects on it. If you would like to make the Canvas smaller to fit just the objects that are visible, use Trim Canvas. If you would like to make the canvas larger to accommodate objects that may otherwise run off it, choose Fit Canvas. You can also access Image Size, Canvas Size, and Canvas Color from the Modify menu.

Task: Change Image and Canvas Size

Here you'll work with a sample image and resize it with the Property Inspector. If you want to resize the entire image in Fireworks, you use the Image Size command. You can also access the Image Size command from the Canvas commands on the Modify menu.

1. Download and unzip the example materials for Hour 04 into the Fireworks_Examples folder.

2. Use the Open command on the File menu to open the JPEG image honokaa_coast. When you open an image in non-Fireworks format, the Canvas takes the image dimensions, and the image is a bitmap object on the Background layer, as in Figure 4.1.

Bitmap object on background layer

FIGURE 4.1

When you open a nonnative bitmap image, it is loaded as a bitmap object on the Background layer, and the Canvas size is set accordingly.

Bitmap object size   Canvas

3. Select the Pointer tool. Click the gray area surrounding the Canvas. If this area is not visible, use the Zoom tool or the Magnification setting in the View menu to reduce the magnification until the entire Canvas is viewable in the workspace.

The Property Inspector, shown in Figure 4.2, will now show the Canvas properties—Canvas color, compression preset, and buttons to bring up the Canvas Size and Image Size dialogs.

Canvas color

FIGURE 4.2
Clicking outside the Canvas in the workspace brings up the Canvas settings in the Property Inspector.

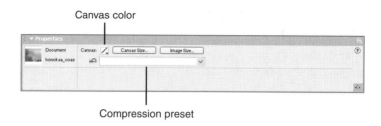

Compression preset

4. Click the Image Size button to change the image size. This image will be a great background for the home page, so go ahead and resize it to fit in a browser window. Changing the image size changes both the Canvas size and the size of all the objects on the Canvas proportionally.

5. Make sure the Constrain Proportions and Resample Image check boxes are checked, as in Figure 4.3. The method for Resampling, to the right of the Resample Image setting, should be set to Bicubic; this generally delivers the best results.

FIGURE 4.3
The Image Size dialog changes the Canvas size and all the objects on the Canvas proportionally.

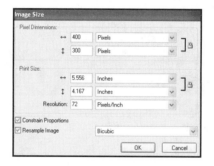

6. Change the width of the image to 400 pixels by typing **400** in the first field. Because the proportions are constrained, the height of the image will change to maintain the original aspect ratio (in this case, the height will change to 300 pixels). Click OK to make the change.

7. Because the image size has changed as the magnification has remained the same, the image will appear smaller in the workspace. Press Control+0 (numeral zero, Windows) or Command+0 (zero, Macintosh) or choose Fit All from the View menu to change the magnification to fit the Canvas within the workspace, as shown in Figure 4.4. To make some room for navigation and graphics, you will need to change the Canvas size, as well.

FIGURE 4.4

When the image size changes, the image magnification stays the same. Choose Fit All from the View menu to fill the workspace. Note that the magnification is now higher (115%) to fit the smaller image in the same workspace window.

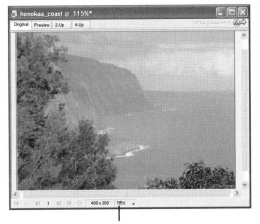

Canvas view magnification

8. Click the Canvas Size button to bring up the Canvas Size dialog. When you change the canvas size, the size of objects on the canvas will not be changed, meaning that bitmap objects will not be resampled. Change the width to 500 pixels by typing **500** in the width field. Change the height to 375 by typing **375** in the next field, as in Figure 4.5.

FIGURE 4.5

Altering the Canvas size does not affect the size of objects on the Canvas.

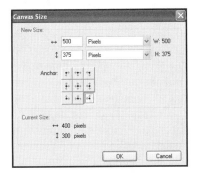

9. The anchor specifies which point the changes reference. In this case, you want the additional Canvas area above and to the left of the image, so choose the bottom right of the current Canvas—the opposite corner—as the anchor. Anchoring in the center would apply the new area equally around each side of the image. Anchoring a point and making the Canvas smaller would remove pixels from the area opposite the anchor. Click OK or press Enter to accept the changes.

10. The new area of the Canvas will appear as a grid of gray and white squares. This grid indicates complete transparency. This is the default Canvas color in Fireworks.

You can change this color with the Canvas setting in the Property Inspector. For now, change it to white by clicking the swatch to bring up the swatch palette and selecting white with the eyedropper. The results are shown in Figure 4.6.

11. Now use Save to create a Fireworks source PNG in the Fireworks Examples folder named home_layout. You'll come back to this image later.

Using the Layers Panel

Fireworks, like many other graphics applications, uses layers to help you manage objects in an image. Layers are like transparent sheets; you can draw on individual sheets and then change how they're stacked, in order to change which elements are in the background and which are in the foreground. In this case, the Canvas is the surface you layer the sheets on.

You can work with layers through the Layers panel (see Figure 4.7). Bitmap editing is considered destructive; when you change a pixel, any information that was previously there is lost. This is why it's so important to back up your source images. By using layers and bitmap objects, you can break your bitmaps into discrete parts, so you can preserve and compare your editing decisions nondestructively.

FIGURE 4.7

The Layers panel is one of the most important tools when working with bitmaps.

At the top of the Layers panel, you'll see a small icon of a gray-and-white grid, which means opacity (see Figure 4.8). The field next to this icon is the Opacity setting for that layer: 100% means fully opaque, and 0% means fully transparent. You can quickly change the opacity of the layer with the slider immediately to the right of the opacity field.

FIGURE **4.8**

The Opacity and blending mode settings for a layer.

Opacity setting   Blending mode

Next to the transparency setting is the Blending Mode menu. Blending modes change how two layers or objects interact based on their color values. There are any number of interesting effects possible with blending modes, and these will be discussed in the section titled "Drawing and Painting."

Underneath the transparency and blending mode settings is the actual list of layers, shown in Figure 4.9. The first, top layer is always the Web Layer in Fireworks. There can be only one Web Layer, and it cannot be duplicated, deleted, or renamed. The Web Layer is where you'll define your slices for HTML table layouts. Information in the Web Layer will not actually be displayed in the image, and you cannot draw or place objects (other than slices) on the Web Layer.

4

Empty expanded layer

FIGURE 4.9

*Each layer is a row in
the Layers panel and
is identified by a
folder icon.*

Active layer

Below the Web Layer are all your other layers; these layers are where you'll assemble
your graphics and images. Each layer will be a row in this table. The topmost layer of
the image will appear above any layers below it. The arrangement of objects in a layer
will also be visible when the layer is expanded; objects, like layers, appear on top of
objects arranged beneath them on the same layer, as in Figure 4.10. Next to each layer's
name is a folder icon. Next to each object's name is a thumbnail of the object. To expand
a layer, click the expand/collapse icon in the leftmost column of the layer row on the
Layers panel.

FIGURE 4.10

*Here two text
objects are added to
the Background layer.
You'll note the stacking
order in the Layers
panel—the word "Over"
appears over the
bitmap object, while
"Under" is covered
by the bitmap object.*

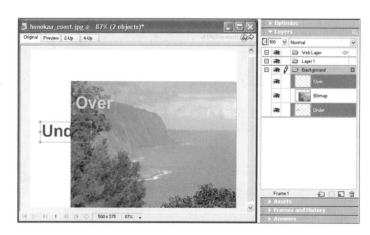

Each row in the Layers panel also allows you to show the layer (second column, eyeball icon visible) or hide the layer (no icon). You can also hide objects within a layer. Simply click the eyeball icon to hide a layer. For a hidden layer, click the empty area next to the layer or object. Hidden layers and hidden objects are not exported with the image—this quality allows you to export many different versions of a document. The column next to the layer's name displays whether the layer is active, inactive, or locked. If a layer is active, a pencil will appear in this column, and the layer name will appear on a blue background. To lock a layer and prevent changes to it, click this column; a padlock icon appears. To unlock a locked layer, click the padlock, and the pencil icon will reappear. To make a layer active, click its row in the Layers panel or select an object on that layer. A locked layer cannot be the active layer.

Each layer and each object in a layer can have a name. This can be critical when organizing a detailed layout or when sharing your graphics with others. To rename a layer or object, double-click its current name. You will be presented with a dialog where you can type a new name. You can also choose to share a layer across frames. This means that the layer will be visible in all the frames of a document. The Web Layer is always shared across frames. If a layer is shared across frames, a filmstrip icon will appear to the right of the layer name. (Frames will be discussed in more detail later in the book.)

At the bottom of the Layers panel are the layer controls: New/Duplicate Layer, Add Mask, New Bitmap Image, and Delete Selection (as shown in Figure 4.11). The New/Duplicate Layer option creates either a blank new layer or a duplicate layer. To create a new layer, click the New/Duplicate Layer button. To duplicate a layer, select an existing layer, click and hold to drag it, and then release it over the New/Duplicate Layer button. The duplicate layer will be created below the selected layer.

FIGURE 4.11

The basic layer controls are New/Duplicate Layer, Add Mask, New Bitmap Image, and Delete Selection.

The Add Mask button allows you to mask a layer with a bitmap alpha channel. A mask reveals some parts of the image and hides others. A black mask hides everything, and a white mask makes everything visible; shades of gray allow for gradation in the mask. This technique is used mostly with bitmap layers because applying a mask to a layer flattens all the objects on that layer into a single masked image.

The New Bitmap Image button creates an empty (transparent) bitmap object of the same dimensions as the Canvas in the selected layer. This is so you can quickly employ a bitmap fill or begin drawing to a bitmap object on the Canvas. The Delete Selection button does just that. Select a layer or object in the Layers panel and click the Delete Selection button to delete it. You can also drag and drop the selection on this button to delete it.

The Layers panel Options menu, the drop-down menu at the top right of the panel, also has some important layer functions, Flatten Selection and Merge Down. Flatten Selection takes all objects or layers selected and creates a single bitmap image on a single layer, much like what happens when you export a Fireworks PNG. Merge Down is similar to Flatten Selection except that it merges all selected objects to a bitmap image residing below the bottommost object. If a bitmap object is not available, Merge Down will not be available on the Options menu.

Choosing Colors and Managing Swatches

Another critical area of working with bitmap objects and the drawing tools is understanding how to work with the color mixer and swatches. The color mixer helps you choose individual colors to use with the drawing tools. Swatches are a way of saving a group of individual colors that you will be using repeatedly. Remember that a bitmap image is simply a grid of pixels with different color values, and a palette is the group of color swatches used in the particular image. Understanding the concepts behind the color palette is very important.

Fireworks uses a 24-bit RGB palette. *RGB* stands for red, green, and blue. A 24-bit image is actually composed of three 8-bit grayscale images—one for each color. The three channels are combined to represent the colors on screen. Your computer monitor is an RGB device; each point, or pixel, is composed of three phosphors—a red one, a green one, and a blue one (in the case of liquid crystal displays, each point is a group of charged crystals). This is the process of additive color. Generally, anyone browsing the Web will be viewing images (and their colors) in the additive color space.

Images for print are different, being made through subtractive color. Unlike a computer monitor, which emits light, paper reflects light. Colors are achieved by adding the inverse of the desired color. Black ink does not reflect as much light as white paper and therefore appears much darker. The inverse, or opposite, of red, green, and blue are cyan, magenta, and yellow, respectively. The subtractive color space is called CMYK, for cyan, magenta, yellow, and black. When a page is printed, all four inks are added to create shades of color. Some image files might have been converted to CMYK for printing; Fireworks will automatically convert them into RGB when they are opened or imported. For this reason, an image printed from Fireworks may not be ideal. When working with images that will be printed, use an application that will perform CMYK separations, such as Macromedia Freehand or the Adobe design products.

The colors in the RGB color space, or spectrum, have names expressed in hexadecimal numbers, or hex codes, which are derived from a base 16 character set (the ten digits, 0 through 9, and the first six letters of the alphabet, A through F). Each color name consists of six characters. The hex code for absolute black is 000000. The hex code for white is FFFFFF. Medium gray is 6C6C6C. It's not important to know how to find a color with hex codes, but it is helpful to know that you can refer to colors by specific names when you want to ensure you're using the same colors as someone else.

Fireworks makes finding and organizing colors easy. The Mixer panel allows you to mix colors by changing their relative values of red, green, and blue (or gray, if you are working with a grayscale image). The Swatches panel lets you save individual colors so you can quickly find them later. The following sections describe the options for these two panels.

Color Mixer Panel

The Color Mixer panel, shown in Figure 4.12, allows you to mix colors numerically or by eye. The Color Mixer panel is always available from the Window menu. The first two settings are for the stroke and fill colors. The stroke color, denoted by the pencil icon, is the color that will be applied to any pencil or brush strokes as well as to vector lines. The fill color can be applied with the paint bucket or as the fill color for a vector shape.

4

FIGURE 4.12

Use the Color Mixer panel to choose and manipulate colors.

Clicking the stroke or fill color swatch will bring up the Swatch menu, shown in Figure 4.13. The current swatch palette will pop up (the default palette is the Web 216 palette). The white swatch with the diagonal red line indicates colorless transparency. To bring up the system color picker, click the color wheel icon at the upper right of the pop-up swatch menu. The arrow at the top right will let you choose different swatch layouts and palette sets. The stroke and fill swatches are also available on the Tools panel, in the Color section.

FIGURE 4.13

The Swatch menu pops up when you click a stroke or fill color.

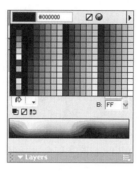

The stroke and fill color settings are also available on the Tools panel, along with the most common color tasks. These are Set Default Stroke/Fill Colors, which automatically sets the stroke to black and the fill to white; No Stroke or Fill, which makes the selected swatch transparent; and Swap Stroke and Fill Colors, which quickly changes the stroke color to the fill color and vice versa.

Below the stroke and fill controls is a color spectrum, shown in Figure 4.14. The hue changes horizontally and the saturation changes vertically. You can use this tool to quickly select an approximate color from the full spectrum. To fine-tune this color, you can use the red, green, and blue sliders to add or subtract tones from the color. As you move the slider, a value will change in the field. You can also edit this value by selecting it and typing a new value. The range of values for each channel is 0 to 255.

FIGURE 4.14

The color spectrum and RGB values can help you define and refine a particular color.

If you need to know the hex code for a color or wish to define a color with values other than RGB, use the Mixer panel Options menu (upper right corner of the panel) to choose RGB, Hexadecimal, CMY (not CMYK, but the equivalent of inverse RGB), HSB (Hue, Saturation, Brightness), or Grayscale. Switching to Hexadecimal will change the values for red, green, and blue to their hex code equivalents. CMY lets you manipulate the colors subtractively; more cyan means less red, and so forth. HSB lets you choose colors by choosing a hue from a color wheel, anywhere from 0 to 360. Saturation is the percentage of saturation of the hue, or the distance from the edge of the wheel from 0 to 100 percent. Brightness is the percentage of white in the color, from 0 (black) to 100 (pure color).

Swatches

The Swatches panel, shown in Figure 4.15, is pretty simple. Using the Mixer, choose a color for the stroke or fill. Then bring up the Swatches panel. When you mouseover the gray area at the bottom of the Swatches panel, the cursor will change to the paint bucket. Click to add this color to your swatch palette. To choose a color from the swatch palette, with the stroke or fill active, mouseover a swatch in the palette. The cursor will change to the eyedropper. Click to change the stroke or fill to this color.

FIGURE 4.15

The Swatches panel shows your palette of selected colors.

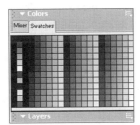

The Swatches panel Options menu also has tools to let you add, replace, save, and clear swatches in the palette. Swatches are saved in color table or ACT files. To save a palette, bring up the Swatches panel Options menu by clicking the icon in the upper right of the panel. Choose Save Swatches, name the file, and select a folder on your hard disk to save it in. To add colors, choose Add Swatches and choose an ACT file from your hard disk. Use Clear Swatches to clear all the swatches from the palette. Replace Swatches clears the current swatches and then adds new swatches from a color table file you select.

Drawing and Painting

The tools you'll use most often when drawing and painting in bitmap mode are the pencil, the brush, and the eraser. The paint bucket is also very useful, and that will be discussed along with the color selection tools in the next hour, "Editing Bitmap Graphics." The pencil is used mostly for editing at the pixel level and for creating fine outlines for masks. The Brush tool is really a set of brushes; it can mimic an airbrush, watercolors, oils, acrylics—you name it. The Brush tool is used for creative bitmap work and retouching. The eraser removes color information from pixels. The paint bucket fills an area of similarly colored pixels. You'll be introduced to the rest of the bitmap tools in the next hour and Hour 6, "Improving Photos."

> The most useful tool when working with bitmaps is undo. Undo has the power to immediately erase your mistakes and return your work to wherever you started. You can undo a drawing step by choosing Undo from the Edit menu or by pressing Control+Z (Windows) or Command+Z (Macintosh). Fireworks saves multiple levels of undo in the History panel, allowing you to go back any number of steps to correct any mistakes.

The settings and options for each tool are available in the Property Inspector when the tool is selected. Before you start working, though, you'll examine each tool's properties.

Pencil

The Pencil tool has only one stroke style—single pixel. To draw with the Pencil tool, select the tool and click an area of the Canvas (if a bitmap object has not been created on the active layer, a new one will be created when the pencil or brush is used). Holding down the mouse button, drag the cursor over an area of the Canvas. Only the pixels directly underneath the cursor are changed to the pencil color (the default is black). Release the mouse button to stop drawing.

> To draw a straight line with the pencil, hold down the shift key while clicking and dragging vertically, horizontally, or diagonally. The shift key will constrain the mouse to 45-degree angles.

The properties for the Pencil tool include the stroke color (which is the same as the stroke color setting on the Tools or Mixer panel) and Anti-Aliased, Auto-erase, Preserve Transparency, Opacity, and Blending Mode settings. The anti-aliased option adds shaded pixels to curves and lines to make them look smoother. Auto-erase means that if you click an existing pixel of the stroke color with the Pencil tool, it will be erased instead of remaining unchanged. Preserve Transparency will prevent you from editing areas of pixels that are transparent; you will be allowed only to draw over existing pixels. Opacity is the transparency setting for the pencil stroke, and Blending Mode can change the interaction between the color being changed and the color being applied. The next section, about the Brush tool, explains blending modes.

Brush

The Brush tool is one of the most versatile tools in Fireworks. You can create any number of images and effects using the brush, from standard 1-pixel lines to airbrush and watercolor effects. To draw with the brush, simply select the brush, choose the appropriate settings, and then click-drag a bitmap object (if there is no bitmap object on the active layer, one will be created for you). Release the mouse button to finish your brush stroke. To restrict your brush to straight lines at 45-degree angles, hold down the shift key while clicking and dragging.

Another of the most useful tools for drawing and painting, in any mode, is a tablet and stylus. You'll find that simple drawing tasks, such as signing your name, are almost impossible with a mouse, trackball, or touch pad. Small, inexpensive stylus tablets are available from Wacom and other manufacturers for both Macintosh and Windows machines with USB or serial adapters.

There are a number of settings for the Brush tool. They are available in the Property Inspector when the Brush tool is selected, as shown in Figure 4.16. The first row of options includes stroke color, stroke width, and stroke style. Set the stroke color by clicking the swatch and choosing a color from the pop-up swatch palette (you can also set the stroke color in the Tools panel or Mixer panel). The stroke width is the width or diameter, in pixels, of a square or round brush, respectively. There are a number of stroke style groups, including Pencil, Basic, Air Brush, Calligraphy, Charcoal, Crayon, Felt Tip, Oil, Random, Watercolor, and Unnatural. The Stroke Options setting lets you specify advanced stroke settings and save custom strokes to the stroke style menu.

FIGURE 4.16

The Property Inspector lets you fine-tune your tools, like the Brush tool.

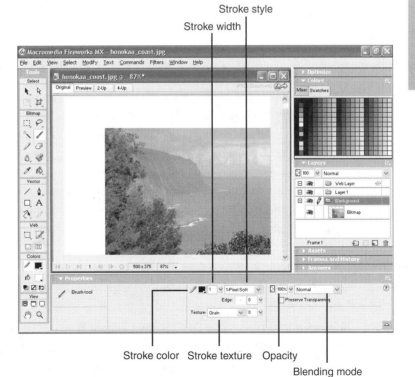

The other rows let you change some of the basic stroke style settings, including edge softness and texturing. Edge softness is the gradual feathering of the brush tip. It is measured as a percentage from 0 to 100 of the total width of the brush tip. A value of 0 means the tip is uniformly colored; 100 means the tip begins to soften immediately from the center.

Textures can be applied to create all kinds of interesting effects. A texture can be created from any Fireworks PNG file by choosing Custom from the Texture drop-down menu. A texture is a tiled image that fills any area covered by the brush. The mix of stroke color and texture is on a percentage scale, with 0 being no texture and 100 no color.

To the right of the brush stroke settings are the Opacity and blending mode settings. Opacity is the measurement of how opaque or transparent the stroke color or texture will appear. A value of 0 is transparent; 100, opaque.

Blending modes is a powerful tool you can use with the brush as well as with other objects and layers. Blending modes change the way the applied blend color affects the base color to which it's applied. For instance, the Normal blend mode replaces the base color with the blend color, and the result is the blend color. The other blending modes:

Multiply—Multiply adds the blend color to the base color, resulting in a darker combination of the two.

Screen—Screen inverts the blend color before adding it to the base color, lightening the base color.

Darken—This mode compares the blend color to the base color and chooses the darker of the two as the result.

Lighten—Lighten is similar to Darken, but the result is the lighter of the base color or the blend color.

Difference—Difference subtracts the lighter color from the darker color. If the blend color is lighter than the base color, the blend color is subtracted from the base color.

Hue—Hue changes the hue of the base color to the hue of the blend color, but saturation and brightness are not changed.

Saturation—Saturation changes the saturation of the base color to the saturation of the blend color, but hue and brightness are not changed.

Color—This changes the base color hue and saturation to that of the blend color but does not change the brightness.

Luminosity—This changes the brightness of the base color to that of the blend color but does not affect hue or saturation.

Invert—This inverts the base color (like a color negative), regardless of the blend color.

Tint—Tint adds neutral gray to the base color.

Erase—Erase removes all color information from the base color.

Eraser

The Eraser tool is pretty straightforward: It removes pixels from a bitmap object. With the Eraser tool selected, you can change its settings in the Property Inspector. These include Size, in pixels; Edge Softness, a percentage of size; Shape, either round or square; and Transparency, where the eraser transparency is inverted—100 means the eraser will make pixels completely transparent, and 0 means the eraser will not change the pixels. To draw with the eraser, click-drag an area of a bitmap object. Holding down Shift will force the cursor to travel in a straight line.

Task: Working with Layers and the Brush Tool

▼ TASK

Now it's time to get creative with the drawing and painting tools. It's important to try your techniques on a scratch file before editing a bitmap. When you do want to open a bitmap for editing, it's wise to create one or more duplicates of the bitmap object on different layers, so you can always return to the original.

1. From Fireworks, open a new file. Set the dimensions to 300 by 300 and the Canvas color to white, as in Figure 4.17. Click OK to continue.

FIGURE 4.17

Create a new file 300 pixels tall and 300 pixels wide with a white background.

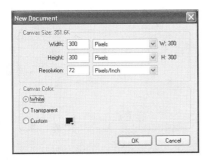

4

2. Make sure the Layers panel is visible. The new file will start with a single, empty layer named Layer 1. Double-click the layer name to change it. Name this layer Background (see Figure 4.18). Click OK to continue.

FIGURE 4.18

Double-clicking the current layer or object name allows you to change it.

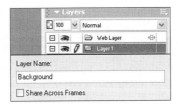

3. Click and hold on the layer called Background. Drag the mouse to the New/Duplicate Layer button. A new layer named Background1 will be created. Double-click this layer to rename it Foreground. Click OK to continue.

4. Because you'll want to draw the background first, click the column to the left of the Foreground layer to lock it. A padlock icon will appear. Click the same column next to the Web Layer to lock it; if it's the active layer, your drawing tools will be disabled. Now click the Background layer to activate it.

5. Select the Brush tool. From the Property Inspector, change the stroke color to green and the stroke style to the Basic Crayon setting (select Crayon from the Stroke Style pop-up menu and choose Basic from the submenu). Change the stroke color to a grass green.

6. Using your mouse, click-drag the Brush tool on the Canvas to begin filling the bottom third of the Canvas with a nice green lawn. When you're done, expand the Background layer in the Layers panel. You'll notice that there is now a bitmap object element under that layer, as in Figure 4.19. Double-click the object name (Bitmap) to change it to Grass.

FIGURE 4.19

By drawing on the Canvas with the Brush tool, you automatically create a new bitmap object on the active layer.

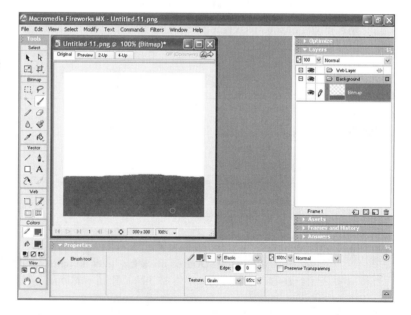

7. While in the Layers panel, click the New Bitmap Image button at the bottom. This will create a new bitmap object in the Background layer.

8. Change the stroke color on the Tools panel to a sky blue. Select the Brush tool. Begin painting in the empty area above the green grass. You'll notice that a thumb-

nail of the new bitmap object in the Layers panel will contain the blue pixels. Go ahead and draw over the grass; the object Grass won't be affected.

9. In the Layers panel, name this new object Sky. If you drew over the edge of the grass horizon, don't worry. Click the object Sky and drag it down until a gray highlight appears beneath the object Grass. Release the mouse button to arrange the object Sky behind the object Grass. The edge of the grass will now overlap the edge of the sky at the horizon, as in Figure 4.20.

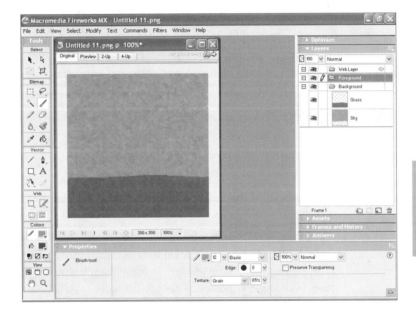

10. Create another new bitmap image with the New Bitmap Image button on the Layers panel. Rename the object Sun. Choose a bright yellow for the stroke color. With the brush tool, draw a circle in the upper right corner of the image.

11. Lock the Background layer by clicking the column to the left of the layer name. Now click the padlock on the Foreground layer to unlock and activate that layer.

12. On the Foreground layer, you're going to draw a red house with white trim. First select a red stroke color and draw a simple house. A new bitmap object will automatically be created in the empty layer. Now change the stroke color to white and add trim around the roof, door, and windows. Because you didn't create a new bitmap object, the white trim replaced the original red pixels in the bitmap object.

13. Go ahead and unlock the Background layer and click the layer name to select it. From the Layers panel Options menu, select Flatten Selection. This will flatten the three bitmap objects on the layer into a single bitmap object.

14. Now click the Foreground layer to activate it. This time select Merge Down from the Layers panel Options menu. The bitmap object from the Foreground layer will now be added to the bitmap object on the Background layer to create a single bitmap object. A masterpiece!

Summary

So far you've explored the tip of the iceberg. You should be familiar with how bitmaps are stored and displayed as a grid of colored pixels, with the difference between destructive and nondestructive bitmap editing, and with using the bitmap drawing and painting tools. In the next hour you'll learn how the bitmap selection tools chop up existing graphics, which you can then start to change and rearrange.

Workshop

These questions will test your knowledge of working with layers and the bitmap tools.

Q&A

Q Why do I need the Pencil and Eraser tools if I can do the same thing with the brush?

A The Pencil and Eraser tools are there for two reasons: First, they've been in almost every bitmap editing application in history and many people would feel uncomfortable without them; second, they free you from having to change your brush settings every time you want to simply edit a few pixels or erase a portion of the image.

Q After a bitmap is flattened, can I unflatten it?

A Unless you just flattened some bitmap objects in Fireworks, which you can simply undo, you're out of luck. Once you save the image and quit Fireworks, the object arrangement is lost. It's important to use Save As or Save a Copy to create a backup before you flatten anything.

Q When I print from Fireworks, why do the colors look washed out?

A Fireworks uses the RGB color space, but your printer uses the CMYK color space. RGB is an additive color method and can reproduce a wider range of the spectrum than CMYK can. The drivers that came with your printer are responsible for automatically converting RGB colors into CMYK colors but may not offer you the kind of control you need for optimizing the output. Use an application like Freehand, Illustrator, or CorelDRAW to convert your RGB images to CMYK and adjust the colors for print output.

Quiz

1. What's the difference between the stroke and fill colors?

   a. The stroke is the foreground color, and the fill is the background color.

   b. The stroke is for vector-drawing tools, and the fill is for bitmap-drawing tools.

   c. The stroke is the color used by the drawing tool, and the fill is used to color shapes.

2. What color system would you use to name a specific color?

   a. RGB numbers

   b. Hexadecimal numbers

   c. Hue, Saturation, and Brightness (HSB) numbers

3. What are swatches?

   a. The individual colors that make up the palette

   b. The tool you use to manipulate individual colors

   c. A disciplinary tool

Quiz Answers

1. c.—The stroke color affects bitmap drawing and painting tools, such as the pencil and brush. The fill color is used by the paint bucket and vector shapes to fill an area or shape with color.

2. b.—Although you can certainly use RGB or HSB values, hexadecimal numbers, or hex codes, are often shorter and more widely understood.

3. a.—Swatches are samples of particular colors. The palette is a group of swatches. The mixer is used to manipulate individual colors. Fireworks does not use disciplinary tools!

HOUR 5

Editing Bitmap Graphics

In the previous hour, "Working with Bitmap Images," you learned how to create bitmap objects and work with colors, layers, and the drawing and painting tools. In this hour the focus will be on editing existing images. With Fireworks you can do all sorts of interesting things to photos and graphics that you can't do in the darkroom or on the drafting table.

In this hour you will

- Become acquainted with the bitmap selection tools
- Learn how to select and change areas of color
- Create multiple instances of a bitmap graphic
- Transform bitmap objects with Scale, Rotate, and Skew
- Add Fireworks effects to enhance bitmap objects

Area Selection Tools

One of the keys to successful graphic design is the ability to focus on critical visual details. One of the most common ways to cut down on visual clutter is to remove or sublimate the unimportant parts of an image. The area selection tools select an area of pixels in a bitmap to be cut or copied and also help define areas on the image that you would like to edit, while preventing other areas from being changed.

First you need to learn about some of the critical tools and their options; then you can start using them on some real photos. These tools include the Pointer and Crop tools in the Select group and the Marquee, Lasso, and Magic Wand tools in the Bitmap group on the Tools panel, shown in Figure 5.1.

FIGURE 5.1

The selection tools can be found in the Select and Bitmap groups on the Tools panel.

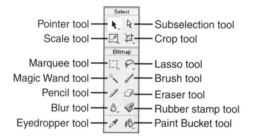

Pointer Tool

You'll be using the pointer much of the time, whether you are editing bitmaps, vectors, or slices. The pointer selects objects on the Canvas. The pointer does not have any settings in the Property Inspector; instead, you use the pointer to select an object to bring up the object's settings in the Property Inspector.

To select an object with the pointer, click the object in the Canvas. It will be highlighted, as in Figure 5.2. The pointer will select an object only if it is arranged on an active layer and is visible. If the object you want to select is arranged behind a selectable object, you can use the Select Behind tool (press V or 0 to toggle between the Pointer and Select

Behind tools). In the case of bitmaps with transparent areas, the pointer will not select a bitmap object if you click an area with no pixels. You must select a colored area to select the object.

FIGURE 5.2

A selected bitmap object will be highlighted by the object selection box, and its settings will be available in the Property Inspector.

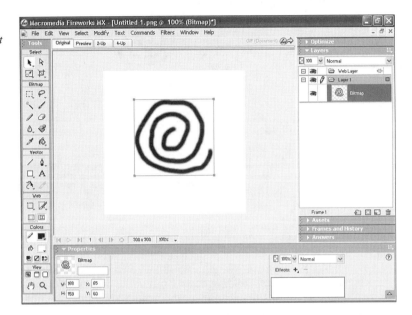

When the Pointer tool is selected, you can browse the objects on the Canvas by mousing over them. When the mouse is over a selectable object, the object will be surrounded by a red highlight box (default). Click to select an object when it is highlighted. The box will change to blue (default). The object is now selected, and its properties will come up in the Property Inspector.

When an object is selected with the Pointer tool, you can move the object by click-dragging the image to where you would like it. You can also use the arrow keys on the keyboard to move the image one pixel at a time (left, right, up, or down). You also can position the object precisely by changing the X and Y position values in the Property Inspector (below the object thumbnail). The values are relative to the top left corner of the Canvas (0,0). Check out the change in properties from Figure 5.2 to Figure 5.3.

5

FIGURE 5.3

*Width, height, and
position can be
changed numerically
in the Property
Inspector.*

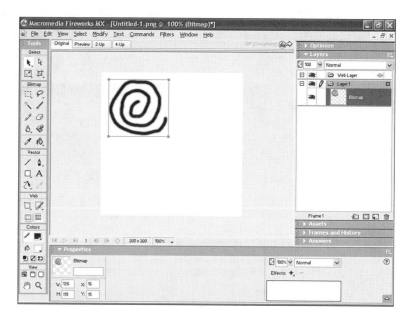

You can also quickly resize and resample a bitmap by clicking and dragging the blue
boxes at the corners. Holding down Shift while dragging forces the width and height
attributes to change in proportion. This can also be done by changing the W and H
dimension values in the Property Inspector. Resizing will be discussed in more detail
later in this hour in the section on transforming bitmaps.

Crop Tool

The Crop tool is very useful for quickly editing images and the Canvas simultaneously.
With the Crop tool you click-drag to create a square area on the Canvas that you want to
preserve, as in Figure 5.4. You can change the crop area by clicking the square handles at
the corners and on the sides. You can also type the crop area width, height, and X,Y position in the Property Inspector when the Crop tool is selected.

FIGURE 5.4

*The crop bounding
box can be adjusted
with the handles on
the sides and at the
corners.*

When you're done selecting your crop area, you can double-click within the crop area or select Crop Document from the Edit menu. The Canvas will be resized to the size of the crop area, removing all of the image that falls outside the selected area, as in Figure 5.5.

You can also select a bitmap object with the Pointer tool and then select Crop Selected Bitmap to set the crop area to the position and dimensions of the selected bitmap object.

FIGURE 5.5

The image and Canvas have now been cropped to the same size.

Pressing C cycles between the Crop tool and the Export Area tool. With the Export Area tool, you choose an area of the Canvas the same way as you would with the Crop tool. Double-click within the area to bring up the Export Preview dialog so you can quickly output the area as a graphics file.

Marquee Tools

The Marquee and Oval Marquee tools select rectangular and elliptical areas of pixels, respectively, in a bitmap object. You can toggle between them by pressing M. With the Marquee or Oval Marquee tool selected, click-drag to draw a rectangle or ellipse over a bitmap object on the Canvas. Holding down Shift while dragging forces the marquee proportions to be equal, creating a square or circular selection, as in Figure 5.6.

5

FIGURE 5.6

The rectangular marquee can be constrained to square proportions by holding down Shift while dragging the mouse.

If you want to change the dimensions or position of a marquee, you can edit the width, height, and X and Y position values in the Property Inspector. If you want to specify an aspect ratio or fixed size for your selection before you draw it, set the marquee Style setting in the Property Inspector to Fixed Ratio or Fixed Size; then set the desired width and height ratio or size in the fields below. Click-drag to create an area with a fixed ratio. If Fixed Size is selected, simply click the top left corner of the area you want to select, and the marquee will appear in that position at the specified dimensions.

A marquee selection edge can be set as either Hard, Anti-aliased, or Feathered. Examples are shown in Figure 5.7. A hard edge means that pixels within the selection are selected and pixels beyond the selection are disregarded, with no gradation. Anti-aliasing creates a softer edge by creating a faint softness around the selection, especially in curved sections. Anti-aliased pixels contain gradual alpha values around the selection. To increase this gradual transition around the selection, select Feather and specify an amount in pixels. Setting Feather to 10 creates a 10-pixel transition around the selection, with pixels toward the outside gradually tending toward transparency.

FIGURE 5.7
To the right of the original (shown with marquee) is a copy of the pixels within the marquee with the edge set to hard. Below the original is the anti-aliased version. To the right of that is a copy with the edge set to a 10-pixel feather.

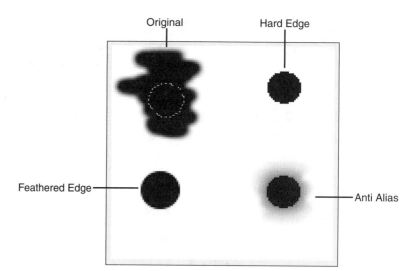

Lasso Tools

The Lasso and Polygon Lasso tools are more flexible versions of the basic marquee tools and can be toggled using the L key. With the Lasso tool you click-drag to draw a line around the pixels you want selected, as in Figure 5.8. With the Polygon Lasso tool, you click points to define corners of a polygon; straight lines are created between the points.

When you return to the point where you started, a small box will appear with the lasso cursor to let you know you are about to close the shape and create the selection (shown in Figure 5.9).

FIGURE 5.8

The Lasso lets you create a freeform marquee around a group of pixels.

FIGURE 5.9

The Polygon Lasso tool allows you to select points linked by straight lines. When you return to the starting point, a small square appears next to the cursor.

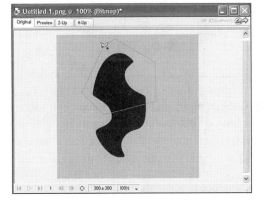

After you've created a lasso or polygon lasso selection, you can change the dimensions or position of the selected pixels on the Property Inspector. This will turn the selection into a new bitmap object with the specified width, height, and X or Y position values. To change the edge of the selection, choose Hard, Anti-alias, or Feather to harden or soften the edges of the marquee.

Magic Wand Tool

The Magic Wand tool is as powerful as it sounds. Clicking a portion of a bitmap object with the Magic Wand tool selects a contiguous area of similarly colored pixels. This is often used to select large fields of color for removal from backgrounds (to restore transparency to a JPEG image, for example) or for selecting natural shapes in an image. A Magic Wand selection was made in Figure 5.10 by clicking one of the original colored pixels, that is, one that has not been affected by applying any feathering.

FIGURE **5.10**

The Magic Wand with the tolerance set to 20 will affect only pixels of a very similar color.

The settings for the Magic Wand include Tolerance and Edge softness. Tolerance is a measurement of just how similar colors need to be in order to be included in the selection. A value of 0 means that only pixels of the same color as the originally selected pixel will be selected. A value of 255 means that the pixels can be of a different hue or shade and will still be selected. In Figure 5.10 the tolerance was set to 20. In Figure 5.11 it has been set to 200; the same color was originally selected in both examples. Notice in Figure 5.11 how the selection has grown to include the gradual shading around the solid color.

FIGURE 5.11

With the Magic Wand tolerance set to 200, you can select any relatively similar pixels.

When an area of pixels is selected, you can add to that area by holding down Shift and starting your additional selection on an unselected portion of the object. To remove an area of a selection, hold down Alt (Windows) or Option (Macintosh) and choose an already selected portion of the object. This will work with any of the selection tools in the Bitmap group on the Tools panel.

The Paint Bucket Tool

The paint bucket is kind of like a combination of the Brush and Magic Wand tools. The paint bucket either fills an area of pixels based on their similarity to the pixel you click or fills an area defined by a marquee selection. First you should learn the Property Inspector settings for the Paint Bucket tool, which are shown in Figure 5.12.

FIGURE 5.12

The paint bucket fills areas of pixels with colors or patterns.

Fill Color—A solid fill color can be chosen from the pop-up swatch menu. If a Web dither, pattern, or gradient fill style is chosen, the Fill Color box will display the appropriate pop-up menu.

Fill Style—The fill style setting lets you choose between the different fill options. These include None, or transparent; Solid, which fills the area with a solid color; Web Dither, which uses up to four colors to create a dithered pattern; and Pattern, which tiles an existing PNG image as the fill. Below these are the different gradient fills.

5

Edge—The edge setting is similar to the selection edge settings, allowing you to choose Hard, Anti-alias, or Feather—except that the setting applies to the edges of the filled area.

Texture—This allows you to add a texture to the fill style. Clicking Transparent turns the texture into an alpha mask so the texture won't influence the color of the fill.

Tolerance—Similar to the tolerance setting for the Magic Wand, the paint bucket tolerance setting allows you to specify how broad the definition of similarity to the selected pixel will be. A value of 0 means only pixels the same color as the original will be changed; a value of 100 means any pixel of a generally similar color will be changed.

Fill Selection—Fill Selection overrides the tolerance setting, filling any pixel within an existing marquee selection.

Transparency—This can be used to set the opacity of the fill. A setting of 0 means that no pixels will be changed, whereas a setting of 100 means none of the original color will be visible through the fill.

Blending Mode—The blending mode settings for the Paint Bucket tool are the same as the layer and object blending modes. These change how the fill color (blend color) interacts with the original colors (base color).

Preserve Transparency—By checking the Preserve Transparency setting, the fill will not affect areas of the bitmap that are fully transparent—only pixels with existing color information will be saved.

Drawing and Painting with Selections

One of the important aspects of bitmap selections is how they affect the drawing and painting tools. When an area of a bitmap is selected, the Pencil, Brush, and Eraser tools will affect only the selected area; areas outside the selection will not be affected. If the marquee is feathered, the feathering will also affect the drawing tool, as shown in Figure 5.13.

FIGURE 5.13

With a feathered marquee selected, the painting and drawing tools will affect only pixels within the selection.

To work on the area that isn't selected, you can deselect the current selection. Otherwise, choose Select Inverse from the Select menu to select the pixels outside the current selection and deselect the current area.

Selection Options

There are also a number of important selection options available from the Select menu. Most are available only when an area of a bitmap object is selected. Superselect and Subselect are for working with groups of objects and will be discussed in Part III (Hours 7 through 10), "Graphic Design: Working with Art and Text."

Select All—Select All can be used with the Pointer tool or with the Marquee tool. When the Pointer tool is chosen, Select All will select all the objects on active layers. To select all the pixels in a bitmap object, double-click the object with the Pointer tool to switch to the Marquee tool and choose Select All. You can press Control+A (Windows) or Command+A (Macintosh) for Select All.

Deselect—Deselect clears any object or marquee selections. Press Control+D (Windows) or Command+D (Macintosh) to deselect any objects or pixels. This does not change the content of the selection in any way.

Select Similar—Select Similar is like the Magic Wand tool but averages the chosen color from the current selection and then adds all similar colors in the object to the selection.

Select Inverse—Select Inverse is an important tool. It selects all the pixels in the bitmap object that aren't selected and deselects the pixels in the current selection. For Select Inverse press Control+Shift+I (Windows) or Command+Shift+I (Macintosh).

Feather—Feather changes the feathering around an existing marquee. After selecting Feather from the Select menu, you will be prompted for a value in pixels, which determines the amount of feathering around the selection.

Expand Marquee—Expand Marquee expands the area of the selection by the specified number of pixels.

Contract Marquee—The inverse of Expand Marquee, this contracts the selection area by the specified number of pixels.

Border Marquee—Border Marquee changes the selection into a new selection that borders on the original selection. The width of the border is specified in pixels.

Smooth Marquee—Smooth Marquee removes any jagged edges from the shape of the selection by resampling the marquee. Smoothing a marquee will eliminate excess pixels along the edges of a pixel selection. This is most useful if excess pixels appear along the border of a pixel selection when you have used the Magic Wand tool.

5

Save Selection—Save Selection saves the current marquee selection with the bitmap object so you can come back to it later.

Restore Selection—Restore Selection restores the selection saved with a bitmap object.

How to Filter Pixel Selections

Another important way to use selections is as a guide for applying filters from the Filters menu. Filters change the values of the pixels within the selection, based on the type of filter and the settings that you specify. Filters can do all sorts of things, such as changing the colors, changing the focus, and creating interesting effects. Filters can also be applied as effects to bitmap objects, as will be discussed later in this hour. Filters are destructive; they will change the original pixels. Effects are not; they are rendered temporarily, preserving the original data.

To apply a filter to the pixels in a marquee or object, simply select the filter from the Filters menu. A filter with additional settings will have its name followed by an ellipsis. After a filter has been applied, the only way to recover the original data is to use Undo from the Edit menu or to replace the altered image with a copy of the original.

Adjust Color

The color adjustment filters improve or change colors in an image or selection. These will be covered in more detail in Hour 6, "Improving Photos."

Auto Levels—Auto Levels analyzes the data in the image and makes mathematical assumptions about the exposure to improve the image. This is not always very effective.

Brightness/Contrast—This quickly adjusts the brightness and contrast of the selected pixels.

Curves—Curves gives you ultimate control over image exposure and color by allowing you to finely adjust the values of individual channels.

Hue/Saturation—Hue and Saturation is used to adjust the color values for all the selected pixels and is used for correction and creative effects.

Invert—Invert changes all the colors to their opposites, creating a negative image.

Levels—Levels provides a histogram display of color values in the image and provides tools to quickly adjust the relative level of channels in an image.

Blur

The blur filters act by blurring detail and high contrast in an image or selection, giving an out-of-focus look. Blur and Blur More are actually just presets of the Gaussian Blur filter.

Blur—Blur adjusts the colors of pixels to merge with the colors of the adjacent pixels, making the image softer. This filter is often used to sublimate high-contrast areas, such as dust, scratches, and creases, or as a focus effect.

Blur More—Blur More blurs the image about three times as much as Blur does.

Gaussian Blur—Gaussian Blur lets you change the radius of pixels that the evening of values will affect, allowing you to control the amount of blur.

Other

The filters in this group are special tools for using bitmaps as creative elements.

Convert to Alpha—This filter converts the bitmap into a grayscale alpha map. Lighter areas are made more transparent; darker areas are made opaque black. This effect is often used to create a mask for another bitmap object.

Find Edges—This filter will create an image in which solid areas are black and areas with high contrast, such as lines, are light, creating an effect similar to a pencil sketch. This can be useful when tracing a bitmap for use as a vector graphic.

Sharpen

These filters improve detail and focus in a blurry image and improve images after they've been resampled. Sharpen and Sharpen More are actually just presets of the Unsharp Mask filter.

Sharpen—Sharpen is the opposite of Blur. Sharpen increases contrast between adjacent pixels, lending an image the appearance of more crisp focus.

Sharpen More—Sharpen More applies an increased level of sharpening, approximately three times as much as Sharpen.

Unsharp Mask—The Unsharp Mask filter is commonly used to increase the clarity of bitmaps used in print and on the Web because the digitization and output processes are very different from the original photographic processes. Unsharp Mask gives you very fine control over how the contrast between pixels interacts.

Eye Candy 4000 LE

These third-party filters are included for free with Fireworks as examples of additional filters that you can purchase and add to Fireworks.

Bevel Boss—This filter bevels the edges of an image as though they were cut with a router. You can adjust the bevel smoothness, lighting, width, and depth.

Marble—Instead of working with your image, Marble replaces it as a type of fill. You can adjust the style of marbling in the dialog.

5

Motion Trail—This filter is very useful when working with action images that seem frozen by a flash or high shutter speed and to suggest motion with limited frames in GIF animations. You can adjust the direction, length, taper, opacity, and color blending of the effect.

Alien Skin Splat LE

Alien Skin is another company that makes filter plug-ins for Fireworks and other applications.

Edges—The Edges filter adds interesting randomized borders to your selection. You can make the image look like a piece of torn paper or add a retro print look with graduated halftone dots.

> Fireworks will accept any third-party plug-in filters that are compatible with Adobe Photoshop 5.x, including those that came with Photoshop. To use these filters, copy them into the Plug-Ins folder in the application folder Fireworks (under the Program Files folder on Windows or Applications folder on the Macintosh).

Selections and the Edit Menu

Now you know how to use selections to designate areas of an image for editing, but you can also use the selection with the Edit commands to repeat or delete pixels selected in a bitmap object.

Cut—Cut removes the pixels in the selected area and copies them to the clipboard so you can paste them elsewhere. Press Control+X (Windows) or Command+Shift+X (Macintosh) to cut the current selection.

Copy—Copy adds the selected pixels to the clipboard so you can paste them elsewhere. Press Control+C (Windows) or Command+Shift+C (Macintosh) to copy the current selection while leaving the original intact.

Paste—Paste will paste the pixels on the clipboard onto the Canvas as selected pixels (if working with a selection tool) or as a new bitmap object (if no bitmap object is currently selected). Press Control+V (Windows) or Command+Shift+V (Macintosh) to paste the contents of the clipboard.

Clear—Clear will clear all color information from the selected pixels, rendering them transparent. If all the pixels in a bitmap object are cleared, the bitmap object will also be deleted. To clear the pixels in a selection press Backspace (Windows) or Delete (Macintosh).

Task: Remove Objects from a Photo with the Selection Tools

▼TASK

Now that you have a new set of tools on your belt, you can play with them to create some interesting graphic effects. In this task you'll remove some elements from the photograph `family_room.png`, which can be found in the `Hour 05` examples folder in your `Fireworks Examples` directory.

1. With `family_room.png` open, as in Figure 5.14, select the Zoom tool by pressing Z.

FIGURE 5.14

This image of a family room has some artwork that you'll want to remove just in case, and you will want to sublimate the room beyond the door. You'll also want to liven up the family room by turning on the TV.

2. Find the image of the whale on the wall toward the middle of the room image. Use the Zoom tool to draw a box around the whale picture and the frame.

3. Change to the rectangular Marquee tool by pressing M. Now draw a box around the image by clicking the top left corner and dragging the cursor to the bottom right corner. Make sure not to select any part of the green matte or wood frame around the image, as shown in Figure 5.15.

FIGURE 5.15

Select the image but leave the green Matte and the wood frame unselected.

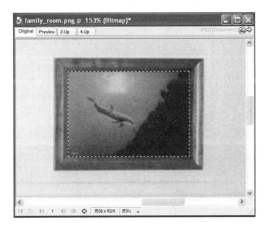

5

4. Press Delete or choose Clear from the Edit menu to clear these pixels.

5. Deselect the selection by pressing Control+D (Windows) or Command+D (Macintosh).

6. Press Control+0 (Windows) or Command+0 (Macintosh) to fit the Canvas within the workspace again.

7. Using the Zoom tool again, zoom in on the doorway to the left of the now-empty picture frame.

8. Choose the rectangular Marquee tool again. This time make sure the Edge is set to Feather on the Property Inspector. Set the feathering to 10 pixels.

9. Using the Marquee tool, click-drag inside the door frame, taking care not to select any of the white molding. You can leave some of the interior around some of the selection, as in Figure 5.16.

FIGURE 5.16

You're selecting the pixels that represent the room behind the door but not the door frame, which is in the current room.

10. Now select the Blur group from the Filters menu and select Gaussian Blur from the submenu.

11. Set the Blur Radius to 3 pixels. This will make the area behind the door seem out of focus, which will draw attention away from it as in Figure 5.17. Click OK to apply the changes.

FIGURE 5.17

The Gaussian Blur filter lets you specify exactly how deep the blur will be in pixels; a higher value means a wider pixel range, which means more blur.

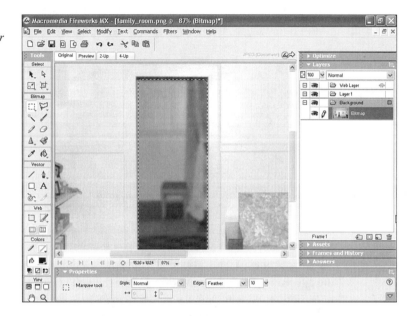

12. Deselect the marquee and zoom out until you can see the whole image again. With the Zoom tool, zoom in on the picture hanging on the wall to the far left. Because of perspective, you can't use a regular rectangle to select this picture.

13. Select the Polygon Lasso tool by pressing L twice. Make sure the edge is set to Anti-Alias this time. With the Polygon Lasso click a corner of the picture within the frame. Now move the mouse to the next corner and click again. Repeat this until you have a four-sided polygon the same shape as the picture in the frame, as in Figure 5.18. Now press Delete to clear the pixels.

5

FIGURE 5.18

*Objects in perspective
can be selected easily
with the Polygon
Lasso tool.*

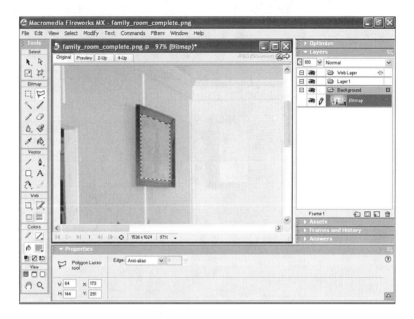

14. Zoom out to fit the Canvas in the window again. This time use the Zoom tool to fit the television in the window by drawing a box around the TV.

15. Press L to cycle to the Lasso tool. This time select the area of the picture tube on the television. Click the corner framed by the yellow burst on the upper right of the television set. Slowly drag the cursor to the left along the top of the picture area. From the next corner follow the slight curve to the bottom. Complete the selection by dragging along the last two sides, as in Figure 5.19.

16. If your selection is too bumpy or jagged, choose Smooth Marquee from the Select menu and set the radius to 10. That should clear up any bad twitches. If you've still made a mistake, deselect and draw the selection again with the lasso. When you're happy with your selection, press Delete to clear the pixels.

17. Finally, select the Crop tool by pressing C. Click-drag to create a crop box that removes a little from the left and right sides of the image and a little more at the top, as shown in Figure 5.20. When you're happy with your crop, double-click the Canvas to apply the crop to the image and Canvas.

FIGURE 5.19

Use the Lasso to select areas with curved and angled shapes.

FIGURE 5.20

The Crop tool is the fastest way to improve most images. Here some unimportant visual information that detracts from the image has been removed.

18. Save this file in the Fireworks Examples folder as family_room_edit.png. A completed copy, family_room_complete.png, is included in the examples folder in case you didn't have good results making selections.

Working with Bitmaps as Objects

Working with pixel selections is very useful, but changes to pixels in a bitmap are destructive changes: They destroy the original information in the bitmap. To mitigate this dilemma, you can work with bitmaps as objects, allowing you to manage multiple elements and compose on the Canvas quickly and easily. Only when changes are made to the object's actual pixels is data destroyed.

To select a bitmap object, use the pointer to click the object on the Canvas or select it from the Layers panel (expand the layer to reveal objects on that layer). To create a new bitmap object from an existing one, choose Duplicate or Clone from the Edit menu. Duplicate puts the new copy below and to the right of the original; Clone creates the new copy in the same location. To create a bitmap object from a marquee selection, choose Copy and Paste from the Edit menu. The contents will appear within a new marquee in the same location as the original pixels.

An easy way to make sure you always have an original copy of a bitmap object handy is to import the object to a backup layer and then paste a copy of the object onto the layer where you would like to work with it. Keep the backup layer locked and hidden, as in Figure 5.21. This way you always have an unaltered copy handy without having to reimport any graphics.

FIGURE 5.21
A locked and hidden layer is a great place to keep copies of all your original bitmap objects.

Transforming Bitmap Objects

You can transform a bitmap object with the Scale, Skew, and Distort tools, available on the Tools panel. You can also transform objects via the Transform commands in the Modify menu. Transformations to bitmap objects are destructive, so keep another copy handy.

Free Transform

Free Transform is not really a tool but rather a set of tools that allow you to transform objects freely with the mouse by eye. Press Q to cycle through the Free Transform tools, Scale, Skew, and Distort. For numeric information while using a Free Transform tool, make sure the Info panel is visible. The Info panel, which can be located via the Window menu, will let you know how far you've moved a handle or the angle of rotation, as well as the new dimensions of the image. The Free Transform mode and Info panel are shown in Figure 5.22.

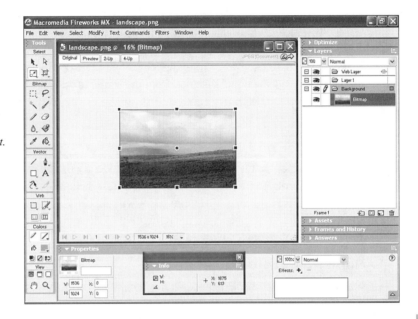

FIGURE 5.22

You can use the Free Transform tools to transform a bitmap object quickly. The Info panel provides real-time feedback on the size and angle of the transformed object.

Scale

When you are transforming the selected objects, a black box that surrounds the objects will appear. At each corner and on the sides of the black box are square handles. Click-drag a corner to adjust the scale of the object proportionally. Click a side to change either the width or height of the object.

> You may transform multiple objects by using Shift+click with the Pointer tool and then choosing a Free Transform tool.

To move the image, click-drag within the bounding box. To rotate the object, click outside the box and drag the mouse around through the desired angle of rotation. To change the point around which the image rotates, click the circle in the center of the bounding box and drag it to where you want the new anchor point to be (it can be outside the

5

bounding box, if necessary). Choosing Undo from the Edit menu removes any transformations and restores the original object. Double-clicking with the cursor will apply your changes to the object.

Skew

The Skew tool allows you to change the relative angles of the bounding box to create perspective effects. Grabbing a handle on one of the sides will move that side parallel to the opposite side, changing the bounding box and the proportions of its contents from a rectangle to a parallelogram. Grabbing a handle on one of the corners will move each corner on that side an equal distance from the center, changing the bounding box into a trapezoid. You can also move and rotate the object as you would with the Scale tool.

Distort

The Distort tool lets you more fluidly change any aspect of the bounding box's angles or size. Each corner handle can be dragged independently of any other to change the shape of an object. Dragging any other handle will adjust the size of the object, but the aspect ratio does not stay in scale. The adjustment will exactly reflect the dragging done, streching or squashing the object from the point the handle was moved.. You can also move and rotate the object as you would with the Scale and Skew tools.

Numeric Transform

When you select Numeric Transform from the Transform commands in the Modify menu, or by pressing Control+Shift+T (Windows) or Command+Shift+T (Macintosh), you will be presented with a dialog. At the top of the dialog is a drop-down menu where you can choose Scale, Resize, or Rotate. Scale will change the dimensions by percentage, Resize will let you specify a new size in pixels, and Rotate will let you specify an angle of rotation down to 1/10 degree. Selecting Scale Attributes applies to vector objects (it will scale or rotate the fill, stroke, and effects, such as feathering, along with the path). Selecting Constrain Proportions maintains the original ratio between width and height.

Applying Effects to Bitmap Objects

You can add effects to bitmap objects with the Property Inspector. Effects are available when an object is selected, as in Figure 5.23, and are nondestructive: After you've added an effect, you can remove it; or change the settings, and the effect will be recomputed from the original bitmap object data. You can add as many effects as you like in a specific order, which determines how they'll work together to create the final result. Effects also can be applied to vector objects, expanding the possibilities for working with vector art.

FIGURE 5.23

The Effects settings are available on the right-hand side of the Property Inspector when an object is selected with the Pointer tool.

The Effects menu includes all the filters in the Filters menu. There are also some Effects that aren't available as Filters because they will work only with object selections.

Options

These are some of the general effects options:

Save As Style—This option will save all the current effects as a style in the Styles panel (part of the Assets Panel group). This way you can apply all the same effect settings to other objects by selecting them and choosing the style from the Styles panel.

All On/Off—This option toggles all the effects on or off simultaneously.

Locate Plug-ins—With this option you can browse your hard drive for third-party filter plug-ins.

Bevel and Emboss

Bevel and Emboss create a simple 3D effect around an object. Settings for each include width, in pixels; depth, a percentage; edge softness, on a scale of 1 to 10; and lighting angle, in degrees.

Inner Bevel—This insets the bevel within the current bounds of an object. Options include the style of bevel curve (Flat, Smooth, Sloped, Frame 1 or 2, Ring, or Ruffle) and depth (Raised, Highlighted, Inset, or Inverted).

Inset Emboss—This makes an object look as though it were stamped on a sheet of paper by adding shadows outside the bounds of the object. You can choose to turn the original image on or off.

Outer Bevel—This is similar to Inner Bevel but adds the beveling outside the bounds of the image.

Raised Emboss—This is similar to Inset Emboss but makes the object appear stamped from behind.

Shadow and Glow

Shadow and Glow add simple lighting effects to an object.

Drop Shadow—This adds a shadow around an image as though it were floating above the Canvas. Settings include Offset, or distance from the image bounds, in pixels; Opacity, a percentage; Color, from the pop-up swatch palette; Edge Softness from 0 to 30; Lighting Angle, in degrees; and a check box to let you knock out the original image.

Glow—Glow adds a glow effect around the object. Settings include Width, in pixels; Opacity, a percentage; Color, from the pop-up swatch palette; Edge Softness from 0 to 30; and Offset, which creates a border between the image and the glow border.

Inner Glow—This is similar to Glow but insets the glow within the bounds of the object.

Inner Shadow—This effect is similar to Drop Shadow but insets the shadow within the bounds of the object.

To apply an effect, simply select an object with the Pointer tool. In the Property Inspector click the plus sign icon next to Effects to bring up the menu of available effects. Choose an effect and specify any settings in the dialog (effects that have additional settings will be followed by an ellipsis). When an effect is applied, it will appear in the list of effects below. Clicking the check mark next to the effect will turn it off; clicking the red X will turn it on. Double-click the effect name to change the settings, or click it and then click the minus symbol to remove it. Click-drag an effect up or down to change the order in which the effects are applied.

Task: Compose Objects with Transform and Add Effects

▼TASK

In this task you will work with three bitmap objects at the same time and then use Fireworks effects to completely change the look and feel of all the objects.

1. Open the file you altered in the previous task, `family_room_edit.png`. If you did not complete the task, open `family_room_complete.png` in the `Hour 05` examples folder.

2. Duplicate the layer Background by dragging it to the New/Duplicate Layer button on the Layers panel.

3. Double-click the new layer, Background1, to change its name to Backup. Press Enter to continue.

4. Click and drag the layer Backup so it is arranged behind the Background layer. Click the eyeball icon to hide the Background layer.

5. Now press Control+R (Windows) or Command+R (Macintosh) to import graphics. Navigate to the Hour 05 example directory. Select airport.png and click OK to import it. Click the Canvas near the top left corner to place the image. Repeat this procedure for landscape.png and sunset.png, placing each a little lower and to the right of the previous image, tiling them for easier selection, as shown in Figure 5.24.

FIGURE 5.24

The three imported images are now tiled on the Backup layer; areas off the Canvas are preserved as part of the object.

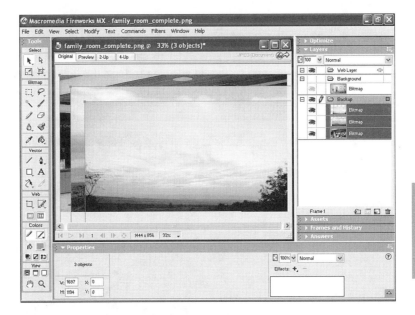

6. Select all three bitmap objects by using Shift+click to click each image. Press Control+C (Windows) or Command+C (Macintosh) to copy these bitmap objects.

7. On the Layers panel click the pencil icon next to the Backup layer to lock it. Click the eyeball icon to hide the layer. Now click the New/Duplicate Layer button to create a new, empty layer. Press Control+V (Windows) or Command+V (Macintosh) to paste copies of the bitmap objects to this new working layer, as shown in Figure 5.25.

FIGURE 5.25

The Backup layer is now locked and hidden, preserving your original objects. The copies are now on Layer 1.

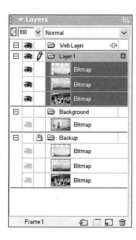

8. Click and drag the Background layer to arrange it above the working bitmap layer. Click the opacity slider to change the opacity to around 50 percent. Now click next to the layer name to lock the layer. This way you can see behind the layer, as shown as in Figure 5.26, and won't accidentally make any changes to it.

FIGURE 5.26

The Background layer is now semitransparent, allowing you to see the bitmap objects underneath.

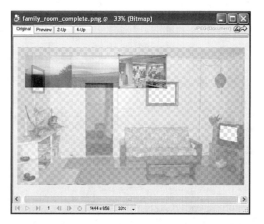

9. Select the top bitmap image with the Pointer tool. In the Property Inspector enter 300 for the width, 200 for the height, with the X and Y positions both set to 50. This will scale the bitmap down and put it near the top left of the Canvas. Repeat this step for the other two new bitmap objects, adding 300 to the X position each time (350, 650).

10. Select the bitmap on the right and drag it until it's behind the TV. Select the bitmap on the left and center it behind the left picture frame. Finally, select the middle

bitmap object and move it behind the middle picture, with the top left corner just overlapping the picture frame, as in Figure 5.27.

FIGURE 5.27

Move the bitmap objects into position with the Pointer tool.

11. With the middle object still selected, click the lower right handle on the object selection highlight. Hold down Shift while you drag the handle toward the lower right corner of the picture frame. When the bottom of the object and the bottom of the frame line up, release the mouse.

12. Now select the object to the left with the pointer. Press Q to change to the Scale tool. Click the handles on the sides to line up the sides of the object with the sides of the picture frame. Now click outside the box, and drag the cursor to rotate the image slightly clockwise, until the horizon in the image is parallel to the bottom of the picture frame, as in Figure 5.28. Double-click to apply the changes.

FIGURE 5.28

Scaling and rotating the object image brings it into the same perspective as the frame.

13. Unlock the Background layer and click the layer name to activate it. Then restore the opacity to 100 percent. You'll have a finished image, similar to the one shown in Figure 5.29, that looks considerably different from the original and has some great new details. You could go further and draw the new images into the picture by selecting them and applying Effect Hue/Saturation to desaturate the colors to match the exposure of the room more closely.

FIGURE 5.29

You just remodeled the family room without leaving your seat!

Summary

Now you should be comfortable editing bitmaps, at both the pixel and the object levels. A lot of bitmap editing is destructive, and care must be taken to preserve copies of original images. Use objects to separate individual bitmap elements and editing decisions and create copies of your layers before merging or flattening them.

The previous hour, "Working with Bitmap Images," and this one have focused on explaining the tools and how you can work with them, with tasks oriented toward understanding basic concepts. In the next hour, "Improving Photos," you'll put together all the skills you've learned in this section, along with some of the new tools available in Fireworks, to accomplish some tasks that are common when working with bitmaps and photos.

Workshop

This final section of the hour is designed to help you remember the topics covered, the tools and techniques. The optional exercises will help you put this hour's learning into practice.

Q&A

Q **I want to draw or paint into a new bitmap object over an existing bitmap object, but my brush is painting into the original object instead. How can I keep from altering the original object?**

A If you begin drawing on the Canvas with a bitmap tool by clicking an existing bitmap object, the changes will be made to that object. You can create a new object by clicking the New Bitmap Object button on the Layers panel or creating a new layer and locking the layer with the bitmap object you want to preserve.

Q **I scaled a bitmap object to make it smaller. Now I want it larger. Why doesn't it look as good as it did originally?**

A When you use the Pointer tool or transform an object, the object's pixels are resampled, creating a new, smaller bitmap image with fewer total pixels. If you make this object larger again, it will resample the smaller image to make it bigger, approximating the picture from the new, smaller bitmap instead of the original. This is why it's important to keep copies of your files and, within a Fireworks PNG source graphic, copies of your original bitmap objects, as well.

Q **When I try to use the Marquee tool, why does it always create the same size or shape of marquee?**

A Make sure that the Normal style is chosen for the Marquee tool in the Property Inspector. The Fixed Size style will let you create a marquee of the specified size only. The Fixed Ratio style constrains the proportions to those specified.

Quiz

1. How do you create a bitmap object from a marquee selection?
    a. Choose Save Bitmap Selection from the Select Menu.
    b. Click the New Bitmap Object button on the Layers panel.
    c. Choose Copy and then Paste from the Edit menu.

2. How do you rotate an image object on the Canvas?
    a. Enter a degree of rotation in the Numeric Transform panel.
    b. Click and drag outside the bounding box when using a Free Transform tool.
    c. Choose one of the standard rotations from the Transform commands in the Modify menu.

3. What's the difference between filters and effects?
    a. Filters are for bitmaps; effects are for vectors.
    b. Effects can be added and removed; filters change the actual pixels.
    c. Effects are included in Fireworks; filters are not.

5

Quiz Answers

1. c.—The other two solutions would definitely not work. Action (a) would simply save the pattern of the marquee, and (b) would simply create an empty bitmap object.

2. a., b., and c.—The option you choose just depends on how much control you want when rotating.

3. b.—Filters change the original pixels, whereas effects are rendered temporarily.

Exercises

These optional exercises are tailored for you to hone the skills and techniques covered in this hour.

1. Rather than work with the supplied images, locate a photograph of a person or animal to work with. Use the tools covered in this hour to remove the background from the photograph. You will be left with a single bitmap object that can then have a new background applied or even be cut and pasted into a new document.

2. As covered in this hour, effects can only be applied to complete bitmap objects, but did you know that you can work around this? Suppose you want to add an effect to only part of a photograph. Try this: Draw a bitmap over an area of a bitmap to be affected, then choose Cut, followed by Paste. This applies an exact copy of the cut pixels in the same location but as a new bitmap. You can now play with the effects only on the new object

3. Did you know that you can convert bitmaps to line drawings in Fireworks, as well? Open a photograph or other bitmap, then from the Effects menu in the Property Inspector, choose Other, Find Edges. See how the outlines in the object are traced.

HOUR 6

Improving Photos

Now that you're comfortable with the most common bitmap creation and editing tools, you will learn some techniques used by professionals when working with bitmap images. Remember that a bitmap image is a lot like a traditional photographic print. Many of the techniques that were used in the darkroom can now be done with Fireworks. These include color and contrast correction, correcting the exposure and detail in particular areas of the image, touching up dust and scratches, and getting creative with multiple exposures or interesting effects.

In this hour you will

- Understand the tools used to correct color and contrast in a photo
- Use the Dodge, Burn, Blur, and Sharpen tools to correct focus and exposure
- Learn how to touch up photos to remove blemishes
- Mask, layer, and filter images to create artistic photo effects
- Selectively compress a photo to keep the file size down while preserving detail in important areas

Color and Contrast Correction with Fireworks

Just because an image is digital does not mean that it is well exposed or color accurate. If an image was taken with a digital camera, it will almost certainly need some sort of correction. If the image originated on photographic film, there are even more steps in the process that could affect the eventual color balance and contrast: the time, temperature, and chemicals used to develop the film; the exposure and development of the print; and the settings used when the film or print was scanned.

Cameras and scanners will make predictable decisions about how an image should be exposed, but that doesn't mean they are always the correct ones. When shooting a subject that is backlit, the camera will average the very light areas with the very dark areas to determine the appropriate shutter speed and aperture. This means that the dark areas will be underexposed and the light areas will be overexposed, because the average is somewhere in the middle. The same goes for developing film; much of the process is done by a machine that uses similar methods to determine how an image should be developed and printed.

Of course, it is best to work with images that have already been color-corrected in the photographic or scanning process. With digital cameras, the image will not have gone through either process and thus will probably need to be color-corrected with graphics software, such as Fireworks. When scanning images, it is best to do as much color correction as possible with the scanner itself using the scanner's software. This is because the color correction will be applied by the hardware while the image is being scanned, as opposed to being applied by filtering the digital data with software.

When working with color correction in Fireworks, it's important to remember that filters change the underlying bitmap data, whereas effects are rendered temporarily and can be removed or changed at any time. If you want to correct a portion of an object that's been selected with a marquee, you must use filters. Keep an unfiltered copy on a locked and hidden layer so that you can refer back to it to reapply the changes (you can also use the Save Selection command from the Select menu to save the marquee before filtering, so that you can restore it later). Effects apply only to objects; they do not affect the original data, saving you the trouble of having to keep a backup. Effect settings and groups can also be saved as styles so that they can be applied to a number of different images, such as an entire roll of film that needs the same type of correction (for instance, daylight film shot indoors).

Evaluating Exposures

The same exposure rules apply whether an image is in color or in black and white. A well-exposed image will contain a full range of tones, with detail—shadows and highlights—present at both extremes of the scale. The same holds true for digital images. If an image is overexposed, details will be lost in the highlights. If it is underexposed, there won't be any detail in the shadows.

The same goes for focus. If an image is photographed out of focus, there is very little you can do about it. No graphics program can magically restore a bad photograph! Fireworks is very good at "tweaking" a good exposure until it's just right, and it's good at creating effects that you just can't achieve with a camera or in a darkroom. What Fireworks can't do is go back and take a better picture for you.

Tones and the Zone System

The information that immediately follows may not be of interest to all of you. However, understanding terminology and the way exposure is determined will certainly be of long-term value if you work with photographs.

Ansel Adams systematized the language of exposure when he created the Zone system. The Zone system is composed of 11 graduated levels, starting with 0 (pure black) and ending with X (pure white). It is usually written with Roman numerals (see Figure 6.1). Zone 0 and Zone X contain no detail; they are meant to represent the boundaries of the potential tonal range. A well-exposed image will typically range from Zone I to Zone IX, the maximum tonal range that can contain detail. Of course, a bride in a white dress seated in a white gazebo might not contain any shadows darker than Zones III or IV, and an image of a dark subject at night might not have any highlights brighter than Zone VI or VII.

FIGURE 6.1

The Zone system breaks tones down into 11 regions from black to white.

The Zone system is used mainly when creating an exposure with a camera or enlarger, but it can also be an important way to understand and describe any image with a full range of continuous tones. *Shadows* in an image range from Zone 0 to Zone III. *Midtones* are from Zones III to VII. *Highlights* are anything above Zone VII. The light meter or auto-exposure feature on a camera will usually average the entire frame and expose it for Zone V, or medium gray. If the image is heavy with Zone III material, this will overexpose the image, and details from Zones VIII and IX will be pushed into Zone X. If it has more Zone VII material, the details in Zones II and III will be lost. These same mistakes can be made when working with digital images; detail in shadows or highlights can be lost when a print is scanned or when the brightness is changed with filters or effects.

6

Understanding Contrast

Contrast in an image can also be described with the Zone system. An image that contains only Zone 0 and Zone X information is considered to have absolute contrast. This is used in lithography, where gradual tones are approximated with a dot screen or halftone. (The pages of this book are a good example; look at a screen shot graphic through a magnifying glass to see how a single black tone creates lighter gradations through lots of little dots of different sizes.) An image that contains information only between Zones IV and VI is considered very low contrast. There are no shadows or highlights in such an image. Everything is a muddy gray.

Contrast in an image is a lot like focus. It is easier to increase contrast than it is to reduce it without losing image information, just as it's easier to make a sharp image look blurry and out of focus than it is to make a blurry image look sharp and focused. Still, contrast can be increased, within limits. It's critical that the image contain a range of tones covering most of the Zone scale and that the image is not cut off at either end, which would indicate a loss of detail. You can judge this very accurately by using the histogram that comes with the Levels effect.

Task: Using Levels to Adjust the Brightness and Contrast of a Black-and-White Image

▼ TASK

You'll work on the image old_honokaa.png, which can be found in the Hour 06 examples folder. Go ahead and open the image in Fireworks. You could adjust the image with the Brightness/Contrast effect, but this method reduces total detail in an image. Making the image brighter would move the shadows toward middle gray, resulting in a loss of shadow detail. Making the image darker would move the highlights toward middle gray, which also reduces detail. With levels, though, you can adjust the shadow tones, midtones, and highlight tones without sacrificing details in the shadows or highlights.

1. Select the bitmap object with the Pointer tool.

2. Click the Plus icon next to Effects on the Property Inspector. Select Levels from the Adjust Color group. You'll be presented with the dialog in Figure 6.2. The histogram is the bar graph in the middle of the dialog. The x-axis represents the tonal range, from black on the left to white on the right. The y-axis represents the relative number of pixels present. This is an example of a good histogram; the curve begins within the bounds of the graph, and there are no gaps where color detail might be missing.

FIGURE 6.2

The Levels dialog allows you to view the histogram, a great tool for evaluating the tonal quality of a digital image.

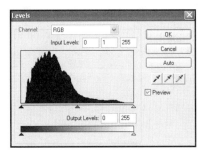

3. At the top is a drop-down menu that allows you to choose the channel you would like to evaluate or adjust—Red, Green, Blue, or RGB (all three simultaneously). This image was photographed on color film and scanned as 24-bit color, but because the subject is black and white, the three colors come out pretty much the same (shades of gray or neutral tones are created by equal values of red, green, and blue). For this reason, you'll edit only the combined RGB values. For a full-color subject, you would edit each channel individually.

4. The sliders at the bottom represent the shadow boundary, the midpoint, and the highlight boundary. Click the black slider and move it to where the bar graph begins, or type **9** in the first Input Levels field. You know that no detail has been lost because no pixels exist below the shadow slider.

A histogram should be an unbroken mass of black that begins and ends between the two extremes of the x-axis. If the histogram is cut off at either end, you know detail has been lost in the shadows or highlights; there probably was information in those areas, but it has now been merged into Zone 0 or Zone X. If there are gaps in the histogram where no pixels are present for a given tone, details and tone continuity have been lost in the midtones. Gaps appear when an image has been compressed or filtered. Some gapping is okay. Heavy gapping means that posterization and noise are present and that a better original should be found.

6

5. Now adjust the highlight slider either by clicking it and moving it to the end of the bar graph or by typing **233** in the last field to the left of Input Levels. This sets the brightest pixel in the image to white, just as the previous slider set the darkest pixel to black. No information has been lost, because there are no pixels after this point on the graph.

6. Finally, adjust the midpoint slider, which is the gray slider between the shadow and highlight sliders. Move it to the left until the middle Input Level field reads 1.5. This adjusts the midpoint toward the shadows, providing more room for highlight detail and lightening some of the shadow detail. The complete settings are shown in Figure 6.3. Click OK or press Return to apply the effect.

FIGURE 6.3

The handles have been adjusted for optimal shadow and highlight contrast, and the midpoint has been set with middle gray closer to the shadows, which lightens shadow detail without making the blacks too gray.

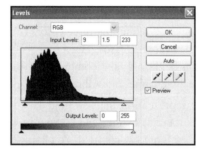

7. You'll notice that the details in the shadows on the right of the image have become more clear and noticeable because of the Levels adjustment, as in Figure 6.4, which shows both the original and the adjusted image.

FIGURE 6.4

By adjusting the contrast with the Levels effect, details in the shadows have been brought out, and the tonal accuracy across the image has been improved. The top image in this figure shows the newly adjusted photograph, with the original below it.

8. There is another problem with this image—a light blue mark from some chemical residue on the print. First, take all the color information out of the image to remove the blue cast and smudge. With the bitmap selected, choose the Hue/Saturation effect from the Adjust Color group.

9. With the Hue/Saturation dialog up, drag the Saturation slider all the way to the left or type **–100** in the Saturation field, as in Figure 6.5.

FIGURE 6.5

After the image is completely desaturated, it is converted into a grayscale, with only tone information and no color information.

10. Use the Color Fill effect in the Adjust Color group to add some color and flair to the image. You can give the black-and-white image a sepia tone effect. When you select the Color Fill effect, a small settings pane opens above the Property Inspector, as in Figure 6.6.

11. Change the Blending mode to Color. Set the color to be blended to **#FFCC99** by clicking the swatch and typing the hex code in the field at the top of the pop-up swatch panel. Change the opacity to **75** percent by typing in the field or using the slider.

FIGURE 6.6

The Color Fill effect allows you to fill an entire bitmap object with a color.

12. Now the image looks more like an antique to match the small-town mood set by the baseball diamond, Main Street, and church steeple. You can easily save this set of effects by choosing Save as Style from the Options group. You can apply this style by selecting an object and then selecting the custom style from the Style panel in the Assets panel group.

Color Theory

Fireworks uses 24-bit RGB color to process images. Each primary color (red, green, and blue) is saved as an 8-bit channel. With these three colors most of the visible color spectrum can be reproduced. The three channels correspond to the three colors of phosphors used to make up each point on a CRT, or cathode ray tube, such as in a computer monitor or television. (LCD, or liquid crystal display, uses a different technology but still adds red, green, and blue values together to create a single point of color.) The absence of red, green, and blue represents black. Full red, green, and blue represents white.

The print process is completely different from RGB. Because a printed piece of paper can reflect only available light, rather than projecting its own light, like a CRT, a subtractive process is used to remove the desired color from the reflected light. This process is called CMYK, for cyan, magenta, yellow, and black. Cyan, magenta, and yellow are the inverse colors of red, green, and blue, respectively. Red is reproduced by printing magenta and yellow on the sheet, which subtracts green and blue from the reflected white light. Nothing is printed to produce white. Cyan, magenta, and yellow are printed in relative densities to reproduce color tones, whereas black is used for detail and shadow depth, with all four combining at full density to create process black.

Because any color corrections made with Fireworks will be for the Web, it's not so important to understand the print process. What's important is to understand how all the colors are related. If you reduce the amount of red in an image, it will appear more cyan, because the levels of green and blue will be relatively higher. Increasing blue will take yellow out of the image. If you add red, green, and blue evenly, the image will appear lighter; decreasing them in proportion will make it darker.

Color Correction Considerations

It's important to remember three things when adjusting the relative levels of color in an image: the color in the actual subject, how the color was captured, and how the color will be output. The color in the subject is determined by the color temperature of the light and by the surface from which it is reflected into the lens of the camera. The capture color is determined by optics and film; color can be adjusted by a filter placed over the lens or by a film coating designed to work with a specific color temperature (such as outdoor or daylight film). In the case of digital equipment, the captured color is determined by the camera's exposure settings, which affect how the CCDs behind the lens interpret colors reflected onto them. Finally, the colors will be output to a subtractive medium, such as a printer, or to an additive medium, such as a television or computer monitor.

When you color-correct, you are usually trying to present an accurate representation of the original colors by changing how the capture colors are output. This can be very subjective, and in many cases you may not know what the actual colors in the subject were. It's also important that the output colors work with the other colors on the Web page, including those in other photographs. It may be more important to preserve a particular color balance throughout a number of photos than for each one to be corrected out of context with the others. If it looks good, do it.

Task: Color-Correct a Photograph

In this task you will work with a photograph that needs some color correction. The image file is very similar to the previous one—in fact, it shows the same subject at a different time. The photograph appears to be far more green that it should be, so adjustments will be made to correct this.

1. Open the file honokaa_today.png in the Hour 06 examples folder. This is a contemporary image of Mamane Street, the Main Street in the previous photograph. Unfortunately, the image has a slight green cast and needs a little magenta to be truly correct.

2. First, you'll examine the histogram and correct the levels. Select the bitmap object with the Pointer tool and choose the Levels effect from the Adjust Color group.

3. You'll notice that the histogram is cut off at the left end; there is data right up to black, with a concentration at pure black. This is not optimal, but because this image was scanned from the negatives at the photo lab, you can't do anything but leave it alone. Instead, you'll concentrate on where there still is room—in the highlights. Change the channel to Red, using the drop-down menu at the top of the Levels dialog. You'll be presented with a slightly different histogram, as in Figure 6.7.

FIGURE **6.7**

You can examine the histogram for each channel independently. In this case you can tell by the black line that's flush with the left end of the graph that detail in the shadows has been lost.

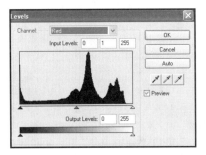

4. Go through each channel and slide the highlight slider on the right until it meets the end of information for that channel. Do not move the midpoint and shadow sliders. If you'd rather enter the values numerically, change the last Input Level field for each channel as follows: Red, **241**; Green, **240**; Blue, **242**.

5. The brightness has been adjusted, but you still have a noticeable color cast. To prove that the image has a color cast, open the Info panel from the Window menu. Look at the Options menu in the Info panel and make sure RGB is selected as the color mode. This will make it easier to calculate colors in the image intuitively. Mouseover an area of the asphalt next to the black truck on the left.

6. Asphalt should be gray, and gray is created with equal parts red, green, and blue. If you examine the color values in the info panel, however, you'll notice that there is a little too much red and not enough blue for the asphalt to be gray. Now mouseover a white area of clouds. White is another neutral color. Here there isn't enough blue, but the red isn't as out of proportion with the green. You need to add blue in the midtones (asphalt) and highlights (clouds), take away red from the midtones, and take away a little green from the shadows.

7. Choose the Curves effect from the Adjust Color group. The Curves effect is a powerful way to correct color imbalances in a photo. You'll use curves to make sure the neutral tones are really neutral across the tonal range. Choose the Red channel from the drop-down menu at the top of the dialog, as shown in Figure 6.8.

FIGURE 6.8

The Curves effect shows a graph with the input values on the y-axis and the output values on the x-axis.

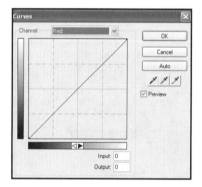

8. Click to create a point, making sure that it is near the middle of the line. Placing the point anywhere else will result in very strange and unwanted results. By adjusting this point, you can change how a pixel of the input value is output. Change the Input field at the bottom of the panel to 160. Now change the Output field to 155. This means that pixels with a value of 150 Red will now be changed to 145 Red. The curve means that input values higher and lower than the adjustment point will also be adjusted toward the output value. Some red has been removed from the midtones.

9. Change the channel again to Blue. Click the line to create an adjustment point. Set the Input field to 130. Set the Output field to 150. This will add blue to the midtones. Now click to create a new point. Change the Input field for this point to 235. Change the Output field to 240. This will add blue to the highlights. Click OK or press Return to apply the effect.

10. Now mouseover the asphalt one more time. You'll notice that the values in the Info panel are more consistently neutral than they were before. The values in Figure 6.9

are for a pixel of asphalt near the bottom of the image. Go ahead and check an area of clouds. You'll notice a similar improvement. You may think the image is a little too magenta, so remove some blue and red or add some more green. Use the All Off and All On features of the Option group in the Effects menu, located in the Property Inspector, to quickly compare the original to the color-corrected version. There's certainly been an improvement!

FIGURE 6.9

The gray asphalt is now much more generally neutral, as evidenced by the Info panel.

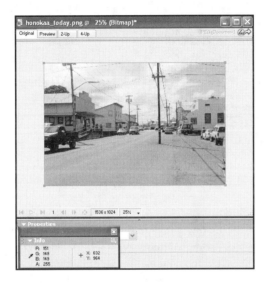

Photo Retouching Techniques

There are a number of tools that can be used for fine photo retouching. Retouching is the process of editing out blemishes, such as dust, scratches, creases, light leaks, and any other small details that detract from the quality of the final image.

Taking Advantage of the Exposure and Focus Tools

Another way to correct an image's exposure and detail is with the Dodge, Burn, Blur, and Sharpen tools. Located in the Tools panel, as shown in Figure 6.10, these tools are similar to the Brush tool except that instead of blending color in, they simply adjust the values of the pixels. Dodging and burning are done in the darkroom by using masks to reduce or increase the amount of light that hits the photosensitive emulsion on the paper. Blurring and sharpening don't really have a darkroom equivalent; you can adjust the focus of the enlarger but only for the whole image, and when critical focus is reached, it certainly can't be exceeded (this holds true for digital images, as well). That's when the important part of your composition is sharp and has the right degree of contrast.

FIGURE **6.10**

Located in the Tools panel, the Exposure and Focus tools allow you to adjust the values of pixels in your image.

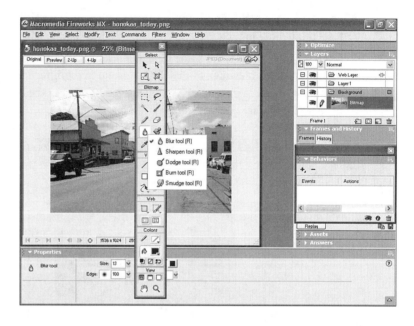

Dodge—Dodge lightens the area under the cursor as you click-drag a bitmap object. This can be used to bring out details in the shadows or to remove details from highlights. The Dodge tool settings in the Property Inspector include Size, in pixels, from 1 to 100; Edge Softness, a percentage; Shape, either round or square; Range, which can include Shadows, Midtones, or Highlights; and Exposure, from 1 to 100. Exposure adjusts the intensity of the dodge.

Burn—Burn is exactly the opposite of dodge; instead of lightening the area, it darkens the area. Burn and dodge change only the luminosity of the color, not its hue or saturation. The Burn tool options in the Property Inspector are the same as those for the Dodge tool, except that Exposure adjusts the intensity of darkness.

While applying the Dodge or Burn tool effect, you can swap between dodge and burn quickly by pressing the Alt (or Option) key.

Blur—The Blur tool is used to add blur to any part of an image simply by clicking, not just to an individual object or preselected area. Blur tool settings in the Property Inspector include Size, in pixels, from 1 to 100; Edge Softness, a percentage; Shape, either round or square; and Intensity, or the level of blur to be applied. An intensity of 100 will completely average the values between two contiguous pixels, and an intensity of 1 will slightly soften areas of high contrast.

Sharpen—The Sharpen tool increases the contrast in a selected area, the opposite of the action performed by the Blur tool. Settings in the Property Inspector are the same, except that the Intensity setting applies to the level of contrast that is added instead of removed. A setting higher than 20 would severely affect the quality of your image; sharpening should be applied lightly and carefully to prevent high-contrast noise from appearing.

> You can use the marquee selection tools to constrain changes to an area of the bitmap. The Dodge and Burn tools will work only on pixels that are within the marquee. Feather the edge of the marquee to make sure that changes will blend more seamlessly into the image and that no unnaturally hard edges will be apparent.

Smudging, Cloning, and Sampling Pixels

Some Fireworks tools are obviously very powerful in design terms, but the value and applicability of others may initially be less obvious. Smudging, Cloning, and Sampling Pixels may well fall into this latter group.

Smudge—The Smudge tool is in the same group as the Burn, Dodge, Blur, and Sharpen tools, but it doesn't really fit in. The Smudge tool acts like a finger in wet paint; colors will be mixed under the tool and moved or wiped in the direction of the tool's movement. Smudge settings include the Size of the smudge area, in pixels, from 1 to 100; the Edge Softness, a percentage; Shape, either round or square; Use Entire Document, which will work with all colors on all visible and active layers if checked and with only the active bitmap object if unchecked; Smudge Color, which applies the selected color to the beginning of the smudge; and Pressure, which determines the depth of the smudge. Low pressure will barely blend and move the colors, and high pressure will completely blend the colors. Colors will persist throughout the smudge stroke.

Rubber Stamp—The Rubber Stamp tool is one of the most powerful tools in the Bitmap group on the Tools panel, and it is often used to retouch blemishes in a photograph by copying an unblemished area of the image over the blemished area. With the Rubber Stamp tool, you first click to select the area of pixels that you would like to use as the source, and then you select the destination for those pixels. If you click and drag, pixels will be rubber-stamped relative to the original relationship between the source and destination cursors. To choose a new relationship, Alt+click (Windows) or Option+click (Macintosh) to reset the source pixels.

Options available for the Rubber Stamp tool on the Property Inspector include Size, in pixels, from 1 to 100; Edge Softness, a percentage; Source Aligned, which if checked maintains the relationship between source and destination cursors, and if unchecked keeps the source cursor at the original location regardless of where the destination is

6

clicked; Use Entire Document, which checked will rubber-stamp data from any visible element on the Canvas, and unchecked will work with only the active element; Opacity, a percentage; and the Blending mode.

Eyedropper—The Eyedropper tool is another incredibly useful tool because it allows you to sample a color value from one or more pixels. To use the eyedropper, select it from the Tools panel, choose the stroke or fill color setting, and then click an area of the Canvas. The stroke or fill color will change to that of the selected pixel. You can also choose to sample a 3 × 3–pixel or 5 × 5–pixel average in the Property Inspector; this takes the average color from an area that big (9 or 25 pixels, respectively) centered on the selected pixel.

Task: Use the Rubber Stamp and Smudge Tools to Retouch Blemishes Seamlessly

▼ TASK

Now that you have an understanding of what these tools can do, you'll make some enhancements to one of the photographs on the CD. This image has already been improved, using the color correction techniques outlined earlier, but as you will see, there is still room for improvement. The following steps take you through the process of retouching blemishes on a photographic image.

1. Open the file `plantation_home.png` from the `Hour 06` examples folder. This image has been color-corrected but not retouched. Problem areas when retouching photographs include smooth, gradual areas of tonal change—skin, water, painted surfaces, and skies. Here the problem is definitely the sky. There must have been some dust on the photograph or on the scanner. Also, there might have been dust on the negative, indicated by the presence of both white and black specks (the dust on the negative would have dodged the image during print).

2. Zoom in on the television antenna, as shown in Figure 6.11. You'll see almost a halo of dark specks in the sky. First you'll use the Rubber Stamp tool to get rid of these by copying good areas of the sky over the dust. Select the Rubber Stamp tool by pressing S.

FIGURE 6.11

When you zoom in on an area of sky, you will notice some obvious dust and scratches, which you can clear up with the Rubber Stamp tool.

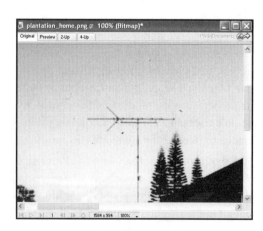

3. In the Property Inspector set the Size to 10, set the Edge Softness to 75, check Source Aligned, and leave Use Entire Document unchecked (you're dealing with only a single bitmap). A target cursor will appear. Click an area of the sky to the left of a dust particle. Try to match the tone of the destination pixels to the tone behind the spot of dust. In Figure 6.12 the source pixels are designated by the light cross to the left and will be redrawn under the cursor to the destination on the right.

FIGURE 6.12

Using the Rubber Stamp tool, you can copy a pixel or pixels exactly from one area of the canvas to another. This will help get rid of image blemishes and other imperfections.

4. Now move around the antenna and click to replace the pixels under the cursor with the source pixels to the left. Notice how the source pixel cursor moves in relation to the destination pixel cursor. Try not to click and drag; excess movement with the Rubber Stamp tool can look artificial (though this is often used creatively). For retouching, you don't want to replace dust and scratches with evidence of brushwork. With just a dozen clicks, you should be able to clean up the whole area (see Figure 6.13).

FIGURE 6.13

The dust problems have been completely cleared up with the Rubber Stamp tool.

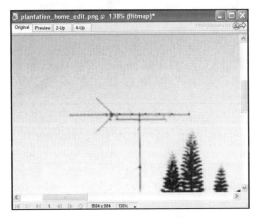

6

5. You may have also noticed some light spots in the sky. Instead of the Rubber Stamp tool, you can use the Smudge tool to get rid of these problems. Just as with the Rubber Stamp tool, using a lot of smudge or setting the Smudge tool to a heavy pressure can create artificial-looking lines and shapes in the photograph, defeating the purpose of retouching. Press R to cycle through the exposure tools to the Smudge tool. Set the Size to 10 and the Edge to 100. Use a round brush tip and make sure Smudge Color is unchecked. Change the pressure to 20. You'll also want to zoom in on the area, as in Figure 6.14.

FIGURE 6.14

The Smudge tool is great at removing spots from fields of color.

6. Click with the Smudge tool and drag across the white spot as though you were rubbing it out with your finger. Smudge lightly across in every direction until the spot blends in with the color of the sky, as in Figure 6.15.

FIGURE 6.15

Now the blue from the sky has been blended into the white spot, and the dark spots of dust have been removed, creating a natural-looking sky.

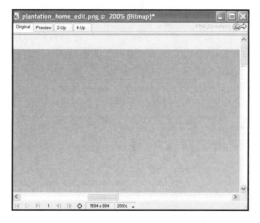

Voila! Remember that retouching is all about trying to remove the marks of the mechanical process or of wear and tear to make the image look more natural. Of course, it can also be used to clear up blemishes in the subject itself, but again the aim is to make things look less artificial, not more. If you would like to compare the original to the retouched image, open plantation_home_edit.png in the Hour 06 examples folder. This is the completed version of the task. The house no longer seems to be surrounded by volcanic dust!

Masking Bitmap Objects with Grayscale Images

Another way to edit a bitmap's appearance is through masks, which can be added to bitmap objects in the Layers panel. A mask is another bitmap image that's used to selectively show and hide areas of the bitmap that it's masking. To add a mask, select the bitmap object in the Layers panel and click the Add Mask button. A new thumbnail will appear to the right of the original bitmap thumbnail. The bitmap object on the Canvas will have a diamond in the center when selected to let you know that it is masked. Double-click the diamond to edit only the mask, not the bitmap itself, or click the mask's thumbnail in the Layers panel. To remove a mask, choose Delete Mask from the Options menu in the Layers panel. You can also choose Disable Mask if you want to keep the mask but don't want it displayed.

When you create a new mask, you will automatically be in Mask Editing mode. The stroke and fill swatches will change to grayscale. Masks are made up of a grayscale image. The darker the area, the more it is hidden. The lighter the area, the more it is shown. Black areas become transparent, whereas white areas are unchanged. You can edit masks with any of the bitmap tools, or you can use Paste as Mask in the Edit menu to paste a bitmap object as a mask to the selected object. If a mask exists, you will be asked whether you want to replace the current mask or add the information to the current mask. Any color information is automatically changed to grayscale.

Masks can be created and used in a number of ways. They are a great way to draw a very accurate outline to isolate a subject from a bitmap. When layered over a color, masks can be used to enhance exposures or create great color fill effects.

Use Invert to quickly reverse the parts that are masked and the parts that are visible. Use Brightness to quickly show more or less of the entire bitmap. Use Contrast to increase or decrease the variation in the mask's depth. You must apply the effects or filters to a bitmap before it is copied and pasted as a mask.

Task: Masking an Image

As explained already, masks show or hide specific parts of an image. Creating an empty mask and then editing the properties will allow you to cover some or all of the underlying image, depending on the selections you make.

If you have used previous versions of Fireworks, please note that MX reverses the action of grayscale masking. Where black used to show whatever was underneath the mask and white hid it, the opposite is now true.

There is more than one way to create a mask in Fireworks. This task will create a mask through the Layers panel.

1. In Fireworks create a new document and set the background to be transparent, then open a photographic image to work with. Show the Layers panel, if it is not already visible.

2. At the bottom of the panel, click the Add Mask button. The blank mask will appear next to the bitmap in the panel, as seen in Figure 6.16.

FIGURE 6.16

A blank mask as indicated in the Layers panel.

3. As soon as it is created, the mask becomes the selected item. When you draw over the mask, the mask will change and reveal the underlying background (or any image behind the photograph on the canvas).

4. Select the Brush tool from the Bitmap area of the Tools Panel.

5. Now draw onto the canvas. In Figure 6.17 the Brush tool was simply applied to write the name of one of the people in the photo. Note that the background shows through quite clearly where the brush was applied.

6. You could now play with the Canvas color and see how the masked area looks as color rather than transparent. Figure 6.18 shows exactly the same image and mask as before but with a colored Canvas—the difference is quite obvious.

FIGURE 6.17

FIGURE 6.17

The Brush tool cuts through the photo to reveal the underlying layer.

FIGURE 6.18

The change in the Canvas shows through the image.

6

Specify Areas in an Image to Apply Selective JPEG Compression

A great way to improve the output of a compressed photograph is by employing selective JPEG compression. This allows you to select one or more areas of the image and apply either more or less compression than that applied to the unselected areas. With a portrait of a seated subject, for example, you could select the hands, torso, and face for light compression. Then compress the background more heavily, preserving more subject detail for the same file size than if the compression were applied equally.

Task: Choose a Selective Compression Area and Optimize for Export

▼ TASK

In this task you will first identify the area of an image that needs to retain maximum quality. You will then choose the correct compression for different areas of the file, before choosing the most appropriate optimization settings in preparation for exporting. The area that is compressed separately, called a selective JPEG, can be as large as you want.

1. Open the file plantation_home_edit.png from the Hour 06 examples folder. This is the file that you retouched with the Rubber Stamp and Smudge tools.

2. Select the Lasso tool. In the Property Inspector change the edge to Feather and set it to 25 pixels.

3. Click-drag to select the garage, the house, and the two trees in front of the house, as in Figure 6.19.

FIGURE 6.19

The Lasso tool has been used to select an area of the image that is to be compressed less than the rest of the image.

4. Just in case you lose the selection, choose Save Bitmap Selection from the Select menu. In this way, the selection is saved independently of the selective JPEG, so you can restore it later, if you need to.

5. Select Settings from the Selective JPEG commands in the Modify menu. Check Enable Selective Quality. You can leave the quality setting at the default for now. After Selective Quality is enabled, you can access it directly from the Optimize panel.

6. Now select Save Selection as JPEG Mask from the Selective JPEG commands in the Modify menu. The selection will be covered by a semitransparent mask of the color specified in the Settings dialog from the previous step, as in Figure 6.20.

7. Now expand the Optimize panel. Choose JPEG as the compression format. Set the Quality to 30. Set the Selective Quality to 60 and the Smoothing level to 2. Finally, select the Preview tab above the Canvas, as in Figure 6.21.

8. With the Zoom tool you can view how the selective compression is applied. Zoom to 100% on the area underneath the tree in front of the house, as in Figure 6.22. Notice how the lawn that was outside the selective area is now heavily compressed, whereas the base of the tree and the house behind are still pretty clear. The feathering you applied to the marquee helps this transition somewhat.

6

FIGURE 6.22
*You can see how the
more heavily com-
pressed area looks
when compared with
the area that is com-
pressed at twice the
Selective Quality.*

Summary

You should now be very familiar with all the bitmap editing tools and what they're used for. Don't be afraid to experiment with the images included or with your own images. Play around with the tools or try out an idea you might have come up with while reading this book. There are an infinite variety of things you can do with bitmaps!

In the next section you'll be working mostly with vectors, but many of the same techniques that apply to vector objects in Fireworks apply to bitmap objects, as well, including grouping, gradient fills (very handy with masks), and masking bitmaps with a vector image instead of with a grayscale mask. If you've never worked with vectors before, you'll be delighted with how easy and intuitive it is with Fireworks, even for a dedicated pixel pusher!

Workshop

You are now at the end of what has likely been the busiest hour so far. You have covered many topics in this time as well as completing various color- and photograph-related tasks. No matter how well you have read all of this and done the tasks, this last section of the hour will help you check how much has sunk in. There are also a few optional exercises that will help you get used to the techniques used so far.

Q&A

Q What's the best way to color-correct an image?

A There is no best way to color-correct an image. You studied a method that uses neutral tones, but it can also be done by eye if there's another known color to check with, such as a skin tone. Levels and Curves are used primarily, but you can also use Hue/Saturation or even masks and blending.

Q **What can I do if my histogram has lots of gaps or if it runs off the edge of the graph?**

A All you can do is preserve the darkness of the shadows or highlights. Trying to lighten shadows with no detail will just make them a gray monotone. Trying to darken highlights will also result in gray. As soon as detail is lost, it's gone. Try rescanning, if possible. If it's a problem with the print, take it to a professional photo lab, where they can work on the image photographically.

Q **Why can't I use Paste to paste a bitmap object into a mask I'm editing?**

A You must select the bitmap, not the mask, and use Paste as Mask from the Edit menu. Simply pasting data will create a new bitmap object, regardless of whether or not you're in Mask Editing mode.

Quiz

1. What does the Rubber Stamp tool do?

    a. Fills an area with a texture from a source file

    b. Graphically indicates approval or disapproval of a finished piece

    c. Copies an area of pixels under the source cursor to the area under the destination cursor

2. How would you darken an exposure around a small area, like a bright light, in an image?

    a. Select the object and apply the Brightness/Contrast effect.

    b. Use the Burn tool.

    c. Apply a mask and layer the image over a light background.

3. What happens when you add too much sharpening?

    a. The entire image snaps into focus.

    b. Black and white noise begins to appear.

    c. The image begins to blur.

Quiz Answers

1. c.—The Rubber Stamp tool clones pixels from the source cursor under the destination cursor.

2. b.—Although you could mask and layer (c), it would probably take a lot longer.

3. b.—You can't rescue focus from a blurry image. If you apply too much sharpening, high-contrast noise will appear in the image.

Exercises

1. Spend a little time working on images that have been scanned. If these are older photos, there will always be room for improvement, as age alone causes deterioration. Try removing blemishes and touching up the images. A newly improved photo can not only bring back memories but also make relatives very happy!

2. Use the Clone tool to make a friend or colleague appear at a party or meeting he or she missed. Simply open the image with the scene the person is to be placed into, then import an image of the person. You should then be able to work him or her into the situation unobtrusively.

3. Use masking techniques to see what effects you can create. Try placing more than one photograph or image onto the Canvas, and then create masks to blend the images. This can be a good way of showing off multiple products on a Web site.

PART III

Graphic Design: Working with Art and Text

Hour

HOUR 7

Working with Vector Paths

Fireworks is particularly well suited for working interchangeably with bitmaps and vector paths. Vector paths are derived from calculus, but they are a really useful way to present visual information derived from mathematical functions, or algorithms, instead of using bitmaps or databases for the display. Because of this, vector graphics have many interesting properties. Vector lines and shapes can be resized again and again without a loss of quality.

In this group of hours, you will begin working with the Fireworks Vector tool group on the Tools panel. In Hours 8 and 9, "Creating Text and Typographic Effects" and "Tools and Techniques for Layout and Design," you'll learn how to work with text, and you'll study some advanced techniques for working with vector graphics. The last hour in this part, "Tricks of the Trade," will go over some great techniques that professional graphic designers use to combine vectors and bitmaps to create great-looking work.

In this hour you will

- Learn how to create and edit vector paths
- Control anti-aliasing for optimal output
- Understand the Fireworks PNG vector features
- Organize vector graphics by using groups and layers

Drawing Points and Lines

When you draw with the vector tools, you're not actually editing pixels. Instead, the movements of the cursor are interpreted as points along a continuous path. For instance, when you draw with the brush (see the top object in Figure 7.1), a bitmap object is created, and the color information of the individual pixels underneath the brush tip is changed to match the brush settings. But if you want to smooth out a bump or make the line a little shorter, you'll have to use another bitmap tool to change the color information of those pixels back to the original setting. You can also use Undo and completely redraw the line.

FIGURE 7.1

Here you can see similar figures drawn with different tools. The top one was drawn with the brush. The bottom was drawn with the pen but with the same settings as the brush. Notice how the paths are highlighted individually for the vector drawing, whereas the bitmap is one distinct element.

Bitmap drawing

Vector drawing

With a vector path the line itself is all that matters. Instead of having to edit a bitmap to change the size or shape of the line, you can change the shape of the line simply by moving the points that define it. Furthermore, the stroke settings, such as width and color, can be changed at any time. Only when the vector is rendered through flattening or export does it become bitmap data and lose the path information. If the vector is saved in the Fireworks PNG source format, its appearance can be edited with the vector tools at any time. In Figure 7.2 both graphics were scaled down and then returned to their original proportions. Scaling the bitmap down went smoothly, but scaling it back up ruined it.

Scaled bitmap drawing

FIGURE 7.2

The vector stroke looks perfect even after two transformations have been applied.

Scaled vector drawing

To create a path, you can use any of the drawing tools in the Vector group on the Tools panel. These include the Line, Pen, Vector Path, Rectangle, Rounded Rectangle, Ellipse, and Polygon tools. You'll learn about the rest of the tools in the Vector group in the next hour, "Creating Text and Typographic Effects."

Line—The Line tool is probably the simplest of the drawing tools. Press N to choose the Line tool. Click and drag on the Canvas to create a line that starts where you click and ends where you release. At each end of the line, vector points are created, with the path joining them. Hold down Shift to constrain the line within 45-degree angles. You cannot create shapes with the Line tool, only single line segments. Only the stroke, opacity, and Blending mode settings are available in the Property Inspector.

Pen—The Pen tool is very powerful because it is used for both creating and editing paths. Press P to choose the Pen tool. It's important to watch the cursor when using the Pen tool; it will switch to a different mode, depending on where you click. Click the plus sign under the Pen tool cursor to add a point,

7

and click again to add a corner point. A line will then be created between them. Click-drag to create a curve point to add a curve to the line segment. You'll learn about the other Pen tool features in an upcoming section, "Editing Bézier Curves." Options for the Pen tool in the Property Inspector include fill, stroke, opacity, and Blending mode. Figure 7.3 shows a simple line, with two points, that has been dragged at one end to produce a curve.

FIGURE 7.3

You can use the Pen tool to create simple lines and then add curves at any point to change the shape to suit your needs.

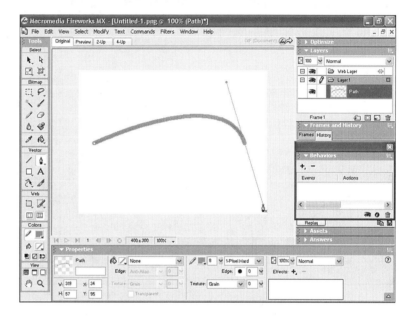

Vector Path—The Vector Path tool is similar to the Brush tool in the Bitmap group. Press P to cycle to the Vector Path tool. With the Vector Path tool, you can click-drag to draw a free-form line. The line, points, and curves in the path are automatically created after you release the mouse button. If the line ends where it began, a closed shape is created, which can then be filled. The Vector Path tool also allows you to employ pressure and angle settings if you are using a tablet and stylus. Options for the Vector Path tool include stroke, opacity, and Blending mode. Figure 7.4 shows two ways to use the Vector path. At the top of the figure is a closed shape with a fill color added, while at the bottom you can see a series of drawn paths.

FIGURE 7.4

Using the Vector Path tool, you can create free-form shapes simply by drawing with a mouse or tablet pen. Paths that start and finish in the same place can be filled.

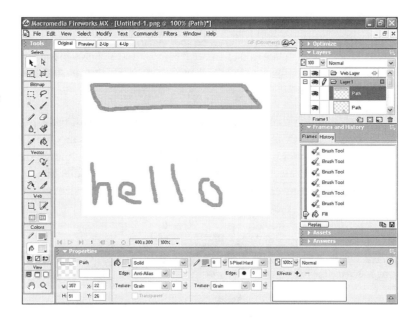

Rectangle—The Rectangle tool creates a closed shape composed of four lines at 90-degree angles. To create a square, hold down Shift to constrain the proportions of the rectangle. Options for the Rectangle tool include fill, stroke, opacity, and Blending mode.

Rounded Rectangle—This tool is similar to the Rectangle tool, but it creates a rectangle with rounded corners. To change how rounded the corners are, change the Roundedness setting in the Property Inspector. A higher setting will create a more rounded rectangle. Other settings include fill, stroke, opacity, and Blending mode.

Ellipse—This tool creates ovals and circles. Hold down Shift to constrain the proportions to a regular circle. Ellipse settings include fill, stroke, opacity, and Blending mode.

Polygon—This tool creates regular multisided figures, from triangles (3 sides) to nearly circular 25-sided figures. In the Property Inspector you can set the type to polygon or star, choose the number of sides (or points, if a star), and select the angle of the corners. Click the box to the right of the angle setting to have Fireworks set the angle automatically. Other settings include fill, stroke, opacity, and Blending mode.

7

If you start drawing your rectangle, rounded rectangle, or polygon in the wrong place, you can move it before it is even finished! Hold down the spacebar, move the object to the desired location, and carry on drawing.

The selection tools and free transform tools work with paths in the same way that they work with bitmap objects. Like bitmaps, each path is an object in Fireworks. Moving the Pointer tool over a path will reveal the points and line segments. Clicking with the pointer will select the path object, as in Figure 7.5. Selecting a path object brings up the Path settings in the Property Inspector, including size, position, fill, stroke, opacity, and Blending mode.

FIGURE 7.5

An entire path object can be selected with the Pointer tool.

Another selection tool that's used with paths and grouped objects, which you'll read about later, is the Subselection tool, located next to the Pointer tool on the Tools panel. The Subselection tool allows you to select individual points in a path. Shift+click selects multiple points. These can then be moved with the cursor keys (Up, Down, Left, and Right) or by click-dragging a selected point with the Subselection tool (see Figure 7.6).

FIGURE 7.6

Use the Subselection tool to select a single point along the path or to select an object within a group of objects.

Using the free transform tools is an easy way to edit paths. The transformations change only the relationships between points, not curves or lines, which means that an object can be endlessly transformed without the risk to quality inherent to transforming bitmaps. Select a path with the Pointer tool and then choose one of the free transform tools to transform a path by eye. You can also transform paths numerically using the Numeric Transform command, which is located in the Transform submenu from the Modify menu. When using Numeric Transform, uncheck the Scale Attributes setting if you do not want to scale stroke widths and feathering along with the path itself.

The Crop tool does not affect paths, only the Canvas. If you crop the Canvas so that paths will be outside the bounds of the cropped Canvas, they will remain in their positions relative to the original Canvas.

> If you have been playing with your preferences, you may find this does not happen. Open the Preferences dialog and then choose the Editing tab; make sure that Delete Objects when Cropping is NOT selected. If it is, then remove the check to retain maximum editability.

You can use the Export Area tool with paths just as you would with bitmaps—click and drag to create an area to export, double-click with the mouse, and specify optimization settings in the Export Preview dialog. The vectors will be exported as bitmap information in the appropriate format.

Task: Trace Line Art to Create Vector Art

Imagine for a moment that you have been given a file to work on that you did not create. You have no control over the quality of the file. You will likely only have a bitmap copy to work on that cannot easily be changed or resized. One way that Fireworks offers to solve this problem is to trace the original line drawing and create a new, editable vector drawing from it. The following steps will take you through this with one of the sample files from the CD:

1. Open the file idol_icon.png from the Hour 07 examples folder. This icon is in bad shape. You could make it smaller, but if you later tried to enlarge it, it would become even worse. Trace it with the Vector Path tool to create a copy you can more fluidly resize.

2. Select the Vector Path tool by pressing P. Make sure that the settings in the Property Inspector reflect those in Figure 7.7. Set the stroke color to red (to highlight the new stroke you're applying), the stroke width to 20, and the brush type to Soft Rounded (from the Basic group). The edge is set to 100 (full softness). Make sure that no texture, transparency, or blending is being applied.

▼ TASK

7

FIGURE 7.7

The Vector Path tool can use any of the strokes available to the bitmap Brush tool in the Property Inspector.

3. Now begin by click-dragging to draw over one of the eyes. Go ahead and fill it in. A vector path will be created, and your red brush stroke will appear over the bitmap. You'll notice in Figure 7.8 that a new path object has been created on the Layers panel on Layer 2.

> When drawing over the shape, try to keep your strokes as fluid as possible. Too much dabbing, or too many small strokes, will result in too many paths and a very complicated layers panel.

FIGURE 7.8

Drawing with the Vector Path tool automatically creates a new path object, which you can arrange in the Layers panel as you can any other object.

4. Repeat this procedure for all the black lines in the bitmap. When you're done, go ahead and hide the layer Background. You'll now have a vector graphic that you can resize, edit, and change the attributes for. You can view the file idol_vector.png in the Hour 07 examples folder to see a completed version.

Editing Bézier Curves

There are two types of points that can define a path—corner points and curve points. Line segments between corner points remain straight, joining a corner point at an angle. Curve points allow you to create smooth mathematical curves from line segments. These are known as Bézier curves, named after Pierre Bézier, who came up with an equation to mathematically describe the shape of Renault auto bodies. Some examples are shown in Figure 7.9.

FIGURE 7.9

There are four paths here. The first is a straight line with two corner points. The next one has a curve point with a vector on the left and a corner point on the right. The third path has two curve points, each with a vector. The last one is a fractured curve that doubles back on itself.

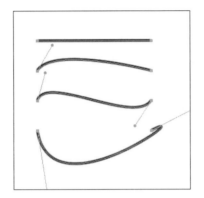

The simplest curved line segment is defined by four points—the *origin point,* the *destination point,* the *origin vector,* and the *destination vector.* The origin and destination points are the points that make up the path. The curve of the line segment is defined by the angle and distance of the vector points from the origin and destination points. A line between two Bézier curve points can be made into a soft roll, a quarter circle, a cresting wave, or even a complete loop.

When you click with the Pen tool, you create a corner point. If you hold down the mouse button and drag away from the point, you'll notice that a straight line is created through the point and that the path begins to curve on either side. You are applying equal and opposite vector points on either side of the origin point. You can edit these vector points with the Subselection tool by selecting the origin point and then click-dragging the circles at the end of either vector. Moving the vector back to the origin point deletes the curve information, creating a corner point. To create a curve point, click a selected corner point and drag with the Pen tool to add vector handles.

You can also add and delete points with the Pen tool to change a line segment. With the Pen tool, mouseover a point that isn't selected. The cursor will change to show a minus sign under the Pen icon. Click to delete this point. To add a new point, click with the Pen tool on a line segment. Click and drag to create a curve point. A new point will be added, with or without vector handles.

7

You can do a lot with the Pen and Subselection tools. They are the core tools for path editing. With the Subselection tool you can change the position of individual points and edit their vector handles. You can also delete points and the adjoining line segment with the Subselection tool—to open a closed shape, for instance. With the Pen tool you can quickly and precisely edit paths by adjusting curves and removing points without removing the line segment and opening a closed shape. You can also use the Pen tool to close a shape by clicking either end of the line path.

Changing the Appearance of a Path Object

You can edit the stroke and fill styles in the Property Inspector before or after drawing a path. These are the same settings used with the Brush and Paint Bucket tools in the Bitmap group. Object settings, such as opacity, Blending mode, and effects, can also be specified for path objects.

Fill settings apply to any path. If a path does not form a closed shape, an empty line segment will be created between the endpoints of the path to define the fill boundary. Choose the no-color swatch (white with diagonal red line) if you don't want to use a fill. The fill color can also be set on the Tools panel or in the Color Mixer panel. All the settings are available in the Property Inspector when a path object is selected. These include fill type, edge softness, and texture. Transparency can be applied to the texture by checking the Transparency box.

Stroke settings include stroke color, stroke type, edge softness, stroke width, and texture. These are the same as the settings for the bitmap Brush tool, and any number of styles can be chosen. If you don't want to use a stroke, choose either the no-color swatch or the None stroke type.

The object settings apply to the entire object, including stroke and fill. You can set the opacity with the opacity slider. Blending modes work the same way that they would with the bitmap tools, except that they can be changed at any time. You can also use any of the effects that you can use with the bitmap tools, and the effects will change along with the path if the stroke and fill settings are changed, if points are edited, or if the object is transformed.

Task: Apply Stroke and Fill Settings to Vector Paths

▼ TASK

You have seen how to use the tools to create your vector objects and paths. Now it is time to move forward and add strokes and fills to change basic lines and shapes into things that are more usable in your workflow.

Fireworks has all of the tools that you require for this. Most are located within the Property Inspector, which offers total control over fills and gradients as well as textures and lines.

1. Open the file idol_vector.png from the Hour 06 examples folder. This is the vector graphic that you created in the last task.

2. Press Control+A (Windows) or Command+A (Macintosh) to select all the path objects on the active layer (see Figure 7.10).

FIGURE 7.10

You can change the settings for multiple paths at once by selecting them and changing the settings in the Property Inspector.

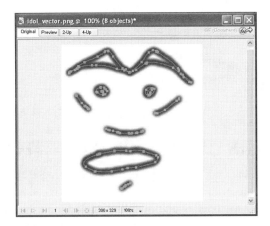

3. Click the stroke swatch next to the pencil icon. The pop-up Swatch menu will appear. At the bottom will be some special vector stroke settings. The first drop-down will let you change the position of the stroke to Inside the Path, Centered, or Outside the Path. You can also choose the Fill Over Stroke option. These apply only to strokes around closed shapes. For now, simply select the color black from the swatches.

4. Change the stroke style to Textured from the Charcoal group in the Stroke Category menu. This is located directly above the Edge setting in the Property Inspector. Make sure that the Texture drop-down menu is set to Grain with a percentage of 85. This will apply a texture of 85% grain to the stroke.

5. Using the pointer, press Shift+click to select the eyebrows and mouth. These are closed shapes, so go ahead and apply a fill to them to add some color back to the icon.

6. Select the fill style to the right of the Paint Bucket icon, and select Solid from the list of fill styles. From among the Edge settings, select Hard. Finally, click the fill-color swatch to select the color blue (#66CCFF was used, which you can type into the color field at the top of the pop-up menu).

7. Now add the same texture to the fill that's applied to the stroke. Select Grain from the Texture menu, and then set the amount to **85** by typing in the field or using the slider. After you're done, you'll be left with Figure 7.11. You'll see that it's an improvement over the example bitmap you started with.

7

FIGURE 7.11

Adding a texture effect and a little color really brings out the life in this graphic.

Arranging Path Objects with the Layers Panel

Like bitmap objects, path objects can be selected and arranged by using the Layers panel (see Figure 7.12). Objects further down in a layer are arranged behind the objects above them. You can change the opacity and Blending mode for all the paths on the layer by selecting the layer and changing the opacity and Blending mode settings in the Layers panel. This will be applied in addition to any opacity or Blending mode settings already applied to individual paths.

FIGURE 7.12

You can name and arrange paths using the Layers panel, just as you would with bitmap objects.

You can also use the Arrange commands in the Modify menu to change the stacking order of paths. Bring Forward (Control or Command plus the up-arrow key) will move the path above the next path on the layer. Send Backward (Control or Command plus the down-arrow key) will move it behind the path immediately behind it. Bring to Front (Control or Command plus Shift and the up-arrow key) will move the path to the top of the layer. Send to Back (Control or Command plus Shift and the down-arrow key) will make it the last element in the layer.

You can also use the Layers panel to show or hide a path or to change the path object's name. Click the Eyeball icon to the left of the object name to hide the path. Click again to show it. To change a path object's name, simply double-click the current name. You can type a new name in the field that appears. Press Return to apply the new name to the object.

Standard output formats, such as JPEG and GIF, do not support Fireworks paths. All paths are flattened into bitmaps before exporting. Make sure to always save an original Fireworks source PNG and back it up; you can't rely on your exported files if you want to continue working with the vector paths.

Working with Groups of Paths

Another important method for organizing path objects is grouping. Paths that are grouped together will be treated like a single path when changes are applied. To group paths, select multiple objects by holding down the Shift key and clicking the Pointer tool (you can also select multiple paths from the Layers panel by using Shift and clicking the path objects). Choose Group from the Modify menu or press Control+G (Windows) or Command+G (Macintosh). The selection highlight will change to four handles around the elements in the group that form the group's bounding box (see Figure 7.13).

7

FIGURE 7.13

A group of objects can include vector and bitmap objects. The entire group can be quickly scaled with the handles at the corners. Notice that the new group object in the Layers panel replaced the individual path objects.

Grouping works with any object, including bitmaps. When you group a number of objects, a new Group object appears on that layer in the Layers panel. Grouped objects cannot span more than one layer; if you select objects on more than one layer, they will be grouped together in the same layer as the topmost selected object. To rename a group on the Layers panel, double-click the group name as you would a bitmap or path object. To ungroup the objects, press Control+Shift+G (Windows) or Command+Shift+G (Macintosh) or select Ungroup from the Modify menu.

When path objects are grouped, you can change the settings for the entire group at once. For instance, changing the stroke settings in the Property Inspector with a group selected applies the new settings to all the paths in the group. The same goes for fill, opacity, and Blending mode. When items are grouped, they are also transformed in their original proportions. Click the handles at any of the four corners of the group with the pointer to resize a group quickly. Hold down the Shift key to constrain the resized group to its original aspect ratio. You can also transform or add effects to a group object in the same way that you would with an individual bitmap or path object.

If you want to edit a part of a group without ungrouping it, you can use the Subselection tool to select an individual path or bitmap object within the group. This way you can change the stroke, fill, effect, or position of an element within a group without affecting other elements in the group. Conversely, you can create a group of groups so that you can edit large numbers of objects very quickly. When a group containing other groups is ungrouped, the original groups are retained.

Opening and Importing Vector Graphics

When you open or import a vector graphic created in another program, such as Adobe Illustrator or CorelDRAW, there are a number of options that you can specify to help

Fireworks interpret the file the way you want it to. You can choose to import the graphic as a single bitmap or preserve specific elements, such as layers and grouping. Some of the file format features supported in other applications may not be supported in Fireworks, but most of the basic graphic features are.

When you choose a vector file with the Open or Import commands on the File menu, you are presented with a dialog that you may remember from Hour 2, "Image Collection and Management." The Vector File Options dialog includes a number of features that are useful when importing vector files (see Figure 7.14).

> For more about working with vector graphics created in other applications, check out Hour 22, which is all about Adobe Illustrator and Macromedia FreeHand, two commonly used vector applications.

FIGURE 7.14

The Vector File Options dialog will let you scale, resample, anti-alias, and render vector graphics before importing.

Scale—The scale setting will resize the vector file automatically. Remember that vector paths can be scaled up or down without sacrificing quality. Changing the scale makes the dimensions of the imported image larger or smaller.

Width and Height—These settings default to the width and height specified in the file. Changing the drop-down menu to the right changes the units that the width is measured in. Changing these settings may change the proportions of the imported graphic.

Resolution—The resolution setting determines how many pixels will be used to define the paths when they are rendered as a bitmap. Vectors can be printed reliably

7

at almost any resolution. If the original resolution is higher than the intended output resolution, change to the lower resolution and scale up the image later if it needs to be bigger.

Anti-Alias—Anti-aliasing refers to adding shaded pixels at the edge of a stroke to give it a smoother appearance when it's converted into a bitmap. You can choose to turn on anti-aliasing for paths, text, or both. You can also choose a Crisp, Strong, or Smooth setting. Crisp gives the most accurate lines, whereas Smooth gives the smoothest appearance, with Strong somewhere in between.

File Conversion—Depending on the type of file, you can choose how Fireworks imports information, such as Page and Layer organization. If a file contains multiple pages, you must choose which one you would like to import; Fireworks will import only one page at a time. Below the page menu is the Layers menu. The Ignore Layers option places all paths and groups on the same layer in the Fireworks file. Remember, the Layers option preserves the original layers in the file. Convert Layers to Frames creates a new frame for each layer in the original file for use as an animation. You can also include Invisible (layers that were hidden in the original file) and Background layers.

Render as Images—The Render as Images feature helps you reduce the complexity of large vector files with lots and lots of paths. Groups, blends, and tiled fills could contain hundreds of points of information and might render very slowly in Fireworks. If this is a problem, you can specify a limit above which the multiple objects are rendered as a single bitmap object. This removes any vector information from the object. You can Open or Import the file again if you need to work with the original vectors.

> Some clip art graphics contain thousands of lines and shapes. Even though simple vectors generally create small files, hundreds of paths—each with hundreds of points—will still create a huge file, and the time it takes your processor to do all that math might slow down Fireworks performance. Set the Render thresholds very low to have complex paths flattened into bitmaps.

Summary

Hopefully, this has been a successful foray into the world of geometric art. Don't fret if the math is confusing. Just remember that you can draw with the Vector Path tool just as you would with the Brush tool in Bitmap mode, but the path is more flexible when you use the Vector Path tool. You can make changes quickly and easily, and the lines will always look clean and smooth—no noise or jaggies, even after scaling or other transformations.

Workshop

This section gives you a chance to see how much you can remember about vector graphics and the subtopics covered in this hour. The quiz will act as a simple test of your memory. Learning to use vector tools is quite complex, and it is worth your while to get familiar and feel confident with them. To increase your skill at using the tools, the exercises will let you try your hand at a few more tasks.

Q&A

Q How do I draw a path by just clicking and dragging with the mouse?

A Use the Vector Path tool (press P to cycle through the path drawing tools). This will create a path in the same way that you would draw with the Brush tool.

Q How do I change an object within a group without having to ungroup it?

A Use the Subselection tool. Changes applied to the group will affect all elements within a group. With the Subselection tool you can also select individual points along a path.

Q I imported a graphic from Illustrator, and now Fireworks is really, really slow. What can I do to speed it up?

A Vector path files are generally smaller than bitmap files, but this is not always the case. Use the Render settings to render elements when importing; this creates bitmap objects that won't require as much processor power to display. Also, saving the file as a PNG will immediately take some stress off the application's memory allocation.

Quiz

1. How many points define a Bézier curve?

    a. 2

    b. 3

    c. 4

2. How do you delete a point from a line?

    a. With the Subselection tool

    b. With the Pen tool

    c. With the Vector Path tool

3. What happens when you scale a vector graphic?

    a. It becomes jagged and noisy.

    b. It changes the relationship between points and paths.

    c. It resizes gracefully.

7

Quiz Answers

1. c.—The origin point, the destination point, the origin vector, and the destination vector define a Bézier curve.

2. a. or b.—Deleting a point with the Subselection tool also deletes the adjoining line segments. Deleting a point with the Pen tool leaves the rest of the line segment intact.

3. c.—Vector paths resize gracefully because they are drawn fresh from the paths whenever they are resized or resampled.

Exercises

The sample files in this chapter showed the Idol graphic, a nice, simple face shape created solely by Vector graphics. The following exercises will enhance your skills and confidence.

1. Without using the sample files, try to create a new face shape. This should have two eyes, a nose, and a mouth. Then add some hair, a hat, and a bow tie. All of these can be created with the Vector tools covered in this hour.

2. Decorate an egg! Use the Ellipse tool to create your basic shape, then see how creative you can be. Think about the intricate designs of Fabergé eggs and see what you can do. It is one thing to create free shapes but quite another to find yourself working in an enclosed area, such as within a shape.

3. Try some body shaping. For all eternity, people have tried to find the easiest way to lose or gain weight, so see how Fireworks does this. Use multiple round shapes to create a roundish person. Then use the vector tools to reshape the paths and turn the round person into something close to a stick person.

HOUR 8

Creating Text and Typographic Effects

One of the core elements of designing graphics for the Web is employing text. Because Web pages are limited by the fonts available on the user's system, rather than those on the author's system, only a small set of fonts is available for text on a Web page. But any font can be used when composing bitmap graphics. These can then be laid out on a Web page in addition to HTML-formatted text to create pages with typographic flair at minimal file sizes.

In this hour you will

- Become familiar with the Text tool
- Enter text on the canvas or paste it from other programs
- Style text using fonts and colors
- Change text flow with typesetting
- Use paths to create dynamic text graphics

Using the Text Tool

Fireworks MX has vastly improved the Text tool from previous versions. Instead of having to use the Text Editor to enter or change text and to apply fonts and styles, you can simply select the Text tool, specify the desired settings in the Property Inspector, click an area of the canvas, and begin typing. It's that simple!

Creating Text Objects

Clicking the Canvas with the Text tool creates a text object, much like painting with the bitmap tools or drawing with a vector tool. And like bitmap or vector objects, text objects can be selected and rearranged on the Layers panel, grouped with other types of objects, transformed, and altered with effects. Like vector objects, text objects can be changed at any time until they're converted into bitmaps through merging, flattening, or exporting. A text object also can be converted into a vector object, which will be discussed in Hour 10, "Tricks of the Trade."

Selecting Text

The Text tool cursor allows you to select portions of a text object. With the Text tool click the area of a text object where you would like to start the selection, and then drag to the point where you would like to end the selection. In this way you can select parts of a text passage and apply different settings to the text within the text object. You can also cut, copy, or paste over the selection, using commands from the Edit menu. To paste text within an object, click with the Text tool to place the text cursor where you want to paste the passage.

The Pointer and Subselection tools can also be used with text objects. Double-clicking a text object with the Pointer tool will bring up the Text tool cursor, so you can edit the text content. Selecting a text object allows you to view the object settings and change them in the Property Inspector. When an object is selected, you can also move it, scale it, or use the Edit commands to cut, copy, or paste it. If a text object is within a group, you can use the Subselection tool in the same way you would use the Pointer tool with an independent text object.

If you are familiar with previous versions of Fireworks and would prefer to use the traditional Text Editor dialog, don't worry—it's still here! Simply select a text object with the pointer, or create one with the Text tool by clicking the Canvas. Now select Editor from the Text menu. This will bring up the classic Fireworks Text Editor dialog that you're used to.

Importing Text from Other Applications

There are three ways to import text from other applications. You can copy text from one application on your system to the clipboard, switch to Fireworks, and then choose Paste from the Edit menu. A new text object containing the text from the clipboard will appear on the Canvas. If the clipboard also contains rich text information, such as the font, size, and style, that information will be pasted, as well. Not all applications will copy rich text information to the clipboard along with the text content. Figure 8.1 shows some of the text from this hour pasted directly into Fireworks from Word.

FIGURE 8.1

Not only can you type directly into Fireworks, but you can also paste text from most well-known applications directly into the Fireworks document window.

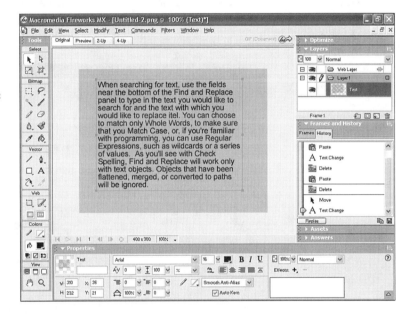

Another method is to use the Import command to import a standard text file (.txt) or a rich text format (.rtf) file. The text from the file will appear as a new text object on the Canvas. If an RTF file is used, information such as font, size, and style will also be applied. You can create RTF files with WordPad for Windows XP or TextEdit for Macintosh OS X.

Finally, when you open or import files from other graphics applications that support editable text (such as Photoshop PSD, CorelDRAW CDR, and Adobe Illustrator AI), you may choose Preserve Editability as the text setting in the Import dialog. Although this may sometimes change the appearance of the text (for instance, if the font specified is not available on your system), it docs allow you to edit and reapply settings to the object. Choose Preserve Appearance in the Import dialog if you want to make sure the text appears as it was intended.

Proofreading Text with Fireworks MX

All of us make mistakes, and there's nothing like a typo to draw attention away from an otherwise good design. Fireworks MX provides two great tools for editing and proofreading text—Find and Replace on the Edit menu and Check Spelling on the Text menu.

Find and Replace

Find and Replace is a powerful feature that isn't just for text. Press Ctrl+F (Windows) or Command+F (Macintosh) to bring up the Find and Replace panel, as shown in Figure 8.2. From this panel you can choose to search the selection, the current frame, the entire document, the files in the Project log, or files you choose using the Open dialog. You can search for text, fonts, colors, URLs, or colors that aren't Web safe.

FIGURE 8.2

The very powerful Find and Replace panel can be used to locate text, URLs, and colors across a whole range of documents.

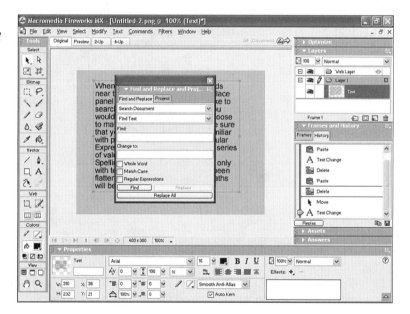

When searching for text, use the fields near the bottom of the Find and Replace panel to type in the text you would like to search for and the text with which you would like to replace it. You can choose to match only Whole Words, to make sure that you Match Case, or if you're familiar with programming, you can use Regular Expressions, such as wildcards or a series of values. Regular Expressions allows you to match part of a word or words as part of the search process. As you'll see with Check Spelling, Find and Replace will work only with text objects. Objects that have been flattened, merged, or converted to paths will be ignored.

Check Spelling

You can check the spelling of any text in a Fireworks file by pressing Shift+F7. By default this checks all spelling in the currently open document. This will check only text objects—if text has been flattened, merged, or converted to paths, it will be ignored by the spell checker. It will check text that has added effects, such as shadows or bevels, attached. Use Spelling Setup from the Text menu to choose a dictionary, edit your custom dictionary, and specify other spell-checker settings.

> It is better to check your text before you apply any formatting. This is not required, but it can help to find spelling mistakes that would change the overall size of the text object. It is also good practice to get it done first rather than risk forgetting when final deadlines approach.

Setting Properties for Text and Text Objects

Once you've placed your text on the Canvas (and have you checked the spelling?), you can start applying formatting to the text. Remember that you can apply formatting to all the text in the object by selecting it with the Pointer tool. If you want to apply formatting to a portion of text within an object, use the Text tool to select a passage by click-dragging. Figure 8.3 shows the Property Inspector with a text object selected. Also following is a list of the options available when working with text.

FIGURE 8.3

With a text object selected in the document window, the Property Inspector offers you many tools and features to format the text any way you want.

Font—You can change the font for a selection by selecting a font from those listed in the Text menu. You can also type the name of a font in the Font field in the Property Inspector or select a font from the pop-up menu.

Size—Font size is measured in points. You can choose a point size from the sizes available under Size on the Text menu. You can also choose Other to specify a font size numerically. When a text object or passage is selected, you can change the size using the Size field on the Property Inspector by typing the new size in the field or by using the slider.

> When you set a text size in points and then transform the text to be smaller or larger, the size setting will remain the same. When you change the size setting of transformed text, it will be resized in relation to its transformed size.

Style—Styles for text include Bold, Italic, and Underline. To remove styles from a text object or passage, select Plain from the Styles available in the Text menu.

Alignment—Alignment specifies how the text content is aligned within the text box. Left and Right align text to the left or right side of the bounding box, respectively. Center will center lines of text within the box. Justified will adjust the space between characters to make each line of text align to both the left and right sides of the box. Stretched Alignment stretches each line to align it equally on both sides.

You can also align text vertically by choosing Top or Bottom alignment. You can also Center, Justify, or Stretch vertically. All of these options are available under Align in the Text menu or from the Property Inspector.

> When you align text vertically, notice that the other alignment options change in the Property Inspector. Instead of Left, Center, and Right, you now have Top, Center, and Bottom.

Color—Use the fill color to specify the color for a text object or passage selection. The color can be changed by using the Property Inspector or from the fill color swatch on the Tools panel. You may also choose to add an outline to the font by changing the stroke color. You can choose the stroke color from the Property Inspector or from the stroke color swatch on the Tools panel.

8

Anti-aliasing—Anti-aliasing can be applied to character edges. You can find the Anti-aliasing menu next to the stroke color setting. No anti-aliasing is best for font sizes below 10 points. Crisp applies a light anti-alias suitable for font sizes from 10 to 18 points. Strong applies more anti-aliasing than Crisp but not as much as Smooth. Strong is generally used for font sizes between 18 and 36 points, Smooth for anything larger than 36 points.

Opacity and Blending Mode—As with any other object, you can set the opacity and blending mode for a text object. This will affect how the object appears when layered over other objects.

Effects—You can also add effects to a text object, just as you would add them to any other object. The advantage of using effects is that you can change or remove them at any time while retaining text editability. Using a filter command with a text object will convert the text into a bitmap object.

Task: Entering, Styling, and Importing Copy

▼ TASK

Now that you have an understanding of what can be done with text, you will put that into practice. The following task will work on a file that you first saw and used in Hour 4, "Working with Bitmap Images." You will add some text into the document and then format and style it accordingly.

1. If you completed the first task in Hour 4, then go ahead and open home_layout.png from your Fireworks Examples folder. Otherwise, open the file home_layout.png in the Hour 08 examples folder.

2. Make sure the Background layer is locked. You won't be working with the bitmap on that layer. Click Layer1 to activate it.

3. Click anywhere on the Canvas or workspace to bring up the Canvas settings in the Property Inspector. Click the Canvas swatch to bring up the pop-up swatch menu. The cursor will now become an eyedropper. Change the background color to a dark brown shade, chosen from the branches of the trees on the left. You can also type the hexadecimal value **#44341A** in the field at the top of the swatch menu, as in Figure 8.4.

FIGURE 8.4

When the pop-up swatch menu is active, you can use the cursor just as you would use the eyedropper.

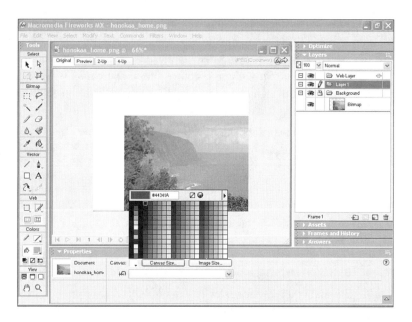

4. Now select the Text tool by clicking the button on the Tools panel or by pressing T. Using the Property Inspector, change the font to Verdana. Now change the size to 20. Click the color swatch to bring up the pop-up swatch menu again. Use the eyedropper to select an area of blue sky, or type **#AED2E0** in the hexadecimal field. Click the Bold button to set the style, and make sure Smooth Anti-Alias and Auto Kern are chosen, as in Figure 8.5.

FIGURE 8.5

This is how the Text tool settings should look in the Property Inspector.

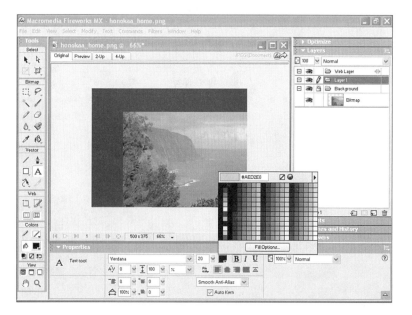

5. With the Text tool as your cursor, click the Canvas near the top left corner. Type **Mamalahoa Highway**. Line the cursor up with the left edge of the photo and click just above it. Type **driving from Hilo to Honokaa**. You can move the type so it looks like it does in Figure 8.6.

FIGURE 8.6

Laying out text is quick and easy with the Fireworks Text tool.

6. Use the Import command from the File menu or press Control+R (Windows) or Command+R (Macintosh) to import the file `mamalahoa_copy.rtf` from the `Hour 08` examples folder. Click with the Place cursor to put the text flush with the left side of the canvas and lined up with the top of the photograph.

7. Once the text is placed, use the Pointer tool to grab the handle on the right side of the bounding box and drag it so it's flush with the left side of the photo. The text wrap will change to fit within the area on the left, as shown in Figure 8.7.

FIGURE 8.7

The text from the RTF file is imported with color, font, size, and style intact. Changing the bounding box with the handle fits the text within the space on the left.

8. Save this image when you're done. A completed version (`honokaa_home_text.png`) is also provided for use in the next task, which involves working on the text flow for the headline and copy.

Fonts are really just paths that define closed shapes. Because of this, you can use fonts as graphics. Some fonts, often called dingbats, are collections of shapes and symbols to be used as graphics instead of as text. Such fonts can serve as collections of ready-made icons.

Changing Text Flow with Text Blocks, Paragraph Settings, and Paths

Once you've entered some text, there are a number of ways to change how the lines of text flow on the page. You can change the style and shape of the text block, change how lines are spaced and paragraphs indented, and even change the text to flow along a curved path or shape.

Text Blocks

When you select a text block with the Pointer tool (or a text block within a group with the Subselection tool), you'll notice that there are handles at the corners of the block and on two of its sides. Text object handles work differently from bitmap or vector object handles—they don't resize the content they contain. They specify the width of the text object, which will affect how the lines wrap within the text object. As you change the handles on the sides, the text box will grow taller or shorter, as more or fewer lines are necessary. Changing the handles on the bottom corners will affect only the width of the block. Changing the handles on the top corners will change both the width and the point at which the text starts. If you choose a vertical alignment setting, the width handles will become height handles to handle vertical text wrapping.

Paragraph Settings

You can adjust the spacing between characters, lines, and paragraphs by using the paragraph settings for a text object in the Property Inspector. Figure 8.8 shows you the Property Inspector with a text object selected. The tools available are also explained.

FIGURE 8.8

The Property Inspector allows you to make amendments to the layout and flow of your text.

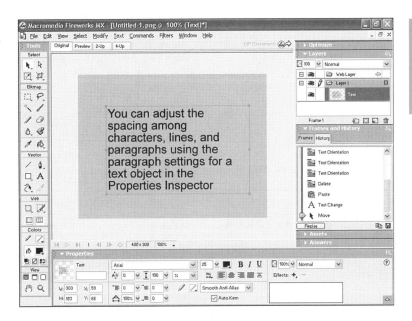

Kerning—Kerning is the space between individual characters. A negative percentage in the kerning field on the Property Inspector indicates that characters are closer together. To move them farther apart, set the kerning value to a positive percentage. Check the Auto-Kerning check box to turn on a font's native kerning. Turn the native kerning off when you are working with small point sizes and when anti-aliasing is turned off.

When working within a text block, you may apply kerning between two characters by moving the cursor between them. You may apply kerning to a passage by selecting the passage with the Text tool. Use the pointer to select a text object and apply the same kerning to all characters. Use Control+Left Arrow (Windows) or Command+Left Arrow (Macintosh) to decrease kerning by 1%; Control+Right Arrow (Windows) or Command+Right Arrow (Macintosh) increases kerning by 1%. Holding down the Shift key with the preceding commands will change kerning in 10% increments.

Leading—Leading is the distance between lines of text. Leading is measured either as a percentage of the character's point size or in pixels. Click the Leading Units menu on the Property Inspector and choose % for percentage, px for pixels. To choose one or more lines for which to set the leading, select the passages of text where you would like the leading change to start and finish. Leading will affect the distance between all selected lines and the line immediately above the selected passage. Select a text object with the pointer to change the leading for the entire object. You may also use Control+Up Arrow (Windows) or Command+Up Arrow (Macintosh) to increase leading by 1 unit. Use Control+Down Arrow (Windows) or Command+Down Arrow (Macintosh) to decrease leading by 1 unit.

Character Width—This changes the width of characters in the selected object or passage. Decreasing the percentage makes them skinnier; increasing it makes them wider. Any character width setting is applied before transformations, allowing you to use character width to affect text within the text block before scaling or transforming the text object.

Indents—To indent text, use the Paragraph Indent field in the Property Inspector to specify a number of pixels to indent text on the first line after a line break.

Spacing—You may also set the spacing between line breaks by setting the distance from the preceding paragraph or the distance from the paragraph after the line break. This is measured in pixels.

Attaching Text to Paths

Another great effect that you can use with text is to attach lines of text to a path. Text is normally placed along a straight line, but by attaching it to a path, you can make text flow along any kind of curve or angle.

You can use any kind of path, either open or closed. If the path is a closed shape, you cannot use line breaks—only the first line will flow around a shape. With an open path, line breaks and word wrapping will work as though the path is the baseline, and new lines will repeat the same path.

To attach text to a path, simply select the text object with the Pointer tool and then Shift-click to select the path to which you would like to attach the text. Select Attach Text to Path from the Text menu or press Control+Shift+Y (Windows) or Command+Shift+Y (Macintosh). To edit text once it's attached to the path, simply double-click with the pointer or insert a cursor with the Text tool. This text can also be spell-checked or searched with the Find and Replace option. To change the path, select Detach from Path on the Text menu, change the path, and then reattach the text to the new path.

> When you attach text to a path, the stroke and fill settings for the path are saved but invisible. Stroke and fill settings in the Property Inspector for the object will now affect the text. When you detach the path, the path will reappear with its original stroke and fill settings intact. In the Property Inspector, when you select the object, you may also change by how many pixels the lines of text are offset from the path.

Orienting Text Along a Path

To change how the characters are oriented along the path, choose an Orientation setting from the Text menu after you have attached the text to the path.

Rotate—This rotates the characters to be parallel with the angle of the path underneath them.

Vertical—This keeps characters along the path parallel to the horizontal axis. The path simply moves them up or down.

Skew Vertical—As the angle of the path increases or decreases, the characters are skewed vertically by the same degree.

Skew Horizontal—As the angle of the path increases or decreases, the characters are skewed horizontally by the same degree.

Task: Attach Text to Path and Use Kerning to Adjust Character Spacing

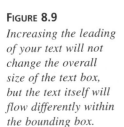

As the preceeding section has shown, Fireworks makes it really straightforward to attach a text object to a path. That is all well and good, but what if the text is not quite the right length for the path? You can use kerning to adjust the spacing between characters, giving a perfect result. The following task will make further changes to the file you have already been working on in this hour.

1. If you worked on the previous task in this hour, open your honokaa_home.png file. Otherwise, open the file called honokaa_home_text.png in the Hour 08 examples folder.

2. Using the Pointer tool, select the paragraph of white text on the left. Using the Property Inspector, increase the leading of the text to 110 percent and the kerning to 10. The bounding box won't change, but the text flow will change to accommodate the new character spacing, as shown in Figure 8.9.

FIGURE 8.9

Increasing the leading of your text will not change the overall size of the text box, but the text itself will flow differently within the bounding box.

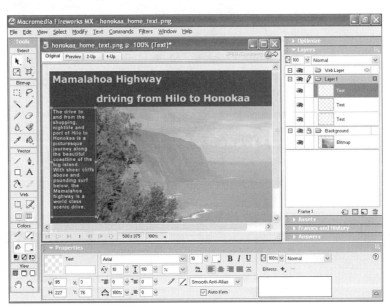

3. Now choose the Pen tool. Set the stroke color to white (**#FFFFFF**) and the style to 1-Pixel Hard from the Pencil group. Click and release with the Pen tool near the left side of the Canvas and above the level of the top of the photo. Click at the bottom of the third "a" in "Mamalahoa" and drag to the right to create a smooth curve between the two points. Put another point at the top of the "g" in "driving" and drag to create another curve (the two arcs almost making a semicircle). Finally, put a point near the end of the top headline, as shown in Figure 8.10.

FIGURE 8.10

Use the Pen tool to create a path to attach the headline to.

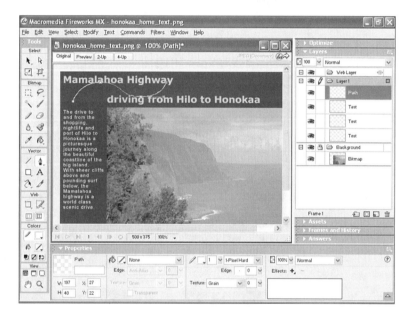

4. With the Pointer tool, use Shift+click to select the headline "Mamalahoa Highway" and the path you just created. Now choose Attach to Path from the Text menu or press Control+Shift+Y (Windows) or Command+Shift+Y (Macintosh).

5. With the new object still selected, change the kerning to 10. Changing the kerning will affect the flow of the text, pushing the word "Highway" off the end of the path. This text will wrap to a new line following the same path as the first. Now set the leading to 120 percent. The text will appear as it does in Figure 8.11.

FIGURE 8.11

After you've attached text to a path, you can still change settings, such as the kerning and leading.

6. You can make more room for the curved headline by rearranging the other two text blocks. Using the pointer, select the subtitle and use the Right Arrow key to move the text until it ends on the right side of the canvas. Now select the white copy on the left, and use the Down Arrow key to move it until it's aligned on the bottom of the canvas.

7. Select the curved headline with the pointer one more time. Select the Scale tool from the Tools panel or press Q. While holding down the Shift key, click-drag the bottom right handle until the right side of the bounding box is flush with the start of the subtitle, as in Figure 8.12. Double-click to apply the transformation.

FIGURE 8.12

You can emphasize the headline by making it bigger, filling the space created when the other two text blocks were moved.

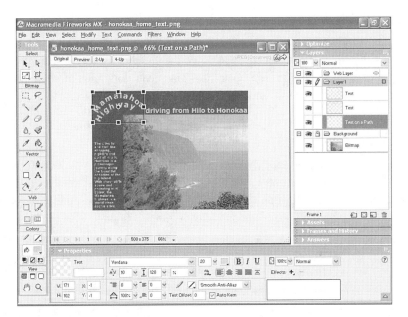

8. With the curved headline still selected, use the Property Inspector to add an effect. Use Drop Shadow from the Shadow and Glow group. The first field on the Drop Shadow panel is the offset. Change this to 5. Click the color swatch and use the eyedropper to select a shade (such as **#95C0C5**) from the overcast area in the sky. When you're done, your Canvas should look something like the one shown in Figure 8.13.

FIGURE 8.13

Some simple effects and text flow techniques have really improved this layout.

9. You may save this image. If you like, you can also open the honokaa_home_mamalahoa.png file from the Hour 08 examples directory for comparison.

Summary

By now you should be comfortable working with text in Fireworks. Because of the typographic constraints of HTML, you'll find that for really distinctive text effects, you'll want to export text as GIF files. This gives you much more flexibility in applying fonts, colors, text flow, and effects.

Workshop

Now you have a chance to review what you have learned about working with and enhancing text objects in Fireworks. Here are some exercises to help you practice. Although they don't present step-by-step instructions, these exercises should only require you to apply the techniques covered in this hour.

Q&A

Q I've pasted a passage of text from another application. Why doesn't the text have the same font, style, and size settings that it did in the original application?

A If the system or application does not support a rich text clipboard, only the characters will be copied. Fireworks will apply default text settings to the pasted text.

Q **I've exported a number of files with text from Fireworks into JPEG format. When I use Find and Replace to search the exported files for a word, why don't I get any results?**

A Once text has been flattened, merged, exported, or converted to paths, all character information is gone—it's been rendered into pixels or vectors. You can search text only within Fireworks PNG source graphics created with the Save command on the File menu.

Q **I've attached text to a path, but I want the path to appear along with the text. What can I do?**

A Before you attach the text to the path, make sure to create a copy of the path by selecting Clone from the Edit menu. When you attach the text to the cloned path, the original path stroke and fill underneath will appear with the text around it. Shift-click to select the text object and original path, and group them to create a single object.

Quiz

1. How can you make sure that text from an Adobe Photoshop file will look like it did in Adobe Photoshop?

    a. Choose Preserve Editability as the text setting in the Import Options dialog.

    b. Choose Preserve Appearance as the text setting in the Import Options dialog.

    c. Render as Images any groups with more than one object.

2. What kind of text file is used to import font, style, and size information along with the text content?

    a. HTML

    b. ASCII

    c. RTF

3. Why do you have to use graphics to show special fonts on a Web page rather than use text coded in HTML?

    a. Because somebody viewing the Web page may not have the font.

    b. Because you don't want someone to steal your fonts.

    c. Because text on a Web page can be only black or white.

Quiz Answers

1. b.—Use Preserve Appearance to make sure the text and fonts appear as they were intended, even if you don't have the same fonts on your system.

2. c.—RTF, or Rich Text Format, files can contain font, style, and size information along with the text.

3. a.—Text on a Web page can use only the fonts that are available on the system of the user viewing the Web page. To display special fonts on a Web page, you must export them as GIF image files.

Exercises

Using text on the Internet to avoid the problems of restrictive fonts is a really common technique. In this hour you have looked at ways of making text work the way you want. These little exercises will test your understanding of text in Fireworks.

1. Create a star shape by using the drawing tools you learned about in Hour 7, "Working with Vector Paths." Then use this shape as a path for text, maybe a celebrity's name following the line segments. Once the text is on the basic path, adjust the leading, kerning, and font size to fit the shape exactly.

2. Import some text from a word processor, then choose key words to create headings for a Web page. This will sharpen your ability to remove words, create new text objects, and reformat existing text to suit your needs.

3. Create a greeting card. Start with a graphic that you wish to use, maybe even a photo of the recipient, and then add text for the greeting message. Remember that you must consider size and color when placing text onto existing colors. Make some of the text vertical, or create a balloon shape to hold a personal greeting, sized and shaped to fit.

Hour 9

Tools and Techniques for Layout and Design

Now that you're familiar with all the potential graphic elements in Fireworks—bitmap, path, and text objects—you can work on effective design and composition with a number of different objects. The flexibility of paths makes it easy to create a variety of graphics from just a few simple lines and shapes. You'll also learn how to use layout tools, such as rules, grids, and the Align panel, to make composition a breeze.

In this hour you will

- Use path operations to manipulate path objects
- Convert text objects into path objects to use as graphics
- Create masks from paths for any object
- Correctly space and align graphics with layout guides

Reshaping, Altering, and Combining Paths

So far you've looked at a number of ways to edit paths—stroke, fill, opacity, and effects settings in the Property Inspector; position, rotation, and scaling with the Selection and Transform tools; and editing paths with the Pen and Knife tools. Fireworks MX also includes a number of other path tools to aid graphic design.

Freeform Path Editing

There are three tools you can use to edit the shape of a path by eye. These include the Redraw Path tool, the Freeform tool, and the Reshape Area tool in the Vector group on the Tools panel. These are very useful for smoothing out freeform paths and for making small adjustments by hand, such as changing the facial expressions on an animated character. Fireworks will adjust all the points and curves along the path for you.

Using the Redraw Path Tool

To use the Redraw Path tool, first select with the pointer the path to be edited and then press P to cycle through the Pen and Freeform path tools to the Redraw Path tool. When you mouseover the selected path, the selection outline will change color. Click where you would like to start redrawing and drag to create the new shape of the path. Returning the cursor to a point along the original path and releasing it will change the path to the new shape, as shown in Figure 9.1. Releasing it at a point off the original path will cause the path to end at the release point, creating a line instead of a closed shape. The edited sections of the path will automatically inherit the original path object properties. If no path is selected, the Redraw Path tool acts the same as the Vector Path tool and will default to the most recent Vector Path object settings.

FIGURE 9.1

As you can see from this before-and-after figure, redrawing the path allows you to totally change the direction and shape of a path.

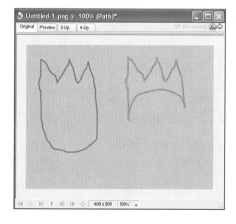

Pushing and Pulling Paths with the Freeform Path Tool

The Freeform path tool lets you push and pull lines and shapes much like they were strings laid out on a table. Select a path to edit with the pointer, and then press O to select the Freeform path tool. Mouseover a line segment along the path to bring up the Freeform pointer. Click-drag to edit the line segment; as you drag, the points and curves will be changed for that line segment.

To make changes along a larger segment or the entire path, click with the Freeform path tool on a blank area of the canvas. A round, red cursor will appear. Drag the cursor along the path to push or pull the line when it comes into contact with the outer edge of the cursor. Press the Left Arrow key while holding down the mouse key to make the Freeform tool area smaller. Press the Right Arrow key to make it bigger. The size can also be set in the Property Inspector along with pressure sensitivity (when used with a tablet stylus) and Preview (to see the changes as you're making them). In Figure 9.2 the path that you just redrew has been edited with the Freeform path tool.

FIGURE 9.2

Use the Freeform path tool to click and drag a line segment, nudging it anywhere along the path.

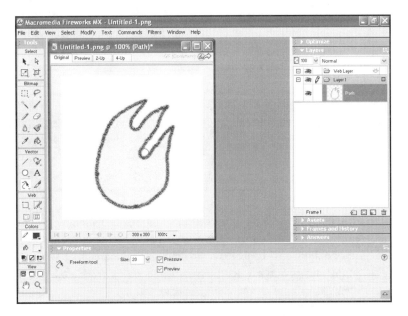

 To increase the size of the Freeform tool's tip while working, click the up or right arrow. To decrease it, use the down or left arrow.

Massaging Shapes with the Reshape Area Tool

Grouped with the Freeform tool is the Reshape Area tool. Press the letter O to toggle between the Freeform tool and the Reshape Area tool. The Reshape Area tool uses the inside of the circular cursor as its bounds, instead of using the outside of the circle like the Freeform tool. Use the Reshape Area tool to bring curves within the boundaries of the cursor. Click-drag with the mouse to bring up the cursor and reshape an area of the path. Figure 9.3 shows an image in which a small area in the lower left-hand corner has been reshaped.

FIGURE 9.3

You can change the shape of a path within the bounds of the Reshape Area cursor.

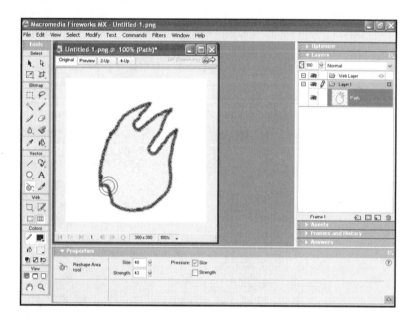

The Reshape Area tool has two settings: size and strength. These correspond to the two circles of the cursor. The size, in pixels, is the outer limit of the cursor, whereas the strength, a percentage, is the amount of the area that's changed within the boundary of the cursor. You can set the pressure feedback from a tablet stylus to affect the size, strength, or both as you click and drag.

If you want to change the size of the Reshape Area tool's tip while working, click 2 on the numeric keypad to increase it; click 1 to decrease it.

Adding or Subtracting Pressure Information with the Path Scrubber Tools

The Path Scrubber tools can add or subtract pressure information from a path drawn with either the Vector Path tool or the Pen tool. Fireworks has some pressure-sensitive stroke categories, such as Calligraphy, Charcoal, and Air Brush. If you use a digital drawing tablet, you can affect both the pressure and the speed of these strokes, whereas using a mouse, you can adjust only the speed. The effect of the stroke is directly affected by the amount of pressure when applying a stroke. This works in the same way as the different appearances achieved when you use old-fashioned crayons: Press hard and fast, and the outcome will be very different from slow, gentle strokes.

You can select the Path Scrubber tools only by clicking the tool group arrow below the Freeform tool or the Reshape Area tool. Additive adds pressure or speed; Subtractive reduces pressure or speed. Use the Property Inspector to choose between changing the pressure, speed, or both and the rate at which pressure or speed is changed. With the additive or subtractive Path Scrubber selected, click-drag along a path to add or subtract pressure or speed.

To set how pressure and speed affect the stroke, you can bring up the Edit Stroke dialog by selecting an object or vector drawing tool, selecting Stroke options from the Stroke style in the Property Inspector, and then clicking the Advanced button. At the top of the dialog is the Sensitivity tab, where you can choose from among the different stroke properties that can be affected by the pressure, speed, and angle of the stroke. Click OK to save and apply the changes. From the stroke options box, click Save Custom Stroke to save your settings as a stroke style in the current stroke style group.

Combining Paths

By combining multiple paths, you can create any number of new shapes. To combine two or more paths, select them with the pointer and select a combination method from the Combine Paths commands in the Modify menu.

When you employ a path operation from the Modify menu, you will lose any speed and pressure information for the stroke. This includes speed and pressure applied either from a tablet stylus or with the Path Scrubber tools.

Join and Split

Use the Join command to create a composite path from multiple paths. Any filled areas that overlap will be removed. Layering a circular path over a larger square path and joining them will add the circular stroke inside the other path and remove the fill where the circle and square overlap, creating a transparent void in the larger path, as in Figure 9.4. Although Join will create a single path object, it will not create a shape that can be filled from disconnected paths. Use the Pen tool to join the ends of two or more paths to create a shape that you can fill. Use Split to return joined paths to their original states as individual objects.

FIGURE 9.4

A circle has been added inside the original path by using Join. Notice that the selected object in the Layers panel is now a composite path.

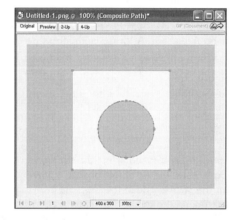

Union

Union creates a single shape from two or more paths. All selected path objects are turned into a single, contiguous shape around their outline, as shown in Figure 9.5, which shows before-and-after shots of a Union being created. This works only with overlapping paths. The stroke and fill attributes of the new path are applied from the path that's furthest back in the stacking order (closest to the bottom in the Layers panel).

Intersect

Intersect creates a new shape from the common area between all selected paths. For example, laying the corner of a rectangular path over the edge of a circular path and choosing Intersect would create a new path in the shape of the area where both paths meet. The result would be a three-sided object: a corner formed by two straight line segments, which are connected by an arc, as shown in the before-and-after shots in Figure 9.6. The stroke and fill properties are inherited from the path that's furthest back.

FIGURE 9.5

A Union takes multiple overlapping paths and creates a single path from them. Here you can see the before-and-after effect of this.

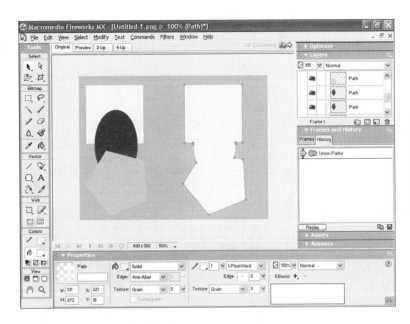

FIGURE 9.6

Intersecting paths will result in the creation of a new shape, which will come from the overlapping area of the joined paths.

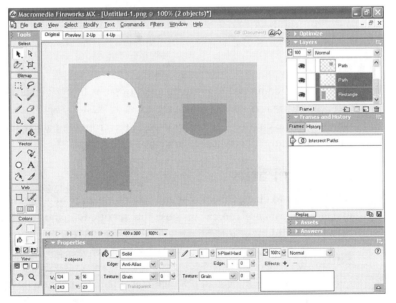

Punch

Punch is used to remove the area of a shape that's covered by another shape. A rectangle layered over a circle would punch out a section of the circle, as shown by the before-and-after shots in Figure 9.7. Selecting more than one object will punch out any area in the bottom object covered by another path layered over it. The new shape will retain the stroke and fill settings of the bottom object.

FIGURE 9.7
Punching an area removes the overlapped section of the shape below. Here you can see that part of the circle is removed by punching a rectangle.

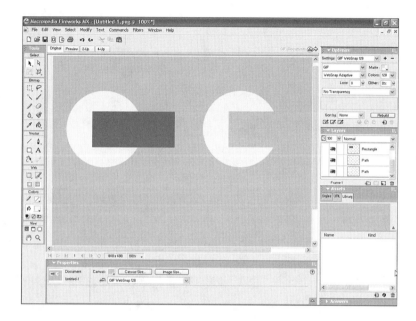

Crop

Use the Crop command to preserve areas of paths layered underneath the topmost path and remove areas of paths outside the topmost path—similar to the way the Crop tool works with the canvas. The object used as the cropping path will disappear, and cropped paths beneath it will retain the stroke and fill settings.

Altering Paths

Another way to change the shape and size of a path is by using the Alter Path commands in the Modify menu. You can also use this set of commands to change the edge setting for a path fill to make it hard, anti-aliased, or feathered.

Simplify

Simplify removes unnecessary points from a path that would otherwise result in jagged paths or large vector graphics files. You can set the amount of simplification from 1 to 25. A setting of 1 will remove the fewest points and best preserve the original shape of the path. Setting 25 will remove the most points and may change the path so much that it would be no longer recognizable. Three levels of simplification are shown in Figure 9.8. You can always use Undo to discard changes.

FIGURE 9.8

The object in the top left has not been simplified. To the right is a copy that has been simplified by 5. The next object (lower left) has been simplified by 15, and the last by 25. Each has fewer points than the previous, which results in less visual similarity.

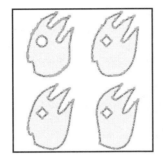

Expand Stroke

Expanding the stroke of a path is useful for creating a fill in the same shape as the selected stroke. The fill is removed, but the selected stroke is retained on the inside as a composite path, and a new, expanded stroke is created around it, with the original fill in between. Expanding the stroke of a circular path would create a toroid, or donut, shape. Expand Stroke settings include the width, in pixels, between the original and expanded strokes. Other Expand Stroke settings determine the style of corners—miter, round, or beveled— and the miter limit, if mitered corners are chosen (the miter limit sets the ratio between the length of the corner and the width of the stroke). Furthermore, Expand Stroke settings establish how the line segments are end-capped—butted, squared, or rounded. Figure 9.9 shows the same rectangle three times, with different stroke expansion options applied.

FIGURE 9.9

Expand the stroke of your path to create a composite path. Here you can see the same rectangle after the stroke has been expanded three different ways.

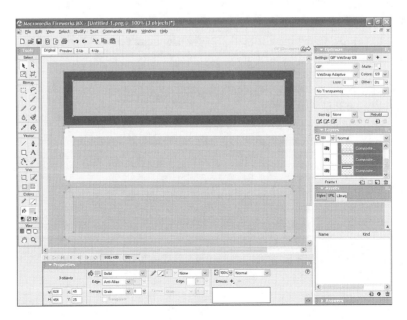

A miter is a joint made by beveling each of two surfaces to be joined, usually at a 45° angle, to form a corner, usually a 90° angle. The most obvious
use of mitering is in the creation of picture frames.

Inset Path

Inset Path can actually be used to expand or contract a selected path. The end result is to
create a larger or smaller path object with the same fill and other settings as the original,
while retaining the aspect ratio. You can choose Inside to create a smaller path or Outside
to create a larger path. When you inset a path, the stroke and fill settings and relationships
are not changed. You can set corners to be miter, round, or beveled and set the miter limit,
if miter corners are selected. Very interesting effects can be created when layering an outside inset path behind the original or an inside inset path on top. Use Clone or Duplicate
to create a copy of the selected path and to inset the copy to work with both.

Task: Altering Paths to Create Effects

In this task you will create a series of layered shapes on top of each other. While not tech-
nically difficult, this will show you how having the facility to adjust a path by a specific
amount of pixels, rather than through manual or percentage scaling, can be beneficial.

1. Start by drawing an ellipse. Then use the Subselection tool to change the ellipse to
   be more egg shaped, with a flatter bottom and more pointed top.

2. Select the newly drawn path object and then from the Edit menu choose Duplicate.
   An exact replica is created on top of your original.

3. Change the fill color of the duplicated item. Then from the Modify Menu choose
   Alter Path, Inset Path, to open the Inset Path dialog, as seen in Figure 9.10.

FIGURE 9.10
*The Inset Path dialog
opens to allow you to
choose the settings you
want for the new path.*

4. Choose an option from the direction radio buttons (the type where only one can be selected at a time). Inside will contract your path, and Outside will expand it. For this task select Inside.

5. Use the Width slider to set the number of pixels by which the path will be altered. If you prefer not to use the slider, you can type a value into the field. For this task choose **25.**

6. Since you are working with an ellipse, ignore the options for corners.

7. Click OK to continue.

8. Select All paths. Then from the Modify Menu choose Align, Center Vertical. The result should look something like Figure 9.11.

FIGURE 9.11

After insetting a path and aligning the two objects, you have a smaller path object inside the original.

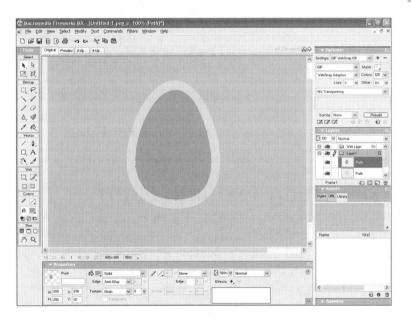

9. Repeat Steps 2 through 8 three more times. For alternate paths use the two fill colors you have in the document. The final result of this can be seen in Figure 9.12.

FIGURE 9.12
By overlaying multiple instances of the inset path on top of each other, you can create many effects. A simple effect is shown here.

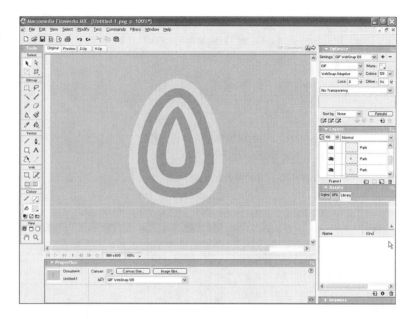

You can see that the advantage of using this method is in the exact rescaling of one path to another.

Converting Text into Paths

Text objects are made up of many paths that define the characters in a font. When you convert a text object into a path, you are sacrificing control over the text content (the characters you typed or pasted) to gain control over the shapes of the characters in the selected font. This means that the spell checker and the Find and Replace panel will not work with text objects that have been converted into path objects.

To convert a text object into a group of path objects, simply select a text object with the pointer and then select Convert Text to Paths from the Text menu or press Control+Shift+P (Windows) or Command+Shift+P (Macintosh). The text object will change to a group object on the Canvas and in the Layers panel, as in Figure 9.13. Press Control+Shift+G (Windows) or Command+Shift+G (Macintosh) to ungroup the object so that you can select individual characters with the Pointer tool. Many text characters that contain voids, such as P, Q, and R, will be composite paths. Use Split from the Combine commands on the Modify menu to break these paths apart, or use Join to restore them.

FIGURE 9.13

The first object is a text object; note the text object bounding box. The next is the same object converted to paths; converted text is initially grouped. Below that are the ungrouped paths. Each character is an individual path object.

Once you've converted text to a path, you can work with the paths through any of the tools in the Vector group or any of the path operations in the Modify menu. This technique is often used when designing logo graphics to lend more flexibility to how characters appear graphically. Remember to always keep an original copy of the text object on a locked or hidden layer, in case you need to change a character later.

Converting text into paths was a common operation for working with documents that were to be moved from one machine to another, to make sure font decisions were preserved. Fireworks MX caches a copy of all fonts used in a source PNG so that the file can travel freely without your having to worry about what fonts are available on the system. You can still use this technique when exporting a Photoshop PSD or Adobe Illustrator 7 file; any fonts in the exported document will have to be available on the system the document is destined for. Remember to keep a text object original in case the text needs to be changed!

Using Paths as Masks

You've learned how to add bitmaps as masks to other bitmaps. You can also use path objects as masks in much the same way. A mask selectively shows or hides the object or group being masked. You can use path or text objects to mask bitmaps, paths, text, or groups. You can also use grayscale or alpha-channel bitmaps to mask paths, text, or groups just like you would mask a bitmap.

To use a path as a mask, draw or paste the path over the objects you would like to mask. Make sure the path you intend to mask with is the topmost object. Now use Shift+click to select the masking path and all the objects you would like to mask with the Pointer tool. From the Mask commands on the Modify menu, select Group as Mask. In the topmost object, areas within the path outline (the area covered by the mask's fill) will be visible. Areas outside it will not.

When an object is masked, the mask will appear next to the object on the Layers panel. Vector masks are marked with a pen tip icon in the lower right corner. Select the masked object and then select Disable Mask from the Mask commands in the Modify menu to remove the mask and restore the paths within the mask. Choose Delete Mask to delete the mask and any paths in it. You can also use the Paste as Mask command in the Edit menu to add a mask. Simply copy the path you would like to use as a mask, select with the Pointer tool the objects you would like to mask, and choose Paste as Mask from the Edit menu (it's also available from the Mask commands in the Modify menu).

> There's one more way to apply a mask. Instead of copying an object and pasting it as a mask, you can copy the objects to be masked, select the objects with the Pointer tool to mask them, and choose Paste Inside from the Edit menu, or press Control+Shift+V (Windows) or Command+Shift+V (Macintosh). The objects in the Clipboard will be pasted within the outlines of the selected path object.

Click the mask icon in the Layers panel to bring up the mask setting in the Property Inspector. You may choose to mask to the Path Outline (default) or use the grayscale appearance properties of the path's fill and stroke like you would with a bitmap mask. Darker areas hide more, and lighter areas reveal more. When Path Outline is selected, you can also choose the Show Fill and Stroke command. The fill and stroke settings for the masking path are available at the bottom of the Property Inspector. The opacity, Blending mode, and effect settings affect the entire masked object as a group. Use the Subselection tool to select elements within a masked group to change their stroke, fill, opacity, Blending mode, or effect settings individually.

Task: Apply Converted Characters as a Mask

In this task you will import an image file and then, using text and a mask, create a text object filled with an image of Honokaa. This will help give the Web site visitor a good impression of this Big Island location.

1. Start by creating a new canvas with the width set to 400 and the height set to 150. Make sure the background is set to Transparent.

2. Use the Import command on the File menu, or press Control+R (Windows) or Command+R (Macintosh), to import the file sunset.jpg from the Hour 09 examples folder. Place the image in the top left corner. Use the Property Inspector to make sure it is at 0 in the X position and 0 in the Y position once it's been placed on the canvas.

3. Select the text tool from the Vector group on the Tools panel. Make sure the color is set to black and the size is set to 65. Click with the text tool cursor near the left edge of the canvas and type **HONOKAA.** Using the Pointer tool, move the text object to the center of the image, as in Figure 9.14. The exact position in the Property Inspector is X = 10 and Y = 30.

FIGURE 9.14

Some text has been layered over an image that will be masked.

4. With the text still selected with the pointer, choose Clone from the Edit menu or press Control+Shift+D (Windows) or Command+Shift+D (Macintosh). The cloned text object will be selected. Choose Convert to Paths from the Text menu, or press Control+Shift+P (Windows) or Command+Shift+P (Macintosh). The text will then become a group of path objects. Use the show/hide column in the Layers panel to hide the original text object.

5. With the group selected, copy the object, using Copy from the Edit menu or Control+C (Windows) or Command+C (Macintosh). Hide the group by using the show/hide column in the Layers panel. Select the bitmap with the Pointer tool, and choose Paste as Mask from the Edit menu. The image will be masked to reveal only the area within the path outlines, as in Figure 9.15.

FIGURE 9.15

The group of paths has been pasted as a mask onto the bitmap. Note the mask thumbnail next to the bitmap in the Layers panel; because it is a vector mask, it has an added Pen tool icon on the mask thumbnail.

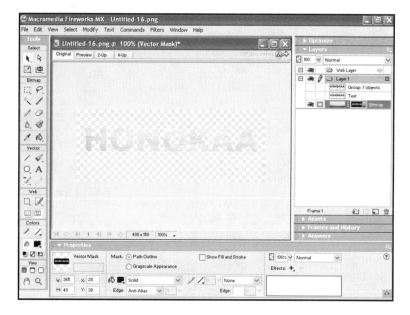

6. Make sure the Show Fill and Stroke check box is checked. Change the stroke color on the Property Inspector to black. Set the stroke style to 1-Pixel Soft from the Pencil group. A black outline will now appear around the paths in the mask. Click outside the canvas to deselect the object.

7. You can edit the entire masked object by selecting it with the Pointer tool. You can also edit the masked objects and the mask itself independently of each other. On the Layers panel between the masked object and mask thumbnails is link icon. Click this icon to unlink the mask from the image. Now click the mask thumbnail to select it.

8. Press Q to choose the Scale tool from the Select group. Use the handles on the top, bottom, and sides to scale the masking path to the edges of the canvas, as in Figure 9.16.

FIGURE 9.16

You can edit the mask independently of the masked objects by unlinking them in the Layers panel. Here the mask is transformed without changing the masked objects underneath.

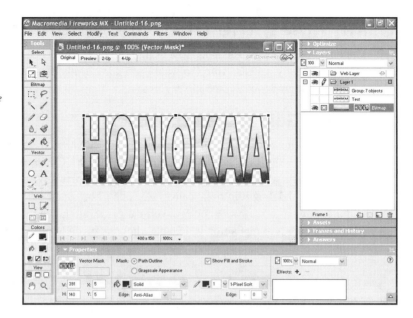

9. Press Q again to cycle to the Skew tool. Click the lower left handle on the bounding box and drag it toward the center of the canvas until it's even with the edge of the first character. Double-click or choose the Pointer tool to apply the transformations.

10. Now you can see more of the masked image, hopefully giving you a better sense of place. By giving the text some vertical stretch and skewing it toward the center, you've added some visual dynamics to the characters. The finished graphic, `honokaa_headline.png`, is included in the `Hour 09` examples folder and is shown in Figure 9.17.

FIGURE 9.17

The finished graphic combines a photograph with text to give the viewer a sense of what Honokaa, Hawaii, can be like.

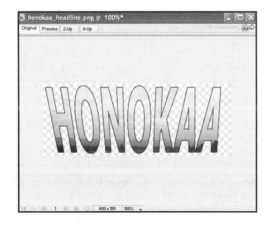

Using Rules, the Grid, and Alignment

Once you begin adding elements to a design or layout, things can start to get pretty cluttered. Eventually, you are going to want everything neatly placed on the canvas. This is where layout guides can come in very handy.

Placing Guides with the Rulers

To begin placing vertical or horizontal guides, select Rulers from the View menu, or press Control+Alt+R (Windows) or Command+Option+R (Macintosh). This will toggle the rulers in the workspace. The ruler units default to pixels. With the rulers visible, click the top ruler and drag it into the canvas to place a horizontal guide. Click the left ruler and drag it over the canvas to place a vertical guide, as shown in Figure 9.18. Click the guide and drag it to reposition it. Double-click the guide to enter a numerical value for the position.

FIGURE 9.18

Use the rulers to place guides on the canvas for help in aligning objects.

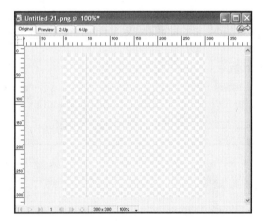

Select Show Guides from the Guides commands in the View menu to show or hide the guides. Choose Lock Guides to lock the guides in their current positions. When Snap to Guides is checked, the cursor will automatically position itself along the guide while drawing or moving an object or point. Selecting Edit Guides will let you change the color of the guidelines and also let you choose Show, Snap to, or Lock Guides.

Ruler guides are different from slice guides, which are used to lay out slices on the Web layer. Ruler guides are used only for laying out artwork on the canvas. Ruler guides are not objects and don't exist within a particular layer. They are never exported as part of an image.

Laying Out and Drawing with the Grid

You can also use a grid in place of or in addition to rulers and guides. To show the grid, select Show Grid from the Grid commands in the View menu, or press Control+Alt+G (Windows) or Command+Option+G (Macintosh). The grid will appear on the canvas, as shown in Figure 9.19. Choose Snap to Grid to have the cursor snap to the nearest line on the grid when drawing or moving objects or points. Choose Edit Grid to change how the grid is shown and laid out. You can choose the color of the grid and the sizing of the gridlines. You can also choose Show or Snap to Grid.

FIGURE 9.19

You can use a grid instead of guides for aligning objects. Neither the grid nor the guides are exported with the image.

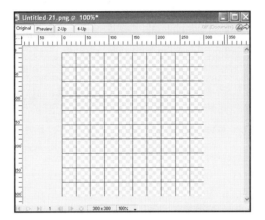

Aligning Objects with the Align Panel

Another way to make sure two objects line up horizontally or vertically is to use the Align panel or the Align commands on the Modify menu. Aligning to the left will align all selected objects to the leftmost point among them. Center Horizontal will align them all down the middle. Distribute Widths or Heights will distribute the objects evenly between their current bounds.

Choose Align from the Window menu to bring up the Align panel, where you can see icons representing how the alignment would look, as shown in Figure 9.20. With the Align panel, you can also select the To Canvas button to align objects on the sides or down the middle of the canvas. You may also choose to distribute objects, match the vertical or horizontal dimensions of the objects, or space the objects evenly. Choosing the Anchors button will let you align points selected with the Subselection tool within a path. You may choose to align to the preceding control points of selected anchor points, the selected anchor and control points, or the succeeding control points of the selected anchor points.

FIGURE 9.20

The Align panel can align a bunch of paths along the left edge of the canvas.

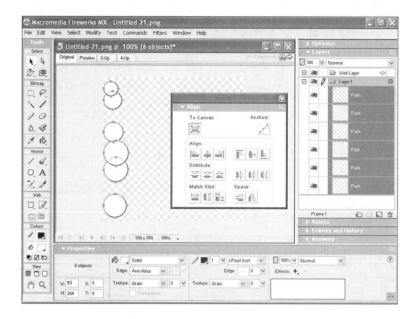

Summary

Give yourself a hand; you should now have a firm grasp of the fundamentals of Fireworks MX vector graphics. If you've worked with vector graphics before, you should now be able to find most of the tools you would ever need to do your work directly in Fireworks. And because you can also create and edit bitmaps in the same application, you will be able to save time that you otherwise would have spent switching from one application to another. In the next hour, "Tricks of the Trade," you'll get tips on some techniques used by professional designers to create stunning graphics.

Workshop

The following questions will test your knowledge of vector graphics, applying masks, and other topics discussed in the past hour. Answers are provided for your reference. The exercises will put into practice what you learned in this hour, helping you build experience.

Q&A

Q How do I set the pressure of my stylus on the tablet to affect the stroke width?

A Choose the Vector Path tool. In the Property Inspector select Stroke Options from the Stroke Style menu. Click the Advanced button at the bottom of the Stroke

Options menu. At the top of the Edit Stroke dialog, select the Sensitivity tab. Now select Width from the Stroke Property menu. Change the Pressure setting to a percentage from 0 to 100. The percentage defines the ratio between the maximum stroke width (set in the Property Inspector or Stroke Options menu) and the minimum stroke width at the lightest pressure. Click OK to close the dialog and begin drawing. Full pressure will allow you to draw a line of the full width. When less pressure is applied, the stroke width will change within the percentage set in the Edit Stroke dialog.

Q When I use a path object as a mask, how do I make the stroke of the masking path visible?

A Click the Vector Mask icon on the Layers panel. In the Property Inspector choose Path Outline for the mask and make sure Show Stroke and Fill is checked. Now select a stroke color and style from the Property Inspector. The stroke of the masking path will now be visible over the masked objects.

Q I've copied some text that was converted into paths. Why can't I paste it into a word processor or text editor?

A When you convert text into paths, the actual text characters are lost. They are now individual path objects and cannot be copied and pasted the same way you would work with editable text. Make sure to save a copy of the original text object before converting it into paths.

Quiz

1. You can use the Add Mask button on the Layers panel to add a bitmap mask to a path, text, or group object.

    a. True

    b. False

2. How would you align a number of objects along the left side of the Canvas?

    a. By setting their X position value to 0

    b. By adding a guide along the left edge of the Canvas and dragging the objects along it with the Pointer tool

    c. By selecting To Canvas in the Align panel and choosing Left alignment

3. Which file format does not cache or embed fonts for text objects?

    a. Flash SWF

    b. Adobe Illustrator 7

    c. Fireworks PNG source template

Quiz Answers

1. a. True—You can add a bitmap mask to a path, text, or group object by selecting it in the Layers panel and clicking the Add Mask button. You can edit this mask with any of the tools in the Bitmap group.

2. a., b., and c.—Any of these methods would work, but certainly option c would be the fastest.

3. b.—Adobe Illustrator 7 files will not cache or embed fonts, meaning that any editable text objects with fonts not present on a system will not appear correctly. Flash SWF automatically converts the fonts into paths, meaning the font is cached but text is no longer editable. Only Fireworks PNG source templates created with the Save command on the File menu will cache and embed fonts for use on any system.

Exercises

These optional exercises are designed for practice with combinations of the techniques you have covered in this hour.

1. Practice creating masks and mask effects. Create a photographic montage using masks of different shapes. The path of a vector mask object crops or clips the underlying objects to the shape of its path, creating a shaped effect. When working with multiple images, you can create interesting and effective displays.

2. Use the shape skills you have just covered to create complex paths manually. You can turn a circle into a square by the addition and movement of points, although this is not easy. Practice the different path-joining techniques to better understand how they work and their relative strengths. Punching and combining paths accurately will give you limitless options in your design work.

3. Create a complex path object and then use the Simplify command to remove some of the points. As mentioned in the text, you need to be careful not to remove too many points, or you will adversely affect the intended object. Again, trial and error is a good way to come to grips with the best methods to apply to different objects.

Hour 10

Tricks of the Trade

This hour will cover some of the most complex tools available in Fireworks for creating and editing graphics and will show you how to apply the fundamentals you've learned in this group of hours to create professional-quality graphics. For example, you'll learn how to work with gradient fills, such as using them to create incredible masking and transparency effects. You'll also learn how to create great custom brushes and textures. Finally, you'll discover how to use anti-aliasing and effects to create more realistic drawings.

In this hour you will

- Add gradient fills to path objects and edit them
- Create gradual masking and transparency effects
- Manipulate advanced stroke and fill settings
- Use your own bitmap and vector graphics as patterns
- Work with effects to make elements blend seamlessly together

Creative Fill Techniques

You can employ a number of tricks with fills to give your graphics a little extra snap. Simple filled shapes can make great design elements in a Web design. You can use gradients and patterns to add more visual flair. You can also use these techniques in purely creative work to add style and realism to vector drawings.

Working with Gradients

Gradients are a very powerful graphics tool. A gradient is a fill that gradually shifts between two or more colors, as in Figure 10.1. Gradients use math to make very accurate transitions that span a full range of possible tones. You won't have to worry too much about this. Fireworks MX makes it easy to apply and edit gradient fills.

FIGURE 10.1

A linear gradient fill applied to a vector shape. Note the gradient-fill control handles across the middle—they determine the distance and direction of the transition.

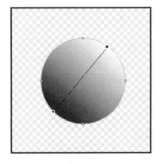

To apply a gradient fill to a selected object, choose Fill Options from the Fill category menu next to Fill Color on the Property Inspector. You can select the type of gradient from the Styles menu at the top of the Fill category menu. A number of gradients are available, ranging from Linear to Folds. Each style produces a different gradient effect. Experiment to find the ones that you like. Linear, Radial, and Ellipse are the most common gradients used.

Below the style is the color setting for the gradient. You can choose a preset from the drop-down menu on the left, or you can click the Edit button to customize the colors and transparency settings for the gradient. When you click the Edit button, you will be presented with the Gradient Editor, as in Figure 10.2. At the top are sliders for the alpha, or transparency, of the gradient. Below the gradient bar are the color sliders. Click a slider to change the opacity or color setting for that point on the gradient. Click anywhere along the gradient bar to add a new slider at that point. Click and drag a slider to change its position along the bar. Drag a slider off the end of the bar to delete it (note that there must always be at least two sliders, however). Select a preset to see how the preset gradient colors are achieved. Click the Fill Options menu above to make the changes. You can return to this menu by clicking the fill color swatch whenever it's a gradient.

FIGURE 10.2
The Gradient Editor, available in the Fill Options menu, allows you to adjust transparency and color ranges for a gradient.

After you choose a gradient style and colors, you can change how the gradient is applied relative to the object. Select a gradient-filled object with the Pointer tool; the gradient-fill handles will appear with the object. The round handle is where the gradient starts (if linear) or where it is centered (if radial or elliptical). The square handle (or handles if an ellipse) defines the range and angle of the gradient. Click and drag a handle to move it. You can move either handle outside the area of the fill if you want the gradient to start or end outside the shape. The handles will scale in proportion to the object when transformed.

You can save a gradient fill as a style for later. Click the Add Effects button in the Property Inspector and choose Save as Style from the Options group. You can name the style in the field at the top. Make sure that Fill Type is selected among the Properties check boxes. Click OK to save the new style. You can access it from the Styles panel, which is in the Assets panel group by default.

You can easily create gradient transparency effects for one or more objects by creating a rectangular path around the objects and giving it a grayscale gradient fill (the Black and White preset is very handy here). Use Cut or Copy to add the filled shape to the Clipboard and then select the objects to be masked. Use Paste as Mask from the Edit menu to add the rectangular path with the gradient fill from the Clipboard as a vector mask. Select the Mask thumbnail in the Layers panel and click the Grayscale Appearance button on the Property Inspector. Darker areas of the gradient will become more transparent, whereas lighter areas will become more opaque. You can even edit the gradient fill handles for the mask object at any time by unlinking the mask and selecting the masking path with the Pointer tool to bring up the handles.

Task: Create a Gradient for Future Usage

▼ TASK

In this task you will look at using gradient fills that can be saved for future applications. The following steps will take you through the process of editing an existing gradient and then saving it to be used again.

1. Start by creating a new blank document in Fireworks. Set the canvas to have a black background and to be 400×300 pixels in size. Use the Text tool and type the word Silver. Format the text to be Verdana font, white in color, and the font size to be 100. The file should look like Figure 10.3.

FIGURE 10.3

Start with a basic document that only has some formatted text. This will be the basis of the new style.

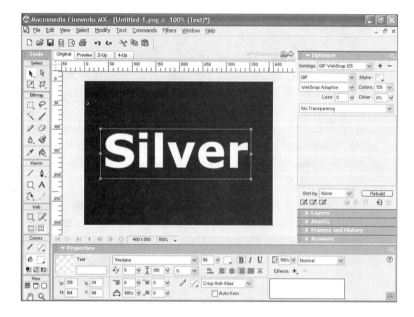

2. Select the text and then click to open the color swatch in the Property Inspector. Click the Fill Options button and then choose Linear from the fill categories and Black, White as the preset gradient fill.

3. Click the Edit button next to the Black, White preset gradient setting. The Edit panel opens, ready for you to add the points needed to create a silver metallic effect. To give a smooth effect, you need five points in total. These need to be black at each end, white in the middle and grey in between. Simply click where you want the new point to add it, as in Figure 10.4.

FIGURE 10.4

Simply click to add a new point into the gradient fill. For silver you use five points that give a nice smooth transition.

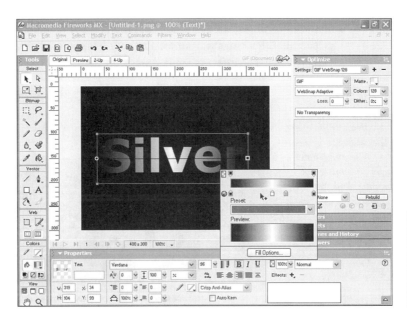

4. Grab the circular end of the gradient handle. Move it to be level with the top of the text. This will move the whole gradient line. Then grab the square end and drag it diagonally so that the gradient line is at the left edge of the text. Notice how the effect changes as you move the gradient. You can see the intended result in Figure 10.5.

FIGURE 10.5

Moving the gradient handles changes the angle of the gradient. Here the gradient appears to be top to bottom rather than left to right.

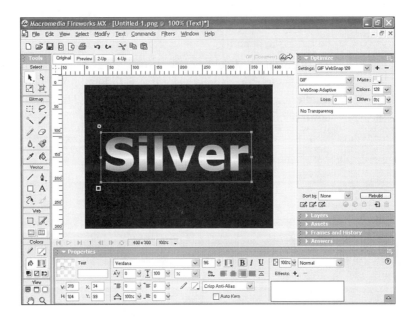

5. Now you will add a Fireworks effect to make the fill look more silver and metallic. Open the Effects menu from the Property Inspector. Choose Bevel and Emboss, Inner Bevel. The effect is applied immediately; it can be seen in Figure 10.6.

FIGURE 10.6

Adding a bevel will give depth to an effect. The settings will need to be changed, however, to remove the pointed look that the default gives.

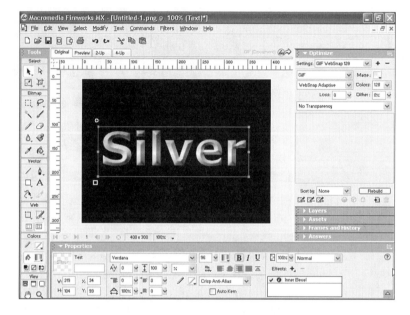

6. Now you need to edit the effect to make it look less pointed and more silvery. Double-click the Inner Bevel effect in the Property Inspector. In the panel change the Bevel Edge Shape to Smooth and the width to 6. All of the other settings can be left at the defaults.

7. The gradient fill should now be a shiny silver. If you are not happy with any part of the fill, simply make edits accordingly. In Figure 10.7 you can see that the gradient handles have been adjusted to be a little longer. This gives the effect of light farther down the fill.

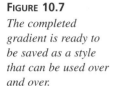

FIGURE 10.7
The completed gradient is ready to be saved as a style that can be used over and over.

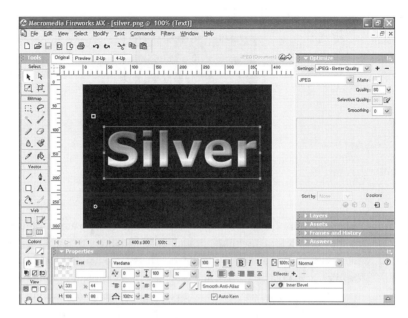

8. To save the fill as a style, click the Add Effects button in the Property Inspector. Choose Save as Style from the Options menu. This will open the New Style dialog.

9. In the dialog type a name for this new style; Silver would be appropriate. Check the Fill Type, Fill Color, and Effect check boxes to ensure that all of the information for the fill is retained. Click OK to continue.

10. Show the Styles panel (Window, Styles). Your new style is immediately added at the bottom of the panel.

Using Preset and Custom Patterns

Another way to distinguish filled areas is to use patterns. Fireworks comes with a number of custom patterns, but you can use any Fireworks PNG, GIF, JPEG, BMP, or TIFF image. To choose a patterned fill for an object, select the object with the pointer and choose Fill Options after clicking the color swatch. Choose Pattern from the Type menu at the top. Use the texture menu to choose one of the preset fills, or choose Other to select an image file from your hard drive. The pattern Leaves is shown in Figure 10.8. When you choose an image file for a pattern, it is added to your list of preset patterns.

FIGURE 10.8
Patterns can tile bitmaps as a fill instead of a solid, Web dither, or gradient fill.

When a pattern fill has been applied to an object, the pattern-fill handles will appear when the object is selected with the Pointer tool. Moving the round handle will change where the tiling is centered relative to the object. The square handles can be moved to scale or skew the tiles in the pattern. Click and drag any of these handles to move them. In Figure 10.9 the pattern-fill handles were used to change how the pattern is applied. Graphics used for patterns are always treated as bitmaps (even if they were vectors in a Fireworks PNG file) and will be resampled if scaled with the pattern-fill handles.

FIGURE 10.9
The pattern-fill handles allow you to reposition, scale, or skew the tiles in the pattern.

To change the pattern used in a pattern fill, simply select the fill color to bring up the Pattern Fill menu and preview. You can also use the Fill Options menu. You can save pattern fills as styles or apply them as masks in the same way you would for a gradient fill. Pattern and gradient fills can also be applied to bitmaps through the Paint Bucket tool. You can also combine gradients and patterns with textures for even more flexibility. You'll learn more about textures in the next section after this tip.

> You can also use patterns to mask a bitmap image. Simply select a vector object you would like to use as a mask and apply the bitmap you want to mask as a pattern. You can scale the bitmap relative to the path by using the pattern-fill handles. The bitmap pattern will be transformed in proportion to the path when scaled, skewed, or distorted.

Advanced Stroke Options

If you want the ultimate control over how the stroke on a path appears, you can use the Stroke Options menu and the Edit Stroke dialog to specify every little detail. These custom strokes can then be saved as a stroke style or as part of a style on the Styles panel. Custom strokes can be used for vector objects or for the Brush tool in the Bitmap group on the Tools panel.

To create a custom stroke, simply select a vector object, a drawing tool, or the Brush tool. On the Property Inspector select Stroke Options from the Stroke category menu next to the stroke color swatch. From this menu, you can select the style, color, tip softness, stroke width, texture, and path orientation—inside, outside, or centered. You can also choose to place the fill over the stroke in places where they intersect. Click the Advanced button to bring up the Edit Stroke dialog, shown in Figure 10.10.

FIGURE 10.10

The Edit Stroke dialog gives you the ultimate control over creating custom strokes to use with vector and bitmap drawing tools.

The Edit Stroke dialog has three tabs. The Options tab has settings for Ink Amount, the density of the stroke color; Spacing between points of color applied by the tip; Flow Rate, which increases the amount of ink applied over time; and Build-up, for adding density by scrubbing with the tip over a point. You can apply Texture to the stroke center or the stroke edge, and you can also try one of the Edge Effects to further stylize a line. For cross-hatching and other techniques, you can choose more than one tip. If more than one tip is selected, you can use the Variation menu to set the spacing relative to the stroke width and to choose how the colors vary between each tip. A preview screen at the bottom lets you preview your changes.

 You must select a preset stroke style as a starting point for your custom stroke. Some features, such as spacing and flow rate, are available only for certain stroke styles, such as the Air Brush tips.

Select the Shape tab to specify the shape of the stroke tip. Checking the Square box will create a square tip, and leaving it unchecked will make it round. You can set the size of the tip in pixels, the edge softness percentage, and the aspect, or ratio, of width to height. For square tips or tips with an aspect less than 100 percent, you can set the angle of the tip for calligraphic effects.

The Sensitivity tab can be used in conjunction with a stylus and tablet to vary the stroke relative to the pressure or speed of the stylus. You can also vary a stroke property depending on its angle by assigning horizontal or vertical variation to a property. The Random function will randomly change the property as it's applied, regardless of pressure, speed, or angle. Select a stroke property from the menu at the top, and then select what input variable it will be affected by. You can vary any of the stroke properties with any input variable and combine variations to create interesting effects.

To save your custom stroke, press OK to exit the Edit Stroke dialog and save your changes, and then click the custom stroke Save button at the bottom left of the Stroke Options menu. You can also save the stroke as a style on the Styles panel by clicking the Add Effect button and choosing Save as Style from the Options group. Make sure that the Stroke Type check box is selected before giving it a name and clicking OK to save the new style.

Creating Your Own Textures

Textures are a lot like patterns except that they can be applied to strokes or fills and do not contain any color information. Textures are used to add brightness details to strokes and fills. A texture has been applied to the fill in Figure 10.11. Textures will not change the hue of the stroke or fill color; they will only vary the brightness or alpha. To add a texture to a fill or stroke, select the texture from the Texture menu on the Property Inspector or in the Fill or Stroke Options menu. Select a percentage of intensity for the texture. For fills, lighter areas of the texture can be made transparent by checking the box next to Transparent.

FIGURE 10.11

*The preset texture
Line-Horiz 3 has been
added at the default
50% intensity. Notice
how light and dark
horizontal lines are
imposed on the
pattern fill.*

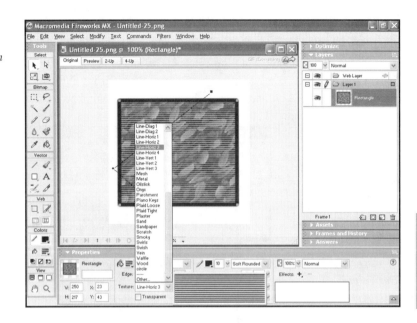

10

To create your own texture, simply choose Other from the Texture menu. You may select
a Fireworks PNG, GIF, JPEG, BMP, or TIFF file to use. Color information will be
ignored, and the image will be tiled to fill the textured area. After you have chosen a
custom texture, it will be added to the texture menu for use at any time.

Adding Effects to Vectors

Another way to stylize your vector graphics is to employ effects. Some effects are particularly well suited for vector graphics, such as the Bevel and Emboss effects and the
Shadow and Glow effects. By using effects with your vector graphics, you can create
the appearance of three dimensions through lighting, shadow, and focus. Effects can be
applied to any object, including bitmaps, paths, text, and groups. To further expand the
possibilities, effects can also be applied to objects that have been masked. Use Save as
Style from the effects Options to save your effect decisions as a style on the Styles panel.

You can use the Gaussian Blur effect to blur a vector graphic, making it look out of focus. This is also a good way to create a diffuse shadow or highlight, and it is the basis of the shadow and glow effects. The object in Figure 10.12 has been blurred with Gaussian Blur. Gaussian Blur is also useful because it blurs the vector object in the same way it would a bitmap object—there is no distinction between the stroke and the fill.

FIGURE 10.12

Gaussian Blur with a radius of 10 pixels has been applied. Note that the object and pattern fill handles are still available. If any aspect of the object is changed, the results of the effect will change, too.

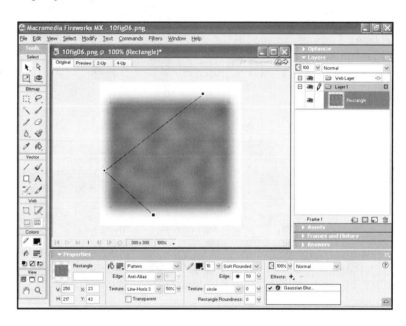

To add lighting effects to a vector object, use the Shadow and Glow effects. Using Drop Shadow will make the object appear lit from the front. A drop shadow has been added to the object in Figure 10.13. To cast a bigger shadow, change the offset. Changing the color cast and intensity of the shadow will alter the color and opacity, respectively. Change the angle of the shadow to match the angle of the light source. Use Knock Out to treat the shadow as a separate object and to remove the original object from the effect output. Inner Shadow can be used to simulate shadows cast on the object by other objects. Glow and Inner Glow are useful for making an object appear to be a source of light, and they can also be used to create shadow effects by choosing a dark glow color.

FIGURE **10.13**

Drop Shadow has been used to add a shadow behind the object, making it appear to be above the Canvas and lit from the top left. You can change the depth and angle with the Drop Shadow effects at the bottom right of the screen shot.

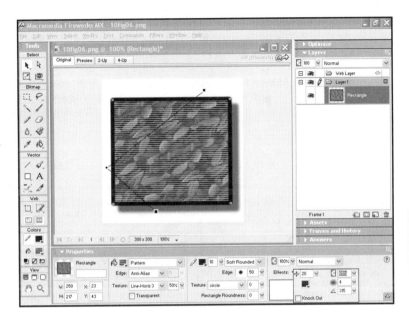

10

Use Bevel and Emboss to give three-dimensional shading to an object. Raised and Inset Emboss will make something appear as though it has been stamped onto a surface, such as a sheet of paper. Raised Emboss has been used on the graphic in Figure 10.14. You can set the width, or apparent depth, of the embossment, as well as the contrast, softness, and angle of the lighting. You also choose whether to show or hide the object. Bevel can be used in the same way, except that Bevel allows you to add color to the depth shading. Inset Bevel and Inset Emboss can be used to make the object appear to recede instead of protrude. This is often applied to buttons on a Web site to make them appear more like real push buttons.

FIGURE **10.14**

Using the Raised Emboss effect gives an object the appearance of being stamped or raised, like a seal on a document or a key on a keyboard.

Another great effect to use with vectors is the Motion Trail effect from Eye Candy. The Light version of this software ships with Fireworks and is available via the Filters menu. Change the Direction to suggest which way the object is moving. Change the Length and Taper to suggest distance and speed. Choose Bleed Color from Edges to create a more abstract effect. Leave it deselected for a more realistic visual appearance.

Task: Put It All Together to Create a Button Graphic

You have read about the different ways Fireworks can change your images simply by adding and editing effects. In this task you will put all of the theory into practice and create a button complete with effects.

1. Create a new file by using New from the File menu or by pressing Control+N (Windows) or Command+N (Macintosh). Set the width to 50 and the height to 50. Make the background color transparent. Click OK to continue.

2. Zoom in on the blank Canvas with the Zoom tool or by changing the magnification in the View menu. Zoom in to 400% magnification.

3. Using the Rectangle path tool, click and drag from the top left corner to the bottom right corner. Leave some room on the sides. Don't worry about the current fill or stroke settings—you can change them later. After you've finished drawing, use the Property Inspector to set the width to 40, the height to 40, the X position to 5, and the Y position to 5.

4. Choose Stroke Options from the Stroke Styles menu on the Property Inspector. Choose Pencil from the Style menu at the top. From the menu below that, choose Graphite. Change the stroke color to black and the stroke width to 1. You'll notice in Figure 10.15 that the graphite pencil uses the Grain texture at 80% to achieve a mottled effect like a real pencil. Click in the workspace outside the Canvas to apply the changes and hide the Stroke Options menu.

FIGURE **10.15**

A graphite pencil stroke that's one pixel wide has been applied around the path by using the Stroke Options menu.

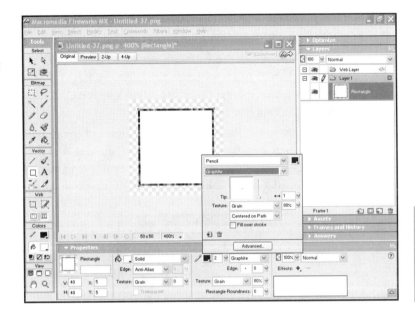

10

5. From the Property Inspector click the Fill Style menu and choose Pattern. Now click the fill color swatch to bring up the Pattern menu. Change the pattern listed at the top by clicking to bring up the menu and then choosing Other. Navigate to the Hour 10 examples folder and choose the file HI-Clouds.png. If you click the menu again, you'll notice that "HI-Clouds" has been added to your list of patterns.

6. You'll notice a faint line in the middle where the pattern has been tiled. Select the Pointer tool from the Tools panel and click the path object. The pattern fill handles will appear. Click the round center handle and drag it below and to the left of the Canvas, as in Figure 10.16. This will reposition the pattern tiling in relation to the fill.

FIGURE **10.16**

The pattern fill handles have been used to change the point where the pattern is tiled so that it doesn't appear within the path.

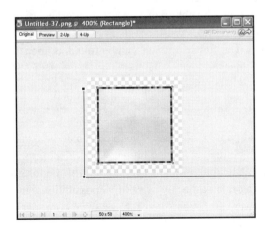

7. Use the Import command from the File menu or press Control+R (Windows) or Command+R (Macintosh) to import the file `icon_drawing.png` from the `Hour 10` examples folder. Click above and to the left of the Canvas to place the graphic.

8. The imported objects will automatically be selected. Choose Group from the Modify menu or press Control+G (Windows) or Command+G (Macintosh) to group the imported objects.

9. Choose Numeric Transform from the Transform commands on the Modify menu or press Control+Shift+T (Windows) or Command+Shift+T (Macintosh). Choose Scale from the menu at the top and make sure Scale Attributes and Constrain Proportions are selected. Change either the width or the height to 10, as in Figure 10.17.

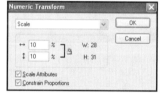

FIGURE 10.17
Numeric transform will be used to quickly resize the imported graphic. The size in pixels will reflect the results of the percentage change.

10. If the scaled graphic disappears from the workspace, zoom out to 100% by using the Zoom tool or by changing the Magnification in the View menu. Select the Pointer tool, and click-drag to move the graphic within the button. You can also simply change the X position to 11 and the Y position to 8 in the Property Inspector without having to change the view. Return the magnification to 400%.

11. Click the square path with the Pointer tool to select the object. Click the Add Effects button in the Property Inspector to add the Outer Bevel effect from the Bevel and Emboss group. Select the Flat bevel style and set the bevel width to 5. Click the bevel color swatch to choose medium gray, or hex code #666666. The contrast should be set to 75%, the softness to 3, the angle to 135, and the lighting style to Raised. The finished image can be found as `icon_button.png` in the `Hour 10` examples folder.

Summary

Phew! You've covered pretty much everything you can do with vector and bitmap graphics in Fireworks. By combining vector and bitmap tools, Fireworks MX makes it easy to work in either mode. Blending bitmaps and effects with vector graphics and masks will allow you to explore a vast array of creative possibilities. In Part IV, "Creating Animations: The Power of Motion," you'll bring them both together as you learn how to animate graphics with Fireworks MX.

Workshop

In this hour you have looked at many of the tools and options that really highlight the power of the Fireworks application. Use the questions and quiz below to review your learning and test how much you remember about fills and stroke effects. The exercises at the very end will help you put some of these techniques into practice.

Q&A

Q **I've applied a grayscale gradient fill to a path and pasted it as a mask. Why isn't the result a gradual transparency?**

A Select the mask by clicking on its thumbnail next to the masked object in the Layers panel. In the Property Inspector make sure the Grayscale Appearance button is checked and that the fill color swatch shows the gradient fill. Vector masks default to the Path Outlines setting.

Q **I created a Fireworks PNG graphic with vectors to use as a pattern. When I scale the pattern with the pattern fill handles, why am I getting jagged bitmap edges?**

A Even if the graphics in a Fireworks PNG file are vector paths, they will be treated as bitmaps when used as a pattern or texture. Scaling the patterned or textured object will scale these bitmaps along with them, potentially creating jaggies when the bitmaps are resampled.

Q **I'm trying to create a stroke with flow so that more ink is applied as I hold the cursor over a point. Why aren't the spacing and flow properties available to me in the Edit Stroke dialog?**

A Some of the preset strokes do not allow for spacing and flow properties. If you want to use these properties, choose an Air Brush stroke as the starting point for your custom stroke.

Quiz

1. Where do you change how pressure and speed affect the stroke?

   a. In the Property Inspector

   b. In the Stroke Options menu

   c. In the Edit Stroke dialog

2. What kind of file can't be used as a pattern or texture?

   a. JPEG

   b. PSD

   c. TIFF

3. What effect would you use to make an object look like it was moving?

    a. Motion trail

    b. Gaussian blur

    c. Emboss

Quiz Answers

1. c.—Use the Sensitivity tab in the Edit Stroke dialog to assign pressure and speed variables to a stroke property, such as width or ink.

2. b.—You can use PNG, GIF, JPEG, BMP, or TIFF images but not Photoshop PSD, Illustrator, or CorelDRAW files.

3. a.—Motion trail from the Eye Candy effects group can give the appearance of motion with a directional blur.

Exercises

1. Try working with perspective. You know all about creating shadows, so try expanding that to create perspective shadows by skewing cloned objects and applying masks.

2. Use the opacity settings available in the Property Inspector to fade out and image. You can overlay one object over another and use a gradient fill with reduced opacity to create a nice faded effect.

3. Try creating 3D objects of your own. Remember that the use of shadows and perspective will add to the effect. Gradient fills can give a nice metallic effect, as you saw earlier in the hour.

PART IV

Creating Animations:
The Power of Motion

Hour

HOUR 11

Planning and Creating Animation for the Web

In this hour you will begin working with animated graphics. You'll learn the basics of animation theory and techniques as well as some of the tools you'll use to create animations in Fireworks MX. These tools include frames, symbols, and shared layers, which can be used to aid Web site design as well as to create motion graphics.

In this hour you will

- Understand the steps involved in planning an animation
- Learn visual tricks and optimization techniques for Web animations
- Use frames to animate graphics and organize templates
- Use tweens to convert graphics into symbols for distribution

Animation Theory and Storyboarding for the Web

Animation is hundreds of years old, having existed even before photography. The basis of all animation is changing an image over time. Eadweard Muybridge practically anticipated motion pictures when, in order to win a bet, he used a number of cameras to photograph a horse in motion, as shown in Figure 11.1. Although film, video, and computers have made incredibly realistic animations possible, even big Hollywood productions involve traditional drawing, painting, sculpture, and photography skills. These techniques are used to previsualize computer-generated characters and backgrounds. This is critical because creating even a few seconds of an animated motion picture can take weeks, with or without a computer.

FIGURE 11.1

Professional animators still refer to the work of Eadweard Muybridge, who was the first to use photography to document creatures in motion.

When working on the Web, you won't have to spend the same amount of time for every second of an animation. Because of the file size constraints, most Web animations are very simple, consisting of a dozen or fewer frames for a second or more of play. Motion pictures are displayed at 24 frames per second and are of a much higher resolution and color depth than you can use on the Web.

You can benefit from techniques developed by film and television animators, however. The most important technique is storyboarding the concept for your animation. A storyboard is simply a sketch for each frame or scene in an animation, as shown in Figure 11.2. Once you've drawn a storyboard, it is much easier to visualize exactly how the animation will eventually look and how much time or skill it will take to animate it.

FIGURE 11.2

This simple storyboard was sketched in pencil, inked with a felt-tip pen, and scanned. The images can be copied into a series of frames to create a preview of the animation.

When drawing your storyboard, try to keep a few things in mind. First, you will be able to put much more detail in your drawing with a pencil and paper than you will be able to create on the Web. Text and objects such as characters should be very large in proportion to the viewable area. They will be very small when viewed on a high-resolution monitor. Gradients, shading, high-detail, and lots of colors can all make file size unmanageable. Web animations use GIF compression, which limits the palette and compresses fields of solid color more efficiently.

Another technique is to minimize the area of motion in the viewable area. For example, moving just the lips and the eyes on a character's face means you have to draw the rest of the head or body only once. Areas of an animated GIF image will have to be saved only once for the duration of the animation if they don't change. Keeping background detail low and the area of movement small will go far to keep file size down.

You can also use looping and timing to create a small number of drawings that can work over a long stretch of time. You can set the time between individual frames in an animated GIF to expand or compress the time between changes. You can also loop the frames, repeating them over and over. This is good for motion that's supposed to represent a continuous activity, such as walking. Especially for simple animations on a Web page, looping can be used to repeat the animation *ad infinitum*. You've probably encountered a banner advertisement that slowly cycles through a few simple frames and then repeats itself. This is done with looping and frame timing. The fewer the frames, the smaller the file.

You can use some tricks to make lifelike animations even with limited frames. The Motion Trail effect creates the illusion that an object is moving very quickly. (Fireworks includes this and a couple other effects from the Eye Candy filter set, which was developed by Alien Skin Software; see note box on the following page.) Apply the Motion Trail effect in the direction opposite the object's motion and adjust opacity to vary the degree of blend with the background. As the object slows down, make it more opaque and make the motion trail shorter, lighter, and broader. You can also use the Drop Shadow effect or create

11

a duplicate copy, distort it to apply perspective, and use Gaussian Blur to adjust the softness. When the object is still, remove the effects. An example is shown in Figure 11.3.

FIGURE 11.3
Play with Eye Candy's Motion Trail and opacity to give a smoother appearance to fast motion at low frame rates.

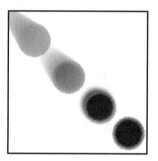

Another trick is to use more frames per second for a small movement, such as a winking eye, but very few frames for large movements, such as text scrolling across the viewable area. A grayscale palette can also be used when detail and shading are more important than being colorful. If you must use gradual transitions, limit them to one, two, or three frames—this is often enough to effectively suggest a smooth transition.

Eye Candy is an effects application produced by Alien Skin. There is a light version included with Fireworks. Located in the Filters menu, there are three possible effects that can be applied. To learn more, either play with the included filters or check out Alien Skin's Web site at http://www.alienskin.com.

Among the key concepts here is to plan your animation thoroughly with storyboards. Also, make sure important information, such as text, will be legible. Minimize the size of the viewable area, the area of motion, and the number of frames to keep file size down. Use solid colors, line art, and simple transitions to avoid inefficient compression, dithering (the process of using colors not in the current palette to create an approximate color match), and posterization (when an area of gradual color transition is rendered with an abrupt color change instead of a smooth, sequential transition). Finally, carefully time your frames and use looping to extend the duration of the animation.

Creating and Organizing New Frames

When working with animations, you'll be using the Frames panel, which by default is grouped with the History panel. All images in Fireworks MX have at least one frame. This is all you need to create a static image. To add a frame, simply click the New/Duplicate Frame button (the frame icon with a plus sign) at the bottom of the Frames panel, shown in Figure 11.4. This will add a frame after the last frame in the list. You may also use the Add Frames command in the Frames panel Options menu. You can choose to add one or more frames at the beginning, before the current frame, after the current frame, or at the end.

FIGURE 11.4

The Frames panel is where you can choose which frames to view, edit, add, rearrange, or delete.

To select a frame, click the frame in the Frames panel. It will become the active frame shown in the canvas, and the frame row in the Frames panel will be denoted by a dotted border. To select a group of contiguous frames use Shift+click. To select a group that is not contiguous, as in Figure 11.5, use Control+Shift+click (Windows) or Command+click (Macintosh).

FIGURE 11.5

Multiple frames are selected, but only the bordered frame is active and visible in the workspace.

To duplicate one or more frames, select them and then click-drag the selected frames to the New/Duplicate Frame button on the Frames panel. Select one or more frames and click the Delete Frame button to delete the selected frames (if all the frames are selected, the first frame will not be deleted).

All frames in a document share the same Canvas. You cannot change the Canvas size for individual frames. For that you will have to create a new document. Naturally the frames also share all the other Canvas settings, including resolution and background color.

If you would like to change the order of the frames, select one or more frames and then click-drag them to their new positions in the frame sequence. A black bar will show where the frames will be inserted. To step through frames or preview an animation, use the controls in the workspace below the Canvas, as shown in Figure 11.6. The first left arrow will bring you to the first frame. The white right arrow will play the animation. The next right arrow will bring you to the end of the animation. The number of the current frame in the sequence is noted here. The next two arrows step one frame backward and forward, respectively.

While the animation is playing, the white arrow changes to a black stop button. It then automatically changes back when the animation is stopped.

FIGURE 11.6
The frame navigation buttons at the bottom of the workspace let you step through frames or preview the animation.

Specifying Frame Names, Timing, and Looping

By default, frames are named in the order they appear in the sequence, beginning at 1. When you rearrange frames, the default names will change to remain in numerical order. When you change the name of a frame, as in Figure 11.7, the custom name will not be changed when the frame's position in the sequence is changed. To name a frame, double-click the current frame name listed in the Frames panel. A field will appear in which you can type the new name. Press the Enter key to apply and save the new name.

FIGURE 11.7

The frames in this sequence have been named to help organize them.

By double-clicking the right column of a frame's row, you can change the duration of the frame in the sequence, as shown in Figure 11.8. Durations are specified in hundredths of a second. A value of 100 would display the frame for 1 second. A value of 6000 would display the frame for 1 minute. To calculate the frames per second (fps), divide 100 by the desired frame rate. A rate of 5 fps would mean each frame's duration would be 20/100ths of a second. You can also disable a frame from export by unchecking the Include when Exporting box. A red X will appear in the duration column, but the frame will not be deleted or changed.

FIGURE 11.8

Now you've specified the time for each frame to be displayed. The first frame is faster than the next couple to better simulate a decelerating object, and then the fourth frame is held for 2 full seconds.

To specify sequence looping, click the GIF Animation Looping button at the bottom of the Frames panel, as in Figure 11.9. You may choose No Looping if you do not want the animation to repeat. You may also specify a number of times to loop from 1 to 20. Forever will loop the animation endlessly. The current number of loops will be listed to the right of the button. You may also specify an exact number of loops using the Export Preview dialog, which will be discussed in the next hour, "Improving and Finishing Your Animation."

11

FIGURE 11.9

You can repeat an animation as many times as you want, or not at all, by clicking the GIF Animation Looping button at the bottom of the Frames panel.

Working with Layers and Frames

Layers created for any frame will be present for all frames in the document but may not contain graphics on individual frames. The content of the layers can change from frame to frame, but their names, settings, and stacking order in the Layers panel do not. You may share a layer to make its contents the same for all frames. To share a layer from any frame (the frame name will be noted at the bottom of the Layers panel), double-click the layer name in the Layers panel and check the Share Across Frames box. The objects on the shared layer from the current active frame will be available on that layer in all frames. A filmstrip icon, with arrows pointing left and right, will appear in the layer's row to denote a shared layer. The Web layer is always shared—slice objects on the Web layer cannot change from frame to frame.

Frames can also be a great tool for laying out Web pages. Template elements such as guides, symbols, buttons, and background graphics can be placed on a shared layer. New frames can be created for each page that uses the template, and text or graphics for each page can quickly be composed within the template. Guides and grids don't change from frame to frame, making it easy to align graphics and text from page to page. Comparing pages against each other becomes a snap!

Task: Create a Basic Animation

In this task you will work through the process of creating a nice, simple animation that fades text from the screen. The steps involved will take you through the topics covered so far in this hour.

1. Start by creating a new document in Fireworks. Set the dimensions to be 300×300 pixels.

2. Add some text to the document. **Learning Fireworks MX** is seen as typed in Figure 11.10. Format the text to be whatever fonts and colors you want to use. However many fonts and colors you use, be sure to retain the text as a single object.

FIGURE 11.10

Start by adding the content you want to animate in a new document. When working with text, you have complete formatting options, even when animating.

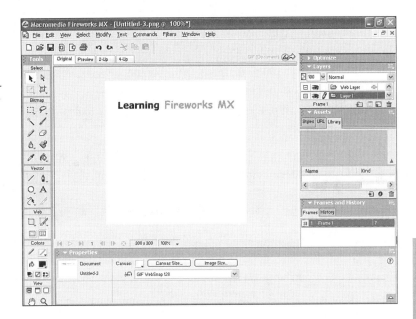

3. From the Modify menu, choose Animation, Animate Selection. This will open the Animate dialog, as shown in Figure 11.11. For this task we want the text to disappear completely and travel down the Canvas as it does so.

FIGURE 11.11

The Animate dialog offers you full control over the settings for your animation. Simply type in the values you want.

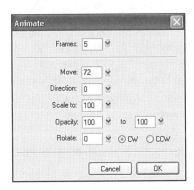

Use the following settings in the dialog:

Frames: 15. This will give a nice, smooth movement.

11

Movement: 170. This should move the text almost to the bottom of the canvas at the point it fades from view.

Direction: 270. Using the slider, set the direction to 270. As you turn the slider, you will see that the indicator is pointing straight down when you get to 270.

Scaling: 100. You do not want the text to change in size, so leave scaling at the default of 100.

Opacity: 100 to **0.** These settings will take the text and fade it completely from view as it travels down the screen.

Rotation: 0. Again, you do not want the text to change direction, so leave rotation set to 0.

4. Click OK to continue. The alert box shown in Figure 11.12 is displayed. Click OK to add the required frames for your animation.

FIGURE 11.12

You must allow Fireworks to add the required frames to your animation. Click the check box if you don't need to be reminded again.

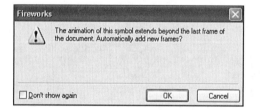

The animation of this symbol extends beyond the last frame of the document. Automatically add new frames?

☐ Don't show again   OK   Cancel

If you would rather not see this dialog in the future, click the Don't show again check box at the bottom left of the dialog.

5. Select the text in the document window again. With the text selection you can see the selection handles for the animation. The green circle is the starting point of the animation, and the red circle is the final point. If the movement of the text is not great enough, you can drag the red circle to the bottom of the document. If it goes too far, you can drag it upward.

6. Test the animation by clicking the play button at the bottom of the document window. Click the stop button at any time to stop the animation at the current frame.

7. With the animation stopped, view the Frames panel. Notice how the frame you stopped the animation at is automatically selected. In Figure 11.13 you can see the animation stopped at Frame 11. Notice how the text is almost at the bottom of the screen and has almost faded.

FIGURE 11.13

You can see the status of your animation in any frame simply by stopping the animation using the stop sign or else selecting the frame in the Frames panel.

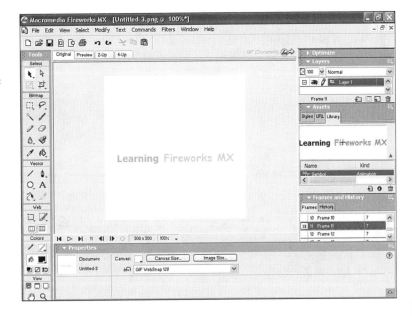

Converting Objects into Symbols

11

An important feature of Fireworks is its ability to convert graphic objects into symbols. Any object in Fireworks can be converted into a bitmap, path, text, or group. Symbol objects are like groups but have special features, such as the capability to edit instances of the symbol individually or universally and to apply behaviors (such as button interaction or animation) to them. When one or more objects are converted into a symbol object, a new item is created in the Library panel, so you can simply drag and drop symbols from the Library onto the Canvas.

There are three types of symbols—graphic symbols, animation symbols, and button symbols. In this hour you'll use graphic and animation symbols to create some simple animations. For more information on button symbols, the Symbol Editor, the Library panel, and editing symbol instances, refer to Hour 15, "Creating Interactive Graphics." For now you'll be using the familiar menus and the Layers, Frames, and Properties (Property Inspector) panels to work with symbols.

To create a symbol from objects on the Canvas, select them with the Pointer tool and choose Convert to Symbol from the Symbol commands on the Modify menu or press F8 (Windows and Macintosh). You can choose to create a symbol object of the Graphic, Animation, or Button type. To remove the objects from a symbol, select the symbol with the Pointer tool and choose Break Apart from the Symbol commands on the Modify menu.

Task: Create an Animation Symbol to Animate an Object

In this task you will create an animation symbol from a text object. This will lead to the creation of an animated Web banner, which can be used to advertise a company, product, or Web site.

1. Open the file background.png from the Hour 11 examples folder. This file is in standard Web banner dimensions, 468 pixels wide by 60 pixels tall. There is only one frame.

2. There are three layers: Visit Hawaii, Animated Text, and Background. Visit Hawaii and Background are shared across frames and are locked. Expand the layer Animated Text and select the text object contained on that layer. Notice that it's below the Canvas, as in Figure 11.14.

FIGURE 11.14

There's a text object on the Animated Text *layer, but for now it's placed so it's not visible on the Canvas.*

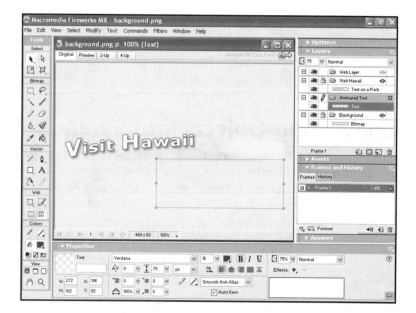

3. With the text object selected, choose Animate Selection from the Animation commands on the Modify menu or press Alt+Shift+F8 (Windows) or Option+Shift+F8 (Macintosh). This will automatically convert the selected object into a symbol of the Animation type.

4. When you choose to animate an object, you'll be presented with the Animate dialog. In this dialog you choose the number of frames, movement distance (in pixels), direction of movement (in degrees), scaling percentage, change in opacity, and rotation angle and direction. For this task set Frames at **7,** Move to **94,** and Direction to **90,** as in Figure 11.15. This will move the symbol 94 frames from bottom to top over the course of seven frames.

You can bring up the Animate dialog again at any time, enabling you to change the settings. Simply select the animated symbol with the pointer and choose Settings from the Animation commands on the Modify menu.

FIGURE 11.15

The Animate settings dialog allows you to specify motion, scaling, opacity, and rotation for an Animation symbol.

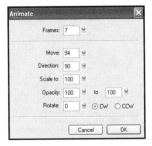

5. You will be warned that the animation you are about to apply extends beyond the last frame of the document. Check the Don't Show Again box if you do not want to be warned in the future. Click OK to add the new frames and Continue.

6. The text object will become a symbol object, which is denoted on the Canvas with a static marquee border around the graphic, as shown in Figure 11.16. Because it is an animation symbol, the symbol also has movement handles, which are the round circles along the line extending from the center of the symbol. Reposition the green handle to change where the symbol starts on the Canvas. Reposition the red handle to change where it ends. The handles in between show the positions of the regular steps in between. Other animation settings are available in the Property Inspector. Click the play button in the workspace below the Canvas to view the animation.

FIGURE 11.16

Note how the object selection box changes when an object is converted into a symbol. The handles can be used to change the Animation symbol's movement.

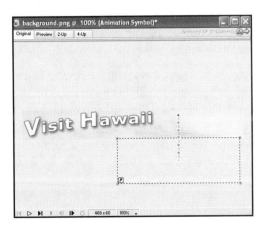

11

7. Changing the frame timing will allow you to pause on each of the lines of text and smooth the motion as the first line scrolls. First double-click in the right column of the Frame 2 row to change the frame delay for the second frame. Enter **300** in the field and press Enter. Change the delay for Frames 3 through 6 to **25.** Now change the delay for the last frame to **500.** The finished settings are shown in Figure 11.17.

FIGURE 11.17

By changing the frame timing, you can pause on particular frames to give users time to read the text.

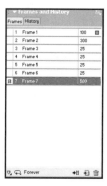

8. The optimization settings were saved with the file, so the image will export as an Animated GIF image. Use the Preview in Browser command on the File menu or press F12 (Windows and Macintosh) to view the finished animation in a Web browser. The entire animation will take about 10 seconds (to compute the total time, add the delay for each frame and divide by 100).

Inserting Motion Tweens

Another way to animate an object across multiple frames is to use tweening. In traditional animation the artist drew the keyframes for character motion and interaction, and the assistant drew the frames in between. These in-between frames ended up with the nickname *tweens.* Fireworks can act as your animation assistant by drawing all the necessary steps between two copies of a graphics symbol.

To tween one or more objects, select them with the pointer and use Convert to Symbol from the Symbol commands on the Modify menu or press F8. Name the symbol and choose the Graphic type. The objects will now be a selected symbol on the Canvas. Use Duplicate from the Edit menu to create a copy of the symbol on the same layer. Click and drag with the pointer or use the Transform tools to move and modify the copy. You can also use tweening for copies with a different opacity, as shown in Figure 11.18.

FIGURE **11.18**

These are two copies of the same graphic symbol, but the one on the right has been transformed, and its opacity has been halved.

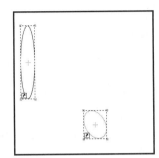

Use Shift+click with the Pointer tool to select both copies of the symbol. Select Tween Instances from the Symbol commands on the Modify menu, or press Control+Alt+Shift+T (Windows) or Command+Option+Shift+T (Macintosh). The Tween Instances dialog will open. This small dialog has only two fields, as follows:

Steps—Use this text field to input the number of steps of changes you want between the two objects. The greater the number of steps, the smoother the resulting animation will be. The more steps there are, the larger the file size, however.

Distribute to Frames—Distributing across frames will place all the tweened symbol instances on successive frames. The symbol instances are distributed based on their stacking order, starting at the bottom, with the topmost instance being last in the sequence.

New frames will be created automatically if there are currently not enough for the number of steps indicated in your settings. Each symbol instance will also be on the same layer throughout the frames. Unchecking the Distribute to Frames check box will place all instances of the symbol on the same frame, as shown in Figure 11.19. You may distribute them later by selecting them with the pointer and then clicking the Distribute to Frames button on the Frames panel.

FIGURE **11.19**

New instances of the symbol are created between the two copies, with scale, rotation, and opacity gradually adjusted for each step.

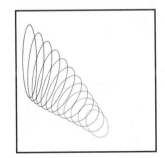

11

Tweens are not only used with animation. They can also create exciting geometric effects within a static image, lending dynamic motion effects to backgrounds and borders. Using a path object, convert it into a symbol and place another copy of the new symbol object elsewhere on the Canvas. Use the Transform tools, opacity setting, or effects to change the copy. Select both symbols and use Tween Instances to create new instances between them. Choose a number of steps but don't distribute to frames. More steps means a smoother transition. A cool morphing effect is achieved as the symbol changes incrementally.

Summary

You've gotten started working with animations in Fireworks MX by learning how animation works, how best to plan an animation for the Web, and how to add motion to objects by using frames. In the next hour, "Improving and Finishing Your Animation," you'll learn about some tools to help with more advanced animation as well as how to export your animation for use on a Web page.

Workshop

In this hour you have been introduced to the basic concepts of creating Web animations in Fireworks. For a single hour you have covered a large amount of information, so use this final section to review what you have learned. The exercises at the very end will give you the opportunity to practice these new techniques.

Q&A

Q I'm not any good at drawing, so why should I bother with a storyboard?

A Even if you're no Da Vinci, you should still take the time to sketch out an idea. This may mean just sketching three or four still frames or drawing some text with an arrow pointing the way you want it to move. You also can try combinations and sequences of images very quickly with notecards. Especially when working with other people, such experimenting with changes can take time, so it's better to know what you want to accomplish before you set out.

Q I'm navigating from frame to frame, moving an object on a shared layer a little bit each time. Why isn't it animated when I click the play button in the workspace?

A When a layer is shared, you can edit the objects on that layer from any frame, but the change will affect that layer for all frames. You want to create an unshared layer and place a copy of the object you want to animate on that layer in each frame.

Q **When I create a symbol from a path or bitmap object, how come I can't edit the individual objects with the Subselection tool?**

A A symbol is a graphic that's meant to be repeated over and over again with slight variations. When something has been converted into a symbol, you must edit the symbol through the Symbol Editor dialog. You can bring this up by double-clicking the symbol on the Canvas. If you edit one copy of the symbol by using the Symbol Editor, though, all the copies of that symbol will be changed as well. You may use Break Apart from the Symbol commands on the Modify menu if you want to remove the objects from that symbol instance.

Quiz

1. What's the frame rate in frames per second if each frame's delay is set to 10/100ths of a second?

   a. 1

   b. 5

   c. 10

2. How can you make an object move across the Canvas?

   a. Place a copy of the object on an unshared layer across a number of frames, each time in a slightly different position on the Canvas.

   b. Use the Animation symbol type, set the steps in the Property Inspector, and move the motion handles.

   c. Convert the object into a Graphic symbol, duplicate it at another location, and use Tween Instances to create copies between them.

3. Which layer is always shared across every frame?

   a. The Background layer

   b. Layer 1

   c. The Web layer

Quiz Answers

1. c.—10. Divide 100 by the frame delay number specified to determine the frame rate.

2. a., b., and c.—You can use any of these techniques to create the illusion of the object moving across the Canvas.

3. c.—The Web layer is always shared and does not change from frame to frame.

Exercises

1. Create a new document in Fireworks and add a series of shapes. Place each shape on a new layer, then convert each shape to be an animated symbol. Once each shape is converted, add animation settings for it to create the illusion of not only movement but also shapes fading in and out. The Opacity setting in the Animate dialog will allow you to do this easily.

2. Take the new document from the previous exercise and develop it into a Web banner for a new company. Remember to think about the recommended size for banners and the intended usage. Plan to have movement but not a flashing effect. Make sure the company name or product is visible at all times during the animation—this is the part you want the customer to remember.

HOUR 12

Improving and Finishing Your Animation

You've learned about most of the basic animation techniques, but you may want to use Fireworks MX for more than just advertising banners. In this hour you'll look at some more ways to control motion by working with objects on more than one frame using multi-frame editing and onion skins. With these tools you can select objects across multiple frames and change how an object moves throughout a sequence by previewing nearby frames. You'll also learn how to export animations for use on the Web and in other applications.

In this hour you will

- Use tweens to animate symbols across one or more frames
- Adjust the motion of animated elements by using onion skins and multi-frame editing
- Work with the Export Preview dialog to optimize an Animated GIF for the Web
- Export optimized layers and frames to individual files

Inserting Motion Tweens

At the end of the previous hour, "Planning and Creating Animation for the Web," you looked at motion tweening. Now you will have a quick recap of the concept and then put it into practice.

To tween one or more objects, select it with the pointer and use Convert to Symbol from the Symbol commands on the Modify menu, or press F8. Name the symbol and choose the Graphic type. The objects will now be a selected symbol on the Canvas. Use Duplicate from the Edit menu to create another copy of the symbol on the same layer. Click and drag with the pointer, or use the transformation tools to move and modify the copy. You can also use tweening for copies with a different opacity, as in Figure 12.1.

Figure 12.1

These are two copies of the same graphic symbol, but the one on the right has been transformed, and the opacity has been halved.

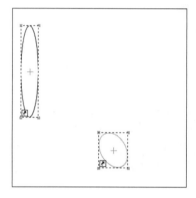

Task: Creating a Simple Motion Tween

▼ TASK

In this task you will create a moving line effect by using the tweening techniques introduced so far. Although this is not the most complicated use of tweening, this will certainly get you used to how it all comes together.

1. Start by creating a new Fireworks document. Set the Canvas to be 400 pixels wide by 100 pixels deep. Leave the Canvas color set to white.

2. From the View menu choose Rulers. Although this is not necessary, it does help to give a visual representation.

3. Select the Brush tool from the Bitmap section of the Tools panel, and then in the Property Inspector set the stroke color to something really bright. Use the Stroke category drop-down menu to choose Hard Line, and then set the tip size to 15, but leave all other settings untouched, as shown in Figure 12.2.

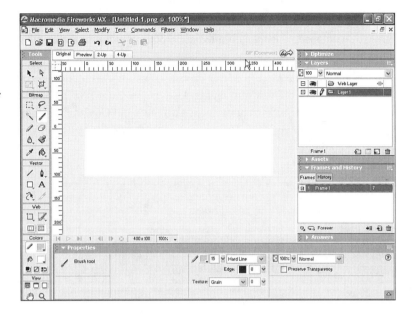

FIGURE 12.2

Use the Property Inspector to set the style and width of the line to be drawn. This line will form the basis of your motion tween.

4. On the Canvas draw a line that is around 30 pixels wide. Hold the Shift key while drawing the line to ensure that it is completely straight.

> If you are uncertain about the length of the line, select it in the document by using the Pointer tool. Then in the Property Inspector, adjust the length manually by changing the value in the W field.

12

5. From the Modify menu choose Symbol, Convert to Symbol, in order to open the Symbol Properties dialog. Name the symbol **Line** and set the Type to Graphic, as shown in Figure 12.3. Click OK to continue.

FIGURE 12.3

Use the Symbol Properties dialog to name your symbol and set the Type.

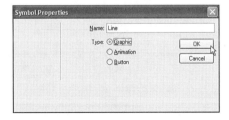

6. With the symbol selected in the document, choose Clone from the Edit menu. The cloned instance is immediately placed on top of the original and is selected by default.

7. From the Modify Menu choose Transform, Numeric Transform. This opens the Numeric Transform dialog. Use the drop-down menu and select Resize. Remove the checks from both Scale Attributes and Constrain Proportions. Then in the width section type **600**. The settings should look the same as Figure 12.4. Click OK to continue.

FIGURE 12.4

The Numeric Transform dialog is used to set the properties for the cloned instance of the symbol.

8. Select both symbols by choosing Select All from the Select Menu. (If you are using an existing document with existing content, use the Select Behind tool to select the original instance.)

9. From the Modify Menu choose Symbols, Tween Instances, to open the Tween Instances dialog. Select 15 as the number of steps, and check the Distribute to Frames check box. Click OK to continue.

10. From the Modify Menu choose Canvas, Trim Canvas, to remove the excess workspace. All that should be visible is the initial small line segment and white space after it, as shown in Figure 12.5.

FIGURE 12.5

Removing the excess area of the Canvas will leave you with only a small line visible on the screen. When the animation is previewed, the line will grow before your very eyes.

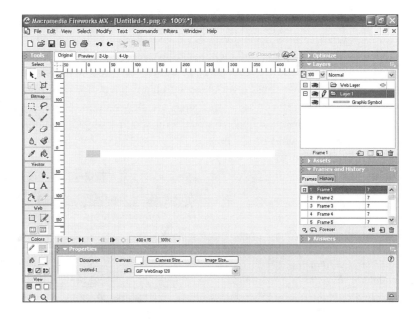

11. Select the Preview tab at the top of the document window and then click the Play button at the bottom. Your line will appear to grow across the screen.

12. Save the file as `line.png`.

To make this file usable as a Web graphic, export it as a GIF animation that is set to loop. Exporting animated GIFs is covered in detail later in this hour.

> You can jazz this up a little by changing the fill on the different instances. Try using a gradient fill or feathering the edges of the lines. It's amazing, the different effects that can be achieved by one simple change.

12

Viewing and Selecting Objects Across Frames

If you have a lot of objects distributed across a number of frames, it could take a long time to adjust each one individually. Imagine that you've tweened a pair of symbol instances and distributed them across frames so that they appear to move from left to right across the bottom of the Canvas. If you now want them to move across the top of the Canvas, you don't want to have to move each step. You can use the Multi-Frame Editing option in the Frames panel to work with an object from more than one continuous frame.

To view objects from more than one frame, you can use onion skins, shown in Figure 12.6. Onion skins were used in traditional animation drawings when drawings were sketched on translucent paper and then layered to show their motion over time. The onion skins were often used by tweeners. The character artist could sketch the first and last drawings, and the tweener could layer these with blank sheets for each frame in between. In Fireworks objects on adjacent frames are shown on the Canvas semitransparently, although their actual opacity settings remain unchanged. The object on the currently active frame will be fully opaque.

FIGURE 12.6

Show All Frames has been chosen. Objects within the onion skin range markers in the left column of the Frames panel are shown as semitransparent. The opaque object is the object on the active frame, Frame 5.

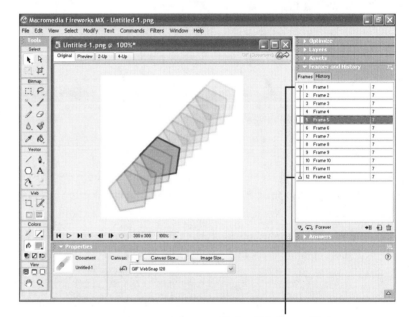

Onion Skin Range Markers

The onion skin options can be easily accessed from the Frames panel by clicking the Onion Skinning button, located at the bottom left next to the GIF Animation Looping button. Click this button to select whether you want no onion skinning or whether you want to see only the next frame, the frames before and after, or all frames. Selecting Custom will bring up the Onion Skinning dialog, shown in Figure 12.7, where you can specify the number of frames you would like to see before and after the selected frame, as well as the opacity at which they will be displayed.

FIGURE 12.7

Choosing Custom from the Onion Skinning button menu brings up the Onion Skinning settings dialog.

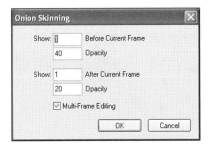

You can turn multi-frame editing on or off with the check box on this dialog or from the Onion Skinning button menu. Multi-frame editing allows you to select objects displayed as onion skins and edit them, even if they aren't on the active frame. This means you can change properties for any object on any frame. You can use the pointer, Transform, Align, or the Property Inspector to edit objects selected across frames. When multi-frame editing is turned off, objects shown as onion skins cannot be selected or changed.

When onion skins are turned on, the frame range markers will expand across onion-skinned frames in the left column of the frame rows on the Frames panel. Clicking a frame row with the mouse will make it the currently active frame, and the range markers will adjust themselves in the sequence. If you click the left column of a frame row above the top marker, the top marker will move to include that frame. Clicking below the bottom marker will display a frame further along in the sequence. Clicking between the markers will make the range shorter. You can also adjust the frame range markers by typing values into the Show fields in the custom Onion Skinning dialog.

To select an object visible on a frame other than the currently active frame, make sure the Multi-Frame Editing check box is checked. Select the Pointer tool and move it over the object. The object's handles will become highlighted. Click to select it. The object's settings will now be available in the Property Inspector. To select other objects visible on the active frame or in another onion skin, as in Figure 12.8, simply hold the Shift key and click the objects you want selected. You may use the pointer or the Property Inspector to change their position, opacity, or effects. Grouping objects will move all selected objects to the first frame between the onion-skin range markers.

12

Contains a Selected Object

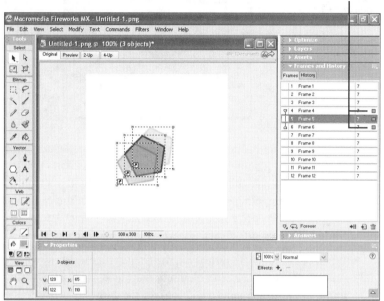

FIGURE 12.8

*One or more objects
can be selected and
changed by using
multi-frame editing,
even if they are on
different layers or
frames. You'll notice in
the right-hand column
of the Frames panel
that a frame with a
selected object has a
selection marker in its
frame row.*

Exporting an Animated GIF

There are two ways to export an animated GIF from Fireworks. The first is to set the document's optimization settings in the Optimize panel. From the Export File Format menu, choose Animated GIF. You can choose the color palette settings just as you would for a regular GIF image, including Matte background color, preset or custom palettes, and color depth. You can also set the amount of acceptable loss to reduce file size and the amount of dithering to approximate lost colors. Animated GIFs also support index transparency, just like regular GIFs. You can also edit individual colors directly on the palette. The Remove Unused Colors setting can be found on the Optimize panel's Options menu, located at the top right of the panel.

You can preview the optimized GIF image by using the Preview tabs at the top of the workspace window. Onion skins are disabled in the preview mode. You can use the animation controls at the bottom of the workspace to jump to the beginning or end, play the animation, or step through the frames. You can also click a frame in the Frames panel to jump to that frame. Use the Export Preview command on the File menu to bring up the Export Preview dialog. You can optimize the palette and compression with the Options tab. Use the Animation tab to change the Animated GIF settings.

On the Animation tab each frame will be listed in rows on the left (see Figure 12.9). The first column can be used to enable or disable frames to be exported. The following columns show a frame's name, disposal method, and delay. To change the delay for a frame, click the frame's row and enter a new value in the Frame Delay field above the frame listing. Any change will be reflected in the Frames panel after you're done.

The disposal method is used for optimizing a GIF's file size by specifying how frame information is repeated or changed. The four options are outlined here:

- The Unspecified setting will simply replace the current frame with the next frame when the delay period is over.
- The None setting will show both the current frame and the new frame.
- The Restore to Background setting will replace unchanged areas with the Matte background color.
- The Restore to Previous setting will repeat unchanged areas from the last frame. You can also select the Auto Crop and Auto Difference check boxes on the Animations tab in the Export Preview dialog, if you want disposal method decisions to be made for you.

To change the disposal method, select the frame from the list and choose a method from the Disposal Method button menu. U stands for Unspecified (default), N stands for None (or Do Not Dispose), B stands for Restore to Background, and P stands for Restore to Previous.

FIGURE **12.9**

The Animation tab in the Export Preview dialog allows you to completely control the export settings for an animated GIF file.

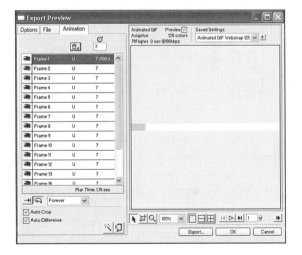

12

Some early Netscape browsers (before 4.0) do not support the Restore to Background and Restore to Previous disposal methods correctly, so be careful when using these methods.

Task: Optimize and Export an Animated GIF File

This task will reinforce the settings required when preparing a file to be exported as an animated GIF.

1. Open the file `visit_hawaii.png` from the `Hour 12` examples folder. This file is a completed version of the animation created in the last hour, "Planning and Creating Animation for the Web."

2. Choose Export Preview from the File menu or press Ctrl+Shift+X (Windows) or Command+Shift+X (Macintosh). You will be presented with the Export Preview dialog, as shown in Figure 12.10.

FIGURE 12.10

Using the Export Preview dialog, you can access some features of GIF animation that you can't access from the Optimize panel.

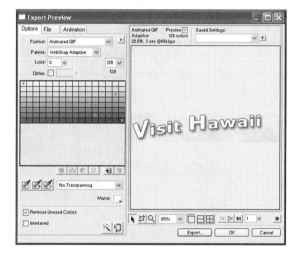

3. You want this animation to be under 10KB, or less than half the size it will currently export at. The export size is displayed over the Preview window on the dialog, along with an estimate of how long it will take for the image to download over a 56Kbps modem. The first frame will display for one and a half seconds— just long enough to download 10KB over a 56Kbps modem. You'll have to cut down on the number of colors and maybe adjust the value in the Loss field to achieve this. With WebSnap Adaptive as the palette, choose 32 from the Colors menu that is directly to the right of the Loss value.

4. The image will now be a little over 13KB. That's good, but you're not there yet. To get rid of another 3KB, change the value in the Loss field to 50 by typing it in or using the slider. The size will decrease to just under 10KB.

5. The image preview in the Preview window on the right side of the dialog hasn't changed. It's still showing the full-quality PNG file. To preview the Animated GIF

export, you must click the play button, located below the Preview window (and above the OK button). Go ahead and click it now.

6. Change the magnification by choosing 400% from the Magnification menu or by using the Zoom tool on the left. Click the play button again to render the preview. Because of the fewer colors and the loss setting, some of the blue from the background will bleed into the yellow of the title. It is the most noticeable on the capital H, as shown in Figure 12.11. You can use the Pointer tool below the Preview window to check the value of a preview pixel against the GIF palette on the left.

Original Color

Highlighted Swatch   Color Bleed

FIGURE 12.11

The heavy loss value has caused some of the colors to bleed. The cursor is positioned over a blue pixel in the H character, and the color is highlighted in the palette to the left and is written out numerically in RGB and hex values below. This color should be the Websafe yellow color that is first in the palette.

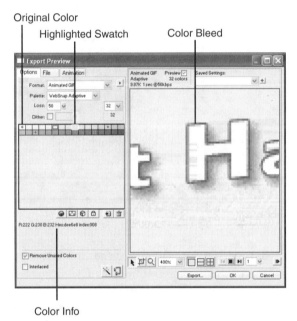

Color Info

7. Reduce the loss to 40 and use the play button to preview the animation again. You've solved the problem with color bleed, but now your file is a shade over 10KB. (Many banner servers have strict limits on the size of GIF animations.) You'll have to make another compromise.

8. You might have noticed that reducing the number of colors has a greater impact on the size of the file than increasing loss. Select the current value of 32 in the Color Depth field and type **28**. Press Return. The size of the exported file will now be under 10KB again. Preview the animation with the play button. Although it's not as good as the original, the colors are accurate, and the text is legible, with a few noticeable compression artifacts.

9. One of the reasons this file is so small is that by default, Fireworks employs Auto Crop and Auto Difference for animated GIF images. Click the Animation tab at the

12

top of the Export Preview dialog and uncheck the Auto Crop and Auto Difference
check boxes. Note in Figure 12.12 that the output size has ballooned to more than
four times the current size; this is because each frame is being exported in its
entirety, as opposed to only the pixels that change from frame to frame.

File Size

FIGURE 12.12

*With Auto Crop and
Auto Difference turned
off, the file size in this
example will more than
quadruple. Turning
them on does not affect
the appearance of the
exported file.*

Automatic Frame Optimization

10. Restore Auto Crop and Auto Difference and click OK to apply these settings to the
    document. Use the Save command from the File menu to save the settings and
    the document. You can use the Preview in Browser command by pressing F12
    (Windows and Macintosh) to see how the image will appear in your Web browser.

Exporting Individual Frames as Files

Another method for exporting animation is to export each frame as an individual file.
The settings in the Optimize panel will be applied to each frame in the document so that
you can export into any of the Fireworks export formats. Choose the Export command
from the File menu, and then choose Frames to Files from the Save as Type menu, as in
Figure 12.13. After this option is selected, you can specify whether you want to Trim
Images by checking the corresponding check box. If this box is selected, each frame will
be cropped to include the objects in that frame. If it is unchecked, the entire Canvas will
be exported for each frame. You can also export Layers to Files from the Save as Type
menu. This will export each layer of the current frame into the format specified in the
Optimize panel. You can use Trim to Images as you would when exporting frames.

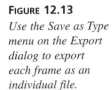

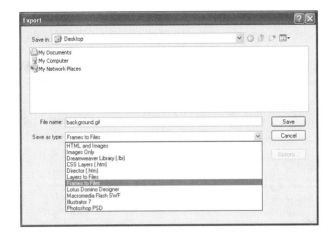

Importing Animated GIFs

Another important feature in Fireworks is the ability to import and refine animated GIFs from previous projects. This feature can also be used to study the work done by other animators. You can save an animated GIF from the Web in the same way that you would any image visible in your Web browser. When you use the Open command to open an animated GIF file in Fireworks, the document will open with multiple frames. Each frame will contain a bitmapped object that appears the same way the frame would appear in your browser. The exact palette from the GIF will automatically be loaded in the Optimize panel, and Frame Delay settings will also be preserved in the Frames panel. Use the Save command from the File menu to save the animated GIF as a Fireworks source PNG.

When you import an animated GIF into an existing document, it is placed on the current active layer and frame as an Animation symbol. If the animation has more frames than are available in the document, you will be asked whether you want to add enough frames to complete the animation. Now you can add even more motion, rotation, scaling, or transparency to the animation by changing the settings from the Animation commands in the Modify menu. You can access the individual frames in the symbol either by using the Symbol Editor and double-clicking an instance that is present on the Canvas or by selecting the symbol in the Library panel, double-clicking to change the properties, and clicking the Edit button to bring up the Symbol Editor.

12

Summary

Now you should be familiar with all of the tools available for animation with Fireworks MX. These include motion tweening, onion skinning, and multi-frame editing. After you finish your animation, you can export it as an animated GIF image, a series of individual images in a static format, or as a Flash SWF animation, which you'll learn about in the next hour, "Working with Flash MX."

Workshop

You have just about completed the second hour of learning about animation techniques in Fireworks. This final section tests your memory, and the exercises at the end take these techniques a little further.

Q&A

Q When I use the Tween Instances command, all copies end up on the same frame. How do I get them placed on consecutive frames?

A When indicating the number of steps for a motion tween, make sure the Distribute to Frames check box is checked. If the check box were not checked and all instances were created on a single frame, select all instances with the pointer and click the Distribute to Frames button at the bottom of the Frames panel.

Q I've turned on multi-frame editing, but I can see only the active frame. Where are the onion skins?

A You can use the Onion Skinning button to turn on the onion skins for just the next frame, for the frames before and after, or for all frames. You can also click the left column of a frame row in the Frames panel to move the range markers for onion skins to include that frame and any frames in front of or behind the currently active frame.

Q My animated GIF files are way too big when I export them. What can I do to make them smaller?

A The major culprit is usually too many frames. Cut down on the total number of frames to cut down on size. Change the palette to use fewer colors, if possible. Make sure that the motion in the image takes up only a small portion of the Canvas. Finally, increase the Loss setting in the Optimize panel or in the Export Preview dialog to further reduce size.

Quiz

1. What are tweens and onion skins?

   a. Tweens are objects available in the Library panel, and onion skins are the frames in the Frames panel.

   b. Tweens are the start- and endpoints of an animation, and onion skins are the steps in between.

   c. Tweens are the small changes between two graphic symbols, and onion skins are semitransparent views of objects on frames adjacent to the active frame.

2. What file format must be selected in the Optimization panel for the exported file to animate on a Web page?

   a. GIF

   b. Animated GIF

   c. Fireworks PNG

3. What happens when you use the Group command on the Modify menu to group objects you've selected across a number of frames when using multi-frame editing?

   a. The group will combine all objects on the first frame with a selected object.

   b. The group will be created on each frame with an object.

   c. The group will become an animation symbol with each object on its own frame.

Quiz Answers

1. c.—Tweens are the images created in between the two key symbols. Onion skins let you view a semitransparent preview of frames before and after the active frame.

2. b.—Animated GIF. The GIF format will create only a static image of the currently active frame. Fireworks source PNGs cannot be viewed in a Web browser.

3. a.—If you've selected objects across a number of frames and grouped them, the group will be created on the first frame in the sequence that contains a selected object. This may not necessarily be the currently active frame.

Exercises

1. Earlier in this hour you created an animation of text fading out down the screen. Try expanding that animation to do a little more: Add a new set of text that fades into view up the screen where the current text disappears. You should be able to achieve this seamlessly.

12

2. In other hours you have looked at many different tools and techniques. Now try putting them together in an animation. Create a sphere with a gradient fill, and then animate some text so that it appears to move around the sphere.

3. Spend a little time thinking about how animation could enhance your Web site but also think about how it could affect it adversely. Too many people put animations, flashing text, and bright colors on a Web site just because they can. Spend a little time planning your animation tasks so that they help your site and don't send visitors running.

HOUR 13

Working with Flash MX

Because of the advantages of Flash animation over GIF animation, more Web sites than ever are replacing regular GIF animation graphics with Flash animations in the Shockwave Flash, or SWF, format. Flash has many features that make it easier to create smaller files for animations. Fireworks can also be used to accomplish bitmap editing and optimization for graphics in Flash.

Fireworks can be used to create Flash SWF animations, or you can import Fireworks source PNGs with native features, including layers and frames, directly into Flash. With the improved loadMovie command in Flash ActionScript, it's easier than ever to create dynamic Flash movies with images from Fireworks. Plus, Fireworks is the perfect tool for optimizing graphics from Flash for backward compatibility.

 If you do not have Flash MX, you may skip this hour, or you may download a free trial copy from
http://www.macromedia.com/software/flash/

In this hour you will

- Export graphics and animation as Flash SWF files
- Use Quick Export to export files for other applications
- Open Fireworks source PNGs with editable objects in Flash
- Export graphics from Flash for use in Fireworks

Exporting as a Flash SWF File

The quickest way to start working with Flash from within Fireworks is to simply export your document as a Flash SWF file. Unlike animated GIF images, Flash SWF files have full support for alpha transparency, motion, vector graphics, embedded text, and all sorts of other great features. Furthermore, Flash can use the JPEG format for bitmap objects, meaning you can use a broader color palette. You can then reference the Flash SWF file from another Flash animation by using Flash ActionScript, or place the necessary tags in an HTML file, using Dreamweaver or a text editor.

To export a Flash SWF file using Fireworks, select the Export command from the File menu or press Ctrl+Shift+R (Windows) or Command+Shift+R (Macintosh). From the Save as Type menu, choose Macromedia Flash SWF. Now click the Options button to bring up the Flash SWF export options, as shown in Figure 13.1. Settings include settings for Objects, Text, JPEG Quality, Frames, and Frame Rate. The Flash SWF files exported are also compatible with latest versions of Apple's QuickTime media architecture, making them available to lots of other applications.

FIGURE 13.1

Flash SWF export settings are available from the Options button in the Export dialog, when Flash SWF is chosen from the Save as Type menu.

For vector objects you can choose Maintain Paths or Maintain Appearance. By maintaining paths you can generally make smaller files for export, but effects, textures, and patterns will not be shown for a vector object unless you select Maintain Appearance. Then it will be flattened into a bitmap object. For text you can choose between Maintain Editability and Convert to Paths. If you choose Maintain Editability, you can import the exported

SWF and edit the text in Flash. However, if the font used is not available on the system with Flash, the characters may not look right on the screen.

Change the JPEG Quality setting to change how much compression is applied to bitmap objects in the animation. This will also affect vectors that have been rendered to maintain appearance. A lower number means lower quality, as well as a smaller file size. You can also choose to export all frames or a range of frames. Finally, you must specify a frame rate. Flash doesn't use the same frame delay settings that GIF animations do. Instead, it maintains a steady frame rate, specified in frames per second. Divide the number of frames in the animation by the frame rate to determine the total duration in seconds. Click OK to close this window, and click Save to export the file as a Flash SWF animation.

Using Quick Export for Flash and Other Applications

Fireworks makes it easy to export files quickly for other applications. The Quick Export button, a round "fw" icon with an arrow, is located on the upper right-hand side of the document workspace, as shown in Figure 13.2. Click it in order to bring up a menu of applications to export the document for. You can export code for Dreamweaver, animations for Flash, vector paths for FreeHand, and images for Director or launch these applications from within Fireworks. You can launch your browser to preview your document as a Web page or graphic. You can also export to products not in the Macromedia Web Design Studio, such as Adobe Photoshop, GoLive, Adobe Illustrator, and Microsoft FrontPage.

FIGURE 13.2

The Quick Export button will help you copy an object, export a document, or launch an application with just a few clicks.

Another way to move graphics quickly from one application to another is simply to use Copy. You can copy bitmap objects, path outlines, or text to the system Clipboard by choosing Copy from the Edit menu or by pressing Ctrl+C (Windows) or Command+C (Macintosh). Use Ctrl+V (Windows) or Command+V (Macintosh) to paste them into applications such as Flash, FreeHand, Illustrator, Photoshop, or FrontPage. Of course, special Fireworks elements, like textures, patterns, effects, or symbols, may have to be flattened or merged to display properly in another application.

13

Working with PNGs in Flash

Flash SWF is a quick way to get your animations into the SWF format, but it isn't necessarily the best way to import graphics or animations from Fireworks. You can use the Import command from the File menu in Flash to import a SWF created in Fireworks. However, layer information is not preserved, and images shared across frames will be repeated on multiple frames, a method that is not optimal for SWF file size. A Flash SWF created in Fireworks and imported into Flash is shown in Figure 13.3.

FIGURE **13.3**

If you export a Flash SWF file from Fireworks and then import it into Flash, all objects will be on the same layer and repeated in every frame.

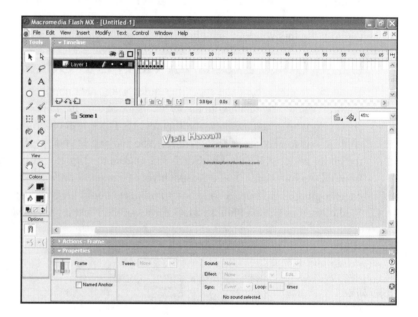

You may, however, import Fireworks source PNGs directly into Flash, complete with vector paths, editable text, layers, and frames. While in Flash choose Import from the File menu, navigate to your Fireworks source PNG, and click OK. Note the difference between the imported PNG in Figure 13.4 and the imported SWF in the previous figure. You'll be presented with the Fireworks PNG Import Settings dialog. From here you can choose how you want the structure of the PNG file preserved and how to import objects and text.

FIGURE 13.4

Importing a Fireworks PNG allows you to maintain layers, objects, and symbols from Fireworks, making it easier to optimize shared layers quickly by cutting down on repetitive data.

Importing as a movie clip and retaining layers will create a Flash Movie Clip symbol in the Flash Library panel with the same layers and frames as in Fireworks. You may also choose to import the file on a single layer in the current scene. Objects such as vector graphics can be rasterized to maintain appearance or editability. Text can also remain editable or be rasterized as bitmaps. You can also import the source graphic as a single flattened bitmap object, discarding any source file features.

Editing Bitmap Symbols in Flash

When you import a PNG, GIF, JPEG, or BMP image into Flash, a bitmap symbol is added to the library for that image. One of the ways that Flash can make smaller animations with the SWF format than other formats is because the symbol is compressed and coded only once in the SWF file. Every time it reappears in the player, it's being called with a small line of code, instead of repeating all data in the bitmap. Use the Library panel in Flash to view all symbols in a project, as in Figure 13.5. Each bitmap symbol will have a green icon decorated with a tree image. You can sort the symbols by type by clicking the Type column-heading button.

When you import a Fireworks source PNG with layers and objects intact, each bitmap object in the Fireworks file will become a bitmap symbol in Flash. If you choose to maintain the appearance of paths, they also will become bitmap symbols in Flash. If you've imported an animation, any bitmap object on a shared layer will be repeated in

13

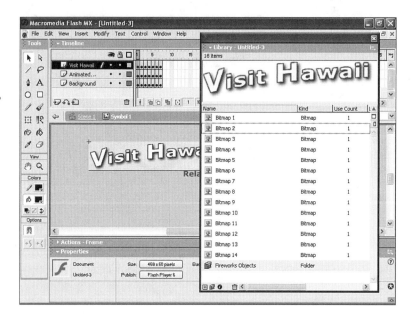

FIGURE **13.5**

The Flash Library panel allows you to view all bitmaps and symbols in a project and organize them into folders, sort them by type, and keep track of how often each item is used.

the Flash library for each frame—exporting the scene or movie clip in this way would repeat data for identical bitmap symbols. This is not optimal, and it is why only animations in which file size is not critical should be exported directly from Fireworks.

To restore the functionality of shared layers, you can delete all but the first keyframe for a layer in the Flash timeline by clicking them with the mouse and pressing Shift+F5 (Windows and Macintosh) and then adding frames to those layers to make up the difference by using F5 (Windows and Macintosh). This technique is illustrated in Figure 13.6. When you're done, you can use the Update Use Count Now command from the Library panel Options menu in Flash to update the list of symbols in the library. Unused bitmap objects will have a value of 0 in the Use Count column. Use Ctrl+click (Windows) or Command+click (Macintosh) to select unused bitmap symbols and then click-drag to the Delete button on the Library panel to delete these and ensure that they won't be exported. You can always import the source PNG again.

Another important reason to import Fireworks source PNGs is that Flash uses its own compression for bitmap objects, so it's best to import bitmap files in an uncompressed or non-lossy format. To change the compression settings for a bitmap in Flash, double-click the bitmap symbol icon to the left of the symbol name. You may change the name in the field at the top. The path to the file, the modification date, the dimensions, and the color depth are all displayed, as well as a preview of the object on the left. You may choose to allow smoothing when the image is scaled in Flash. See Figure 13.7.

FIGURE 13.6

This Flash movie has been optimized to eliminate repeated bitmaps. The Animated Text layer uses a motion tween to animate the text object. Frames have been added to restore the timing to that in the GIF animation.

FIGURE 13.7

Double-click a bitmap object in the library to bring up the Bitmap Properties dialog. Here you can update or replace the image file, change the compression, and test the compressed file size.

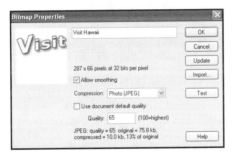

There are two types of compression presented: PNG/GIF, which uses non-lossy compression, and JPEG, which uses lossy compression. If compression is set to JPEG, you can choose to use the document default quality specified in the Publish Settings dialog, which can be accessed from the File menu. Unchecking this box will let you directly specify a compression value. Click the Text button to update the preview with the compressed version. The file size and compression ratio will also be shown at the bottom. Use the Update button to update the bitmap object from a changed original. Use Import to exchange the bitmap with data from another image file. All bitmap files are saved in the Flash Movie source FLA file and do not necessarily need to be available on the system on which you open the Flash source movie.

Task: Import a PNG into Flash

Again, when you import a Fireworks PNG file into Flash, you will have a variety of options to choose from. In this task you will work through the process of importing a Fireworks PNG and working out which options best suit your needs.

1. Open Flash and create a new document to hold the imported Fireworks file. From the Modify menu choose Document. Set the document size to be 490 × 330 pixels. This will ensure that the document is large enough to accept the imported content.

13

2. From the File menu choose Import.

> If you are already proficient with Flash and wish to import the PNG file as a
> movie symbol into an existing document, then you can select the layer and
> keyframe that you want to import the file into.

3. In the Locate dialog, browse to the file named `flashlayout.png` from the `Hour 13`
   examples folder. Click Open to continue to the Fireworks PNG Import Settings
   dialog, as seen in Figure 13.8.

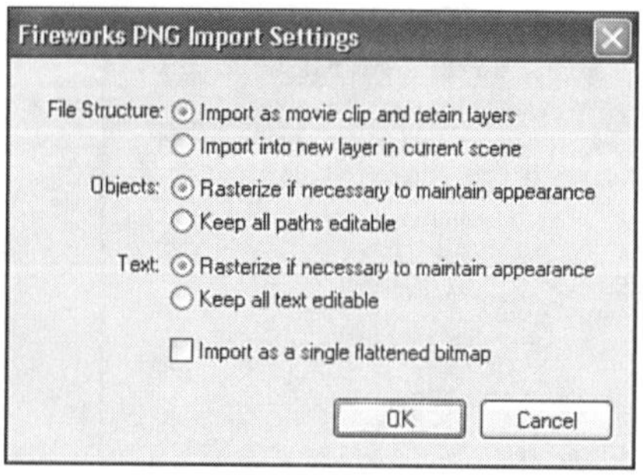

FIGURE 13.8

*The Fireworks PNG
Import Settings dialog
allows you to decide
how the content of
your PNG file will be
imported into Flash.*

Fireworks PNG Import Settings

File Structure: ⦿ Import as movie clip and retain layers
⃝ Import into new layer in current scene

Objects: ⦿ Rasterize if necessary to maintain appearance
⃝ Keep all paths editable

Text: ⦿ Rasterize if necessary to maintain appearance
⃝ Keep all text editable

☐ Import as a single flattened bitmap

[OK]   [Cancel]

4. Choose an option for File Structure:

Import as movie clip and retain layers—This option will import your Fireworks file
as a movie clip. All original layers are also imported as they appear in Fireworks. The
movie clip is inserted into the current layer and keyframe. This is the recommended
option in this task because there are multiple layers in the PNG file.

Import into new layer in current scene—This will import your Fireworks file onto a
single, new layer, regardless of how many layers appear in the original PNG file.
Where frames are used in a Fireworks file, they are retained.

5. Select an option for the handling of vector paths and objects:

Rasterize if necessary to maintain appearance—Selecting this option will import
vector objects while retaining their editability. However, any unsupported effects will
be converted to bitmaps within Flash. This option is recommended because it best
retains the overall look of the imported file.

Keep all paths editable—This will import vectors and objects as editable, with no
conversion to bitmaps. The drawback of this option is that any unsupported effects are
completely lost.

6. Decide on text handling:

Rasterize if necessary to maintain appearance—This option will retain the editability of text, unless it has special fills, strokes, or effects that are unsupported in Flash. Where these strokes are found, Flash will convert the text to a bitmap—this retains appearance over editablility. For this PNG-importing task, this is the option that you want to use.

Keep all text editable—As with importing vector paths, this option preserves the editability of all text. The drawback of this option is that any unsupported effects are completely lost.

> If you simply want to import your PNG file (a photograph, for example) as a single bitmap, then choose the check box reading Import as a single flattened bitmap. This will override all other options in the dialog.

7. Click OK to continue and import the file into Flash. The imported file is seen in Figure 13.9.

FIGURE 13.9

The imported PNG file is imported onto the Flash stage, based on the settings you chose in the dialog.

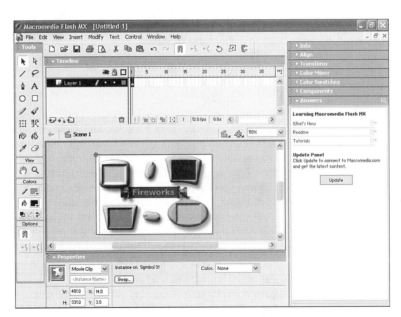

13

8. Notice that even though you chose to retain layers, the image initially appears as a single object. This is because it has come in as a movie clip symbol. To see all of the individual layers ready for editing, double-click the symbol on the stage. All layers are now visible in the Timeline, as shown in Figure 13.10

FIGURE 13.10

Double-clicking the newly created movie clip symbol will display all imported layers and their objects that are ready for editing.

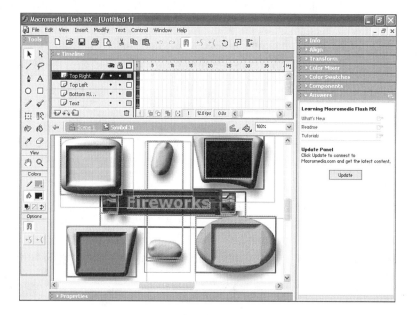

It's a good idea to create a graphics symbol or movie clip with a copy of your bitmap symbol in it. Place the bitmap object on the Canvas, select it with the Flash Pointer tool, and press F8 (Windows and Macintosh). Give the symbol a name similar to that of the bitmap, and use the symbol on the Flash Canvas whenever you would want to put in a copy of the bitmap. In this way you substitute another file for the the bitmap without using the update feature in the Bitmap Properties dialog, which would irreversibly erase the old bitmap data from the Flash source movie.

Use the symbol to add a mask layer to the bitmap or reposition the bitmap relative to the symbol center for scripted movement. Place it in another symbol, scene, or movie clip with other graphics. By transforming the symbol instead of the bitmap, you can replace the bitmap with another while preserving any modifications that you would otherwise have to repeat. When finished, you can delete the bitmap object from within the symbol before publishing and use a loadMovie command to load the bitmap into the animation from a JPEG file that was created in Fireworks. The Flash SWF will be much smaller, and you can update the bitmap whenever you like without having to open the source movie!

Exporting as JPEG or GIF for Image Call

If you're an advanced Flash user, you may be familiar with the loadMovie command in Flash ActionScript. In Flash MX you can use the loadMovie command to load Flash SWF animations, JPEG images, and MP3 sounds from external files. Fireworks can create SWF files or JPEG graphics for use in dynamic Flash movies. By using ActionScript to call an external SWF or JPEG file, you can change the contents of the file without having to publish the Flash movie again. To export a JPEG from Fireworks for use in Flash, simply choose the JPEG file format from the Format menu on the Optimize panel. Use the Export command from the File menu and choose Images Only from the Save as Type menu on the Export dialog.

Task: Use loadMovie to Load a JPEG Image into an SWF Animation

The loadMovie command in Flash allows you to call an image directly into a Flash symbol by using ActionScript. This task will take you through the steps required to do this using a prepared Flash file.

1. Using Flash MX, open the file `visit_hi_optimized.fla` from the `Hour 13` examples folder. Make sure the Flash Tools, Timeline, Actions, and Properties panels are visible, even if they are not expanded, as shown in Figure 13.11.

FIGURE 13.11

The file `visit_hi_optimized.fla` *will open to the first scene of the animation you originally created in Fireworks MX. The animation is all contained in the movie clip instance selected on the stage.*

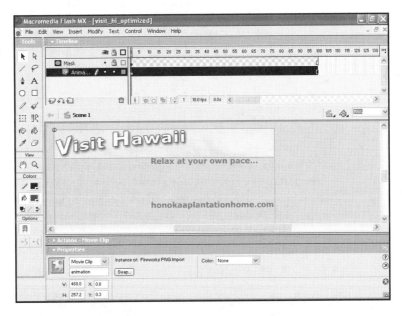

13

2. The first and only scene, Scene 1, has two layers: a mask layer named Mask and a
    masked layer named Animation. The mask layer is shown as a red outline; lock
    both layers to preview the mask. Notice that in Flash the settings for changing
    layers are located in the Timeline panel. Unlike Fireworks, Flash doesn't have a
    dedicated layers panel. The Animation layer has an instance of a Fireworks PNG
    Import movie clip named Animation on the keyframe at frame 1. With the bottom
    layer unlocked, double-click anywhere in the animated movie clip on the stage to
    edit it in place, as done in Figure 13.12.

FIGURE 13.12

*Double-click a symbol
on the stage to edit the
symbol in place.
Changes made to
a symbol will be
mirrored in all
symbol instances in
the movie, just as in
Fireworks.*

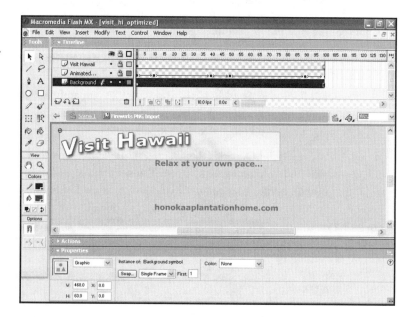

3. Above the stage will be a bar noting that you're working on the movie clip
    Fireworks PNG Import under Scene 1. You're going to replace the bitmap object
    within the symbol on the background layer with a dynamically loaded file. Click
    the graphic of clouds, an instance of the Background symbol. In the Flash Property
    Inspector, change the instance from a Graphic to a Movie Clip, using the symbol
    type menu in the upper left-hand corner. A field will appear below, so that you can
    name the symbol instance **background**, as in Figure 13.13, and press Return.

FIGURE 13.13

By changing the type of symbol instance, you can give it an instance name for reference in ActionScript.

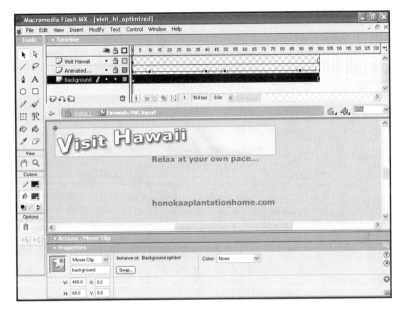

4. Double-click the Background symbol instance to edit it in place. There is one frame with a copy of the bitmap object background on it. Select this frame by clicking it in the Timeline, and expand the Actions panel above the Property Inspector by clicking the white arrow next to the word "Actions." The expanded Actions panel is shown in Figure 13.14.

FIGURE 13.14

Clicking the frame and expanding the Actions panel allows you to add a scripted action to that frame.

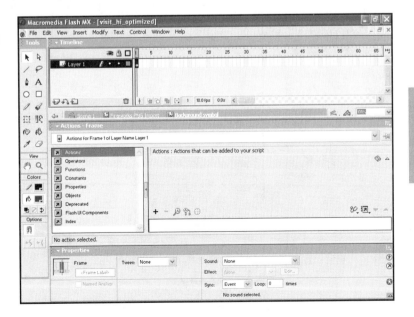

13

5. On the left of the Actions panel is the list of commands. Click Actions to expand the Actions commands. Click Browser/Network to expand this group, as well. Double-click the loadMovie command to add it to the script window on the bottom. Notice that the top of the panel displays a description of the command.

> With a command selected in the Actions panel, you click the blue book icon to see the reference material available for the command. This information is very helpful when learning about scripting. The Reference panel will open and display correct usage, parameters, and code examples.

6. The loadMovie settings will appear above the Script window. Set the URL field to `background.jpg`, a file in your Hour 13 examples folder. You can use any absolute or relative URL and can reference a JPEG image, SWF animation, or MP3 audio file.

7. The Location field allows you to specify where the external file will be loaded. You can specify a Level or Target to load the movie into. A Level can be from 0 to 9 and can be used to layer Flash movies. A Target is a specific movie clip instance. In this case you'll want it to load in the instance background in the movie clip instance named Animation within the current movie. Type **_root.animation.background** in the Location field as the path to the target movie clip for the loaded file. When you're done, check the Actions panel against Figure 13.15.

FIGURE 13.15

You've added a loadMovie command to the first frame in the symbol in order to load an image from an external JPEG file into the symbol.

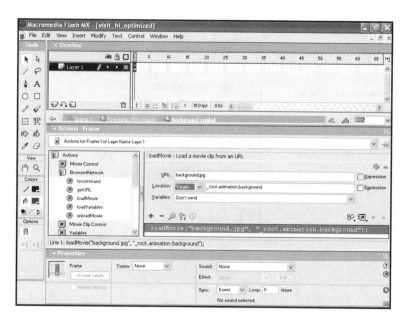

8. Collapse the Actions panel to reveal the stage. Now you can delete the bitmap object instance in this symbol. Select it with the Pointer tool and press Delete. To test whether the movie works, press Ctrl+Return (Windows) or Command+Return (Macintosh). As long as visit_hi_optimize.fla and background.jpg are in the Hour 13 examples folder together, it will work. A Flash SWF file named visit_hi_optimize.swf will be created in the Hour 13 folder when you test the movie.

Exporting from Flash to Fireworks

Fireworks is the perfect tool for working with images exported from Flash. You may need to export images as an alternative for users who don't have Flash, for use in other applications, or as previews or thumbnails of a Flash movie. Fireworks can be used for scaling, color adjustment, or Web compression optimization. Using the Batch Process feature discussed in Hour 18, "Batch Processing and Configuration Sharing," you can process whole directories of images at once.

To export an image file from Flash, choose the frame that you would like to export on the Timeline or within a symbol. Choose Export Image from the File menu in Flash. Choose a format for export. If you want to preserve vectors for editing in Fireworks, choose the EPS or Adobe Illustrator formats. If you want a flat bitmap image, choose PNG, JPEG, GIF, or Bitmap BMP. After choosing a file name and clicking Save, you will be asked for the image dimensions and format settings. The options for PNG export are shown in Figure 13.16. Choose Minimum Image Area if you want the image trimmed to contain only the objects on the Flash Canvas. Choose Full Document Size if you want the entire area of the Flash Canvas. Set the compression and file options, and click OK to continue.

FIGURE 13.16

PNG export is your best bet for a quality bitmap export from Flash. Use Full Document Size to export only the stage area.

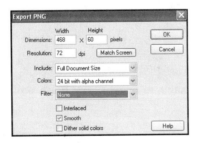

13

To export an entire scene or symbol as a series of images, choose Export Movie from the File menu in Flash. You can choose to export a sequence of EPS, Adobe Illustrator, PNG, JPEG, GIF, or Bitmap images—one for each frame in the scene or symbol. The file name that is typed will be appended with a number, such as `flash_frames0001` if **flash_frames** were typed. Choose the format specifications as you would for a single image. Images exported from Flash can be opened in Fireworks, imported into an existing Fireworks source PNG, added to a batch list or project log, or even used as a pattern or texture.

It's important that you make critical content available to users who do not use Flash. You can simply export a keyframe as a 32-bit PNG, open it in Fireworks, optimize it as a JPEG, and export it as HTML and Images. Save the file, along with your published Flash movie. Put a link in the HTML exported from Flash with the Flash movie to the alternate JPEG version that you created in Fireworks. Check the Macromedia Web site, at `http://www.macromedia.com/`, for information on how to test for the Flash Player and redirect users automatically.

Summary

Fireworks MX and Flash MX are now much more powerful when combined, thanks to the similarity in their user interfaces and in the compatibility of their tools. You can work fluidly with vector paths, bitmap objects, text, and animation in either application. Fireworks offers all bitmap-editing tools that are missing in Flash, although Flash can take your Web graphics and interactivity to the next level with its advanced animation and scripting features. To learn more about Flash MX, why not try *Sams Teach Yourself Macromedia Flash MX in 24 Hours* by Phillip Kerman?

Workshop

In this hour you have learned to use Flash MX with Fireworks. Review the questions, answers, and exercises in this section to sharpen your Flash skills.

Q&A

Q When I export a SWF animation from Fireworks, why is the file so big?

A Fireworks is not the best place to produce optimized Flash SWF files. Features such as shared layers are not used as efficiently as they could be. Exporting a SWF from Fireworks should be used only when file size is not critical or as a way to export one or more bitmapped objects for reference from another SWF by using the loadMovie command.

Q **I've imported a Fireworks source PNG into my Flash movie. Where did all the effects go?**

A Flash does not support Fireworks effects—items must be merged into bitmap in order to import with effects into Flash. This can be achieved by choosing to preserve appearance instead of to maintain path outlines when importing.

Q **Using ActionScript, I reference a JPEG file for a bitmap object. When I e-mail the animation to my friend, though, why doesn't the image appear as part of the movie?**

A The JPEG file must reside on a Web server or on the other user's hard drive. If it was e-mailed with the SWF as an attachment, the loadMovie command will not be able to access the JPEG content. Place the JPEG file on a Web server, and use an absolute path in the loadMovie command to make an SWF that can be attached and e-mailed while still loading the appropriate file. It's recommended that you also post the SWF to the Web server and e-mail a link to the movie instead because some e-mail systems will block attachments entirely.

Quiz

1. What file format should you use to import vector paths from Flash into a Fireworks document?

   a. PNG

   b. Adobe Illustrator

   c. Flash SWF

2. What compression formats are supported by Fireworks SWF export?

   a. JPEG

   b. GIF

   c. PNG

3. At a rate of 15 frames per second, for how many seconds would a 45-frame animation play?

   a. 15

   b. 5

   c. 3

Quiz Answers

1. b.—The Adobe Illustrator format supports most of the Flash vector path and editable text features and can be opened or imported into a Fireworks document.

13

2. a.—Fireworks SWF export can use only JPEG compression and often creates a file that can benefit from further optimization. Import the graphics into Flash straight from the Fireworks source PNG for more control over SWF optimization.

3. c.—Divide the number of frames (45) by the frame rate (15) to determine the duration in seconds: 45 frames / 15 fps = 3 seconds.

Exercises

1. Try importing more PNG files into Flash. Change the settings in the Import dialog to see how this changes the editability of the imported items. These settings need to be analyzed with each individual image to ensure that you always get the best from the integration.

2. Use the animation skills you learned in Hour 11, "Planning and Creating Animation for the Web," and Hour 12, "Improving and Finishing Your Animation," to create an animation. Then export your Fireworks animation to Flash and use the power of Flash to extend your animation capabilities.

3. Spend a little time learning more about Flash. It's not only a powerful tool in its own right but also a very handy companion application when working with Fireworks. Using the drawing tools in Fireworks is a great way to get started with more complex animations in Flash.

PART V

Designing Web Pages: Layout, Interactivity and Publishing

Hour

HOUR 14

Slicing Layouts

One of the most powerful strategies for designing Web pages is to quickly cut up an image into small parts to add links, save file size, and arrange graphics and animation on a page along with text. Using the Web Layer in Fireworks MX, you can create slice objects to partition your template layout into areas that are then exported into separate files. Slices can also be named, optimized individually, and then exported with HTML code for the Web and other applications.

In this hour you will

- Learn how to fit slices into your workflow
- Create slices on the Web Layer
- Use slices to refine optimization
- Export slices as individual images along with HTML table code

What Are Slices, and Why Should I Use Them?

In the early days of the Web, the people who put many current standards in place didn't necessarily envision the explosion of color, sound, and movement that Web pages now use regularly. The basic language of Web pages—Hypertext Markup Language, or HTML—was designed very specifically for academic documents. The early developers thought only scientists and professors would likely use the Web, since it was largely intended as a research and communication tool.

When commercial interests began to hire graphic designers to create visually compelling Web pages, the designers had to work around the limitations of HTML as a design medium with what were sometimes inelegant solutions. The most important innovation was with HTML tables, which were originally meant for laying out rows and columns of statistics and data. Using tables, text and graphics could be laid out together with more control, and file sizes could be kept minimal. Being able to hand-code, or hack, tables became a fundamental Web design skill. But coding these intricate tables and cropping all the graphics to fit were complicated and time consuming—making small changes took almost as long as reworking the whole layout.

Fireworks came to the rescue with a system for cutting up source images and automatically computing the HTML code necessary for the table layout. A slice represents an area of the source image that will be exported as an individual file and laid out with other slices using an HTML table. Of course, slices can also be used for simply making multiple crops from a single image or for cutting graphics up for use in Flash or Director as individual symbols or cast members. Fireworks can export slices for use as a graphics library for a site in Dreamweaver MX, for instance. And because designers are beginning to move away from HTML, Fireworks can create layouts using cascading style sheets (CSS) or XHTML, as well.

According to the World Wide Web Consortium, which governs such matters, HTML will be phased out in favor of XML. It declares, "XHTML ... is the next step in the evolution of the Internet." In other words, XHTML is the "bridge language" that will get us to XML. In theory, XHTML provides a markup language that doesn't force developers to re-create the same document for different browsers or different devices, because the extensibility mechanism will eventually be able to sniff out the client and return the right information in the right form, whether the device is a high-resolution computer monitor or a four-line PDA.

Creating Slices on the Web Layer

To create a slice on the Web Layer, simply select the Slice tool by pressing K, and click-drag to create a rectangular slice, as in Figure 14.1. Most slices are rectangular since bitmap image files and HTML table cells are also rectangular. A transparent green box with red outlines will appear on the canvas. Lines will also appear, running away from the top and bottom of the sliced image. Because of how tables work, slice guides are created. This ensures that when loading into a browser separately, the slice and the rest of the image come together accurately to form a complete image. You can arrange other slices along these guides or choose not to export areas that aren't actually part of a slice.

FIGURE 14.1

The Slice tool can create a slice object on the Web Layer. Each slice object represents an HTML table cell and can contain either an image file or HTML code.

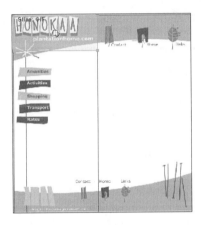

When a slice is created or selected, the Web Layer will automatically become the active layer in the Layers panel. A slice is an object just like a bitmap, path, text, group, or symbol and can be copied or pasted, but it cannot be grouped or placed on any layer other than the Web Layer. Slices also apply to all frames—the Web Layer is always shared across frames. Slices on the Web Layer can be selected with the Pointer tool. To change the dimensions of a slice, click any of the square handles at the corners of the bounding box with the Pointer tool and drag to change the position of that corner, as shown in Figure 14.2.

14

FIGURE 14.2

Click any of the square handles with the Pointer tool to change the dimensions of a slice.

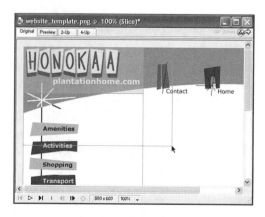

While changing or creating slices, the cursor will snap to other slices or slice guides already on the Web Layer. This is important, since overlapping slices will not display correctly when laid out using HTML tables. Use the Zoom tool to magnify slice borders to make sure that slices are correctly aligned before finally exporting. You can also use the slice guides, which are the lines that extend from the slice bounding boxes into areas of the document that aren't sliced. You can use the Pointer tool to click and drag these guidelines to change any of the bounding boxes along the guide, as in Figure 14.3.

FIGURE 14.3

Click any of the slice guides with the Pointer tool to change the dimensions of any slice adjoining that guide.

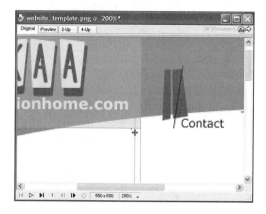

When working with graphics, you can lock or hide the slice layer to make sure you don't make any inadvertent changes to the image slicing. You can change the color of the slice guides and decide whether to show or hide them by choosing Edit Guides from the Guides commands on the View menu. For the same reason, it's also good to lock layers with graphics before working with the Web Layer. Slices and their settings can be saved with the document only by using the Save command from the File menu to create a Fireworks source PNG.

Sometimes you may need to create slices that aren't rectangular. You can press K to toggle between the Slice tool and the Polygon Slice tool. You can also select a vector path object on the Canvas and choose Slice from the Insert commands on the Edit menu to convert it into a rectangular or polygon slice on the Web Layer. Polygon slices are exported as regular rectangular bitmaps with a polygon image map hotspot. For more information about using Polygonal Slices and hotspots for image maps, check out the next hour, "Creating Interactive Graphics."

Task: Slice a Web Page Layout

▲ TASK

In this task you will develop an image that already has some basic slices in place. You will add and size further slices in appropriate parts of the file.

1. Open the file `website_template.png` from the `Hour 14` examples folder. The file, shown in Figure 14.4, already has three slices that have been named. The title has been sliced at the top, and the footer has been sliced at the bottom, with the body of the page in the middle. You'll be creating slices for the icons on the top and for the column of topics on the left.

FIGURE 14.4

*The file
website_template.png
has all the graphics
layers locked in the
Layers panel so that
you can work with
slices without worrying
about changing the
design.*

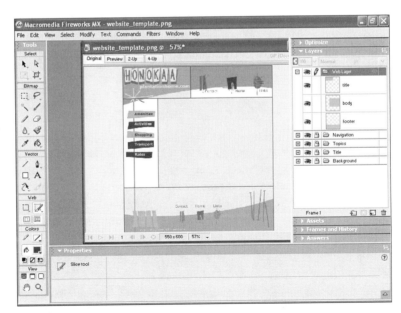

14

2. Select the Slice tool from the Tools panel. Begin by clicking at the top right corner of the title slice and dragging to cover the contact button, with the bottom adjoining the top of the middle body slice. You don't have to be too accurate—the slice will snap to the existing guides so that it will appear as in Figure 14.5. If there's a problem, change the dimensions in the Property Inspector to 108 pixels wide, 115 pixels tall, with an X position of 250 and a Y position of 0. Using the Property Inspector, name the slice **contact** and type **E-Mail to reserve now!** into the Alt field.

FIGURE 14.5

With the Slice tool, you've created a new image slice for the top contact link. Using the Property Inspector, you've named the slice and given it an alternate text description.

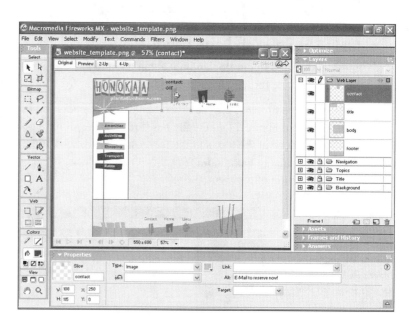

3. Continue to create slices for the Home and Links buttons across the top, until you have four slices across the top of the image, as shown in Figure 14.6. Name the home button slice **home** and type **Home** in the Alt field. Name the links button slice **links** and type **Links** in the Alt field. The exact dimensions are 102 wide, 115 tall, 358 X position, and 0 Y position for the home button slice; and 90 wide, 115 tall, 460 X position, and 0 Y position for the links button slice.

FIGURE **14.6**

The top navigation elements have now been sliced, allowing you to add links, a text description, and individual optimization to areas of the document.

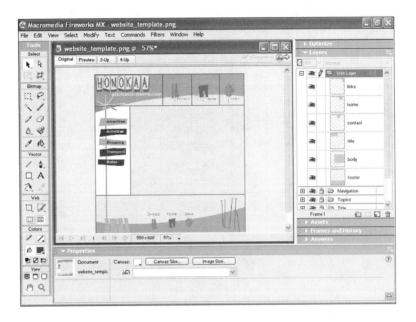

4. Now go ahead and slice up the left column for the topic buttons. First slice the area between the title and the first button and name it **left_top.** There is no need for an Alt description, since there is no text or link for this slice. Continue slicing each button, giving it a name and Alt description to match the text for the topic. Finally, slice the remaining area above the footer slice and name it **left_background**—this can be tiled in its table cell so that the line will continue unbroken if the text in the body extends past the length of the images. There is no support for Alt tags with background images. The slices are shown in Figure 14.7 for your reference.

Leaving the alt field for a slice blank will result in "" for the image's alt tag in the exported HTML, which is recommended accessibility practice for images without content.

14

The dimensions you choose are not critical, just as long as each button is completely contained in its own slice. Also sliced are the areas above and below the buttons. Each slice has been named for easy access from the Layers panel.

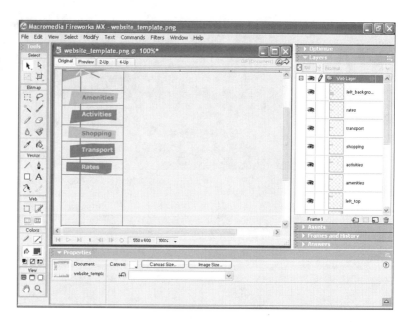

5. Use Save from the File menu to save your slices. A completed version, `website_sliced.png`, has been saved in the `Hour 14` folder for use in the next task.

Specifying Slice Properties

To change the settings for a slice selected with the Pointer tool, simply use the Property Inspector panel. Slice settings include the slice name, dimensions, position, and type. The names are automatically appended with row and column designators. The slice name in the Property Inspector will be used to name the file when the area is exported. You can change the width, height, and X and Y positions by entering new values in the Property Inspector. You can also change the color of the slice if it's interfering with the graphics layered below. Click the color swatch in the middle of the Property Inspector to change the color of the slice.

Other settings depend on the type of slice. A slice can be either an Image slice or an HTML slice. An image slice area will be exported as an image file and laid out on the page in a table cell. An HTML slice area will add a portion of HTML code, such as HTML tags or text.

When using the Reconstitute Table command on the File menu to import an existing Web page and graphics as a Fireworks source PNG, or when working with Dreamweaver MX, you can edit non-image portions of the HTML source within areas defined by an HTML slice. No graphics are exported in areas covered by an HTML slice.

Image slice settings include the compression preset to be used; a URL, or Web link, that's activated when a user clicks the image; a value for the Alt tag, which is used as an alternate text description for systems that don't display images; and a target attribute for the link to open the link in another frame or window. If you don't want to use a compression preset for the selected slice, change the optimization settings through the Optimize panel. Each slice can be optimized with different settings. To apply new settings to multiple slices simultaneously, use Shift+click with the Pointer tool to select more than one slice, and then specify settings through the Optimize panel or choose a preset from the Property Inspector.

It's important to use Alt tags to describe images whenever possible—especially if the image contains text, such as a title or link. Though only a small percentage of users use Web browsers or systems that don't display images, they are still part of a global audience. Many users with slow systems or Internet connections choose not to display images because of the slowdown. This is especially true of handheld wireless users, whose screens are small and with very limited bandwidth. Alt tags also help search engines better categorize the content on your site, potentially increasing valuable traffic.

Task: Apply a Common GIF Palette to All Slices

Ensuring that your exported HTML exports and is rebuilt correctly is a vital part of using slices. Ensuring consistency of your colors is a major part of that process. In this task you will create a single palette for all of your slices.

1. Open the `website_template.png` from the `Hour 14` examples folder if you completed and saved your changes from the last task. Otherwise, open the file `website_sliced.png`, which contains all the changes made in the last task.

2. First you'll create a common palette for each slice. If you apply an adaptive palette to each slice, Fireworks may sometimes choose a slightly different approximate color for two slice areas, which is not what you want at all. Choose Select All from the Select menu or press Ctrl+A (Windows) or Command+A (Macintosh). Now choose Cut from the Edit menu or press Ctrl+X (Windows) or Command+X (Macintosh). This will delete the slices but copy them to the clipboard.

3. Expand the Optimize panel. Choose GIF from the file type menu and Adaptive from the palette menu. Set the color depth to 256 colors. The palette will show the 256 colors chosen for the entire image, as in Figure 14.8. Use the Save Palette command from the Optimize panel Options menu to save this set of colors for use as a custom palette. The file `website_palette.act` has already been saved in the `Hour 14` examples folder for you.

14

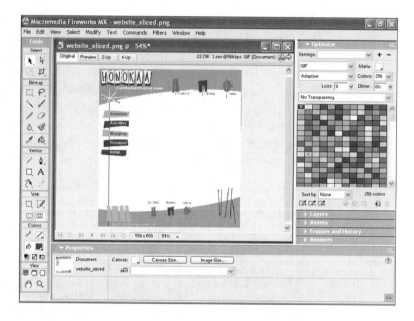

4. Use Paste from the Edit menu or press Ctrl+V (Windows) or Command+V (Macintosh) to paste the slices back onto the Web layer. This will restore all the slices on the clipboard.

> You can copy and paste slices within Fireworks, but they will paste as paths or bitmaps into other applications and will not retain any slice data.

5. With all the slices selected and the Optimize panel expanded, choose GIF from the file type menu. From the palette menu choose Custom. Select the palette you just saved or choose website_palette.act from the Hour 14 examples folder. Make sure the color depth is set to 256 colors—with Remove Unused Colors checked in the Optimize panel Options menu, each slice area will use only the colors in the custom palette it needs, reducing file size. Leave the Loss and Dither settings at 0, with no transparency. The settings are shown in Figure 14.9.

FIGURE **14.9**

Using the custom palette, you can be sure every slice area will use the same set of colors as the others. By removing unused colors, file size is kept at a minimum.

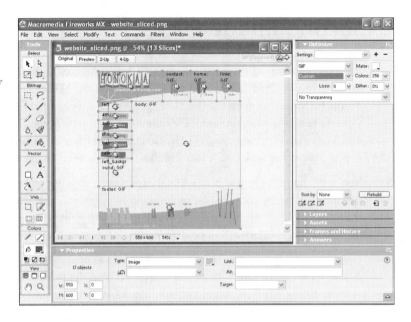

6. Choose Save from the File menu to save the optimized document. To preview the optimized image, click the Preview tab at the top of the document workspace window. Uncheck Slice Guides and Slice Overlay on the View menu to turn off the slice guides and overlay, as in Figure 14.10. Because of the optimized palette and non-lossy GIF compression, the image will be almost identical to the source image.

FIGURE **14.10**

The size of all the exported slices is shown above the preview image—in this case less than 25KB. You should try to keep a Web page under 35KB total, which means you have 10.6KB of room left for the accompanying HTML table code.

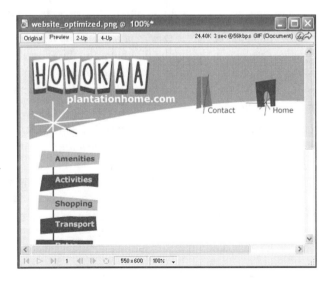

14

Exporting Image Slices

To export a template layout with slices on a Web layer with or without HTML code, use the Export command from the File menu. Choose Images Only from the Save as Type menu if you don't need to export HTML code. Choose HTML and Images if you want to export HTML along with the sliced images. When exporting HTML, you can click the Options button to bring up the HTML Setup dialog, which you'll learn about in more detail in Hour 16, "Exporting HTML Code from Fireworks," along with other code export topics. For now you'll focus on how slicing affects image export.

You may choose to turn slicing off and export the entire document at the canvas optimization setting by choosing None from the Slices menu. Export Slices will export all slice objects. Slice Along Guides will use the layout guides placed with the rulers as the slicing scheme but will not export symbol properties like behaviors.

Options for image slicing include a check box to export Selected Slices Only, which exports only one or more slice objects selected with the Pointer tool. Include Areas Without Slices will export areas of the canvas between the slice guides that aren't part of a slice object. If there are more than one frame, you may choose to export all the frames or the Current Frame Only. If you are exporting HTML and Images, you can save the images to a subfolder relative to the location of the HTML file. Click Browse to change the folder.

Task: Export the Layout

Now that you have added all of your slices, it is time to export the layout, ready for Web usage. The following steps will take you through the process and available options:

1. Open the file `website_optimized.png` from the `Hour 14` examples folder. With the body slice selected and using the Edit button in the Property Inspector, the body slice has been changed from an image slice to an HTML slice, and some code has been inserted. All the layers are locked, so you don't have to worry about accidentally changing anything.

2. Choose Export from the File menu or press Ctrl+Shift+R (Windows) or Command+Shift+R (Macintosh). This will open the Export dialog. Type **index** in the File name field to make it the home page for a Web site. Choose HTML and Images from the Save as Type menu to export HTML code along with image files. You do not need to type the file extension, as this will be added automatically during the file export process

3. Make sure that Export HTML File is selected from the HTML menu and that Export Slices is selected from the Slices menu. Since none of the document is outside of a slice area, it doesn't matter whether Include Areas without Slices is checked. Leaving the Put Images in Subfolder box unchecked will put the HTML and image files together in the same directory, whereas checking it will allow you to locate a specific images folder. Choose the option that best suits the structure of your Web site.

4. Navigate to the Fireworks Examples folder and create a new directory named Honokaa. You can check your settings against those shown in Figure 14.11.

FIGURE 14.11

These settings will export into Honokaa *folder an HTML file named* index.html *along with an image file for each image slice in the document.*

5. Using My Computer from the Start menu (Windows) or the Finder (Macintosh), navigate to the Fireworks Examples folder. Right-click the Honokaa folder and select Properties (Windows), or click to select the Honokaa folder and press Command+I (Macintosh), to bring up the folder information—this will give you the total size for the Web page with graphics and code. The size in kilobytes should be very close to that shown in Figure 14.12.

14

FIGURE **14.12**

*Using Properties
(Windows) or Get Info
(Macintosh), you can
view the sizes of all the
files in a directory to
make sure your Web
pages are under 35KB.*

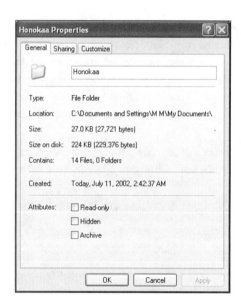

6. Close the Properties dialog (Windows) or the Get Info dialog (Macintosh), and double-click the file index.html to open it in your default browser. The Web page should look something like Figure 14.13. Not all hardware, operating systems, and Web browsers will display exactly the same way.

FIGURE **14.13**

*The Web site home-
page you just created
is shown in Internet
Explorer 6.0 for
Windows XP. You've
taken pains to make
sure the content is
available in almost any
browser or system by
using Alt descriptions
and HTML code.*

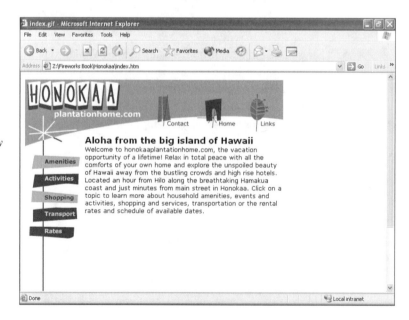

Summary

Whether or not you want to create your graphics in Fireworks, you can still use Fireworks to segment your layout into files for an HTML table layout using slices. With the tricks shown here, you can create Web pages that load really fast and that every user can access and navigate easily. In the next hour, "Creating Interactive Graphics," you'll start adding interactivity, including links and button behaviors that respond to the user.

Workshop

In this hour you have learned about slicing layouts in preparation for use on the Web as well as techniques for changing and formatting sliced layouts. Use this final part of the hour to review these skills and topics.

Q&A

Q What is an HTML table, and why should I care?

A HTML, the standard for coding Web pages, was originally devised as a format for storing text documents like research papers. Tables were meant to lay out numbers, but they also worked for images and became a means for creating advanced graphic layouts for the Web. Fireworks was originally created to help designers and developers create HTML tables with images more quickly and easily.

Q How can I use slices to reduce the file size and increase the quality of an exported layout?

A Slices can separate text and line art from photographs so that different types of compression can be applied to different areas of an image. Slices are not limited to the Web standards GIF and JPEG—slices can be optimized for any format, including PNG, TIF, and BMP.

Q How are Alt image descriptions displayed in a Web browser?

A Alt tags are displayed differently in different browsers. Internet Explorer displays Alt tags when a user mouses over an image with an Alt description. Text browsers, such as Lynx for UNIX, display Alt tags as links to the image file so that the user can choose to download the image described or follow the link from the image. Some browsers read page text to the user through text-to-speech conversion; such a browser will read the alternate description for each image as it progresses through the page. The Alt tags for images in a Web page are ordered on the page from left to right and then from top to bottom.

14

Quiz

1. What makes the Web Layer different from other layers?

   a. The Web Layer cannot be deleted.

   b. The Web Layer cannot be unshared.

   c. The Web Layer can contain only slices.

2. What group of Web users can never view your layout and must rely on image descriptions?

   a. Cellular phone Web browsers.

   b. Users of ASCII terminal Web browsers, such as Lynx.

   c. Users with browsers that convert text to speech.

3. How can you specify the name of the exported file created by a slice?

   a. By selecting the slice with the Pointer tool and changing the name in the Property Inspector.

   b. By double-clicking the slice name in the Layers panel and typing a new name.

   c. By changing the file-naming convention in the HTML Setup dialog.

Quiz Answers

1. a., b., and c.—The Web Layer is particular to Fireworks. It is always shared across frames, cannot be deleted from any Fireworks document, and can contain only slices. Slices cannot be stored on any layer but the Web Layer.

2. a., b., and c.—Most major Web browsers allow you to disable image downloads to speed up Web browsing. They will display HTML formatting and image Alt descriptions, however. Users on wireless systems, such as cell phones, rarely display images, because of the size and color constraints on handheld devices. People with older mainframe systems or who use UNIX/Linux may use a text-only Web browser, such as Lynx. Of course, a user who is blind or otherwise has poor eyesight may have a browser that reads the page back or outputs it to a Braille pad; for such a user an alternate description is the only way to get this information.

3. a., b., and c.—Any of these methods will work for naming exported slices. You will go over the HTML Setup dialog in more detail in Hour 16, "Exporting HTML Code from Fireworks."

Exercises

1. Now that you have an understanding of how slicing works as a concept, try putting it into practice on your Web pages. In the next hour you will look at interactive graphics. Before you get there, however, try experimenting with simply slicing large images to enhance download time. The benefits of this can be hugely beneficial to your Web site in terms of reduced download time alone.

2. Learn a little more about HTML slices, which are a great way of being able to add editable text atop an image. Try this technique: If you have a message that you want to be editable within a graphic layout, simply add an HTML slice. Then, when the file is exported, you can format and edit the text in Dreamweaver without needing to edit the source file at any time

3. Try creating nonrectangular slices in an image. Even if this seems a little strange as a concept, it gives you the opportunity to use Alt tags to identify different areas of an image. This is a perfect thing to do on an old school or work photograph where you want to identify numerous people.

14

HOUR **15**

Creating Interactive Graphics

Fireworks MX isn't just a tool for laying out graphics and tables for Web pages. Another important feature is the ability to add interactivity to these graphic elements. Interactivity includes linking an image to another Web page, creating button rollover effects, and creating navigation elements, such as drop-down menus.

In this hour you'll learn how to use slices and symbols to make a Web page more responsive to users. You will

- Assign links to slices and image map hotspots
- Add behaviors to slices, such as a Rollover button
- Create interactive button symbols for use across a Web site
- Use the Library panel to edit and organize symbols

Adding Links and Hotspots to Slices

The simplest way to add a link to an element on the Canvas is to draw a slice over the graphic and type a URL into the Link field on the Property

Inspector with the slice selected. A URL is a link to another file, such as an HTML Web page. *URL* stands for Uniform Resource Locator, and this is a standard way to refer to files on Web servers.

A URL defines a path, starting with the domain name of the server and moving through the server's directories, to find a particular file name. A URL path can be absolute, which means that it contains the protocol, domain name, directory path, and file. An absolute path would look like `http://www.domain.com/folder/file.jpg`. A URL can also be relative, which means that the path to the file is written out in relation to the current file. A link to `file.jpg` would look for the specified image file in the same directory as the current file. A link to `folder/file.jpg` would look for the image file in the directory named `folder` below the current directory. Use the special designator `../` to move up to the parent directory from the current directory, as in `../folder/file.jpg`. Use it more than once to move up through multiple parent directories, such as `../../../file.jpg`.

An absolute URL can work without knowing the current server and directory context; links in an e-mail are almost always absolute URLs because the e-mail could end up on any system. Relative URLs must link to documents on the same system because the full URL is determined from the context of the page that references it. Relative URLs are often used so that a set of files can exist on more than one system, allowing the author or designer to create a functional copy on the local hard drive.

By default, the Library panel is in the Assets panel group. Another panel in the Assets panel group is the URL panel. The URL panel makes it easy to organize common links in a document or a Web site. Links are stored in an HTML file in the URL Libraries folder under the Fireworks MX application folder. You can add a URL to a library by typing it in the Link field at the top of the URL panel and then clicking the Add Current URL to Library button to the right of the Link menu. Use the Import URLs or Export URLs command from the URL panel Options menu to add URLs from an existing HTML file or to create an HTML library file. You can use the New URL Library command to create a new URL library file in the URL Libraries folder. Select a URL from the URL panel list, and choose Edit URL or Delete URL from the URL panel Options menu to edit or delete the selected URL. Select a slice or hotspot object on the Web Layer with the Pointer tool, and choose the link from the URL panel URL list or from the Link menu in the Property Inspector to apply it.

Another way to add a link to an image is with an image map. An image map is a portion of HMTL code that describes areas of an image that will respond to a user's mouse-click with a URL link. Image map information is contained in the Web page, not in the image itself, and is invisible. Linked areas of an image are called *hotspots*. A hotspot can be a

15

rectangle, any polygon, or an ellipse, for example. Hotspots can be used to add multiple links to a single slice or to designate a specific area of the slice as a link instead of the whole slice image. Hotspots are stored on the Web Layer along with slices.

Task: Add a Link and Hotspots to a Sliced Layout

In this task you will take the website.png file, which you have worked on previously, and add links to the appropriate slices. The end result will be correctly linked slices and hotspot linking to the main areas of the Honokaa Web site.

1. Open the file website.png from the Hour 15 examples folder. This is the Web site layer that you worked on in the previous hour, "Slicing Layouts." You'll just be adding links, so only the Web Layer is unlocked.

2. Expand the Assets panel group and click the URL panel tab to bring up the URL panel. Click the URL panel Options menu and select the Import URLs command. Select the file HonokaaLinks.htm, also in the Hour 15 examples folder. A list of URLs for the page will appear in the URL panel URL list, as shown in Figure 15.1.

You can build up your library of common URLs either by typing them all into a single HTML document and then following Step 2, or by importing them from multiple files. You can also import them from any saved .png file that has URLs within it. Using a .png file, choose the Add Used URLs option.

FIGURE 15.1
You can import URLs from any HTML file and add them to the URL Library.

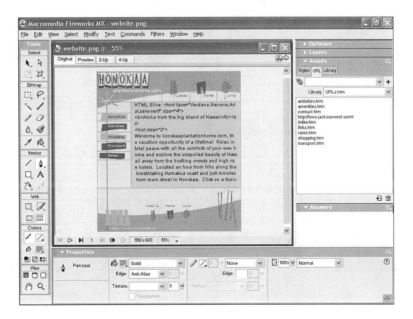

3. Go ahead and apply the appropriate link to the slices with icons at the top and the five topic slices on the left. These include the `contact`, `links`, `amenities`, `activities`, `shopping`, `transport`, and `rates` slices that you created and named in the last hour. Simply match the name of the link to the name of the slice— `contact.htm` for the `contact` slice, `links.htm` for the `links` slice, and so on. The only exception is the `home` slice. Because this is the home page, this link won't be active, so do not add a link to this slice for now.

4. At the bottom of the page is a single large slice that has four images you want to link from—the three navigation icons and the design credit. To add separate links for these areas of the slice, select the rectangle Hotspot tool by pressing J or clicking it on the Tools panel. Click and drag to create rectangular areas over the four link elements, as in Figure 15.2. It's not critical if the hotspots aren't exactly aligned, as long as they cover the graphics and text in the image.

FIGURE 15.2

You can create multiple links within a single image slice by using the Hotspot tool.

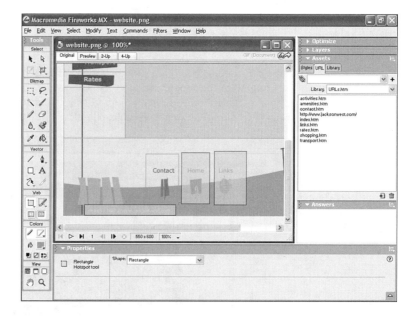

5. Select a hotspot object with the Pointer tool. Type any text covered by the hotspot into the hotspot name and the Alt field in the Property Inspector. Name the design credit hotspot `credit`, but type the full text into the Alt description. You can also use the Link menu in the Property Inspector to apply the appropriate link from the URL

library. Apply the link `contact.htm` to the `contact` hotspot, `index.htm` to the `home` hotspot, `links.htm` to the `links` hotspot, and `http://www.jacksonwest.com/` to the `credit` hotspot, as in Figure 15.3.

Once created, a hotspot is just like a slice in that you can simply click a URL in the URL tab of the Assets panel to apply a link.

FIGURE 15.3

The Property Inspector shows the properties for the design credit hotspot. Hotspot objects are also available on the Layers panel by expanding the Web Layer.

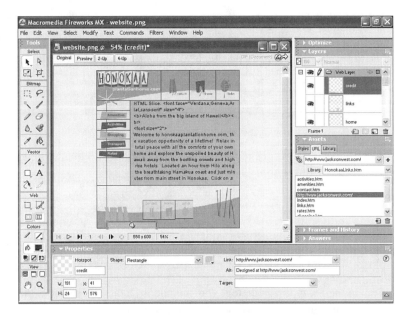

Adding Behaviors to Slices and Hotspots

Fireworks behaviors are actions that you can assign to slices and hotspots and that will respond to mouse events. These actions are performed by JavaScript, which Fireworks includes in the exported HTML code. JavaScript is a scripting language that can control how a browser displays elements of a Web page. You don't have to worry about coding any JavaScript if you simply use Fireworks behaviors to do the work for you.

When a slice or hotspot is selected with the Pointer tool, a behavior handle is visible in the center of the object. You can create a simple image swap by clicking the handle of the slice or hotspot you want to use as the trigger (when the mouse rolls over) and dragging the cursor to the slice you want to use as the target, including the same trigger slice. A hotspot can be a trigger, but it can't be a target. The target image can be swapped with an image in the same location on the Canvas in another frame. Choose the frame to be swapped with the target image from the Swap Image dialog, shown in Figure 15.4, which pops up when you assign a swap.

FIGURE 15.4

The Swap Image dialog allows you to choose the slice you want swapped and what to swap it with—an image on another frame or from another file.

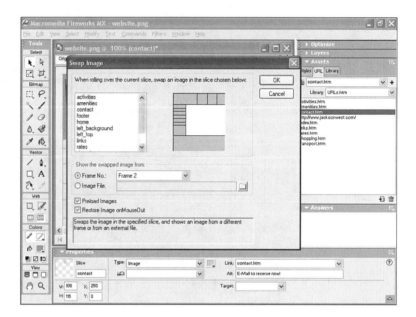

In the Swap Image dialog, you can choose a target slice from the list of slice names on the left or from the slice thumbnails on the right. You can swap the target slice with another frame from the document or from another image file. Click the Preload Images check box to have the browser download the swap image when the Web page loads and store it for faster swap response. Click the Restore Image onMouseOut check box to restore the target image when the mouse leaves the target area. Click OK to apply your changes. A curved blue line, as in Figure 15.5, will now connect the trigger slice to the target slice. You can add more than one target to a trigger slice to swap more than one image with a single mouseover.

FIGURE 15.5

Once a behavior has been selected, a curved blue line is added to the slice to indicate the presence of a behavior (see Contact button).

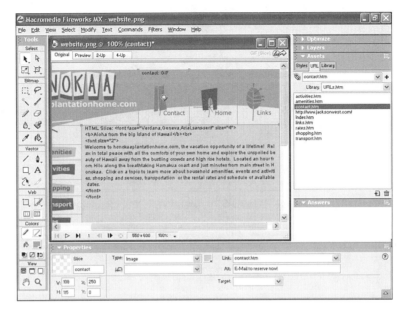

15

Click the behavior handle to bring up the Behavior menu for the selected hotspot or slice. This menu lists behaviors that can be applied to the selection and also allows you to clear any behaviors. The Behavior menu for a slice includes Add Simple Rollover Behavior, which simply swaps the selected slice on Frame 1 with the image on Frame 2; Add Swap Image Behavior, which brings up the Swap Image Options dialog to assign an image swap instead of dragging-and-dropping with the behavior handle; Add Status Bar Message, which changes the message in the gray status bar at the bottom of the Web browser window; Add Nav Bar, which expands the simple swap image behavior to enable you to have all four states of a navigation bar (this allows you to add third- and fourth-image swap states, not only swapping on mouseover but also showing where the user has visited); Add Pop-up Menu, which displays a customizable menu of links that appears when a user moves the mouse over the target area; and Delete All Behaviors, which clears any behaviors from the selected slice. You cannot use the simple rollover or nav bar behaviors with hotspots, but you can use any of the others.

To examine and edit the behaviors assigned to a slice or hotspot, use the Behaviors panel, shown in Figure 15.6, by selecting it from the Window menu or by pressing Shift+F3 (both Windows and Macintosh). From the Behaviors panel you can add, edit, or delete individual behaviors from a selected slice or hotspot. Click the Add Behavior button to add a behavior from the menu. Select a behavior and click the Remove Behavior button to delete it. Double-click a behavior for information on how to edit behavior options.

FIGURE 15.6

Use the Behaviors panel to add, edit, or remove behaviors associated with slice or hotspot objects. Clicking the Plus icon allows you to add a behavior from the list on the left.

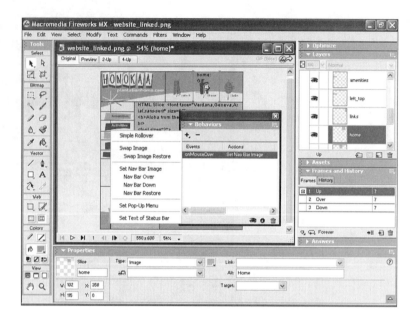

To change the event that triggers the behavior, select the behavior and use the arrow to the right of the current event trigger to bring up a menu of other events that can trigger the selected behavior. onMouseOver will trigger the behavior when the user places the mouse cursor over the trigger slice or hotspot area. onMouseOut will trigger the behavior when the cursor leaves the trigger area. onClick will trigger the behavior when the mouse is over the trigger area and the user clicks the mouse button. onLoad will trigger the action when the page loads in the browser window and does not require user intervention.

Task: Set Up Behaviors for Topics and Navigation

Now that you have seen how easy it is to add links and hotspots into your file, you will move on and add swap image and navigational behaviors to a Web site file. In this task you will use a new copy of the file called website_linked.png. This is the same file as used in the previous tasks but with all of the links in place. These links will act as the basis for your behaviors.

1. Open the file website_linked.png from the Hour 15 examples folder. This is the file you worked on in the previous task. All the slices already have interactive hyperlinks. You'll add rollover and nav bar behaviors to the linked elements.

2. Select the contact slice object with the Pointer tool. Click the behavior handle in the center to bring up the behavior pop-up menu, shown in Figure 15.7. Select Add Nav Bar by clicking it.

FIGURE 15.7

Clicking the behavior handle on a selected slice object allows you to select a behavior to apply from a pop-up menu.

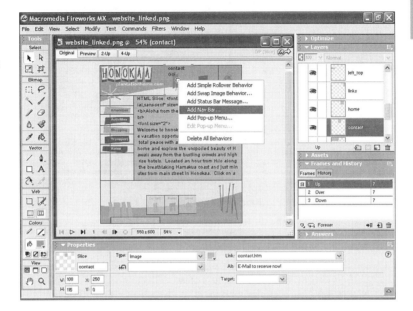

3. The Set Nav Bar Image dialog will appear, as in Figure 15.8. The Nav Bar behavior uses three frames that are already included in the document. The first frame, named Up, is how the slice will appear when the cursor is not over it. The second frame in the Frames panel, here named Over, is how the slice will appear with the cursor floating over it. The third frame, here named Down, is how the image will appear when clicked. The Nav Bar behavior also supports a fourth frame, called Over While Down; this is used when a button that's in the down state has another mouseover effect or link. Click the Include Over While Down State check box (Frame 4) if you will be using this behavior. For now, leave all boxes unchecked and click OK to continue.

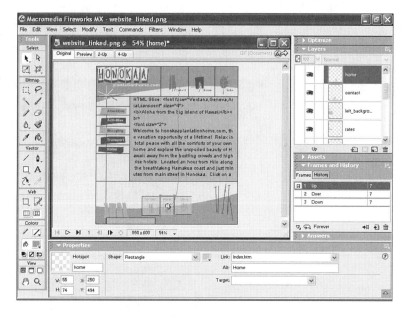

FIGURE 15.8
You can create a simple swap image behavior by simply clicking the selected slice's behavior handle and dragging to release the mouse over the target for the swap.

4. Now select the home slice with the Pointer tool. Click the behavior handle and choose Set Nav Bar, as before. This time check the Show Down Image Upon Load box. Because this is the home page, you don't need this part of the navigation to be active. Checking this box will show the slice from the third frame, Down, and the slice will not react when the mouse rolls over (unless a fourth frame is available and the Include Over While Down State box is checked).

5. Continue applying the Nav Bar behavior to the links, amenities, activities, shopping, transport, and rates slices as you did for the contact slice, leaving the check boxes in the Set Nav Bar Image dialog empty. When you are done, you can preview the navigation elements by pressing F12 to open the page in your favorite browser. The links won't function, because the pages haven't been created yet, but you can move your mouse around to activate the Over states for each nav element.

Creating Interactive Button Symbols

Another way to animate and activate graphics is to use symbols to create ready-made elements with behaviors intact. Symbols are stored in the Library panel for repeated use in the document. A sample Library panel is shown in Figure 15.9. Symbols are kind of like documents within the main document; a symbol can have its own layers, frames, and objects, including bitmaps, paths, text, groups, slices, and hotspots. Symbols can even include other symbols, which is called *nesting*.

FIGURE 15.9

The graphics in the layout have been broken down into symbols so that you can edit a symbol and cascade the changes across frames.

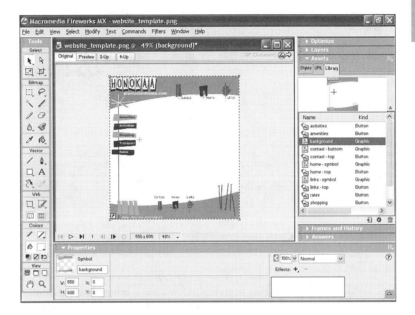

The advantage that symbols have over objects is that when you edit objects within a symbol, all the copies, or instances, of that symbol in the document reflect the change. If you change a symbol that's nested in another symbol, the change will cascade through both symbols and every instance of the two symbols in the document. You can create a hierarchy of symbols by nesting them together and then making changes anywhere in the chain. In Figure 15.10 the title symbol has been placed within the background symbol. If the content of the title symbol is changed, the instance placed inside the background symbol will also change, along with any instances of the background symbol in the document.

FIGURE 15.10

You can nest a symbol by placing an instance within another symbol. Note that when the symbol is in the Symbol Editor, it has its own frames and layers independent of the document.

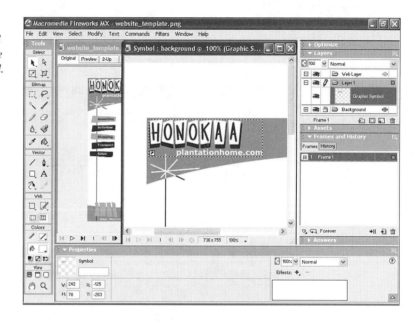

You can nest a Graphic symbol inside an Animation or Button symbol, but nesting Button or Animation symbols inside a Graphic symbol may produce unpredictable results. The same is true of nesting Animation symbols in Button symbols, or vice versa. Button and Animation symbols should be placed in the main document Canvas.

You've worked with Graphic symbols and Animation symbols in previous hours. A Graphic symbol, the simplest type of symbol, contains objects arranged on layers and across frames within the symbol to be placed on the Canvas for display. An Animation symbol can have motion, scaling, and opacity changes applied to the symbol instance, allowing you to move and change the symbol in an animation.

The third type of symbol is used for creating interactive elements called buttons. A button is a symbol that has a frame corresponding to each possible button state. A Button symbol is very similar to a slice with a Nav Bar behavior attached. Buttons have up to four frames—an Up frame, an Over frame, a Down frame, and an Over While Down frame. Another tab setting for buttons is Active Area; this allows you to create a standard slice area for the button. Use Button symbols to create a standard button for your project. A new feature of Button symbols in Fireworks MX is that when you place an instance on the Canvas, you change the content of the text for each instance by using the Property

Inspector, as in Figure 15.11. If you change the appearance of the text object or graphics in the symbol, the appearance of each instance will change, but the text content for each instance will not.

FIGURE 15.11

The Home *Button symbol is selected on the Canvas, and instance-level settings are available in the Property Inspector. These include instance name, text (*Home*), effects, links, and alternate description settings for the button.*

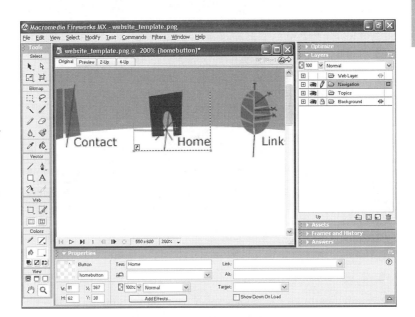

Working with Symbols and the Library Panel

Symbols are edited in the Symbol Editor window, which is very similar to the document workspace. Symbols are like documents within the document; each has its own frame, layer, and Canvas setting. Figure 15.12 shows the Symbol Editor for a button. Note the tabs at the top for each button state. To bring up the editor, you can double-click an instance of the symbol you would like to edit, or you can double-click the symbol icon in the left column of the Library panel. To change the symbol's name or type, double-click the symbol's current name in the Library panel; otherwise, click to select the symbol and select Properties from the Library panel Options menu.

FIGURE 15.12

Button symbols have only four frames—one for each button state—accessible from tabs at the top of the Symbol Editor.

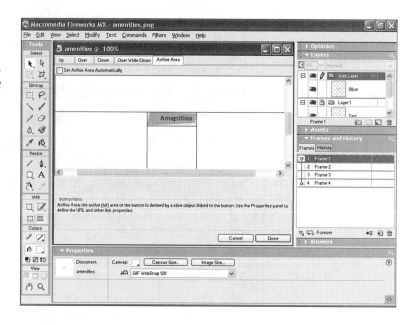

When editing a symbol, you can use any of the tools available in the Tools panel. You can add or remove layers, add or remove frames, and even create optimization slices or hotspot links on the symbol's Web Layer. You can even use image size to resample the symbol, import and paste graphics from other files and applications directly into the symbol, and do anything else you might do in a normal document. The crosshairs on the Symbol Editor Canvas represent the registered center of the symbol when it is placed in another symbol or on the document Canvas. This center is also shown with the symbol selection handles when a symbol instance is selected. Moving objects in relation to this center will change their positions in all instances.

To place a symbol instance on the Canvas, simply click the symbol name in the Library panel and drag the symbol onto the Canvas. The symbol will be placed and selected on the Canvas, and you can edit instance-level settings, such as Button text, Graphic effects, or Animation changes. Instance-level settings do not affect all symbols, only the particular instance placed on the Canvas. You can also use the transform tools to transform the instance. Changes made to the symbol will be reflected in the transformed instance. To remove objects from a symbol, copy them from within the Symbol Editor and paste them onto the Canvas, or use Break Apart from the Symbol commands on the Modify menu.

Other Library panel features include the ability to import and export symbols for use in other Fireworks PNG documents. Symbols are document-specific; when you create a new document, the Library panel will be empty. You can move a symbol from one document to another by dragging a symbol from the library onto another document workspace window or by using the Copy command to copy a symbol instance from one document to paste into another. Use Export Symbols in the Library panel Options menu to create a blank Fireworks PNG document that contains symbols from the document you've selected. The Export Symbols dialog, shown in Figure 15.13, allows you to select the symbols you want to export. Symbols are saved into a Fireworks PNG file on your hard drive.

FIGURE 15.13

The Export Symbols and Import Symbols commands allow you to preview and select the symbols you would like to copy.

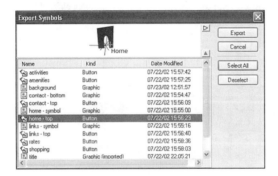

To import symbols from another document, choose Import Symbols from the Library panel Options menu and select an existing Fireworks PNG file. You can preview and select the symbols you would like to import. If you import symbols in this way, you can use the Update command on the Library panel Options menu to have Fireworks check the file that you imported the symbols from and update them with any changes. This allows you to nest a set of symbols from one file into any number of other files and update them from a central source. This will not work, however, for objects or symbols pasted or dragged from the library of another document.

Task: Import and Export Symbols

In this task you will move away from the files you have been using and look at the process of simply importing and exporting symbols. As you will be starting from scratch, the reality is that you will export a new symbol and then import it into a .png file. The steps take you through the process of exporting a copyright disclaimer image that you might want to use in many files.

1. Start by opening Fireworks and creating a new document of around 300×200 pixels. Set the Canvas color to meet your site colors or requirements.

2. Add text and any graphics that you want to act as your copyright information, as shown in Figure 15.14. Trim the Canvas to get rid of any excess space around your content. From the Select menu choose Select All; the contents of your file will all be selected, ready to become a symbol.

FIGURE 15.14

Any type of graphic or information can be converted to a symbol. In this case you are creating useful information that can be reused in many graphics.

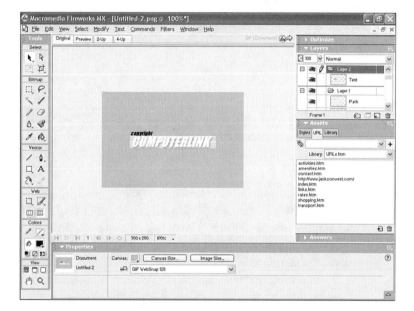

3. From the Modify menu choose Symbol, Convert to Symbol. This will open the Symbol Properties dialog.

4. Choose Graphic as the symbol type and name the symbol copyright. Click OK to continue.

5. Show the Library panel, if it is not already visible. Your new symbol is immediately placed in the panel and is ready to be used at any time.

6. From the Library panel Options menu, choose Export Symbols to open the Export Symbols dialog, as shown in Figure 15.15. Make sure that your new symbol is selected.

FIGURE 15.15

The Export Symbols dialog lets you choose symbols to export for use in other files.

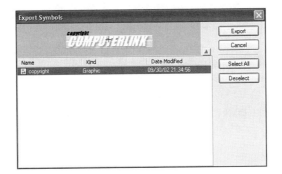

7. Click the Export button in the dialog and then browse to a location to save the file. This need not be within the Fireworks structure. The location can be anywhere on your hard drive. Type a name for the file or accept the default of Custom Symbols. Click Save to complete the export process.

8. Now open a Fireworks document that you want to use the symbol in. This can be any type of image file, even a blank one.

9. In the Library panel click the Options menu and then choose Import Symbols. The Open dialog opens, ready for you to locate the file you saved earlier in this task, as shown in Figure 15.16. Browse to the saved file and click Open to continue.

FIGURE 15.16

Make sure you remember where you saved the exported symbols. Later simply browse to the file and choose Open.

10. The Import Symbols dialog now opens (as shown in Figure 15.17) for you to select symbols to import. In this example there is only one, so make sure it is selected, then click Import to make the symbol accessible in your new file.

FIGURE 15.17

*From the Import
Symbols dialog, you
can import a single
symbol from the saved
file, or if you have
saved more than
one, simply select
the symbols you
want to work with.*

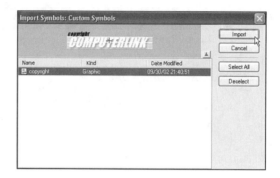

11. The symbol is immediately placed in the Library for the new file. The word "imported" appears in brackets after the name of the symbol, identifying that it has come from another location.

> If, like most people, you are using Fireworks to create multiple graphics for a Web site or sites, it makes good sense to save all of the required files and assets into a single folder. That way, finding symbols to import will be as simple as possible.

Summary

You should now be able to add interactive features to almost any element in your document. You can use a hotspot to swap an image in another slice, link a slice and give it a simple rollover effect, or create a nav bar using slices or Button symbols. If you spend a little time using symbols to create a hierarchy of elements—a Graphic symbol shape nested in a Button symbol with text and interactivity, for instance—you can save time when making otherwise repetitive changes to similar objects. Changes made to a symbol in the Library are reflected in all instances, and each instance can be further transformed to make it more individualized.

Workshop

You should now be able to create whatever kind of interactive and behavior-driven links you want within your image files, from simply using the URLs and creating basic hyperlinks, to having fully developed navigation bars popping up whenever triggered. This final section will test your memory and give you ideas for tasks that will utilize the skills from this hour.

15

Q&A

Q **I just created a slice with a link, and I want the image underneath the slice to change when the user moves the mouse over it. What's the fastest way to do this?**

A Select the slice with the Pointer tool and then click the behavior handle in the center. Select Simple Rollover from the pop-up menu and choose what you want the image to change to—the same area of the Canvas on another frame or an image from another document.

Q **How do I change the Active Area for a Button symbol? When I click the slice with the pointer, nothing happens.**

A Underneath the Active Area tab in the Symbol Editor window for a Button symbol is a Set Active Area Automatically check box. Uncheck this box and then click the active area slice to bring up the slice handles and change the size or position of the active area.

Q **I placed multiple instances of a symbol on the Canvas. When I double-clicked on one to edit it, they all changed. How do I edit just that symbol instance?**

A You can apply transformations, effects, opacity, and Blending modes to symbols through the Property Inspector. These are instance-level settings, so they won't affect the appearance of other instances of the same symbol. Double-clicking a symbol instance brings up the Symbol Editor, where changes are made at symbol level, which means they will be reflected in all instances of that symbol. You can also choose Break Apart from the Symbol commands on the Modify menu to remove the objects from a symbol instance, but any connection to the symbol in the Library panel will also be removed.

Quiz

1. What is the proper way to import a symbol so that you can update the symbol with any changes made in the original file?

   a. Copy the symbol from the source file and paste it into the destination file.

   b. Drag the symbol from the source file library onto the Canvas of the destination file.

   c. Use Import Symbols from the Library panel Options menu to select the source file and symbol to import.

2. Which of these behaviors cannot be applied to a hotspot?

   a. Swap Image

   b. Simple Rollover

   c. Status Bar Message

3. Which URL is an absolute URL?

    a. `http://www.macromedia.com/software/fireworks/index.html`

    b. `index.html`

    c. `../../index.html`

Quiz Answers

1. c.—You must use the Import Symbols command in the Library panel Options menu if you want to be able to update a symbol from the source file later.

2. b.—Hotspots can trigger a link, an image swap, or a status bar message, but not a simple rollover or nav bar behavior. Only slices can use these last two behaviors.

3. a.—An absolute URL includes the protocol (`http://`), domain name of the server (`www.macromedia.com`), directory path (`/software/fireworks/`), and filename (`index.html`). The other two choices are relative URLs.

Exercises

These exercises are purely optional, but undertaking them will certainly help hone the skills you worked on in this hour.

1. Try finding an image of a map, and then slice it into shapes based precisely on the borders of states, provinces, or countries. Create hotspots that are each the correct shape for an area. Then link the hotspots to other Web sites or files.

2. Once you have your map image, try adding mouseover interactions so that when the user moves the mouse over a region, he or she sees an image associated with it. Create the mouseover images yourself and store them as symbols.

3. Create a list of all the links you need to use in your current Web site project. Import them into the URL Library. Then continue developing your management skills by organizing all of the other files you need into a logical structure so that you can import or open them quickly and easily.

HOUR 16

Exporting HTML Code from Fireworks

To make a Fireworks file full of interactive graphics into a Web page, the graphics and interactivity must be laid out and scripted by using HTML and JavaScript. Fireworks can export fully functional code along with all the necessary image files. Fireworks can even export all the code for a custom pop-up menu or XHTML-compliant code for the next generation of dynamic Web pages. XHTML will likely replace HTML as the standard language for displaying Web content. The advantages of XHTML over HTML are too great to list here, but one of the most notable facts is that it can be read by a far wider range of products than the simple Web browser. Current-generation PDAs and mobile phones can also read it, making Web content accessible to a wider audience. To learn more about XHTML, you can either go to the World Wide Web Consortium's Web site, at `http://www.w3.org`, or get yourself a good book on the subject, such as *Sams Teach Yourself HTML and XHTML in 24 Hours* by Dick Oliver.

In this hour you will

- Learn about the different Web page export options
- View and change exported HTML source code
- Create pop-up menus for easy site navigation

Specifying HTML Export Settings

There are a number of ways that you can configure Fireworks to export your HTML files. You may specify settings for HTML export through the HTML Setup dialog, shown in Figure 16.1. Choose HTML Setup from the File menu, or click the Options button when HTML and Images is selected on the Export dialog. With the HTML Setup dialog, you can choose which style of HTML you would like to export for use in another application, what kind of table spacing you would like, and what filename convention will be employed for exported images.

FIGURE 16.1

The HTML Setup dialog allows you to set up how your HTML files are exported and encoded as well as how slices from the current document are named.

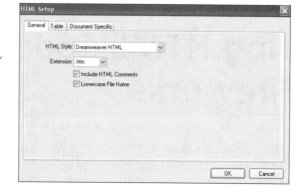

The first tab in the HTML Setup dialog is the General options tab. The HTML Style menu will let you select which style of HTML you would like to export—Generic HTML is best for hand-coding or working with an HTML editor that isn't listed. If you want to be able to edit Fireworks behaviors and interactivity in Dreamweaver, make sure you choose Dreamweaver HTML as the style. You can also choose the extension for exported HTML files from the drop-down list or by typing it in the field. If you are a Macintosh user, you may choose the File Creator Type to set which application will open the file when double-clicked in the Finder. Choose an XHTML format if you want your code to conform to the more rigid XHTML syntax. This will not affect how your pages are displayed in a Web browser.

Checking Include HTML Comments is recommended if you are unfamiliar with cutting and pasting HTML code, although it adds a small amount to the size of the exported

HTML file. Checking Lowercase File Name will change any uppercase characters in the filename to lowercase for better server compatibility; this does not affect the filename extension in the field above.

The Table tab allows you to choose how you would like Fireworks to compute the HTML table spacing (Figure 16.2). Spacing with Nested Tables—No Spacers produces code that is easy to work with by hand. Single Table—No Spacers creates the simplest table and the smallest amount of code, but the results can be unpredictable when multiple slices are employed. A 1-Pixel Transparent Spacer will export a single-pixel transparent file called shim.gif along with your slices. This forces table cells to the proper width and height dimensions. This guarantees a uniform appearance in browsers, but more code is exported, meaning a bigger and more complicated HTML file.

FIGURE 16.2

The Table tab gives you complete control over the exported HTML. Careful selections here will give you complete control over the exported file.

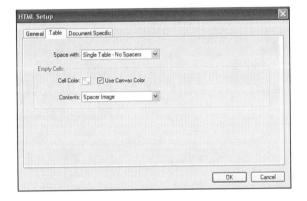

For every table cell you may also choose what color will appear if the cell contains no slice or contains an HTML slice. This color will also appear under any transparent pixels in an exported GIF image. Uncheck Use Canvas Color and select a color by clicking the Cell color swatch to bring up the Swatch pop-up menu. The contents of an empty cell can be None; Spacer Image, which forces the cell into the proper dimensions; or Non-breaking Space, which is a bit of code that adds an invisible space character in the cell.

The General and Table settings will be saved as the default for all your Fireworks documents. The Document Specific tab settings, as shown in Figure 16.3, will be saved and recalled for the Fireworks PNG file you are currently editing for export. You can set how you want the exported slice files to be named with the Auto-naming fields. Make sure at least one field contains a Slice # or row/column setting; otherwise, all slices will be exported to the same file. Do not use the Space character to separate values because this would not work with Web servers. The last two fields determine how the slice will be named for each exported frame. Make sure at least one field has a Frame #, Rollover, or

Abbreviated value. An example of how a slice might be named is shown below and to the left of these fields in the figure.

You may specify an Alternate Image Description for exported slices. This is for areas not covered by a slice or for slices that do not have an Alt tag specified in the Property Inspector when selected. Checking the Multiple Nav Bar HTML Pages box will export an HTML page for each element of a Nav Bar in your document (for example, if your Nav Bar has links to six pages, you will export six HTML documents).

FIGURE 16.3

Document-specific settings can be amended to make individual settings for each file that you export. Unlike the General and Table tabs, this information relates to the current file, not Fireworks in general.

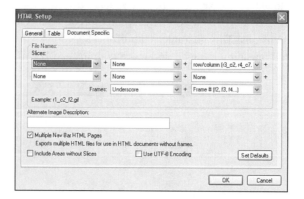

Each page will load with a different element in its Down state. A page will be named after the Nav Bar slice or Button symbol instance.

Check Include Areas without Slices if you want to export areas of an image on the Canvas not covered with a slice. Use UTF-8 Encoding if you will be placing non-Latin characters on the same Web page with Fireworks content. This includes characters in the Chinese, Japanese, Korean, Arabic, Hebrew, and Cyrillic alphabets. This does not apply to text objects on the Fireworks Canvas because they are exported as GIF or JPEG images.

Task: Export HTML Layout with Graphics and View the Page in a Browser

▼ TASK

In this task you will further develop the website.png file that you worked with in previous hours. Exporting the file into a Web browser will enable you to see and test the functionality of the Fireworks layout in a live environment. Once exported, all of your links, rollovers, and buttons should work as you intended.

1. Open the file website.png from the Hour 16 examples folder. This is the file that you sliced in Hour 14, "Slicing Layouts," and then made interactive in Hour 15, "Creating Interactive Graphics."

16

2. Choose Export from the File menu or press Control+Shift+R (Windows) or Command+Shift+R (Macintosh) to bring up the Export dialog. In the `Fireworks Examples` folder, create a new folder named `honokaa_export`. Type **template** in the name field and choose HTML and Images from the Save as Type menu if it is not already selected. Make sure Export HTML File and Export Slices are selected from the HTML and Slices menus, respectively. Leave all the boxes below unchecked, as in Figure 16.4.

FIGURE 16.4

These settings will export an HTML file and image files for each slice. All the files will be created in the same folder since Put Images in Subfolder is not checked.

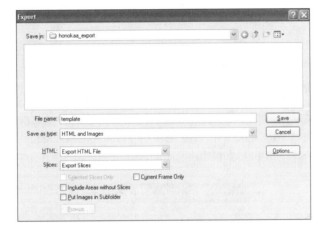

3. Click the Options button on the Export dialog to bring up the HTML Setup dialog. From the General tab choose Dreamweaver HTML as the HTML Style, .htm as the Extension, and check the Include HTML Comments and Lowercase File Names boxes. From the Table tab choose Nested Tables—No Spacer.

There are no empty cells, so disregard the Empty Cells options. Continue to the Document Specific tab.

4. On the Document Specific tab, you've done most of the work already by naming all of the slices. Just in case, set the first slice's drop-down menu to say row/column. For the Frames fields choose Underscore, followed by Rollover. The following example should read `r1_c2_over.gif`.

You've also set the Alt tag for each slice already, so you can ignore the Alternate Image Description setting. You do have multiple Nav Bar elements, each with its own down state—make sure the Multiple Nav Bar HTML Pages box is checked. No areas are not sliced, and you will be using only Latin characters, so ignore the last two check boxes, as in Figure 16.5. Click OK to apply these settings and return to the Export dialog. Click Save to export the HTML and image files into the `honokaa_export` folder.

FIGURE 16.5

By selecting Multiple Nav Bar HTML Pages, you will export pages corresponding to the different down states of slices or button elements with Nav Bar behavior.

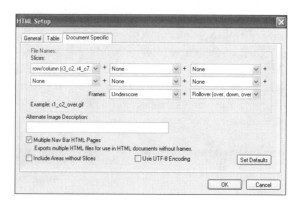

5. Minimize Fireworks MX and navigate to the `honokaa_export` folder you just created in the `Fireworks Examples` folder. A number of HTML files corresponding to Nav Bar elements have been created along with `template.htm`, and each slice and Nav Bar state will have been exported to an image file named for that button and state, as in Figure 16.6.

FIGURE 16.6

The `honokaa_export` directory now contains an HTML file for each Nav Bar down state, an image for each slice, and an image for each frame or state of the Nav Bar slices.

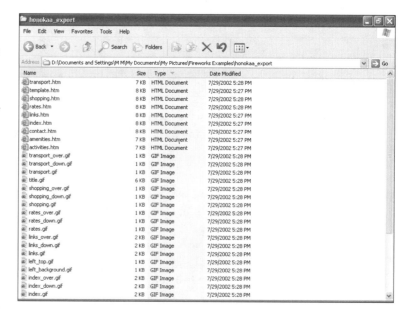

6. Double-click the file `index.htm` to open the file in your browser. Figure 16.7 shows the page as it appears in Internet Explorer. Only the text in the HTML Slice area may change in appearance if a font is not available or if the user has changed the browser's font size. The Home icon at the top doesn't change when you

mouseover—since you already are at the homepage, the button is in the down state. Click another button to change to that HTML page. You were careful to apply links to the slices that correspond to the names of the exported HTML files. Notice that for each Nav Bar element, the link goes to the page with the corresponding down state. Good work!

FIGURE 16.7

Double-clicking an exported HTML file will bring it up in your browser. You can preview any interactive element and the appearance of any HTML slice.

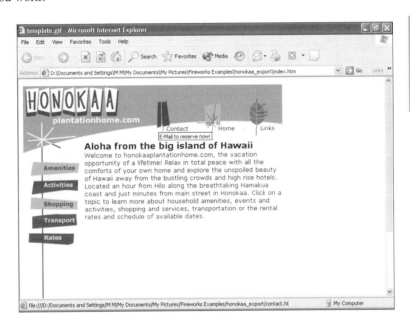

Editing HTML Source Code

There are a number of ways to look at the source code for your Web pages. HTML files are text files and contain no graphics or compiled code. HTML is a markup language for structuring content for display in a Web browser; it is not a programming language. The code can include descriptive information to help classify the content for search engines; scripts that give the browser commands, like for computing an equation or resizing windows; text content to be displayed in the browser; and formatting to specify position, sizes, fonts, and links to other documents. This book is not a complete HTML primer, but you'll pick up a couple of coding tricks along the way and learn the basics of cutting and pasting code within files.

All that you need to view the source code for an HTML document is your Web browser. When using Netscape or Internet Explorer, simply right-click (Windows) or Ctrl+click (Macintosh) an area of the page. Choose View Source from the pop-up menu. The HTML code will appear in your default text editor. The HTML code for the index.htm page viewed at the end of the previous task is shown in Figure 16.8.

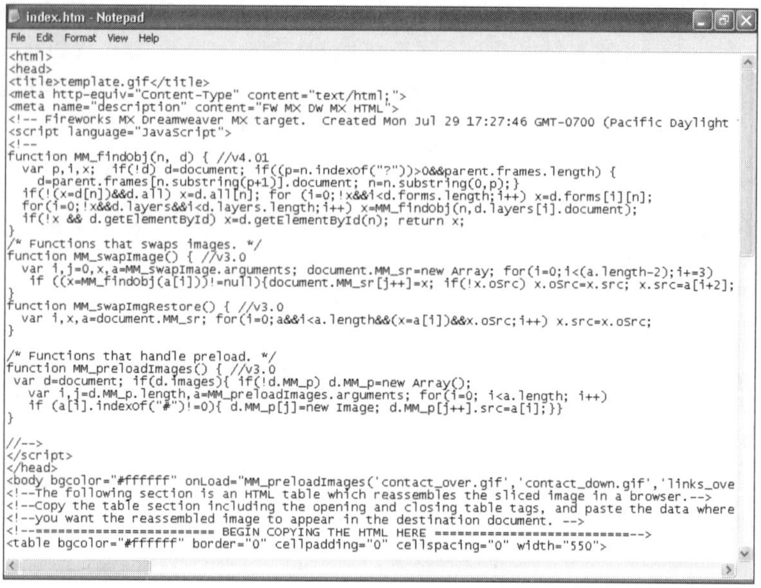

FIGURE 16.8

*Viewing the source of
an HTML document
may seem complicated,
but Fireworks can
include HTML
comments that give
detailed instructions
for copying and
pasting the code.*

```
index.htm - Notepad
File Edit Format View Help
<html>
<head>
<title>template.gif</title>
<meta http-equiv="Content-Type" content="text/html;">
<meta name="description" content="FW MX DW MX HTML">
<!-- Fireworks MX Dreamweaver MX target.  Created Mon Jul 29 17:27:46 GMT-0700 (Pacific Daylight
<script language="JavaScript">
<!--
function MM_findObj(n, d) { //v4.01
  var p,i,x;  if(!d) d=document; if((p=n.indexOf("?"))>0&&parent.frames.length) {
    d=parent.frames[n.substring(p+1)].document; n=n.substring(0,p);}
  if(!(x=d[n])&&d.all) x=d.all[n]; for (i=0;!x&&i<d.forms.length;i++) x=d.forms[i][n];
  for(i=0;!x&&d.layers&&i<d.layers.length;i++) x=MM_findObj(n,d.layers[i].document);
  if(!x && d.getElementById) x=d.getElementById(n); return x;
}
/* Functions that swaps images. */
function MM_swapImage() { //v3.0
  var i,j=0,x,a=MM_swapImage.arguments; document.MM_sr=new Array; for(i=0;i<(a.length-2);i+=3)
   if ((x=MM_findObj(a[i]))!=null){document.MM_sr[j++]=x; if(!x.oSrc) x.oSrc=x.src; x.src=a[i+2];}
}
function MM_swapImgRestore() { //v3.0
  var i,x,a=document.MM_sr; for(i=0;a&&i<a.length&&(x=a[i])&&x.oSrc;i++) x.src=x.oSrc;
}
/* Functions that handle preload. */
function MM_preloadImages() { //v3.0
  var d=document; if(d.images){ if(!d.MM_p) d.MM_p=new Array();
    var i,j=d.MM_p.length,a=MM_preloadImages.arguments; for(i=0; i<a.length; i++)
    if (a[i].indexOf("#")!=0){ d.MM_p[j]=new Image; d.MM_p[j++].src=a[i];}}
}
//-->
</script>
</head>
<body bgcolor="#ffffff" onLoad="MM_preloadImages('contact_over.gif','contact_down.gif','links_ove
<!--The following section is an HTML table which reassembles the sliced image in a browser.-->
<!--Copy the table section including the opening and closing table tags, and paste the data where
<!--you want the reassembled image to appear in the destination document. -->
<!--========================= BEGIN COPYING THE HTML HERE =========================-->
<table bgcolor="#ffffff" border="0" cellpadding="0" cellspacing="0" width="550">
```

Although the HTML for index.htm may look very complicated, all HTML documents
have the same basic structure. The following code is an example of a very basic HTML
page, with descriptions of the elements:

```
<html>
<head>
<title>Basic HTML Structure</title>
</head>
<body bgcolor="#FFFFFF">
This text will appear on the page.
<!-- This text will not -->
</body>
</html>
```

This code is a fully functional Web page. You could type the text into Notepad, save it
as test.htm, and have it appear in your browser, as in Figure 16.9. The elements between
brackets, <>, are called *tags*. Tags structure an HTML document and give the browser instructions on how to display particular elements. The first tag, <html>, tells the browser what kind
of document this is. You'll notice that the last tag, </html>, has a backslash after the first
bracket. This tag closes the first tag, and tells the browser that the page is done being
described. Nested between the <html></html> tags are tags that define the heading of
the document and others for the body of the document. Placed within the <head></head>
tags are descriptive tags and sometimes scripts. In this case the document has been given
a title between <title></title> tags. The title is then displayed in the title bar of the
Web browser window and is also used by search engines to help categorize a page.

FIGURE 16.9

The very simple code example was copied and pasted into Notepad, saved as test.htm, *and opened in Internet Explorer. Note that the title appears at the top of the browser window and that the text in the comment tag does not appear.*

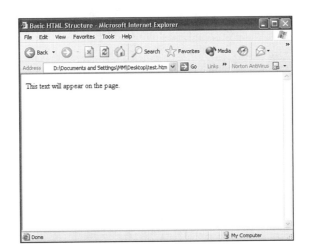

16

You'll notice that the <body> tag itself also has some text —bgcolor="#FFFFFF". This is called an *attribute*. Many tags have attributes, which specify further options for displaying the content within the tags. The bgcolor attribute sets the background color for the Web page. You'll recognize that the color, white, is specified as a hex (hexadecimal, or base 16) code—this is how you will generally define colors within an HTML file.

Between the <body></body> tags is the actual content to be displayed in the browser window. The first line of text will appear to the site visitor. The second line will not appear because it is a comment, which is written to help someone unfamiliar with the code understand the author's intentions when making changes. Comments never appear in the browser. HTML comments always start with <!-- and end with -->. There is no need for a closing tag.

It is vital to realize that although the comments are not immediately visible to the site visitor, they can be read by anyone looking at the HTML code. Never put sensitive or secure information into comments.

Most applications creating Web pages, such as Dreamweaver, let you edit the HTML code by hand in a source code window. You can also use Notepad or Wordpad (Windows) or Simpletext or TextEdit (Macintosh) to edit any HTML file. An HTML file is just a plain text file and must be saved as such (you cannot save HTML code as a Rich Text RTF or Word DOC file). When Include HTML Comments is checked on the General tab in the HTML Setup dialog, Fireworks will also add instructions within the source code to help you determine what parts can be copied and pasted into another file.

To export HTML from Fireworks for pasting into another Web page or for editing the source code, use the Copy HTML Code wizard, available from the Edit menu or the QuickExport menu. Shown in Figure 16.10, this will export your slices and copy the HTML code to the system clipboard so that you can paste it into another HTML file. You will be asked for an HTML code style; then click Next. You can specify a base name for the slices, and you may change the HTML export settings by clicking the HTML Setup button during the next step.

Figure 16.10

The Copy HTML Code wizard will export any necessary slices and copy the HTML source code to the system clipboard.

If you are given an existing Web page and want to make changes to the graphics without having to look at the source code, Fireworks makes it pretty easy. Using the Reconstitute Table command on the File menu and selecting the existing HTML page will create a new document for each HTML table with slices and behaviors, which you can save as a Fireworks PNG file. Images will be stitched together on the Canvas, and slices will be created on the Web Layer and will inherit links, alternate descriptions, and optimization settings, as well as behaviors or HTML code.

To open only the first table, use the Open command from the file menu and select the appropriate HTML file. To import a single table into an existing document, use Import from the File menu and select the HTML file that contains the table. You may experience unpredictable results when importing nested tables or layered files. Remember that in order to appear, any images in the table must be available on your hard drive with the proper relative path relationship to the HTML file.

When you're done, you can use the Update HTML command on the File menu to update any changes you've made in Fireworks back into the document. You will be asked to update just the changes (to preserve any code added to the document after export) or the entire document (to replace the current document with a freshly exported copy of the images and code).

Task: Editing HTML Source Code

Now that you have had a good look at the basics of HTML, how it is structured, and ways of customizing your exported Fireworks HTML, it's time to move on to actually editing HTML source code. This may sound a little complex, but the hints and tips should make it a nice, straightforward process for you. First go over some simple code changes to a file exported from Fireworks, so that you'll be more comfortable working with the code that Fireworks exports.

1. Using Notepad (Windows) or TextEdit (Macintosh), open the file `index.htm` from the `honokaa_export` folder that you created in the last task. A copy is available in the `Hour 16` examples folder. Note that if you are using TextEdit, you need to check the check box reading Ignore rich text commands in HTML files.

2. The document starts with the familiar `<html>`, `<head>`, and `<title>` tags. Go ahead and change the text between the `<title>` and `</title>` tags (`template.gif`) to this:

```
<title>Home - honokaaplantationhome.com</title>
```

3. Below the title are some `<meta>` tags. These help describe a document to other applications, such as HTML editors, Web browsers, and automated search engines. After that is a comment put in by Fireworks with the creation date and time. Next is a `<script>` tag that contains JavaScript. These four functions make the buttons work. If they look unintelligible, don't worry—you should not change them.

   Scrolling down past the closing `</script>` and `</head>` tags, you come to the `<body>` tag. There are two attributes—`bgcolor` and `onLoad`. The `bgcolor` attribute is set by the canvas color of the Fireworks PNG document. The `onLoad` attribute executes a JavaScript function when the page loads. Insert the following four attributes, on the same line but separated by spaces, between the `bgcolor` and `onLoad` attributes:

```
topmargin="0" marginheight="0" leftmargin="0" marginwidth="0"
```

   These attributes are for Netscape and Explorer browsers, and the values are the margins above and to the left of the page content, in pixels. Setting them all to 0 will place any content flush with the top left corner of either Web browser. The default value is 10.

4. After the `<body>` tag there are some comments with instructions on how to copy and paste the code following this paragraph into another document. Between the BEGIN and STOP comment lines are the nested tables created by Fireworks to accommodate your image slices. The `<table>` tag starts a table, the `<tr>` tag creates a row, and the `<td>` tag creates a column within that row. Since you don't necessarily know how much text will eventually be added to the page, you need to create a table that can expand without breaking up visually. Fireworks has put in a comment for each row. Find `<!-- row 2 -->`. Within this row is another table:

```
<tr><!-- row 2 -->
   <td><table bgcolor="#ffffff" border="0"
      cellpadding="0" cellspacing="0" width="550">
      <tr><!-- row 1 -->
       <td><table bgcolor="#ffffff" border="0"
          cellpadding="0" cellspacing="0" width="130">
```

16

You'll tile a background image within the cell that contains this table and also align the table within to the top of the cell. To the second `<td>` tag shown in the preceding, insert the line of attributes as shown:

```
<tr><!-- row 1 -->
  <td background="left_background.gif" valign="top">
    <table bgcolor="#ffffff" border="0"
     cellpadding="0" cellspacing="0" width="130">
```

The image `left_background.gif` is given for the background attribute because it is just a vertical line, the same at the top as at the bottom. The `valign` (vertical alignment) attribute, when set to `top`, forces the contents of the cell to start at the top of the cell.

5. Go ahead and add some copy to the home page before you finish. Included in the `Hour 16` examples folder is the file `copy.txt`. This file contains some text that you'll copy and paste into the home page. Open another instance of Notepad (Windows) and use Open from the File menu to open `copy.txt` (simply choose Open from the File menu in TextEdit for the Macintosh—the file will open in a new window). Select the entire contents of the file and choose Copy from the Edit menu.

6. Return to `index.htm`. Scroll down toward the bottom until you see the text `Welcome to honokaaplantationhome.com` between the `<font size="2">` and `</font>` tags (`<font>` tags and their attributes are a way of specifying font appearance, size, and color for text in HTML). Place the cursor before the closing `</font>` tag and choose Paste from the Edit menu to paste in the new text. This will add the contents of the file to the existing page content.

7. Save your changes to the file by choosing Save from the File menu in either Notepad or TextEdit. Now open the file using the Open command from the File menu in your Web browser. The page is shown in Figure 16.11. Notice that the graphics are flush and that as you scroll down, the line on the left-hand side remains unbroken, even though you extended the length of the page by adding more text. Also, the title of the page is now much more descriptive. The file `template.htm`, in the `honokaa_export` folder under the `Hour 16` examples folder, is a completed copy of these changes.

FIGURE 16.11

By making a few small changes to the code, you've vastly improved how the pages will look and function.

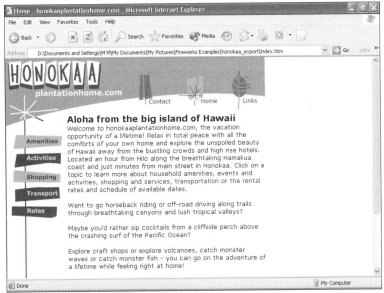

More Automated HTML Code Tools

Fireworks has some tricks up its sleeve for making some advanced Web design tasks easier. A nice feature with Fireworks is the ability to create a pop-up menu that appears when a user clicks or mouses over a hotspot or slice. To add a pop-up menu to a slice or hotspot, simply select the Web Layer object with your Pointer tool and then click the behaviors handle in the center. Choose the Add Pop-up Menu command. The Pop-up Menu Editor dialog, shown in Figure 16.12, allows you to customize the look and feel of the pop-up menu.

FIGURE 16.12

The Pop-up Menu Editor dialog can be brought up by adding the Pop-up menu behavior either with the object's behavior handle or through the Behavior panel.

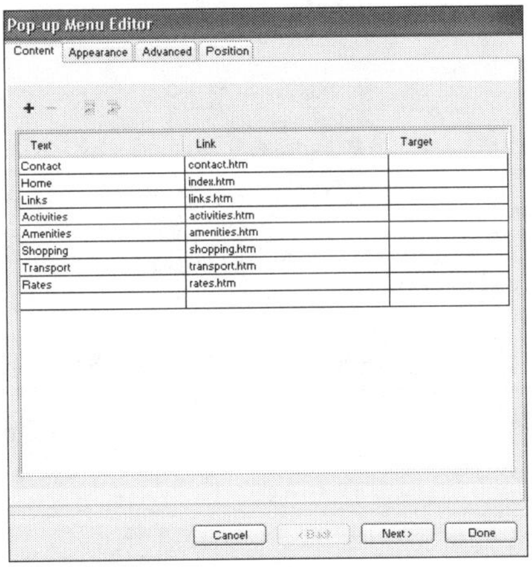

On the Content tab you can add entries to the menu. The text is what will appear in the menu. The link is where the user will be taken when clicking the text. The target allows you to specify a target frame or window, such as _blank to create a new window.

Double-click a field with the mouse to edit that field. You may use the Tab key to cycle through the fields or to create new entries. Add or delete entries by using the Add Menu and Delete Menu buttons. Select a menu item and click the Indent Menu button to indent the option under a heading (the first item cannot be indented). This will create a sub-menu that appears when the heading item is moused over.

The Appearance tab lets you choose how the menu appears. First, the menu can be either a Vertical Menu, with items reading from top to bottom, or a Horizontal Menu, with items leading from left to right. There are two basic types of pop-up menus—HTML cell, with a solid color background, and Image cell, with an image background. You can choose which style you would like by selecting HTML or Image cells at the top of the Appearance tab. For both types of cells, you may select a font group, size, style, and alignment. You may also change the text and background colors for both unselected (Up State) or selected (Over State) items. Image cells allow you to apply a background image with a bevel style from the Style menu, as shown in Figure 16.13. A preview of how the menu will appear is shown at the bottom of the dialog.

If you do not like any of the styles offered by Fireworks for a pop-up menu, then you can create your own. Use a simple rectangle object, apply all of the effects and colors you want, then save it as a style. Export the style file to the New Menu folder in the Fireworks directory on your hard drive. Your style then appears as an option in the dialog.

FIGURE 16.13

Image cells allow you to apply a style to the menu item backgrounds for a beveled button effect.

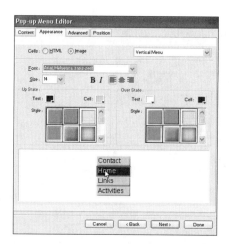

On the Advanced tab in the Pop-up Menu Editor dialog, you can be more specific about how the menu operates (see Figure 16.14). Fireworks will automatically set the width and height of menu cells, but you can change this by selecting Pixels from the menu and typing values into the Cell Width and Height fields. You can add padding between the cells, which is the margin area around the text, or spacing, which creates a space between each cell. You may indent the text a number of pixels or change the amount of time the user has to hold the mouse over the slice or hotspot that triggers the menu before it appears (measured in milliseconds, or 1/1000ths of a second). You can also choose whether to have borders around each cell and specify border width and color. The preview at the bottom of the dialog will reflect your changes.

Remember that you can preview and test your menu in a browser as soon as it is created, simply by pressing the F12 key.

FIGURE 16.14

The Advanced tab allows you to set specific width and height settings for an exported table, choose cell padding and spacing, if required, and generally take complete control of the exported menu.

The Position tab allows you to specify where the pop-up menu appears in relation to the hotspot or slice (see Figure 16.15). Click any of the preset buttons at the top or enter a specific value in the X and Y fields. The position is measured from the top left of the slice. If you have indented items on the Content tab, then you may also specify the offset for the submenu panels that appear. When you are done, click OK to continue. If you want to edit the settings for the pop-up menu, bring up the Behaviors panel from the Window menu, select the slice with the pop-up menu with the pointer, and then double-click the Pop-Up Menu behavior in the Behaviors panel.

FIGURE 16.15

The Position tab lets you set the exact location of the pop-up menu in relation to the hotspot or slice that triggers it.

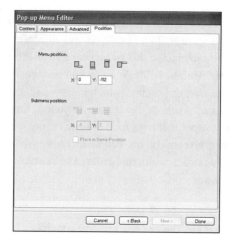

When working with pop-up menus, it is vital to remember that when uploading your files to the Internet, you send the mm_menu.js file. This is generated by Fireworks, and without it your menu will not function.

Summary

HTML is the language of the Web. While other languages, such as JavaScript, CSS, and XML, aid in the design of Internet applications, the core layout of any Web page is still expressed largely as HTML. While you don't need to know any HTML to create a fully functional Web site with Fireworks MX, a familiarity with HTML documents will definitely help you down the road. This hour got you started customizing HTML export settings, importing and updating exported HTML, and exporting the source code for copying and pasting HTML code into an existing page.

Workshop

Use the questions and quiz below to check that everything in this hour made sense to you. Working with HTML can be quite a difficult process if your background is image based. Understanding the complexities of the language—not only in Fireworks but in general—is a little like learning to play chess. You can understand the basic concept in minutes, but it can takes years to master.

Once you have looked at the questions and quiz, there are some optional exercises to help you move onward.

Q&A

Q **I've put some Chinese characters in an HTML slice on the Web Layer. When I export, the characters don't appear correctly. How can I work with non-Latin alphabets when using Fireworks?**

A Either in the HTML Setup dialog available from the File menu or in the Options button in the Export dialog, choose the Document Specific tag. At the bottom of the dialog, make sure to use UTF-8 encoding. This will preserve special characters and double-byte codes for non-Latin character sets.

Q **I edited some HTML source code exported from Fireworks into Microsoft Word. When I saved the file and loaded it into my browser, nothing happened. What went wrong?**

A If you did not save the file in the Text Only format, then it cannot be loaded by a Web browser. You must save the file in a text-only format in order to display it in a Web browser. Microsoft Word also uses some special characters that may not appear correctly in a Web page, such as em dashes and smart (curly) quotes. It is recommended you use a text editor, such as Notepad or TextEdit, to edit HTML source code.

Q **I exported an HTML layout using the Nested Tables—No Spacer option on the Table tab in the HTML Setup window. Why won't Fireworks let me use the Reconstitute Table command to open it up?**

A Fireworks can reconstitute only non-nested table layouts. Use the Single Table—No Spacer option or the 1-Pixel Transparent Spacer option to create layouts that can be Opened, Imported, or Reconstituted. You can edit the table source code yourself to create a series of single, non-nested tables and then reconstitute the HTML. Fireworks will also have trouble if the images and HTML are not in the right folder paths relative to each other. Check the src attribute of the <img> tags to determine the relative paths to the image files or change absolute URL paths to relative paths.

Quiz

1. What HTML tag tells the browser that the content that follows is to be displayed?

    a. <head>

    b. <body>

    c. <html>

2. Which text below contains an HTML comment?

    a. This is an HTML comment < This is not >

    b. < This is an HTML comment >This is not</>

    c. <!-- This is an HTML comment --> This is not

3. What extra image file is exported when 1-Pixel Transparent Spacer table export is chosen?

   a. `shim.gif`

   b. `spacer.gif`

   c. None

Quiz Answers

1. b.—The `<html>` tag opens an HTML source document. Items within the `<head>` tag describe the document for other systems and scripts. Items between the opening `<body>` and closing `</body>` tags are displayed in the Web browser window.

2. c.—The appropriate format for an HTML comment, which is not displayed regardless of where it lies in the document, is with `<!--` to begin the comment and `-->` to end the comment. No closing tag is necessary.

3. a.—The single-pixel, transparent GIF image named `shim.gif` will be created in the folder with the sliced images and reference in the HTML document to make sure the table lays out correctly.

Exercises

Learn a little more about HTML. Although you do not need to know the language to use Fireworks, basic understanding and some code literacy will certainly help you troubleshoot if things go wrong.

1. Try creating your own style and saving it into the New Menu folder, as mentioned in a tip earlier. This will give you total control over matching your pop-up menu to the style and colors of your Web site.

2. Change the settings in the HTML setup dialog to find the mix that best suits your needs. See how changing the settings can give very strange results. You may never need to make amendments to these, but having a complete understanding will again lead to better overall results and successful exporting of your images.

HOUR 17

Working with Dreamweaver MX

Fireworks is the perfect complement to Dreamweaver for working with Web page layouts. You can export code from Fireworks, edit it in Dreamweaver, and return it to Fireworks to edit graphics or slices for the page at any time, using the Roundtrip editing features. The integration between the applications is such that you can even change Fireworks-generated HTML code and JavaScript within the Dreamweaver interface, or edit individual button graphics or image slices from Dreamweaver by using Fireworks. Layouts created in Fireworks can be turned into Dreamweaver templates very easily, and pages on a site can be updated through Dreamweaver's site-publishing tools.

In this hour you will

- Use roundtrip editing to edit pages seamlessly in both Fireworks and Dreamweaver
- Edit behaviors from Fireworks directly in Dreamweaver

- Create Dreamweaver page templates from layouts created in Fireworks
- Use Dreamweaver's Web publishing tools to post your site to the Web

Roundtrip Editing

Roundtrip editing refers to the ability for a single document to be worked on in two different environments. With Fireworks and Dreamweaver this means that graphics layouts exported from Fireworks can be opened and edited in Dreamweaver. If changes are made to the layout in Fireworks, the exported image slices and HTML files with Fireworks tables can be updated for use in Dreamweaver. If links, hotspots, alternate descriptions, or behaviors are edited in Dreamweaver, the changes will be reflected in the Fireworks source document when launched for editing.

To set up the launch and edit defaults for your Fireworks PNG files in Dreamweaver, choose Preferences from the Dreamweaver Edit menu. Choose File Types/Editors from the list on the left, as shown in Figure 17.1. From the list of extensions that appear on the bottom, choose a Web graphics extension, such as .gif, .png, or .jpg. When you choose a file extension, a list of editors will appear to the right. Click Fireworks and then click the Make Primary button just above. This will make Fireworks MX your primary image editor. Repeat this process for each image extension.

FIGURE 17.1

The Preferences dialog in Dreamweaver allows you to set Fireworks as your default editor for any image file type and associated extension.

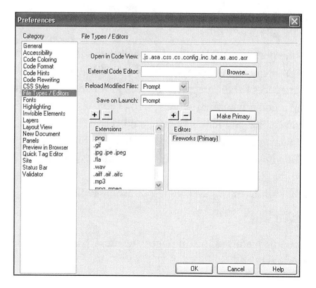

When you want or need to make changes in Dreamweaver to a graphic or table that has been created in Fireworks, you can choose to edit either the source PNG or the placed image file. To indicate which you would prefer, select Preferences from the Edit menu in Fireworks (if you are a Macintosh OS X user, Preferences is under the Fireworks menu). Choose the Launch and Edit tab (or pop-up menu on a Mac) from the top of the Preferences dialog, as shown in Figure 17.2. These options let you select how Fireworks will behave when it is selected to edit an image from an external application (such as Dreamweaver) or to optimize from an external application. The choices include Always Use Source PNG, which searches for the file the slice or table was exported from; Never Use Source PNG, which opens only the chosen image file slice; or Ask When Launching, which lets you decide to edit the image from either the source PNG or the exported slice.

FIGURE 17.2

Configuring roundtrip editing includes setting Launch and Edit options on the Fireworks Preferences dialog.

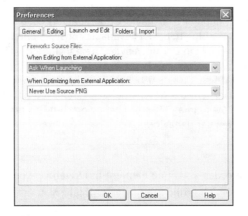

It is important to keep a copy of all your source PNG graphics within the local site folder in Dreamweaver. This will make it easier for others to edit the site from the same source graphics that you are using. The relationship between graphics and tables in a Dreamweaver document and the Fireworks source PNG they are exported from is saved in the Dreamweaver Design Notes for a site. To add PNG files to the site, simply copy them into the site folder. To create a new site folder, choose New Site from the Site menu in Dreamweaver and select the folder that contains the source PNG files and any exported code and images you created using Fireworks. If Dreamweaver cannot find the source PNG for a selected image or table, you will be prompted to locate it or to edit the exported graphics in a new PNG document.

Editing Fireworks Elements from Within Dreamweaver

When you launch a document in Dreamweaver, there are a number of ways you can use Fireworks to edit the graphics and tables in the document. You can edit or optimize images in Fireworks even if you don't have the source file available. If the table or graphics were created in Fireworks and either opened in Dreamweaver or copied and pasted into an existing document, you could refer to the source PNG that created the table or graphic and edit them interchangeably in Fireworks and Dreamweaver. Fireworks will recognize changes to links, hotspots, HTML code in HTML slices, and shared behaviors made in Dreamweaver and will automatically update them in the source file when launched.

> There are a number of behaviors that Fireworks and Dreamweaver have in common. All of the behaviors available for slices and hotspots in Fireworks are also available in Dreamweaver. These include the Simple Rollover, Swap Image, Swap Image Restore, Status Bar Message, and Pop-up Menu behaviors. When a Nav Bar behavior is exported from Fireworks into Dreamweaver HTML code, the behavior is broken into a series of Swap Image and Swap Image Restore behaviors, but it is preserved in the source PNG as a Nav Bar behavior.

Launching Fireworks in order to edit an element in Dreamweaver, such as an image or table, could not be simpler. The following steps will take you through the process:

1. Start by selecting the image or table you would like to edit by clicking it in Design view or by placing the cursor within the appropriate tag in Code view.

2. In the Dreamweaver Property Inspector, note the Edit button with the Fireworks logo and a second Src field below that. Figure 17.3 shows an example of an editable Fireworks element.

3. The Src field shows the path to the Fireworks source PNG relative to the current document. You may type in a new path or click the folder to the right to browse for a file. Click the Edit button to launch Fireworks even if there is no source specified.

4. You will then be prompted to answer whether you would like to use the source file or simply edit the existing graphic (assuming Ask When Launching is chosen from the Edit from External Application menu on the Launch and Edit tab in the Fireworks Preferences dialog).

FIGURE 17.3

FIGURE 17.3

With Fireworks set as the editor for image types, the Dreamweaver Property Inspector will allow you to launch Fireworks to edit the image by clicking the Edit button.

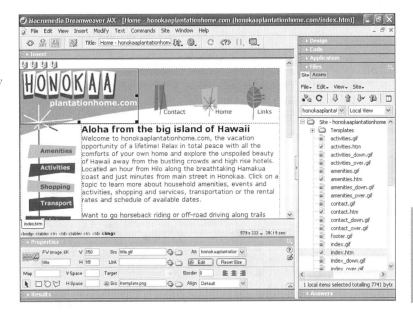

If you choose to use the source file, it will open in the Fireworks document work-space and import any changes already made to the table or graphic in Dreamweaver, including slice settings and behaviors.

When you are done editing, note that Fireworks does not close automatically. If your system is close to the minimum of resources, then remember to manually close the application when you are done.

If you choose to edit the existing graphic, it will open in a new document in the Fireworks workspace. This document will become the source PNG for the graphic, for later reference. If Fireworks does not support changes made to the graphic or table, you will be warned that they will be overwritten when you are done updating the source file in Fireworks. For this reason it's important to make drastic changes to table layouts in Fireworks first and then update the changes in Dreamweaver.

5. At the top of the document workspace will be the Dreamweaver and Fireworks icons and the text "Editing from Dreamweaver," as shown in Figure 17.4. To the left will be a Done button. When you are done, make any changes to the table or graphic that you require and then click the Done button to return to Dreamweaver.

17

6. Any changes to the code and image slices will be reexported and are immediately reflected in the Dreamweaver Design or Code views.

> To cancel any changes you've made, simply close the Fireworks document window, using Close from the File menu, and then return to Dreamweaver. No changes will be made to the Dreamweaver document.

FIGURE 17.4

Clicking the Edit button on the Dreamweaver Property Inspector launches the image or source document in Fireworks. Clicking the Done button after making changes will save the changes to both the source PNG and its exported code as well as image files in Dreamweaver.

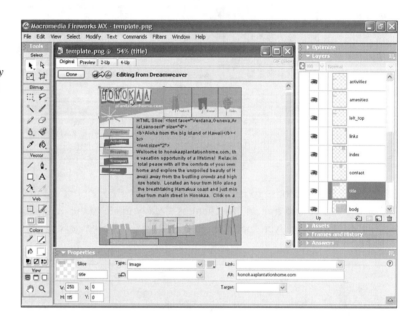

Fireworks can also be used for designing content for Dreamweaver placeholder images and for optimizing image files created in another application. To insert a placeholder image, select Image Placeholder from the Insert menu in Dreamweaver. Specify the name, color, width, height, and alternate text. When you've selected the image placeholder, click the Create button on the Dreamweaver Property Inspector, which is shown in Figure 17.5. Fireworks will be launched with a blank document Canvas so that you can create a graphic for this image.

FIGURE 17.5

Inserting an image placeholder allows you to lay out a Web page quickly and then replace the temporary elements with graphics or tables designed in Fireworks.

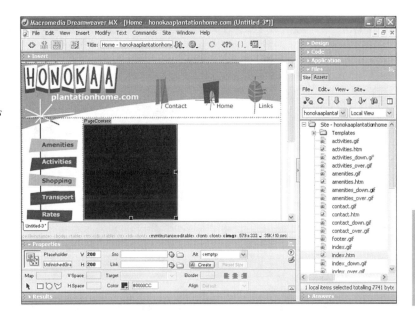

To optimize an image, select it in Dreamweaver and choose Optimize Image in Fireworks from the Commands menu. You will be presented with the export preview dialog, shown in Figure 17.6, where you can specify optimization settings for the image, including file type, palette depth, and compression level. Click the Update button to apply the new optimization settings to the image file. If you have changed the file type and therefore the image extension (from .jpg to .gif, for example), Dreamweaver will prompt you to update all links to the image in the site to reflect the change in the image file name.

FIGURE **17.6**

Choosing Optimize Image in Fireworks from the Dreamweaver Commands menu allows you to change an image file type quickly or to optimize an image created in another application.

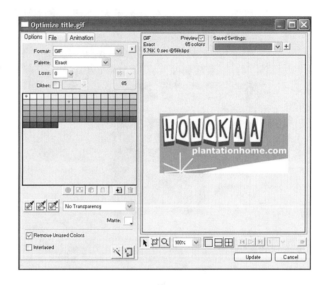

You may also make changes directly in Dreamweaver to an HTML-style pop-up menu created in Fireworks. Simply select the image or hotspot that triggers the pop-up menu, and then choose Behaviors from the Dreamweaver Window menu or press Shift+F3 (Windows and Macintosh). Double-click Show Pop-up Menu to bring up the Pop-up Menu dialog in Dreamweaver. Now you can make changes. If the pop-up menu is an image-style menu, you are encouraged to make the changes directly in Fireworks. Alternately, you can select the pop-up menu background image in the Site panel and choose Edit from the Properties Inspector to edit this file separately in Fireworks. You can still make all other changes in Dreamweaver as you would for the HTML-style menus above.

Updating Edits Made in Fireworks

If you would prefer to work with the source images or layout directly in Fireworks, or if you need to make drastic changes to a table layout created in Fireworks, there are a number of techniques you can use to ensure that the updates are reflected in Dreamweaver when you are done. First, you can use the Copy HTML to Clipboard command from the Dreamweaver QuickExport group. This will copy the HTML for the current layout to the system clipboard and export any necessary image slices to the specified folder. You can then paste the updated code into a new or existing Dreamweaver document by using Code view.

You can also use the Update HTML command from the File menu in Fireworks to update any Fireworks code in an existing document. With the edited source PNG open, choose Update HTML from the File menu and then select the HTML file you would like updated. Fireworks will search for existing Fireworks code and replace it with updated code from the source file. Although this is not as elegant as using roundtrip editing, it can be accomplished without having to get the Dreamweaver application up and running.

Another option is to export your image or layout as a Dreamweaver Library item (.lbi file). When this item is added to a Dreamweaver library and placed in multiple documents, changes made to the library item will be reflected in each different document, much like when using Fireworks symbols. To export a graphic or layout as a Dreamweaver Library item, simply select Dreamweaver Library from the Save as Type menu in the Export dialog. Library items must be stored in the Library folder under the root site folder in Dreamweaver.

When you open the Dreamweaver Assets panel for that site and select the Library category, the new image or layout will be available for you to place. Click-drag a library item onto the document to place it. To edit the library item, simply double-click its name in the Assets panel. A new document window will open in Dreamweaver, and you can select the image or table for editing from the Fireworks source. When you are done editing, you can update any instance of the library item by selecting Update Current Page or Update Pages from the Library commands in the Dreamweaver Modify menu.

Creating Dreamweaver Templates from Fireworks Layouts

Another powerful way to use Fireworks and Dreamweaver together is to design the basic graphics template for your Web page in Fireworks and then create a Dreamweaver template from the exported code for use across a number of Web pages. Like a library item, templates reside in their own special folder (Templates folder) in the local site's root directory and have their own file extension, .dwt. Templates are available from the Template category on the Assets panel in Dreamweaver. If you apply a template to a series of documents and then make changes to the template later, the changes will be reflected in each of the documents based on that template. Templates can also be nested, like Fireworks symbols, and can contain editable regions for placing original content within each individual document.

Task: Create a Dreamweaver Template from a Fireworks Layout

Using the power of integration between the two applications makes many tasks easier. Here you will take a Fireworks layout and use it as the basis for a fully functional Dreamweaver template, complete with editable regions. This template will preserve source information between the two applications, ensuring that it is still editable within the Fireworks interface whenever required.

1. Open the Dreamweaver application. Choose New Site from the Site menu. In the Site Definition dialog, make sure the Basic tab is selected at the top and that the site is named honokaaplantationhome, as shown in Figure 17.7. Click the Next button. Choose not to use server technology, and then click Next again. Now choose Edit Local Copies, the first option, and choose the honokaaplantationhome.com folder from the Hour_17 examples folder. Click Next. Choose None from the final menu because you'll be working with only a local copy. Click Next again and click the Done button to finish. You can always edit the site definition later.

FIGURE **17.7**

The Site Definition dialog and wizard will step you through creating a new site or editing a site's properties, such as server location, editing environment, and server scripting features.

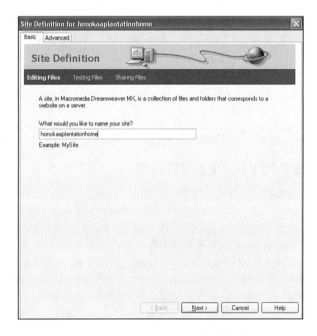

2. Dreamweaver will scan the directory for files and images and will then add them to the Site panel in the Files panel group. Expand this panel group and choose the Site panel tab. Double-click the file Template.htm from the list to open up the document window for that file. Make sure the Design View button (above the document window) is selected, as shown in Figure 17.8. Here you've selected the table that dominates the document; note that Dreamweaver's Property Inspector shows that the table is a

Fireworks table and that the file `website.png` (included in the root folder of the site) is the source PNG for the selected table. Do not click the Edit button for this table, because you made changes to the source code in the last hour ("Exporting HTML Code from Fireworks") that would be overwritten if updated from the source PNG. You may edit individual graphics, however, without altering the table.

FIGURE 17.8

With the table selected in Dreamweaver, the Property Inspector displays the name of the Fireworks source file.

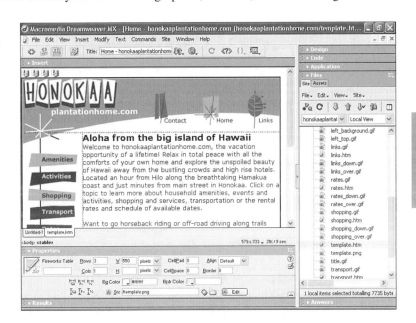

17

3. Choose Save As Template from the File menu. You will be prompted with the Save As Template dialog, which is shown in Figure 17.9. Name the new template `template`, make sure the site `honokaaplantationhome` is selected from the menu at the top, and click Save to continue. The `Templates` folder will automatically be created in your site's root folder, and the new file `template.dwt` will be saved in it. It is important that you save only `.dwt` templates in the Templates folder; furthermore, these files should not be saved outside of this folder.

FIGURE 17.9

When creating a template, make sure you save the layout as a template first. Then add any editable areas or other template-specific features to the template file directly.

4. At the top of the document workspace, the filename will change to `template.dwt` because you are now working on the template and not the original document, `template.htm`. Go ahead and select the text from `Aloha from the big island of Hawaii` down to the bottom of the passage. From the Template Objects submenu on the Insert menu, select Editable Region. You will be prompted for a name for the editable region, as shown in Figure 17.10. Enter **PageContent** and click OK to continue.

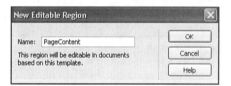

5. Choose Save from the File menu to save the template. Now choose New from the File menu. From the New Document dialog, choose the Templates tab. From the left choose Site "honokaaplantationhome," and then from the right-hand column choose template. At the bottom of the dialog, make sure the box for Update Page when Template Changes is selected, as in Figure 17.11. This will not affect the editable regions of the template. Click Create to create a new document based on this template.

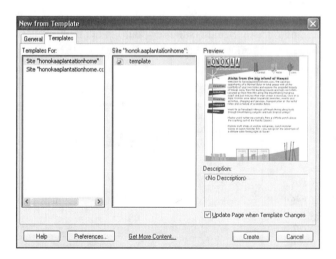

6. Return to the file `template.dwt` by selecting its tab at the bottom of the document window. The Home button is in its down state, and because new files created from the template will probably not be the home page, you need to make this button active. Select the image of the graphic by clicking it with the cursor. In the Dreamweaver Property Inspector, change the source for the graphic from `../index_down.gif` to `../index.gif` and press Return. The original Home button state will appear.

7. At this point you could reapply the Home button's behaviors through the Dreamweaver Behaviors panel, but for now simply save the file `template.dwt` and return to the new file you created earlier in the task. Notice that the new file you created from the template now has the original Home button state visible, as well. Now you can begin customizing the content in the editable region, as shown in Figure 17.12.

FIGURE 17.12

By making a change in the template, you can change any document based on that template.

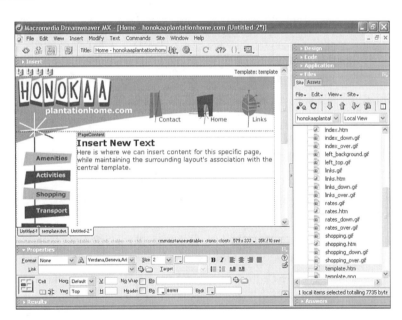

Using Dreamweaver's Web Publishing Tools

Once you've finished a preliminary design for a site or have made changes to the local version of a site that already exists on a server, you can use Dreamweaver's Web publishing tools to upload files from the local site to the remote site on the server. Most users will be using FTP (File Transfer Protocol) to make updates. Refer to the Dreamweaver documentation if you will be using a local network server or a dynamic server environment.

Task: Create an FTP Connection in Dreamweaver

▼ TASK

To transfer your files from a local drive onto the Internet, you need to create a connection to the remote server. The following steps will take you through this process. Before getting started with the task, though, you need to have certain information on hand:

- The domain, or details on other destinations, that your files will be sent to
- The path or directory on the remote server that you must place your files in
- Your username to access the remote server
- Your password to access the remote server
- An FTP account, which should have been created for you when you took out your Web-hosting agreement

If you do not yet have access to a Web server, you can purchase an account for a small monthly fee from many different providers. If you already have an Internet service provider, you might have been given Web-hosting services as part of your account. If not, you can add that service inexpensively. You should look for a server that will offer you a few megabytes of space for HTML files and images and that will allow you to transfer files to and from the server via FTP.

To set up your FTP server connection in Dreamweaver, follow the steps here:

1. Select Edit Sites from the Site menu.
2. Choose the site you would like to set up the information for and click the Edit button on the right.
3. Select the Advanced tab at the top of the Site Definition dialog, and choose Remote Info from the list of categories on the left.
4. Choose FTP from the Access drop-down menu at the top to bring up the settings in Figure 17.13.

FIGURE 17.13

Choosing FTP as the remote host connection type in the Site Definition dialog will allow you to specify the host, path, username, and account for your hosting service, so you can connect to the server to upload your site.

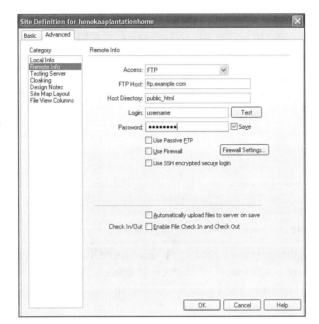

1. Enter your FTP host (this will usually take the form of ftp://hostname.com), host directory (the location for you to place your files), and login (this is usually your username).

2. Enter the password. Click the Save dialog if you are not worried about people accessing the site through your system. Otherwise, leave this field blank, and you'll be prompted for the password whenever you connect to the server.

3. Click Test to test the current settings. If you are a user behind firewalls, such as those maintained at many offices, make sure Passive FTP is selected, or the FTP connection may not work properly. For further FTP connection options, including firewall settings and File Check-in/Check-out features, consult the Dreamweaver documentation.

4. Click OK to continue and then click the Done button in the Edit Sites dialog to finish.

Now you may use the Connects to Remote Host button on the Site panel to establish a connection between your system and the server (assuming you have the FTP host specified correctly and an Internet connection established; contact your service provider if you are having difficulty). Now you may select files from the server to transfer using Get File(s), which downloads files to your site folder, or Put File(s), which uploads them. Select all the files and directories in your site folder and click the Put File(s) button to add the files to the server for the first time.

Once the files have been posted, you may use the Synchronize command on the Site panel's Site menu to update files on the server that have already been updated locally. You may choose to synchronize selected local files or the entire site. You can also choose to Put the newer files (if changes were local), Get the newer files (if changes were made on the remote server), or both (this Gets any newer remote files and Puts newer local files).

You may also choose to delete files on the remote server that aren't in your local site. Clicking Preview will show you exactly which files Dreamweaver will Get, Put, or Delete. You may remove files from this list before commencing with synchronization, if they were chosen in error.

Summary

With the tight integration between Fireworks MX and Dreamweaver MX, it should be easier than ever to work in both environments. You can now design your initial layouts in Fireworks and create a template in Dreamweaver to use in a number of documents. You can return to the template in Dreamweaver, edit graphic elements and table layouts within the Fireworks source PNG, and have the changes reflected in all documents associated with the template. This makes designing an entire Web site using Fireworks a snap.

Workshop

This hour has given you insight into the way that Fireworks and Dreamweaver can work together for enhanced graphic editability and ease of workflow. Roundtrip Editing makes life easier for anyone using the applications, whether as an individual or as part of a development team.

This final section of the hour will give you the opportunity to revisit the topics covered, ending with some optional exercises designed to move you forward and put some of your learning from this hour into practice.

Q&A

Q **When I try to edit a graphic placed in Dreamweaver, Fireworks won't launch and open the original source file it was exported from. Why won't this work?**

A If the path to the source file was unspecified, or if Never Use PNG Source was selected in the Launch and Edit options in the Fireworks Preferences dialog, Fireworks will not automatically open the source PNG for editing.

Q **I made some changes to the source code of a table exported from Fireworks. When I returned to the source PNG to edit the table and clicked Done to return to Dreamweaver, my changes were erased. What happened?**

A Fireworks will have warned you that the table had been changed since export and that any changes made in Fireworks will overwrite changes made in the code or images. Remember to make changes to the table layout directly in Fireworks.

Q **I used the Optimize Image in Fireworks command from the Dreamweaver commands menu to change an image from JPEG to GIF compression. After I clicked through the dialogs and returned to Dreamweaver, instances of the image placed on other Web pages in the site disappeared. Why did this happen?**

A Remember to make sure that you update links sitewide when prompted by Dreamweaver. If you change the name of the file by saving it as a different type, any links referring to the original file name will be broken.

Quiz

1. What folder must Dreamweaver templates be placed in relative to the site's root folder?

    a. Library

    b. Templates

    c. Images

2. Which FTP command sends a file from the local hard drive up to the remote server?

    a. Put

    b. Get

    c. Synchronize

3. What button should you click when you are finished editing a graphic launched in Fireworks from the Edit button on the Dreamweaver Property Inspector?

    a. Save

    b. Close

    c. Done

Quiz Answers

1. b.—The Templates folder in a Dreamweaver site is exclusively for Dreamweaver .dwt templates. These templates should not be placed anywhere else, nor should other files be placed in this folder.

2. a.—The Put command uploads a file from the local host to the remote host. Synchronize is actually a series of instructions for file transfers and may include both Get and Put commands.

3. c.—Clicking the Done button in the document window will save the source PNG and apply the changes to exported files in the Dreamweaver site. The Save button will save changes only to the source PNG, and the Close button will close the source document without updating the changes into Dreamweaver.

Exercises

1. Come to grips with Library items. You may not realize that you can export Fireworks files directly into Dreamweaver as Library items. A Dreamweaver Library item is similar to a Fireworks symbol, which can be reused in many sites. Try creating a symbol or logo you may want to use over and over, then export it to Dreamweaver as an `lbi` file. This is an option from the Export dialog.

2. If you have purchased Macromedia Studio MX, spend a little time looking at the way Fireworks can integrate with Flash. Vector objects can be directly exported, as can Fireworks animations. Not only that, but you can roundtrip edit between Flash and Fireworks. It is well worth exploring these options.

3. Further integration is available between the applications. If you use layers in your Fireworks layout, you can export these layers into a CSS file, which can then be used and applied in Dreamweaver.

PART VI

Speed Up Your Workflow: Automation and Customization

Hour

Hour 18

Batch Processing and Configuration Sharing

There are a number of ways to speed up your workflow and to work better as part of a team. Batch processing in Fireworks allows you to make changes to a number of files quickly and simultaneously.

You can resize and export dozens of images at once without even having to sit at your machine. You can even save the session as a script that you can use later to process images to the same specifications. You'll also learn how to find all the files used to configure and extend Fireworks, so that you can take your preferences, palettes, and compression presets wherever you go or share your styles, libraries, and scripts with others.

In this hour you will

- Learn how to set up and execute a batch process
- Use the Project Log panel to aid you in working with a number of files
- Get down to the nuts and bolts of customizing Fireworks
- Save custom configurations of Fireworks for yourself or others

Batch Processing

Batch processing images is like setting up an assembly line in your computer to process lots of images. Starting with a group of images, you can set Fireworks up to execute a series of commands on each image and save the results. You can use batch processing to export a series of image files quickly; resize the images; find and replace colors, fonts, text, and URLs in source images; and execute Fireworks scripts from the Command menu. After you set up a batch, you can save it as a script, allowing you to execute the same batch process on another set of files.

Something to keep in mind when batch processing is that once you start a batch process, you can't interrupt it except to cancel the entire operation. For instance, you can't stop the batch process when it's working on a specific file, make some more changes to that file, and then continue the batch process. You can cancel a batch process, but this will cancel all further file operations, leaving you with an incomplete set of processed and backup files. (Files are always backed up before processing so that no original information will be lost if the batch process is canceled.)

> It's advisable to create a new folder before beginning a batch process and then copy any files that you would like to process from their original locations into that folder. This way, you have a clear picture of which files you'll be working on, and you won't have to worry about the location or integrity of your original files.

To begin a batch process, simply choose Batch Process from the File menu. You don't even need to have a document open in the workspace. You'll be presented with the Batch dialog, as shown in Figure 18.1. Here you can navigate to the folder of files that you would like to batch process. Simply select the files and click the Add button. If you would like to add the entire contents of the folder, click the Add All button. The added files will appear in the list at the bottom. To remove a file, click its name on the list and then click the Remove button. If you choose to use the Project log, which is explained in detail in the next paragraph, check the box to Include Files from Project Log. You can also check the box to Include Current Open Files, if you would like to add them to the batch, as well. You can add files to the batch process in any of these ways. When you are done adding files, click Next to continue.

FIGURE **18.1**

The Batch dialog allows you to select the files that you would like to batch process. When you save a batch script, this is the only dialog that you will need to execute the script again.

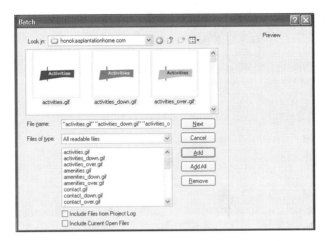

The Project Log panel is a handy way to keep track of multiple files that you would like to work on. Select Project Log on the Window menu to open the panel. By default it is grouped with the Find and Replace panel. This is because when you execute a Find and Replace action, any files that are changed will appear in the Project Log. The Project Log will list the frame number where the change was made and the date and time of the change. Selecting a file in the list will show you the path to the file at the bottom of the Project Log panel.

You can also add files to the Project Log manually by selecting Add Files to Log from the Project Log panel Options menu. Choose Clear All or Clear Selection to clear files from the log, or choose Export Again to reexport the files selected in the log with their current optimization settings. It's recommended that you use the Project Log only with Fireworks PNG files, although the Find and Replace functions will also work with FreeHand, uncompressed CorelDRAW, and Adobe Illustrator files. The actual contents of the Project Log are stored in an HTML file that you can open in your browser to print or share with another user, which you will learn about later in this hour.

After you've selected the batch of files, it's time to select the processes that you would like to execute for the files in the Batch Process dialog, shown in Figure 18.2. Simply select from the Batch Options at the left, such as Export, Scale, Find and Replace, or one of the Commands. Click the Add button to add that step to the Include in Batch list on the right. Click the step in the Include in Batch list to specify the settings for that option. With a step selected, click an arrow in the upper right corner of the dialog to move the step up or down in the sequence, or click Remove to remove it. It's important to consider the sequence of steps; generally, you want to do any image operations, such as a command or resizing, before the export process.

FIGURE 18.2

The Batch Process dialog will guide you step by step through creating a batch. The first step determines what Batch Options you would like to execute during the process.

For the Export option you can choose a compression preset from the Settings menu. Choosing Use Settings from Each File will keep the same file type and optimization as the original. Choosing Custom or clicking the Edit button next to the menu will bring up the Export Preview dialog, where you can customize the optimization settings that you would like to use for the files. There will be no preview available, but you can specify type, palette depth, and compression depth as you normally would by using the Optimization panel or Export Preview dialog.

For the Scale process you can choose No Scaling, which will not affect the image; Scale to Size, which lets you specify an exact width and height for the output; Scale to Fit Area, which will fit the image within the specified width and height but maintain the original proportions; or Scale to Percentage, which will reduce or enlarge the image by the specified percentage. Click Edit with the Find and Replace option selected to bring up the Find and Replace panel, so that you can specify a search value and a replacement value for a color, font, text passage, or URL. Rename will allow you to add a prefix or suffix to the output filename.

You can also choose to execute any of the scripts available from the Commands menu. Saved scripts and Macromedia Extensions can be added to the Commands menu, so that they will be available when you are batch processing. Click the expand icon next to the Commands Batch option to expand the list of available commands. Some commands, such as the Panel Layout, Distribute to Layers, and Reset Warning Dialogs, don't actually affect the image and may work unexpectedly if used as part of a batch process. Instead, use imaging commands such as Convert to Grayscale or Convert to Sepia Tone.

If you want to execute a particular series of steps for each file during a batch process, you can save those steps as a script in the Commands menu and then select it from the Batch Process dialog. A script, such as a filter or effect, can be created from steps in the History panel and saved as a command. Then you can select the script from the list of scripts under Commands in the Batch Process dialog as one of the batch options. To create scripts for the Commands menu by using the History panel, refer to Hour 19, "Creating Custom Scripts for the Commands Menu."

Click the Next button to continue to the final batch process step. This step, shown in Figure 18.3, asks you to specify the output destination and backup options and allows you to save all of your decisions as a script. You can choose to place the batch output in the same location as the original, or you can specify a custom location. Click the Browse button to select the destination folder. Check the Backups box to create backups of the original files. Overwrite Existing Backups will replace any existing backup files from a previous batch with the originals from this batch. Incremental Backups will keep a copy of the original for every batch process, ensuring that no data is lost.

18

If you choose to place the batch output in the original location and do not create a backup or change the output filename by using the Rename option from the previous step, the original files will be completely overwritten.

FIGURE 18.3

The final step before beginning the batch process operation allows you to specify the output destination, select the backup options, and save all decisions as a script in the Commands menu.

Click the Save Script button to save your decisions as a Fireworks script that you can use again at any time. You will be prompted for a filename. By default the script is saved in the Commands folder in the Fireworks MX User Configuration path so that it will be available from the Commands menu in Fireworks. When you select the script from the Commands menu, you will be prompted for a set of files as though you had selected Batch Process from the File menu, but you will not have to complete the preceding steps;

they are saved as part of the script. Click Save to save the script and return to the Batch Process dialog.

Once you've completed setting up your batch, click the Batch button to begin processing the files. A Batch Progress dialog will appear to let you know how the batch process is progressing, as shown in Figure 18.4. Each file chosen from the Batch dialog will be opened, a backup will be created (if specified), the options chosen will be executed, and the results will be exported. To cancel the batch process, click the Cancel button at any time. When all files have been processed, click OK to complete the process. If a file chosen to be processed is not a valid image file or if the disk chosen for the export and backup locations is full, the batch process will cancel automatically.

FIGURE **18.4**

During a batch process Fireworks will let you know which file it's working on and how far through the entire batch it has progressed. When it's done, click OK to continue.

Task: Batch Process a Group of Images

▼ TASK

In this task you will bring together the information you have gleaned so far this hour and actually run a batch process on a selection of images.

1. Start by creating a new folder within your Fireworks working directory. Call it Hour 18.

2. Use your File Management software to copy a few image files into the directory. You can locate some from your hard drive or use some of the existing examples from the book. You will use copies for the task to ensure that your originals remain intact if the batch does not work out as you want it to.

3. From the File Menu, choose Batch Process to open the Batch dialog. Change the Look In drop-down menu to the location you copied your files to, then change the Files of Type drop-down menu to All Readable Files. You should then see all copied files listed in the top panel of the dialog, as seen in Figure 18.5.

4. Click the Add All button to select all of the images in the chosen directory. They will all appear at the bottom of the dialog. Click Next to continue to the Batch process dialog.

FIGURE 18.5

Changing the Files of Type menu will enable you to select all of the files you want to work with. Otherwise, this option is set by default to look for PNG files only.

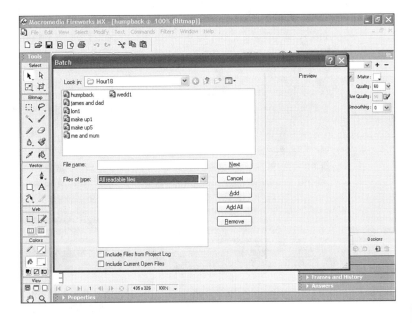

FIGURE 18.6

Choosing different Batch Options causes specific options to be available at the bottom of the dialog. These options change depending upon your selections.

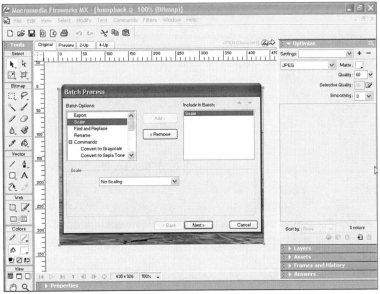

18

5. In the Batch Options category, choose Scale and then click the Add button to move the Scale option to the Include in Batch panel, as shown in Figure 18.6. Notice how Scale now also appears at the bottom of the dialog with a drop-down menu.

6. From the menu choose Scale to Percentage. A % menu (marked only by the percentage symbol) with a slider immediately appears. Use the slider to choose a scale for the images. If you prefer, you can type a percentage value directly into the field.

7. Choose Commands from among the Batch Options, expand the Commands options, and choose Convert to Sepia Tone. Click Add to place it in the right panel. Note in Figure 18.7 that there are no further options for this selection because it is a built-in Fireworks command. Click next to continue.

FIGURE 18.7

Where there are no configurable options for a batch selection, a message is displayed at the bottom of the dialog.

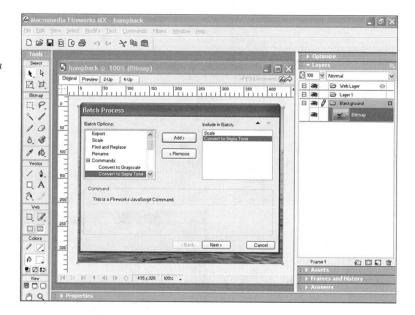

8. From the Saving Files options, choose where the batched files need to go. Select from the location that the files are currently in, or choose Custom Location and browse to where you want the files to go. For this task you should choose the current location.

9. Select Incremental Backups from the backups options. This will leave the files you are working on intact, and after the first process a numeric identifier will be added to the processed file. Note that this does not apply the first time files are processed.

10. Click Batch to process the images; a progress indicator will be displayed, as shown in Figure 18.8. When the process is finished, click OK to continue. All images have had the selected processes applied.

FIGURE 18.8

While the batch is processing, Fireworks displays a status indicator showing you how many files have been completed. If you are processing many images, this is a good time to go get coffee.

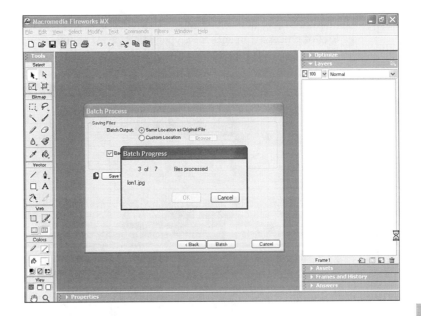

11. From the File menu in Fireworks, choose Open and then browse to the location that you used to select the files. Notice that there is now a new directory called `Original Files`, as seen in Figure 18.9.

FIGURE 18.9

When you choose to back up your files, Fireworks will create a new directory named `Original Files` to differentiate them from the processed ones.

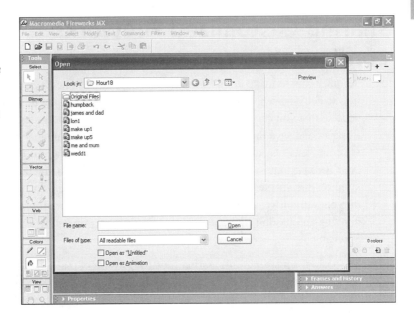

12. All done! You have the original images ready to be used, if required, and a complete set of processed images with your selections. The final figure in this sequence, 18.10, shows an original file with its processed counterpart.

FIGURE 18.10

Here you can see the original file and its processed counterpart after scaling and the sepia tones were applied during the batch process.

Sharing Customized Fireworks Configurations

Another way to make your work go faster is to customize Fireworks to fit your workflow better. For instance, you can add your own image files to the default pattern and texture sets, so that you can use them for any document. You can also create your own symbol libraries and save them for selection from the libraries available in the Edit menu. Custom elements can be configured for the master application or for individual users. And because almost every custom element for Fireworks—including images for patterns, symbol libraries, scripts, compression presets, and palettes—is available as a discrete file on your hard drive, customizing the application for any or all of the users is as easy as copying and pasting files and folders by using your operating system's File Management application.

To locate the master configuration files for Fireworks that affect all users, navigate to the folder that contains the Fireworks application. In Windows XP this is usually `Program Files\Macromedia\Fireworks MX`. For Macintosh OS X users, the files are saved under the `Applications\Macromedia Fireworks MX\` folder. Inside the `Configuration` folder, shown in Figure 18.11, are all the customizable folders for the Fireworks application. Changes to these folders will affect all users on that system. For instance, if you copy an image file into the `Configuration\Patterns` folder, the image file will be available from the list of patterns on the Fill Options menu when the Pattern fill type is selected.

FIGURE 18.11

The master configuration files for all users are stored in the `Configuration` *folder under the* `Fireworks MX` *application folder.*

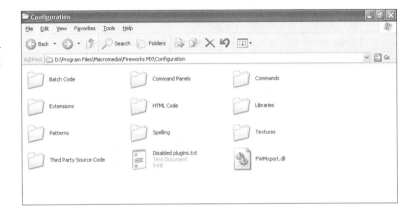

You can customize several other folders. The `Command Panels` folder is for storing custom Flash interfaces for your Command scripts, to make them available in the Fireworks Window menu. The `Commands` folder is where Fireworks JSF scripts are stored, so that they appear on the Commands menu in Fireworks. The `Extensions` folder is where you can place Macromedia Extensions that you've downloaded from the Macromedia Exchange. The `Libraries` folder is where PNG files with symbol elements can be placed, so that they are available from the libraries in the Edit menu. The `Patterns and Textures` folders are where you can place GIF, JPG, or PNG files to use as fill patterns or fill or stroke textures. Finally, the `Spelling` folder is where you can save custom dictionaries for use with the Check Spelling command in the Text menu in Fireworks.

Also under the `Fireworks MX` application folder is the `English` folder (for users of the English-language edition of Fireworks; every edition in another language will have a folder named for that language). Under this folder is the `Keyboard Shortcuts` folder, where the master Keyboard Shortcuts sets are stored as XML files. Choose Keyboard Shortcuts from the Edit menu (on a Mac OS X system, this option is under the Fireworks menu) to customize a set.

The master sets can't be customized. Click the Duplicate Set button at the top of the Keyboard Shortcuts dialog to create a copy of the set in your `User Configuration` folder. You can customize this duplicate set.

18

> Furthermore, you can copy this custom set back into the master Keyboard Shortcuts folder to make it available as a custom set for all users. You can also click the Export Set as an HTML button to create a master list of keyboard shortcuts that you can print as a reference.

All Fireworks defaults are already contained in these folders. You can browse the folders to see what types of files they contain. To add an element to a folder, such as a Fireworks source PNG with symbols to the Libraries folder, simply copy the file from its current location and then paste it into the appropriate folder under the Configuration folder. To create a backup of your custom configuration to share with another Fireworks user or to move it to another system, simply make a copy of the entire Configuration folder and place it on a disk or copy it to your network. Now you can replace the existing configuration file on the new system or copy individual elements from your customized folders into the appropriate folders on the new system. Using Zip or DropStuff compression to create an archive of the contents of your Configuration folder, you can reduce the size of the custom configuration set and help ensure that files are transferred successfully between two systems. Remember that a compressed file will keep a group of files together, so that if you need to restore a configuration later, there is no danger of losing or forgetting any files.

> Fireworks MX configuration files will work with any system. You can use custom configuration files from Windows XP with a Macintosh OS X copy of Fireworks MX, and vice versa.

When working on a multiuser system, such as Windows XP or Macintosh OS X, Fireworks will save many of your custom configuration files to different folders on your hard drive. This way each user on a system can have his or her own individual configuration. For Windows XP the user's configuration is stored in the Documents and Settings\[Username]\Application Data\Macromedia\Fireworks MX folder, where "[Username]" is the name of your user account. The folder for the example user M M is shown in Figure 18.12. For Macintosh OS X users, the User Configuration folder is stored in the Users\[Username]\Library\Application Support\Macromedia\Fireworks MX\ folder. By default any custom elements you have saved while working in Fireworks—such as commands, compression presets (under the Export Settings folder), styles, URL libraries, and custom keyboard shortcut sets (under the English\Keyboard Shortcuts folder)—are stored in your User Configuration folder.

If you are administering a multiuser system and you want to make user-level configuration files available to new users of Fireworks when they log in, then you would add the custom configuration files to the Configuration\First Run folder in the Master Configuration folder. Under the Configuration\First Run folder are the default configuration folders for a Fireworks user configuration. When a new user logs in and uses Fireworks, the custom configuration contained in these files and folders will load for the user automatically.

FIGURE 18.12

Fireworks stores a set of configuration files for each user, allowing multiple users on the same system to customize the application with their own preferences.

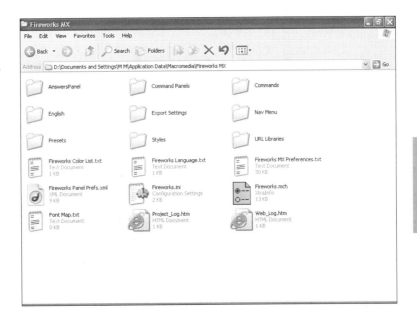

The following list summarizes how to save, find, and manage each type of configuration file, from elements on the Assets panel to URL Library files:

Preferences—Your preferences are saved in the Fireworks MX Preferences.txt file. This is a standard text file that you can open in Notepad, if you like. The file is stored in the User Configuration folder and can be edited by selecting Preferences in the Edit menu in Fireworks (if you are a Macintosh OS X user, Preferences is available in the Fireworks menu).

Keyboard Shortcuts—Keyboard shortcut sets are saved in both the Master Application folder (under English\Keyboard Shortcuts) and the User Configuration folder. Keyboard shortcut sets are saved as XML files that can be opened in any text editor. The master application keyboard sets can't be edited directly in Fireworks MX by using the Keyboard Shortcuts dialog available from the Edit menu. Instead, a copy can be saved in the User Configuration folder, which can then be customized. A new XML file will be created in the User Configuration folder. This can then be copied to the Master Configuration folder to be available to all users.

Project Log—The file Project_Log.htm is found in the User Configuration folder. This file contains the information saved in the Project Log panel in Fireworks. It is a standard HTML file that can be opened in a browser or text editor and printed for reference. It can be copied to another user's configuration folder to make it available to that user in Fireworks.

Commands—Commands are stored in both the Master Configuration folder and the User Configuration folder, under the Commands folder. Commands are Fireworks scripts saved as JSF text files that can be opened and edited in any text editor. Fireworks scripts are based on JavaScript, but they contain special objects for working with Fireworks documents. Scripts saved in the Master Configuration folder are available for all users under the Commands menu. Scripts under the User Configuration folder, in addition to the master set, are available to that user. When a script is saved for a batch process or from the History panel, Fireworks will save it into the User Configuration folder by default.

Command Panels—These SWF Flash animations are available from the Window menu in Fireworks. For both master and user configurations, command panels can be found under the Command Panels folder. An example of a custom command panel is the Align panel that came with Fireworks. Command panels may also require other files, such as text files, XML databases, or ActionScripts. These will usually reside in a folder under the Command Panels folder. The panels under the Master Configuration folder are available to all users. Panels under the User Configuration folder will be available for that user, in addition to the master set. To create custom panels, refer to Hour 20, "Harnessing the Power of Macromedia Extensions."

Compression Presets—Compression presets that you've saved from the Optimization panel, by using Save Settings from the Commands panel in the Options menu, are stored in the Export Settings folder for each Fireworks user. Preset files in this directory are available to the user from the list of compression optimization presets on the Property Inspector for the Canvas, the Optimization panel, the Export Preview dialog, and the Batch Process dialog.

Patterns—The default patterns are stored in the Configuration\Patterns folder. Patterns are simply JPG, GIF, or PNG image files that are tiled to create a fill style. Image files copied into the Patterns folder are available to all Fireworks users from the

Fill Options menu. Users can also specify another folder for patterns through the Folders tab on the Preferences dialog, which is available from the Edit menu (Macintosh OS X users will find Preferences under the Fireworks menu).

Textures—Like patterns, textures are simply JPG, GIF, or PNG image files. They are stored in the `Configuration\Textures` folder under the `Master Configuration` folder. Users can also specify another folder for textures using the Folders tab in the Preferences dialog.

Swatch Palettes—Swatch and optimization palettes are stored as ACT color table files and can be located anywhere. You can save a swatch palette by using the Save Swatches command on the Swatch panel in the Options menu or by choosing Save Palette from the Optimization panel in the Options menu. You can load swatches with the Add Swatches command or the Replace Swatches command from the Swatch panel in the Options menu. Use Load Palette from the Optimization panel in the Options menu to load an ACT file as the optimization palette. You can also use the Create Shared Palette script from Web group in the Commands menu to create a swatch palette from a selected group of image files.

Styles—Styles are saved as special Fireworks Styles (STL) files. Styles can include stroke, fill, opacity, blending, and effect options that you might apply to an object in Fireworks. To create a file for one or more styles, select the styles in the Styles panel; then choose Export Styles from the Styles panel in the Options menu. Styles saved in the `Styles` folder under the `User Configuration` folder will be available from the Styles panel for all documents. Styles saved elsewhere can be loaded into the Styles panel by using the Import Styles command in the Options menu. Styles saved in the `Nav Bar` folder under the `User Configuration` folder will be available in the Pop-up Menu Editor dialog as backgrounds for image style pop-up menus.

Libraries—Libraries are Fireworks source PNG files that contain one or more symbol objects. Simply use Convert to Symbol from the Modify menu to turn one or more objects into a symbol object. The symbol will be added to the document's library. After you save the document in the `Configuration\Libraries` folder under the `Master Configuration` folder, that document's symbol library will be available from Libraries in the Edit menu for all users. You can also choose Other from the Libraries group in the Edit menu, or choose Import Symbols from the Library panel in the Options menu, to pick a Fireworks source PNG symbol library not located in the `Master Configuration` folder.

URL Libraries—URL libraries are specially formatted HTML files. URL libraries can be created with the New URL Library command on the URL panel in the Options menu. To add URLs to the new library, enter them at the top of the URL panel and click the Add Current URL to Library button. You can also choose

18

Import URLs from the Options menu to add URLs from an existing HTML file or to export URLs from the library into a new HTML file. URL libraries saved in the `URL Libraries` folder under the `User Configuration` folder are available from the Library menu in the URL panel.

Summary

Through Fireworks automation and customization tools, you can really begin to save time by processing multiple images at once and setting up the application with all your custom components available directly on the Fireworks interface. In the next hour you'll learn more about creating custom scripts to add to the Commands menu, so that you can execute them for individual documents or when batch processing.

Workshop

The benefits of understanding both batch processing and sharing files will surely be obvious by now, so use the Q&A and quiz that follow to test your memory on the topics covered in this busy hour. Use the exercises simply to put some of the learning to practical use when you have a little time. They are not guided exercises, so do them at your leisure.

Q&A

Q **I'm trying to share a custom batch processing script named** `Thumbnail Batch` **from my Commands menu, but I can't find the file. Where is it?**

A Scripts are saved by default in the `User Configuration` folder under the `Commands` folder. You can also search your system for the file, `Thumbnail Batch.jsf`. For Windows XP users, however, the `User Configuration` folder is stored under the `Application Data` folder, which is a hidden folder and may not turn up in the search.

Q **I have a number of files open that I want to process. How can I select them in the Batch dialog after I've selected Batch Process from the File menu?**

A Simply make sure the Current Open Files box is checked. This will batch process all currently open files. It is not necessary to add files from the Project Log or your hard drive to continue.

Q **I want to save some styles so that they're available from the Pop-up Menu Editor dialog as backgrounds for image style pop-up menus. Where would I put them in my configuration folders?**

A Simply select your styles in the Styles panel using Shift+click. Then select Export Styles from the Styles panel in the Options menu. Save the Style file under the `Nav Bar` folder in your `User Configuration` folder. Now it will be available in the Pop-up Menu Editor dialog when you add the Pop-up Menu behavior to a slice or hotspot.

Quiz

1. What can batch processing be used for?

   a. Deleting files

   b. Moving files

   c. Renaming files

2. Which batch process option will be performed first if they are all selected?

   a. Scale

   b. Rename

   c. Command

3. Under which menu is a saved batch script found in Fireworks?

   a. File

   b. Commands

   c. Window

Quiz Answers

1. c.—Renaming files. You can use the batch process options to add a prefix or suffix to an existing filename.

2. a., b., or c.—Batch processing options are performed in the order they are selected, so any of the answers could be correct.

3. b.—Saved scripts are found under the Commands menu and can be run without going through the batch process dialog.

Exercises

1. Select a single batch of images and then try different batch process options to see the different effects in action. There is no real limit to the number of files that can be processed at once, other than the power and memory of your computer. See how all options can be used singularly or together to save time and effort.

2. Making the most of files and facilities available is another timesaver. Speak to your coworkers about files that would best be shared among all, and then copy the files to the appropriate locations.

3. Spend a little time studying the file configuration on your machine. Notice where all of the files for Fireworks are located. Almost all elements are customizable with a little skill, and the starting point for that is understanding in detail the difference between the user-level files and those available to all users as part of the application.

HOUR 19

Creating Custom Scripts for the Commands Menu

One of the ways you can speed up common tasks and customize Fireworks for your projects is to create custom scripts for the Commands menu through the History panel. To many people the History panel is simply a glorified means of undoing mistakes; however, the reality is that it is much more powerful. The panel records all the recent steps you've taken while using the application. Every click, movement, and keystroke is saved to enable you to save, undo, or repeat the steps. You can then save or copy the steps to a .jsf Fireworks JavaScript file for editing or use on the Commands menu.

In this hour you will

- Undo and repeat steps with the History panel
- Save steps on the History panel as a script
- Examine the text of Fireworks scripts
- Organize scripts on the Commands menu
- Use batch processing to automate tasks

Using the History Panel to View Your Steps

The History panel, grouped with the Frames panel by default, is responsible for recording every step you take while editing an image. Each time you make a change to a document, that change is recorded in the History panel. Changes are listed in sequence, as in Figure 19.1. To the left of the list of steps is a slider handle. This slider handle represents the current place in the sequence of steps. Moving the slider handle back will undo steps. Moving it ahead will redo undone steps. If you undo a number of changes and then make another change, any undone steps in the History panel will be removed and cannot be redone.

FIGURE 19.1

If you slide the handle back to a previous step, you can quickly undo the steps in between. Steps that have been undone are grayed out in the list.

Changes recorded in the History panel are changes applied to a selection. Selection of an object is not recorded in the History panel, though commands from the Select menu, such as Deselect or Select All, are. When you select a new object and start making changes, a line will appear between the last change made to the previous selection and the first change made to the next selection. This includes changes made to other aspects of the document; making changes to the Canvas, layers, or frames is the same as working on the document itself as the selected object.

There are some types of changes that cannot be repeated or added to scripts. A red *X* on the icon for that step will let you know that it cannot be repeated or saved, though it can be undone and redone. These include changes involving the Bitmap tool group and the Freehand Vector tools (Vector Path, Redraw Path, Freeform, Reshape Area, and Path Scrubber). Changes to the View mode or use of the Hand or Zoom tool will not be recorded in the History panel because they do not actually involve any changes to the document or an object. Changes involving menu commands, layer or frame organization, Canvas properties, and adjustments to objects by using the Property Inspector will be recorded, however.

By default Fireworks will save the last 20 steps in the History panel. To increase or decrease the number of steps saved in the History panel, select Preferences from the Edit menu (if you are a Macintosh OS X user, the Preferences dialog is available from the Fireworks menu). Under the General tab and in the Undo Steps field, you can simply change the number of steps recorded in the History panel. Increasing the value in the Undo Steps field simultaneously increases the memory and disk space requirements for Fireworks.

At the bottom of the History panel is the Replay button. The Replay button allows you to repeat one or more selected steps. To select a step, click that step in the list on the History panel. To select multiple steps, use Shift+click. To select steps that aren't continuous, you can use Ctrl+click (Windows) or Command+click (Macintosh). The steps will be executed in the same order in which they appear in the History panel, with the top step first and the bottom step last. After you've selected the steps you would like to repeat, simply click the Replay button to execute them. If you'd like to clear the steps in the History panel to help free up memory and disk space resources, choose Clear History from the History panel Options menu. You will be warned that clearing the history cannot be undone.

Saving a Custom Script from the History Panel

If you would like to save some steps in the History panel so that you can apply the same steps later, you can save them as a Fireworks script. Steps saved in this way can be applied later to any document. The saved scripts have a .jsf extension and can be opened and edited in a text editor; you will look at this later in the hour. You will start by making some edits to a document and then saving the steps as a command to use again.

The first thing to be aware of is the point at which the History panel starts recording. Make sure that you do as much preparation as possible. This will prevent you from saving more steps than you strictly need!

In Fireworks create a new document. Open the History panel (Window, History) and immediately save the file and name it. Notice that the History panel shows the save action.

Now add some text to the document, format it, change the color, and place it in the document where you want it to appear. Notice in Figure 19.2 that the History panel already looks crowded without your really doing much of anything!

FIGURE 19.2

The History panel records every action, no matter how small, even if you do not want it recorded!

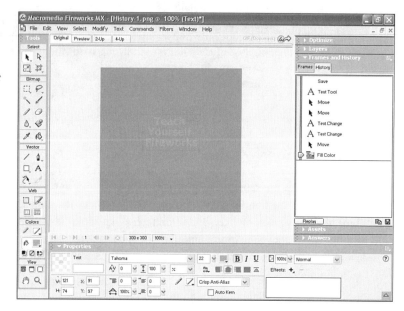

Now try this. Create a document and select the Text tool (but do not touch the Canvas). Choose the font, size, and color that you wish to use, and type the same text. Now look at the History panel in Figure 19.3. Only two steps are visible: one to select the tool and one to move the text. By setting the attributes in advance, you should end up with only the actions you want to save.

When you change your selection on-screen, a dividing line appears in the History panel; this indicates a change in selection. In almost all cases steps on either side of a divider cannot be saved together. This is because different tools are used on different objects—for instance, text effects cannot be applied to a shape.

FIGURE 19.3

Careful planning means that only the actions you want to save are recorded in the History panel. This saves space and makes saving commands far easier.

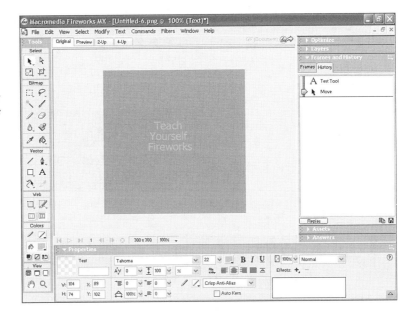

Task: Edit an Image and Save History as Script

In this task you will take a photograph, resize it, fit the Canvas, and then apply the command to another picture. The following steps will take you through the process:

1. Open a photograph directly into Fireworks.

2. From the Modify menu, choose Transform, Numeric Transform, to open the Numeric Transform dialog.

3. Leave the drop-down menu set to Scale and then use percentages to change the size of the picture so that it is more appropriate for Web use.

4. After you have entered the percentages you want, click OK to continue and then resize the image. Note that all of this is shown as a single transform entry in the History panel.

5. Now fit the Canvas to the resized image. Choose Canvas, Fit Canvas, from the Modify menu. All you are left with is the smaller image in a correct Canvas. There are now two steps in the History panel. The second is listed as a crop entry. This is shown in Figure 19.4.

TASK

19

FIGURE 19.4

Fitting the Canvas ensures that the finished article will have no blank space around it, regardless of its size.

 By using the Fit Canvas option, you can avoid having to specify exact sizes for the new Canvas. This is perfect if you want to use your new command on images that are not the same size as the one you are using for the example.

6. You can save the command at this point and use it purely for resizing images. Select both steps in the History panel, and then from the panel Options menu, choose Save as Command.

7. In the Save Command dialog, type a name for the new command and click OK to continue.

8. The new command now appears at the bottom of the Commands menu, as shown in Figure 19.5.

FIGURE 19.5

The saved command appears at the bottom of the Commands menu. It can be accessed and reused at any time. Saved commands are not document specific.

9. Open another photograph and then choose your command from the menu. It is immediately resized, and the Canvas fits.

You have now successfully created your first command, albeit a simple one. This command can be very useful, however, if you use a digital camera where all photographs are the same size (and too big for the Web) and you want to resize them.

Now you will look at creating a command that might be a little more useful when designing a Web site.

Task: Create a Command to Automate Effects Application

▼ TASK

Assume that you want to create text-based graphics as headings for your Web pages. Applying effects can be time consuming, so you will create a command that adds the effects you want each time at the click of a button.

1. In Fireworks create a new document and then draw any background you want for the text headings. In Figure 19.6 a filled, rounded rectangle has been used. Save and name the file. This rectangle will act as a base for future headings but will not be part of the saved command.

FIGURE **19.6**

Saving a file to act as a template will save time and effort. This is handy when you want to apply the same settings and effects to text.

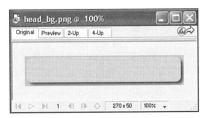

19

2. Type the text you want for this heading, remembering to set the font size and color first.
3. Position the text on the background, if you are using one.
4. Now add effects to the text. In the figure a drop shadow and a raised emboss have been chosen, but you can choose any effects that suit your image.
5. The History panel shows the Text tool, a move, and two effects.
6. Select the last two entries in the panel, choose Save as Command from the Options menu, and then name and save the command.

The effect is now placed in the Commands menu and can be used at any time. Reopen the file you saved to act as a background, type the text for your next header, and apply the command, as shown in Figure 19.7. All your headings will now have the same settings, and you needed to create it only once.

FIGURE **19.7**

When applied, the command script will be displayed in the History panel and will ensure consistency to the items you apply it to.

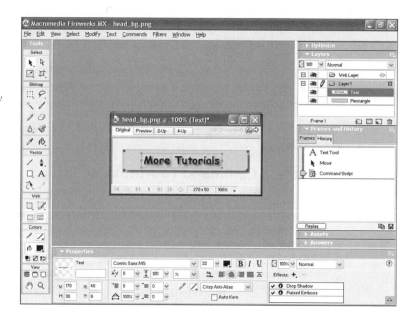

Viewing Custom Scripts as Text

You have now looked at the way the History panel can create reusable commands in Fireworks. This book does not have the scope to delve too deeply into what can be achieved using this method, but the last few pages hopefully have given you some insight into how you can use this time-saving facility even more.

Now you will move on to viewing the script externally. You might wonder why you would want to do this, and for this hour the objective is merely to show you that it can be done. However, in the next hour, "Harnessing the Power of Macromedia Extensions," you will see how editing these files can extend Fireworks and the power of your scripts.

Task: View a Custom Script as Text

▼ TASK

You will start simply by importing an image and placing it onto a Canvas. For this the type and size of image is not important. You are more interested in what happens behind the scenes when this is done.

1. Create a new blank document in Fireworks that has a large enough Canvas to hold the image you want to open.

2. From the File menu choose Import.

3. Locate the image file you wish to import.

4. Click the Canvas to place the image.

The image will appear where you placed it, and a single entry will appear in the History panel, as shown in Figure 19.8.

> Although you may think that placing the image is a second action, the reality is that it is all part of the import function, thus leading to only a single entry.

FIGURE 19.8

Importing and placing an image puts a single entry into the History panel. Just make sure that the Canvas is large enough that you can avoid having to make changes.

5. Select the Import entry in the History panel.

6. From the panel Options menu, choose Copy Steps.

7. Open a text editor, such as Notepad or TextEdit, and from the Edit menu choose Paste. The script for importing your image appears in the text editor, as shown in Figure 19.9.

FIGURE 19.9

The script can be pasted directly into a text editor from the History panel.

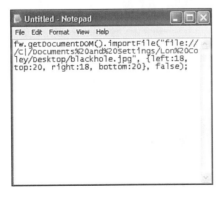

```
fw.getDocumentDOM().importFile("file://
/C|/Documents%20and%20Settings/Lon%20Co
ley/Desktop/blackhole.jpg", {left:18,
top:20, right:18, bottom:20}, false);
```

19

8. You can save this file for future use and editing. Simply give the file a name you can remember so that it can be reused if required.

Understanding the Script

You can now see the script inside a text editor, but unless you have some understanding of JavaScript, it likely looks a little scary right now. The script will now be broken down a little so you can see exactly what has been done to import and place the image. The first part of the script, which will look similar to the following, shows the exact path and filename of the imported image:

```
fw.getDocumentDOM().importFile("file:///C|/Documents%20and%20Settings/
        Lon%20Coley/Desktop/blackhole.jpg"
```

This part of the script shows the exact location that the graphic was imported to:

```
{left:18, top:20, right:18, bottom:20}, false);
```

Assuming that you still have Fireworks open, look at the Property Inspector with the image selected, and you will see these values in the X and Y value boxes.

As you can see, opening and reading the script is really straightforward. You will look at this more closely in the next hour, "Harnessing the Power of Macromedia Extensions," where you will consider how to create a user interface for a script.

Organizing the Commands Menu

Every time you create a command, it is added to the Commands menu in Fireworks. You have complete control over deleting or renaming these at any time. Moreover, commands or downloaded extensions can be managed via the Commands menu, although the process is a little different. Here you will look at both ways of doing this.

To organize your saved command, open the Commands menu and choose Manage Saved Commands to open the Manage Saved Commands dialog, as seen in Figure 19.10. Renaming a command is then simply a case of selecting the command to rename, clicking the Rename button, and then typing a new name for the extension. When you are done, click OK to continue.

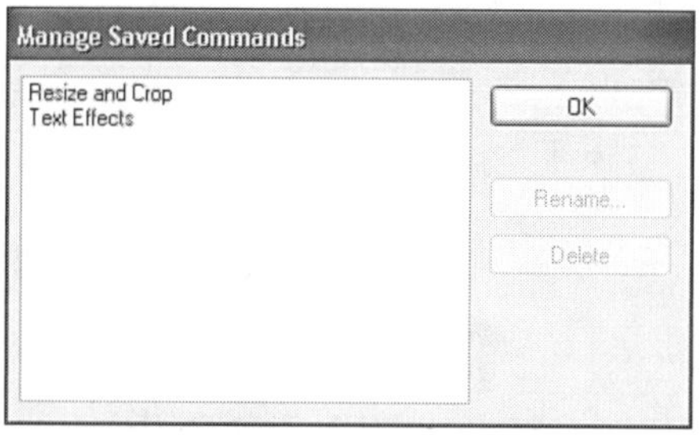

FIGURE 19.10

You can edit, rename, and delete your saved commands through one straightforward dialog.

There are two ways to delete a saved command: You can select the command in the dialog and then click Delete, or you can locate the associated .jsf file on your hard drive and delete it directly from there. The location of this file depends on your operating system. On a machine running Windows XP, the file would be located as follows:

```
C:\Documents and Settings\Lon Coley\Application Data\
        Macromedia\Fireworks MX\Commands
```

For Mac OS X the commands are stored here:

```
/Users/[username]/Library/Application Support/
        Macromedia/Fireworks MX/Commands
```

The name part of this path will vary depending on your username. This Commands directory is specific to commands that you create. Deleting the .jsf file from this directory will immediately delete the command even if Fireworks is open at the time. The effects of any commands that have been used on the current document will not be lost.

Batch Processing Files

So far in this hour, you have looked at the History panel and how to use the saved steps elsewhere in Fireworks. Now you will move on and look at how Fireworks allows you to apply numerous steps to multiple files and then processes the files itself.

The feature is called batch processing, and it seems to be one of the least well-known areas of the application. Batch processing can be used to perform the following operations:

- File conversion to a different format
- Changing the optimization settings for a selected group of files
- Image scaling
- Performing a Find and Replace across multiple files
- Changing filenames
- Applying one or more commands from the Commands menu

The batch processor can be used on almost any number of files, all the way up to many hundreds, although there are obviously constraints based on your processor and memory capabilities. When you open the batch processor, it is then your choice as to which actions or commands are to be performed. You also have complete control over whether the files to be processed are overwritten or backed up or whether a new folder is created.

Always save any open files before you start batch processing if they are to be included. Otherwise, make sure you say Yes to saving the files when prompted. If you were to say No to the prompt, Fireworks would stop the process automatically.

19

Task: Batch Process Selected Files Through the History Panel

The following steps will batch process selected files:

1. From the File menu choose Batch Process. This will open the Batch dialog, as shown in Figure 19.11.

FIGURE 19.11

The Batch dialog is the starting point for your batch processing. Open it from the File menu to get started.

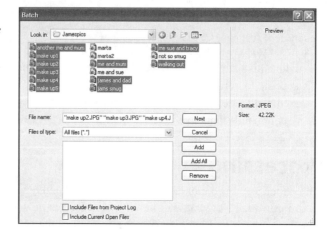

2. Use the Look In (From on a Mac) drop-down menu command to select the folder or drive that holds the files to be processed. Change the Files of Type drop-down menu to say All Readable Files. This will display only files that Fireworks can read.

3. Select the files you want to work with by using Shift+click to choose a group of files or Ctrl+click (Command+click on a Mac) to select individual files. Otherwise, you can click the Add All button to select the entire contents of the current folder.

4. Click the Add button to add the selected files to the process (this is not necessary if you clicked Add All). You can move to alternate folders and continue selecting files until you have selected all the ones you want to work with.

5. If you have been working with a project log, click the Include Files from Project Log check box to include these files.

6. If you want to include any files that are currently open, check the Include Current Open Files check box, as well.

7. Click Next to continue; then open the Batch Process dialog, as shown in Figure 19.12.

FIGURE **19.12**

FIGURE 19.12

The Batch Process dialog lets you choose the options and commands to apply to the files you have selected. You can make and edit selections via this interface.

8. The Batch Options panel on the right contains options for you to select. Choose an option, such as Scale, and then click the Add button to include it in the batch. (You will look at these options more closely in a few minutes.) If you choose any option that has further choices, these will appear at the bottom of the dialog automatically.

9. Choose as many of the options from the list as you want to use on your selected files. You can change the order in which the commands are applied to your selection by using the Up and Down arrows in the Include in Batch panel.

10. Click Next to continue to the Batch Process dialog, shown in Figure 19.13. Then choose one of the following Batch Output options:

    Same Location as Original File—This will save the processed files back into their original location on your hard drive.

    Custom Location—Select this radio button and then use the Browse button to specify a different location (perhaps your Web site folder) for the processed files.

11. Choose a backup location by clicking the Backups check box, as shown in Figure 19.13, and choosing one of the following options:

    Overwrite Existing Backups—This will create a single backup of your original file. If you then batch process the file a second time, the original is lost forever.

    Incremental Backups—This option will create a new backup file each time you run a batch process. Fireworks adds a number to the filename each time. For example, if `file.jpg` were the original, then `file-1.jpg` would be the next one, followed by `file-2.jpg`, and so on.

19

Use the Batch Process dialog to set backup and saving locations for the processed files. If you are unsure about the effects of the process, make sure you choose to back up the files.

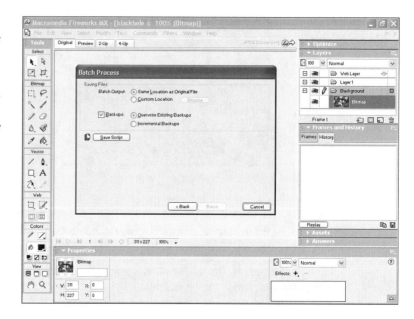

12. If you want to use the same settings again, you can save the settings as a script. Click the Save Script button to do this.

13. Click the Batch button at the bottom of the dialog to run the batch process on the selected files.

Changing Export Settings with a Batch Process

Imagine for a moment that a client has hundreds of files for you to place on a Web site. They have all been used in printed media and are of very high quality and resolution; most likely they are in TIFF format, as well. They might look great on paper but would take forever to download. By using a batch process, you can change the settings for all files at once.

Task: Change Export Settings with a Batch Process

▼ TASK

The following steps will allow you to make the required changes:

1. Open the Batch dialog via the File menu and choose the files to work with as you did previously.

2. From the Batch Options menu, choose Export and add it to the Options panel.

3. At the bottom of the dialog, the Settings menu appears automatically. Choose the optimization setting you want to use with the files as follows:

   • If you are working with files of different formats, choose Use Settings from Each File.

- Choose Custom or Edit if you want to open the Export Preview screen. This will allow you to make some further changes rather than accept the Fireworks default.
- The Preset options will convert all files to the same format, regardless of the original file type.

4. Click Next to continue and complete the batch processing as in the previous task.

Using Find and Replace During a Batch Process

But why would you? This is the usual question that people ask after being told that you can perform a Find and Replace as part of a batch process. There is nothing you can do here that cannot also be done via the Find and Replace panel. Using this as part of a batch process, however, allows you not only to perform this function across many files but also to perform other tasks simultaneously, which again saves time and effort. This is demonstrated in the following section.

Task: Use Find and Replace During a Batch Process

To use Find and Replace during a batch process, follow these steps:

1. As before, open the Batch dialog and choose the files to work on.
2. Select Find and Replace from the options and add it to the Include in Batch list. The Edit button appears in the dialog.
3. Click the Edit button to show the Batch Replace dialog, as shown in Figure 19.14.

FIGURE 19.14

You can find and replace text, colors, and URLs during the batch process. Choose what you want to find from the drop-down menu.

19

4. Use the drop-down menu at the top of the dialog to choose what you are going to find (when using batch processing, this is usually a color).
5. The available options depend on what you are looking for. Figure 19.14 shows the dialog when Find Color has been selected.
6. Click OK and then Next to continue and process the files.

Using Batch Processing to Rename Files

When you looked at the general options for batch processing earlier in this hour, you saw how Fireworks adds a number to the filename when creating backups. You can also modify a filename by adding a prefix or suffix, which is a neat little feature when you want to be able to identify certain image files quickly. For example, if you are running a process to scale a batch of files, then adding a suffix of sma will immediately identify small files. Also, if you are using some sample images that need to be deleted before a final upload, a prefix or suffix is an easy way of making them obvious in a list of filenames.

Follow the steps detailed previously to open the Batch dialog and select the files to work on. This time, select Rename from the available options. The Rename drop-down menu appears at the bottom of the dialog with the following options available:

Original Name—Makes no changes. There is no point in using the Rename option if you are going to make this selection.

Add Prefix—Type in text to add to the beginning of the filename. This can include numbers, letters, hyphens, or underscores.

Add Suffix—Same as the Add Prefix option except the text is added to the end of the original filename.

After you have made your selections, follow the steps given earlier to complete the batch process.

Creating a Script to Perform Batch Processing

Now that you have a better idea about what can be done using the batch process options, you can take this one step further. What if you want to perform the exact same steps over and over on multiple groups of files? Rather than having to keep making the same selections, why not create a script that contains the exact settings you want to use? This is something else that Fireworks makes nice and easy for you.

Again open the Batch dialog, choose your files, and add all the actions you wish to perform in the dialog. After you have made all your choices and the settings are how you want them, click the Save Script button, as shown in Figure 19.15. Choose a location for your file. This can be the same location you used when you created a command earlier in the hour, which will make the script usable directly from the Commands menu.

FIGURE **19.15**

Saving your script is a quick and easy way to save your options. Once saved, the script can be used as often as you want on as many files as you want.

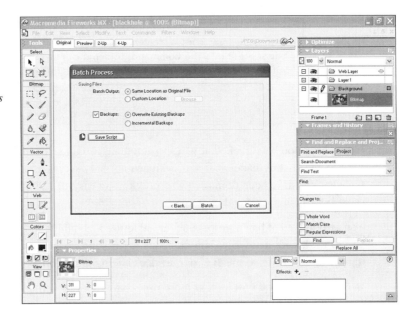

The options that follow are available for running your saved script. If you saved the script into your user-defined commands folder, you can simply access the script from the Commands menu. If you chose an alternative location, choose one of the following options:

- Select the Commands menu in Fireworks and then choose Run Script. This will activate the Open dialog. Locate the saved file and click Open to continue.
- If you prefer to work outside Fireworks, use your File Management application to locate the file in its saved location. Double-click the filename.

After you have selected one of the preceding options, the Files to Process dialog will open automatically. This dialog gives you the choices listed below:

Currently Open Files—As the name suggests, the script will be run on any open documents in Fireworks.

Project Log (All Files)—All files in the project log will have the script applied to them.

Project Log (Selected Files)—Allows you to select files in the project log to process.

Custom—Allows you to choose exactly which files to process.

Finally, click OK to run the script and process your chosen files.

19

After your new script is created and saved, you can run it at any time. If you saved it into the Commands folder, it can be run as a menu item. Alternatively, you can run it directly from the folder it was saved into.

Summary

In this hour you have looked at ways to automate certain tasks in Fireworks. Working through the History panel as it was designed not only serves as a great visual reference for what you have been doing but also provides an easy-to-use interface for reusing the same information over and over again.

You also looked at batch processing, an underused technique in Fireworks that enables you to work with many files simultaneously. Resizing many images without even opening them makes life so much easier, as does adding image effects to preexisting files.

In the next hour you will look at more timesaving options and learn how to expand Fireworks even further.

Workshop

In this hour you have looked at saving information from the History Panel, saving Commands and opening them into a text editor, as well as looking at batch processing in detail. This was quite a lot for a single hour, so use this final section to review your learning. The optional exercises, to complete on your own time, are designed to reinforce the topics you covered in this hour.

Q&A

Q Why can't I save all my steps as a single command? The separator line is always in the way!

A The separator line is perhaps the most significant problem that people come across when creating commands with the History panel. The separator line appears every time you change your selection. Every time you try to perform an action, Fireworks checks to see what is selected and splits areas that cannot be applied to different objects. You cannot apply text formatting to an ellipse, for example, so plan your steps carefully.

Q I want to create a complicated command, but the History panel shows only 20 steps. What do I do?

A Use the Fireworks Preferences panel to change this setting. The default is 20 steps, but you can increase this to meet your needs. Before rushing to make the change, see whether with a little planning you can reduce the number of steps you need to save.

Q **I ran a batch process on some files, but the result was not what I expected. Why?**

A It is most likely that you chose your options in the wrong order. Remember that the order in which the options are listed is also the order in which they are applied. This can cause very strange effects, especially if you are changing colors or adding custom commands.

Quiz

1. Batch processing cannot be used for which of the following?

    a. Changing filenames

    b. Deleting files

    c. Applying commands

2. Which application can be used to view the contents of a script?

    a. Fireworks

    b. Text editor

    c. Web browser

3. What language is commonly associated with scripts?

    a. HTML

    b. Visual Basic

    c. JavaScript

Quiz Answers

1. b.—Although you can use batch processing to perform many actions, file deletion is not one of them.

2. b.—You can use any standard text editor to view and edit the contents of a script. As you will see in the next hour, this can be very useful when you want to make edits or enhancements.

3. c.—JavaScript is the standard language used by Fireworks when creating your scripts. It is also the language others use to create downloadable scripts that can be used with Fireworks.

19

Exercises

Here's a little more practice with some of the new skills you've just been working on.

1. With the History panel see how you can combine sets of operations to create useful commands for yourself and your colleagues. (Remember that the separator line usually splits different tools or objects.) Build yourself a set of commands that will be timesaving within your specific workflow.

2. Take some time out to learn more about JavaScript and how it works within Fireworks scripts. The more you are able to learn and understand, the more complex the scripts you will be able to create. By editing command scripts, you will have even greater control over the power of the application.

3. Expand your knowledge of batch processing. Once you have built up your set of commands, you are able to use them as part of a batch process. With a solid working knowledge of commands and batch processing, you will almost never need to perform the same action twice.

HOUR 20

Harnessing the Power of Macromedia Extensions

One of the first things that you realize about Fireworks, along with any other Macromedia product you may use, is the way that Macromedia encourages you to expand and extend the product's basic capabilities. Now, this may sound a little scary, but it doesn't need to be. The Macromedia Exchange is a dedicated part of the company's Web site, and it is open to anyone. The exchange is full of handy downloads that have been developed by Macromedia itself, along with many that have been created by users who chose to share their innovations with everyone else.

Before going any further, you need to grasp exactly what an extension is. The name is self-explanatory—an extension is an addition to the program that extends its capabilities. An extension can be either additional JavaScript commands or, in some cases, an entirely new panel or panel group.

Fireworks doesn't have its own area within the Macromedia Exchange. Instead, Fireworks extensions are located in an area with Dreamweaver.

In this hour you will

- Download and install extensions
- Learn about the Extension Manager
- Create a new command with a Flash interface
- Install and test the new command

Downloading and Installing Fireworks Extensions

The Macromedia Extension Manager is installed by default, so no action is required before you are able to install extensions. This single Extension Manager is all that is required for working with Dreamweaver, Fireworks, and Flash extensions.

> If by any chance you do not seem to have the Extension Manager installed, visit the Macromedia Exchange Web site at http://www.macromedia.com/exchange. There it can be downloaded at any time.

To view the Extension Manager from within Fireworks, choose Commands, Manage Extensions. The Macromedia Extension Manager, as shown in Figure 20.1, will be displayed. In this figure you can see that some extensions have already been added.

Task: Start to Use the Extension Manager

To get started with the Extension Manager, make sure you have saved all open documents in Fireworks and have a live Internet connection. Then follow these steps:

1. Open the Extension Manager by choosing Manage Extensions from the Commands menu.

FIGURE 20.1

The Extension Manager is a simple, easy-to-use interface for downloading and installing your new extensions.

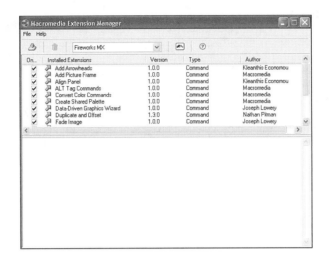

2. Click the Go to Macromedia Exchange button (the Macromedia Logo) on the toolbar. (On a Macintosh choose Go to Macromedia Exchange from the File menu.) Your default Web browser will open directly to the Dreamweaver Exchange Web site.

3. Before you are able to download any extensions, you need to log in or register to the site. To log in, simply type your username and password in the boxes. To register, click the Get a Macromedia ID link on the screen. Once you are logged in, you have full access to the facilities offered in the exchange, which include these:

   - Downloading extensions
   - Searching for extensions by using various options
   - Browsing lists of extensions
   - Rating and reviewing extensions that you have downloaded and used
   - Learning more about extensions that you might download and asking questions about them
   - And for the brave, uploading your own extensions for others to use

4. From the Browse Extensions drop-down menu, choose Fireworks to display a list of available Fireworks extensions, as seen in Figure 20.2.

20

FIGURE 20.2

The Fireworks extensions are displayed with useful information to help you select the best option.

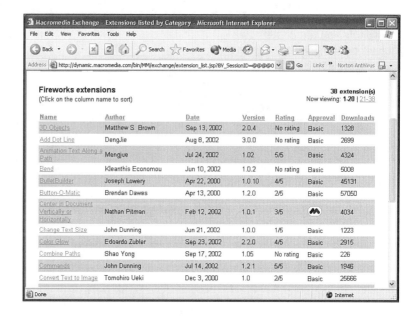

The list is displayed with the following information:

Name—The name of the extension.

Author—The name of the extension's author.

Date—The date the extension was uploaded to the exchange.

Version—The release version the extension applies to; many extensions are revised for new versions of the software.

Rating—The rating, a number up to 5, is an average of the ratings given to the extension by people who have downloaded and used it.

Approval—In most cases, an extension is listed as having "basic" approval, meaning that it has not been officially tested. However, some extensions are actually tested by Macromedia staff. These have the Macromedia logo next to them as an identifier and are guaranteed to work as advertised.

Downloads—The number of times that an extension has been downloaded from the exchange.

5. Click the name of an extension that you're interested in downloading and installing. The link will open an information page for your selection. Make sure that your choice, such as Animation Text Along a Path, is suitable for Fireworks MX. Figure 20.3 shows the information page for this extension.

FIGURE 20.3

Each extension has an information sheet that can be viewed before you choose to download the extension.

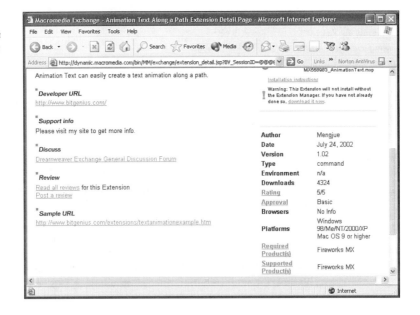

6. Locate the download link on the information page, and choose to download the correct file for your operating system.

7. Save the file to your hard drive and make sure that you remember where you saved the file, because you will need this information in a few minutes.

Task: Install a Downloaded Extension

▲ TASK

You have now successfully navigated your way around the Exchange site, found the Fireworks extensions, and downloaded one that suits you. All that is left to do is to actually install the extension via the Extension Manager. Note that if you are on a Macintosh that runs OS X, you will jump straight from the download to Step 3 of this task.

1. In the Extension Manager click the Install New Extension button or choose File, Install Extension.

2. Locate the file that you downloaded in the previous task and click Install, as shown in Figure 20.4

20

Figure 20.4

Clicking the Install New Extension button in the Extension Manager allows you to browse to the saved file and install it via the interface.

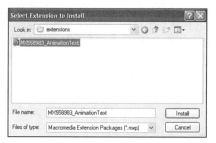

3. You will be presented with a disclaimer about the extension, which you should read before clicking Accept to continue. Note that if you click Decline, the process will end immediately.

4. Once the installation is complete, an alert box confirms this on-screen. Click OK to continue.

5. Look at the bottom panel of the Extension Manager. It now contains descriptive text about the new installation, including where it can be located, as shown in Figure 20.5.

Figure 20.5

Once you've installed an extension, you can read more about it through the Extension Manager, including where to locate the extension for further use.

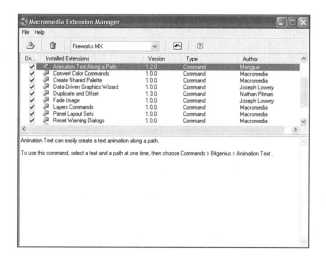

6. Close Fireworks and relaunch it. Although this is not necessary for all downloaded extensions, it is still a good practice to do this for every extension after installation.

If you want to install an extension without even opening the Manager (which must still be installed), locate the downloaded file on your hard drive and double-click it.

You are now ready to use the extension that you downloaded. The information in the Extension Manager will have told you where to locate the newly installed file, so now it is time to go back into Fireworks in order to use it.

Task: Use Your New Extension

Many extensions take advantage of the interaction between all Macromedia products and have been developed with nice user interfaces that make utilizing them even easier. The following steps will enable you to use the new extension:

1. Open a Fireworks document.

2. Add some content appropriate for the file that you installed. In the case of the figures presented this hour, this requires some text and a path.

3. Locate the new extension (commonly located in the Commands menu).

If you cannot find the new extension, return to the Extension Manager, locate the file, and read the instructions in the panel. This should tell you where within Fireworks the extension is located.

4. Select the command. In most cases, a user interface or dialog will open, ready for you to input your parameters, as shown in Figure 20.6

FIGURE 20.6

Most Fireworks extensions now have nice user interfaces for you to input your parameters and get the most out of your downloaded file.

20

5. Make the selections that you want in the interface. If you want more information first, though, most extensions have a Help menu or icon. Use this to learn more about how to apply the associated effects.

6. Click OK to continue and see the effects.

7. Remember, if you are not happy with how your document is affected, you can use the History panel to undo the steps.

As you have seen here, downloading from the Macromedia Exchange is a nice, simple way to increase the capabilities of Fireworks. There are many extensions that will not only enhance Fireworks but also integrate with other Macromedia products, enhancing your design skills and greatly improving workflow. Take some time to read through the downloads available to find out how much more you can do in Fireworks with a little effort.

Using the Extension Manager for Management

In the previous sections you have seen how to use the Manager for downloading and installing from the Macromedia Exchange. It can also be used for the general management of your extensions, no matter which applications they were downloaded for. It may be that you have downloaded extensions that do not perform as you expected. Use the Extension Manager to delete them.

The Extension Manager has these four main functions:

- Downloading and installing extensions
- Removing and disabling extensions
- Packing your own extensions for distribution
- Submitting extensions to share with others via the Exchange

To delete an extension, simply select it in the Manager, and click the trashcan icon (Windows only) or choose Remove Extension from the File menu. This book doesn't delve deeply into the whole process of creating extensions. However, the next section does look at using Flash MX to create an interface for a new command.

Creating an Interface through Flash MX

As you might have noticed in the last section, many extensions now come complete with nice Flash-based interfaces for users to input parameters and other controls. Now, the very idea of creating extensions may seem beyond you at the moment, but you can easily create the basic commands necessary, even with no programming skills. Indeed, in the last hour you saved some steps from the History panel as a Command script, opened the steps in a text editor, and looked at the code.

To recap: Every movement you make in Fireworks is remembered in the History panel. Saving these steps creates a script complete with a code that tells Fireworks what actions to perform on a specific object.

This section refers back to the script you saved in the last hour, "Creating Custom Scripts for the Commands Menu." At that point the script simply imported a file, but now you can look at ways to develop its functionality, complete with a user interface to choose a placement location within your document. There isn't enough time here to develop the command to allow end users to choose a file, but this is still a useful command if you are constantly inserting your photo, a client logo, or even image-based copyright information into Fireworks documents.

Creating commands and extensions comes under the heading of extensibility, and as with previous versions of Fireworks, Macromedia will release a pertinent PDF, available for download from the Macromedia Web site (http://www.macromedia.com), containing all information that you could ever need.

Before even opening Flash, take some time to consider what it is you are trying to achieve with a command. There is no point in creating an interface that makes a command more complicated than the individual actions covered by the command.

If you are unfamiliar with Flash, then check out Hour 13, "Working with Flash MX," before attempting this task.

Plan how you want the interface to look. Maybe draw it as an outline in Fireworks and make sure that you plan only buttons or text fields that are actually needed. An interface that is too cluttered would be confusing and off-putting for users.

Task: Open Flash and Design the Interface

In this task you will work in Flash to create an interface that will be visible to the end user. This interface will work in Fireworks and will allow selections and settings to be made.

1. Open Macromedia Flash MX. (If you do not have a copy, a trial version is available from the Macromedia Web site.)

2. Create a new document. Then, from the Modify menu, choose Document.

▼ TASK

20

3. Change the document size to 180×180 pixels. This will be quite big enough for the interface because the end user will have only two options to select.

4. Set the document background color to be anything you want. Pale blue is used in Figure 20.7, but color is simply up to your personal preference.

FIGURE 20.7

Choose a size and background color for your interface document that will form the basis for the user inputs.

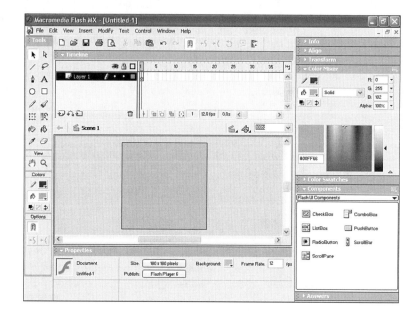

5. Save the file and name it. `Import Helper` or something similar would be appropriate for this.

6. Add any header text or a logo to suit your company or name.

7. Next you will need two buttons, one for the user to accept choices and one to decline. Because this interface is designed to be simple, use Flash-supplied buttons. From the Window menu choose Common Libraries, Buttons, to show the Buttons section of the Library panel, as in Figure 20.8.

FIGURE 20.8

Flash MX comes with predesigned buttons. Even without any design skills in Flash, you can pick and size one of these buttons to suit your needs.

8. Expand a folder by double-clicking it. Then drag a button onto your document. (You will resize it in a minute.)

9. Right-click the button, choose Scale, and then drag diagonally to size the button to suit your document. If you are more confident in Flash, you can type the size you want in the W and H boxes in the Property Inspector.

10. When the button is the right size, you need to add some text to say **Go** or **Yes,** so the user can indicate the desire to proceed.

11. Show the Library panel and rename this button **Accept.**

12. Repeat Steps 8 through 11 for the second button, only this time name it **Cancel** in the Library panel. Your document should look something like Figure 20.9. Save the file again to avoid losing any information.

20

FIGURE 20.9

*At this stage your
interface has a title
and buttons, so that
the end user can
accept or reject
choices.*

Now you have created what looks like a user interface but in reality is simply a pretty
box with buttons. Because this is not a Flash book, it doesn't go far into the concepts of
action scripting. However, you will need to understand a little code to take the leap from
pretty box to user interface. ActionScript is the coding language used in Flash. It is
incredibly powerful when used to its maximum capacity, but even at a lower level, it
makes certain tasks nice and easy.

For this interface you need for something to happen when the user clicks the buttons you
just added (the user accepts or cancels choices). You also need input areas for the user to
choose where the image should appear.

Task: Developing the Interface

▼ TASK

In the next part of this tutorial, you will add a new layer in Flash, create text input areas,
name them, and then add the code needed to make things work. It may sound complicated, but it is actually simple, so let's get straight into it.

1. Start by creating a new layer in your Flash document by selecting Insert, Layer.
   Double-click the new layer name and call it **inputslayer.**

2. Select the new layer and then from the Insert menu choose New Symbol. The
   Symbol Properties dialog opens, as shown in Figure 20.10. Name the new symbol
   textinput, and choose the radio button from the Behavior options. Click OK to
   continue.

FIGURE 20.10

The Symbol Properties dialog allows you to set the names and types of symbols you create in Flash.

3. The stage is blank and ready for you to create the areas for your users to type their selections. Draw a rectangle on the stage, fill it solid with white, and add a solid black line around it. Choose Insert, Convert to Symbol. Convert this rectangle into a graphic symbol named **textbg.** This will act as the area the user sees to input selections.

4. From the Library drag a second instance of the textbg symbol onto the stage and place it directly beneath the original that is already in place.

5. Select the Text tool from the Tools panel, then type a text label to the left of each rectangle. These should say **Left** and **Top,** respectively.

6. Click the Text tool and create a text area directly on top of the first rectangle.

7. Use the Property Inspector to set the following for the text area:

   - In the Type drop-down menu, select Input Text. This will allow the user to type directly into the interface that you are creating.

   - Once Input Text is selected, a second text field appears below it in the Property Inspector. This is for the Instance Name of the symbol; because you will need to refer to the text box in your script in a few minutes, you must name this instance of the text box. Name this **leftpos.**

   - Var: This text box in the Property Inspector is for you to name your variables. As with the instance name, you need to refer to the variables in your script. Name the variables in the field; for the first rectangle type **_root.leftposition.**

   - Set a maximum number of characters for the user to input. As this command will control the placement of an image on-screen, this only needs to be 4. Until screen resolutions become greater than 9999, 4 characters will be just fine.

20

8. Click the text area you typed and insert a value to be used as a default, in this case **100**. This means that if a user clicks the Go button in the interface without first choosing a location, the left position of the image will be at 100 pixels.

9. Repeat Steps 6 and 7, but wherever you had typed **left,** such as the instance name, now type **top.** The screen should now look something like Figure 20.11.

10. Click the Scene 1 tab on the Information bar to return to the Main Document window, and then save your work before you continue.

You now have all of the parts that you need to create the rest of the interface: a nice-looking box, neat text input areas for users to type in, text labels indicating what values need to be placed where, as well as buttons to confirm or cancel the command.

Attach Code to the Accept Button

It is now time to start working with the code to pull it all together. You have already inserted the buttons for a user to either accept or reject his or her own settings. Now you need to ensure that when clicked, these buttons perform the actions they were inserted for.

Select the button that you have named Accept on the stage. In the Property Inspector name the instance **accept;** again, you need this for scripting.

Show the Actions panel if it is not already visible. Because you want the action to be applied when the user clicks the button, type the following code directly into the Actions panel:

```
on (release) {
```

This will trigger an action when the mouse click is released by the user. Now you need to add further code to place the image correctly. You have already discovered the benefits of using layers in your Fireworks files, so you will import your image into its own layer within your document. Type the following as a new line of the release action code:

```
FWJavascript("fw.getDocumentDOM().addNewLayer('image', '');");
```

This line of code tells Fireworks to add a new layer called image to the document. Like most of the coding you will do, it may look complicated but in reality is very simple when broken down.

This next code to be added locates the file and directory to be used:

```
var directory = FWJavascript("fw.appJsCommandsDir");
var logo = "image.png";
var filename = directory+"/"+logo;
```

This code uses a standard Fireworks API (application program interface) call to locate the Commands directory in Fireworks. Then you name the image that you want to import (this assumes that the image will be placed in the Commands directory along with the command itself). You can change this code to match your image name; otherwise, for the purposes of testing, change the name of your image.

The final line of the code brings together the information from the first two lines and joins it to create the path and filename ready to be imported.

Now you have a filename, a location, and something to happen when the button is clicked, but you still need to tell the script to take the information inserted by the user into the text input boxes. The following code will do just that, so add it to the Actions panel:

```
var lefpos = (_level0.leftposition);
var toppos = (_level0.topposition);
```

Now you actually need to load the file onto the Canvas in Fireworks. The following code should be pasted into the Actions panel. This takes all information already inserted and places the graphic at the positions shown in the code. You use a location of 0 at this point, as the user input values have not yet been entered.

```
FWJavascript("fw.getDocumentDOM().importFile(\""+filename+"
        \""+", {left:0, top:0, right:0, bottom:0}, false);");
```

Note that this is all one line of code. It will not function correctly if Flash thinks it is two.

The final line of code, which needs to be pasted into the Actions panel, will take the values inputted by the user and relocate the image accordingly. Again, this is a single line of code:

```
FWJavascript("fw.getDocumentDOM().moveSelectionBy({x:
        \""+leftpos+"\""+", y:\""+toppos+"\""+}, false, false);");
```

As far as your interface and the user details are concerned, you are now all done. This last little snippet of code, however, will exit the interface and return the user to the open Fireworks document. The code is quite self-explanatory—it ends the command:

20

```
FWEndCommand(true, "");
}
```

The complete code for the Attach button should look as follows:

```
on (release) {
FWJavascript("fw.getDocumentDOM().addNewLayer('image', '');");
var directory = FWJavascript("fw.appJsCommandsDir");
var logo = "image.png";
var filename = directory+"/"+logo;
var lefpos = (_level0.leftposition);
var toppos = (_level0.topposition);
FWJavascript("fw.getDocumentDOM().importFile(\""+filename+"
        \""+", {left:0, top:0, right:0, bottom:0}, false);");
FWJavascript("fw.getDocumentDOM().moveSelectionBy({x:
        \""+leftpos+"\""+", y:\""+toppos+"\""+"}, false, false);");
FWEndCommand(true, "");
}
```

Attach Code to the No Button

The No button that you created needs to cancel the command at any time. The code to achieve this is very simple. Again, you tell the script to cancel the command when a user has clicked the button. With the button selected, show the Actions panel and paste in the following code:

```
on (release) {
 FWEndCommand( true, "" );
}
```

This is all that is required, and it uses a code already explained in the previous coding steps.

Export the Flash File

Before you can do anything with the interface in Fireworks, you need to export the file from Flash into Fireworks.

Task: Export the File from Flash into Fireworks

▼ TASK

First, save your Flash document. This is to ensure that it is still available for further editing and enhancements or troubleshooting, if required. Once the document is saved, take the following steps to export your Flash movie:

1. From the File menu in Flash, choose Export Movie.

2. Browse to the Commands folder in the Configuration area of the Fireworks MX directory. On a Windows XP default installation, this path is C:\Program Files\Macromedia\Fireworks MX\Configuration\Commands. In OS X the path is \Applications\Macromedia Fireworks MX\Configuration\Commands\.

3. Name the file Import Helper.swf and then click Save to continue to the Export Flash Player dialog, as shown in Figure 20.12.

4. Make sure that the version number is set to 6 (this should be the default). Then click OK to accept the default settings.

FIGURE 20.12

Use the Export Flash Player dialog to make sure that version 6 is correctly exported.

The Exported SWF file is now saved into the Commands directory and is almost ready to be tested. Before you move to the final step, which is to test the Command directly within Fireworks, make sure that the image file that you referenced in your code is located in the Configuration, Commands directory, as well.

Task: Test the New Command

Now it's time to test all your hard work. Assuming that nothing has gone wrong, you should be able to see and use the new command directly from within Fireworks. Start by creating a new blank document in Fireworks. Then follow Steps 1 to 4:

1. Set the Canvas size to be large enough for the image that you have selected. Otherwise, set it to 400 × 400, which is more than large enough for almost any image to be used on a Web site.

2. From the Commands menu choose Import Helper. Your interface will appear on-screen as shown in Figure 20.13.

▼ TASK

20

FIGURE 20.13

There it is: your
brand new command
interface, nicely placed
in Fireworks and ready
for your input.

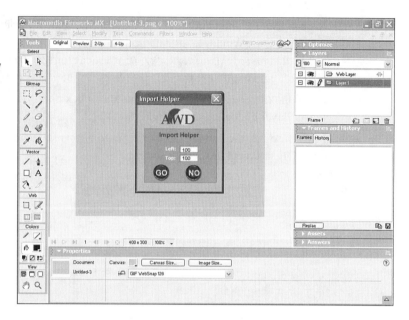

3. Insert values for the positioning options.

4. Click the Go button, and your specified image will appear at the coordinates you specified, as seen in Figure 20.14.

FIGURE 20.14

Your image
appears exactly
on the coordinates
you supplied—all
with a little help from
Flash inside Fireworks.

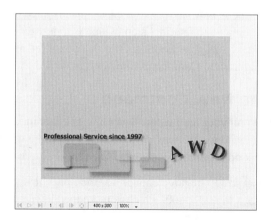

Troubleshooting

Hopefully, you will not have had any problems with your newly created command. If it doesn't function as you expected, however, then the most likely cause is an error in the Flash script.

Work back through this hour's steps and make sure that the code that you have inserted into the Actions panel is the same. If you find no errors there, check that you have named the library items and instances correctly. These are all common areas for making mistakes. After that, check that the Command script and image are both in the same location. Make sure that the file is correctly named, including the file extension.

Summary

Seeing what others have done with extensions and commands is often the inspiration for creating your own. In this hour you have learned about the Macromedia Exchange Web site, where you can obtain extensions for Fireworks. You also downloaded and installed an extension by using the Extension Manager.

The final part of the hour looked at how a simple user interface can be created in Flash MX to offer user input when applying a Fireworks command to an object. Extending Fireworks in this way not only makes using the program more useful but also enhances workflow for you and your colleagues. This hour has given you insight into built-in Fireworks facilities and increased the power at your fingertips.

Workshop

This hour has shown you how Fireworks Commands can be used to develop scripts and has taken that one step further to introduce a Flash interface. This final part of the hour offers some review questions and a quiz to help you review the topics. At the very end are some optional exercises that will take these topics a little further in a practical environment.

Q&A

Q I downloaded an extension, but it does not work. What should I check?

A The first thing to check is that the file downloaded properly. Then look at the information screen for the extension and check that it is suitable for Fireworks MX. If you are still having problems, read the reviews for the extension and see whether others have had the same problem. Peer-to-peer support is always helpful when troubleshooting.

Q I want to make an interface but do not have any Flash skills. Help!

A You can download a trial of Flash MX from the Macromedia Web site. The program comes with some great tutorials to get you started. There is nothing in this hour that can't be learned and re-created easily. Also, check out the support forums

20

on the Macromedia Web site and maybe get a copy of *Sams Teach Yourself Macromedia Flash MX in 24 Hours* by Phillip Kerman.

Q I clicked the Go button in my interface, and nothing happened. Where should I look to fix it?

A The reason that you saved the original Flash file was to make changes, if necessary. Go back to the file and check that all code matches and printed exactly. Then check the names of the library items and instances.

Quiz

1. Fireworks Extensions are located in which part of the Macromedia Exchange?

   a. Flash

   b. Fireworks

   c. Dreamweaver

2. Before creating a Flash interface, which of the following should be considered?

   a. Functionality and workflow

   b. Size and shape

   c. Name and date

3. What does *API* stand for?

   a. adding pretty interfaces

   b. application program interface

   c. application performance improvement

Quiz Answers

1. c.—At the present time Fireworks does not have its own Exchange area, so simply choose Fireworks from the list of categories in the Dreamweaver area.

2. a.—Make sure that you create an interface that will help the user, not one that adds more steps than the user needs or that makes everything more complicated than before. Good planning will lead to a good interface.

3. b.—Before you are able to understand the creation of complex commands fully, coming to grips with the API routines and scripting concepts is really important. This information will help you understand how Fireworks works and how to extend it to meet your needs.

Exercises

1. Now that you have a greater understanding of how Flash can be integrated with Fireworks, spend a little time learning more about Flash and Fireworks together. For example, some of the standard Fireworks panels are SWF files. With a little more understanding and practice, you can create more interfaces to help with everyday tasks.

2. Download and read the `Extending Fireworks` documentation. This is an important file that will enhance your understanding of the way Fireworks interfaces are created and managed. The more you learn about these things, the more you will be able to get from the application.

3. Try developing the interface created here to offer a drop-down menu, allowing the end user to browse or choose the exact file to load. You will need to learn more about action scripting to do this, so take some time and develop your skills.

20

PART VII

Fireworks and Friends: Working with Other Applications

Hour

HOUR **21**

Adobe Photoshop and ImageReady

Many die-hard designers of Web and print graphics still maintain that they "need" Photoshop to create quality graphics. Now, while Photoshop is indeed a professional-standard graphics package, you should see it as an aid to Fireworks and not merely a competitor. By this point in the book, hopefully, that myth of needing Photoshop should have been shot to pieces. Fireworks is a hugely powerful application that can make and edit images and files as complex as your design skills and imagination will allow.

Macromedia is very aware of the number of Photoshop users who are turning to Fireworks to create their Web graphics, so it offers unparalleled support for native Photoshop files. This support allows the importing of PSD files into Fireworks while retaining the bulk of Photoshop features.

It should be noted at this early stage, however, that due to some undocumented changes in Photoshop's plug-ins, API plug-in filters that ship with Adobe Photoshop 6 and 7 do not work in Fireworks MX. However, third-party image filters that work in Photoshop generally also work in Fireworks.

Once inside Fireworks you can optimize files for Web presentation and still export them back to Photoshop, if required.

Adobe ImageReady is less well known. Originally a stand-alone product, it was incorporated into Photoshop at the time of Version 5.5 and was intended to be the Adobe answer to Fireworks.

In this hour, you will

- Use Photoshop graphics in Fireworks
- Place Fireworks graphics into Photoshop
- Use filters and plug-ins
- Open a Fireworks file into ImageReady
- Optimize a Fireworks PNG in ImageReady

Using Photoshop Graphics in Fireworks

After you have a Photoshop file you wish to open in Fireworks, you can either drag and drop the individual parts of the Photoshop file directly into your Fireworks file, or you can import the entire file. Each of the methods has its advantages, depending on your requirements once the file is in Fireworks.

When you drag a graphic from Photoshop into your Fireworks file, each graphic is converted to a bitmap object and thus loses a large amount of editability. This applies to dragging and dropping text, as well. If you want to import text from Photoshop and retain the ability to edit and update it, check out the section "Use Photoshop Graphics in Fireworks" later in this hour.

Importing a Photoshop File into Fireworks

Whether you use File, Open, or File, Import, when working with a PSD file in Fireworks, the Photoshop file is imported into a PNG file as specified by the options set in your preferences. An example of a PSD file open in Fireworks is shown in Figure 21.1.

FIGURE 21.1

Photoshop files should open successfully in Fireworks and retain many of the original features, such as layers and text editability.

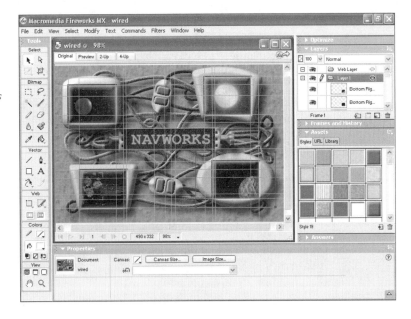

If you want to make changes to the file and then reuse it in Photoshop, you will need to export the file back into the PSD file format.

Task: Set Photoshop Import Options

TASK

Setting preferences for Photoshop file imports allows you to take control of how Fireworks handles the file and to what degree it will remain editable. To set your preferences for handling layers and text in Photoshop files that you import, follow the steps shown here:

1. From the Edit menu, choose Preferences.

2. Select the tab marked Import at the top of the Preferences dialog. Then choose the import options you want from those outlined in Steps 3 through 5 and shown in Figure 21.2.

3. Configure the following options for layers:

    • Convert to Fireworks Objects will import each layer in the Photoshop file as a separate bitmap object on its own layer.

    • Share Layer Between Frames will copy the imported layers across all frames in the Fireworks file, making them visible in all layers. You cannot have the Convert to Fireworks Objects radio button checked to use this option.

21

- Convert to Frames imports each layer in the Photoshop file as an object in its own new frame in Fireworks. If you intend to use the imported file as part of an animation, this is a very handy feature.

4. Here are the options for configuring text:

- Editable converts text in the Photoshop file to editable Fireworks text. This option lets you edit imported text with the Fireworks Text tool and the Property Inspector. The converted text may vary slightly in appearance from the original.

- Maintain Appearance converts text in the Photoshop file to a bitmap object in Fireworks. This option will import text that looks the same as it did in Fireworks, but because it is a bitmap, you will not have any text-editing functions (font, size, and so on) available.

5. The Use Flat Composite Image option can be used only if you saved the file from Photoshop with a composite image. It imports the Photoshop file as a single flattened image with no layers.

6. Click OK.

FIGURE 21.2

Preferences allows you to choose the way Fireworks handles an imported Photoshop file.

In addition to the options you are able to control using the preferences described above, Fireworks also preserves the following Photoshop features:

- Layer masks convert to Fireworks object masks.
- Layer effects convert to Fireworks Live Effects, wherever corresponding Live Effects exist.

Layer effects and Live Effects may vary slightly in appearance.

- Blending modes for layers convert to Fireworks blending modes for corresponding objects, where those blending modes are supported by Fireworks.
- The first alpha channel in the Channels palette converts to transparent areas in the Fireworks image.

Unsupported Photoshop Features

Although the preceding list shows that there is good support for Photoshop files in Fireworks, there are still some features that Fireworks is unable to handle and therefore ignores when a Photoshop file is imported.

- Fireworks supports only a single alpha channel. If the Photoshop file has multiple alpha channels, only the first one is supported.
- Photoshop adjustment layers, which allow you to "play" with color or tone adjustments without making permanent changes to the pixels in an image.
- Clipping groups, where the base layer acts as a mask for the entire group.
- Clipping paths, which let you isolate the foreground object and make everything outside the object transparent when the image is printed.

 In Windows, Photoshop filenames must include a `.psd` extension for Fireworks to recognize the Photoshop file type.

Importing Text and Handling Missing Fonts

If you wish to work on a Photoshop file that contains text, Fireworks will automatically check to see whether you have all the used fonts installed on your computer. If you created the PSD file, you will obviously have them. However, if you are working with a graphic supplied by a client, it is entirely possible that you do not. Even if you work on a network, not all users will have the same fonts installed.

Choosing Maintain Appearance replaces the text with a bitmap image that represents the appearance of the text in its original font. You can still edit the text, but when you do so, Fireworks replaces the bitmap image with a font that's installed on your system. This can cause the appearance of the text to change. As an alternative, you can choose fonts to replace the missing fonts. After you have replaced fonts, the document opens, and you can edit and save the text. When the document is reopened on a computer that contains the fonts specified in the original document, Fireworks remembers and uses the originals.

21

When a Photoshop 6 or 7 file that contains text is opened or imported in Fireworks, a cached image of the text is displayed, so its appearance remains the same as it was in Photoshop. When you edit the text, the cached image is replaced with actual text, which may differ in appearance from the original text.

Task: Choose a Replacement Font in Fireworks

▼ TASK

In a document that contains missing fonts, you can choose a replacement font in Fireworks as follows:

1. If you open a file that calls for a font not present on your machine, the Replace Fonts dialog will open, as shown in Figure 21.3.

2. Click Replace Fonts to open the Missing Fonts dialog, as shown in Figure 21.4.

3. Then do one of the following to decide how the font is to be handled in Fireworks:

   • Choose a replacement font by scrolling down the To category list.

   • To leave the missing font as is, click No Change; the font will be treated as a bitmap object.

4. Click OK.

Because Fireworks is an intuitive program, your choice will be remembered, so that the next time you open a document with the same missing fonts, the Missing Fonts dialog includes the font you chose.

FIGURE 21.3

Fireworks recognizes that a font is missing before the Photoshop file is opened.

FIGURE 21.4

Use the Missing Fonts dialog to select a replacement to work with during your Fireworks session.

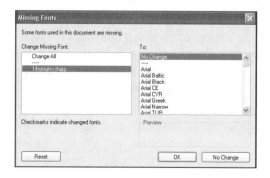

You have just seen that Fireworks can handle text from Photoshop even when you don't have the font. Another great feature is that Fireworks can also support effects that are applied to Photoshop.

It is worth a note of caution here: Although effects may be supported and visible in the two applications, they may not look exactly the same, because the two programs work differently.

Placing Fireworks Graphics into Photoshop

In the previous section you looked at how Fireworks can open Photoshop files while retaining editability. Now you will look at the reverse of that process.

Rather than setting import options, the key to successfully using Fireworks files in Photoshop is how they are exported. These export settings allow you to choose the features that will still be editable within the Photoshop environment. You can choose export options on an individual basis for each Fireworks file you export.

Task: Export a Fireworks File to Photoshop Format

The following steps outline the procedure for exporting a Fireworks file to Photoshop format:

1. When the file is ready to export from Fireworks, either choose File, Export, or use the Quick Export menu shown in Figure 21.5 and select Other, Export to Photoshop.

FIGURE 21.5

The Quick Export menu in the Fireworks interface allows you to export files to other applications quickly and easily.

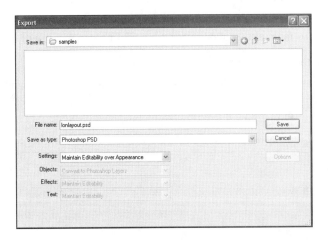

21

2. After the Export menu opens, type a name for your file.

3. Use the Save As drop-down menu to choose Photoshop PSD as the file type for the exported image. This opens the Export dialog, as shown in Figure 21.6.

4. In the Settings menu it is best to choose Custom; this gives you maximum control over the way your file is handled. However, the other options are as follows:

   - **Maintain Editability over Appearance**—This option keeps effects editable, converts text to Photoshop text, and retains editability. This option is the best one to choose if you plan on making major edits in Photoshop.

   - **Maintain Fireworks Appearance**—This option will convert every object in Fireworks to a separate Photoshop layer. This results in a loss of editability but maintains the look of the file as you created it in Fireworks.

   - **Smaller Photoshop File**—This selection will flatten each of your layers into a rendered image, which is ideal when working with very large files containing lots of objects.

5. In the Objects pop-up menu, choose one of the following:

   - **Convert to Photoshop Layers**—This convert option will transform your Fireworks objects and masks into their Photoshop equivalents.

   - **Flatten Each Fireworks Layer**—This option will remove editability from your Fireworks objects by flattening them en masse into a single Photoshop layer.

6. In the Effects pop-up menu, choose one of the following:

   - **Maintain Editability**—Where possible, this option will convert a Fireworks Live Effect to a Photoshop equivalent. However, if there is no comparable effect, it is lost in the export.

   - **Render Effects**—This will flatten all effects into their object; the object will maintain its appearance when in Photoshop but will lose all editability.

7. In the Text pop-up menu, choose one of the following:

   - **Maintain Editability**—Where possible, text will remain editable within a Photoshop layer; any unsupported text formatting will be lost.

   - **Render Text**—As with the other rendering options, this will preserve the appearance of the text, but you will lose the ability to edit it.

FIGURE 21.6
Selecting the PSD format for your export allows you to choose the features that will remain editable within the Photoshop environment.

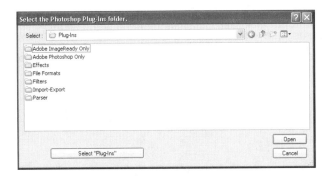

Depending on the version of Photoshop you are running, you should be careful when exporting files with many layers. Photoshop 5.5 and earlier cannot open any file with more than 100 layers. You should therefore merge or delete any layers over 100.

Using Photoshop Filters and Plug-ins in Fireworks

In addition to third-party filters and plug-ins, Fireworks allows you to import and use Photoshop filters and plug-ins.

There are two ways to import filters and plug-ins. They can be imported into either the Live Effects window or the Filters menu. It doesn't matter which location you import them to because once imported, they are accessible from either. There are some constraints when using Photoshop filters: Photoshop 6 and 7 plug-ins and filters are not supported by Fireworks at all, whereas filters and plug-ins for the Mac are dependent on the user's having the correct version of the operating system.

Task: Import Third-Party Filters and Plug-Ins

▲ TASK

Fireworks makes importing or installing plug-ins and filters a really straightforward process. To use the Preferences dialog to import Photoshop and other third-party filters and plug-ins, follow these steps:

1. Save and close any open files in Fireworks; you will need to close the application as a final step before the plug-ins or filters will be made available.

2. From the Edit menu choose Preferences to open the Preferences dialog. Using a Mac running OS X, preferences are located under the Firework Menu.

3. Choose Folders.

21

4. Put a check in the Photoshop Plug-ins check box. The Select a Folder dialog should open automatically; if this does not happen, click the Browse button.

5. Locate the folder in which your plug-ins or filters are installed.

6. Click the Select "Plug-Ins" button to continue, as shown in Figure 21.7.

7. Click OK to close the dialog.

8. Close Fireworks and reopen it. The plug-ins will be loaded when the application reopens.

FIGURE 21.7
Locate the folder that contains your plug-ins and click the Select button to choose this folder. Fireworks must be closed and reopened for the plug-ins to work.

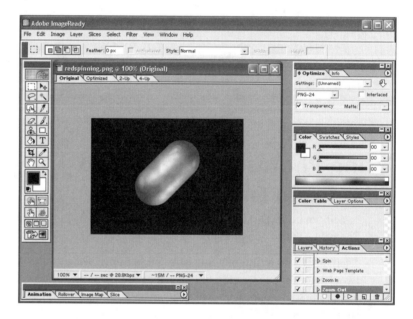

Applying Filters and Effects

Once installed, your filters can be applied either directly from the Filters menu or as Live Effects from the Property Inspector. In most cases it is better to apply filters as Live Effects; this is simply because they can be removed at any time by clicking the delete the current selected effect (–, a minus sign) button.

Applying filters directly from the Filters menu will actually make a permanent change to the pixels.

Opening a PNG File into ImageReady

In this section you will look at a Fireworks layout that has been saved as a PNG file, which can then be opened in ImageReady for further editing and Web preparation. In

ImageReady you can directly add PSD files to an existing layout. You then reexport the file to Fireworks or else save it directly for Web usage.

1. Open ImageReady and then choose Open from the File menu.

2. Locate the Fireworks file you wish to open. A preview should appear in the dialog, as shown in Figure 21.8.

3. Click Open to continue.

4. If necessary, use the View menu to adjust the on-screen size of the image for editing. You will find that files opened in ImageReady tend to be around 50%.

5. After the file is in ImageReady, you can add PSD files directly from Photoshop, if required. This is handy if you have some prepared images already in Photoshop format that you want to add to your layout.

6. Use the Jump To command to open the file in Photoshop and complete any designing you want. As the two applications work hand in hand, you are able to work between them in the same way that Fireworks and Dreamweaver can.

7. In Photoshop apply any plug-ins, filters, or effects that you may want to use. As the image was opened in ImageReady, you can use all Photoshop filters, even those that are not compatible with Fireworks.

8. If you do not intend to return the file to Fireworks, simply jump back to ImageReady to create slices, hotspots, or links that you want in the file.

9. Save the file back to Fireworks for optimization and Web preparation.

FIGURE 21.8

A preview is shown before a PNG file is opened in ImageReady.

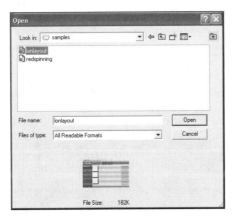

Optimizing a Fireworks PNG in ImageReady

In Figure 21.9 you can see a Fireworks-created PNG file that has been opened into ImageReady, which offers two ways to optimize your image. There is a degree of built-in optimization attached to the Save As command. After you select the file type to use, you

21

can specify image quality, background transparency or matting, color display, and downloading method. However, any Web features—such as slices, links, animations, and rollovers—that you've added to a file are not preserved using this method.

An alternative—and recommended—method is to set the optimization manually, using the Optimize palette.

Task: Optimize a Fireworks PNG in ImageReady

This process is quite similar to optimizing images in Fireworks. The following steps should make the process nice and simple:

1. Click the 4-up tab at the top of the document window to show the file with its default settings in four panes.

2. Select each of the panes in turn and choose an optimization setting from the Optimize tab (if it is not visible, choose Show, Optimize, from the Window menu).

3. As you change the settings, the image is redrawn with the quality and file type that you've chosen.

4. Compare the way the file looks with different settings. Click the Optimize tab to see the image at full size with the options you've selected.

5. When you're done, you can save the file (note that the Save command in ImageReady will always save as a PSD file).

If you want to save the image for use on the Web, save the file into Photoshop and then use the Save for Web command from the File menu.

FIGURE 21.9

In ImageReady you can use the 4-up preview to find the best optimization settings for your file. Each pane can be optimized individually.

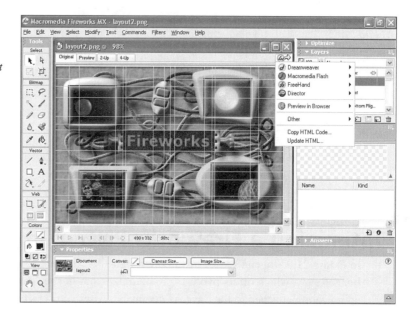

If you are planning on optimizing images in ImageReady on a regular basis, check out the output settings available for Slice and HTML. They allow you to save the settings you use most often.

Summary

In this hour you have looked at using Adobe Photoshop with Fireworks, perhaps the most common integration that occurs with a non-Macromedia product. Careful selection of import and export options will ensure that your files are almost interchangeable between the two applications.

ImageReady is the Adobe application designed for Web graphics, whereas despite many advancements, Photoshop is historically thought of as being for the print industry. These applications work well together, but even their combined power does not come close to overshadowing Fireworks. Perhaps the most important lesson to learn from this is that even though both Photoshop and ImageReady are very good applications, you can work without them when required.

Workshop

The following questions will test your knowledge of image formats, document settings, and other topics discussed in the hour. The exercises will help you put into practice what you've just learned.

Q&A

Q I have been given an old version of a Photoshop PSD file to convert for use on the Web. How should I do this?

A Start by making sure that your import options will suit the image you are going to work with. After the image has been opened in Fireworks, you should be able to make any changes you need, and then you can reexport it as a Photoshop file.

Q Why can't I use all my Photoshop plug-ins and filters?

A Quite simply, Adobe and Macromedia do not make their products in the same way. This means that there are always going to be some compatibility problems.

Q I am interested in learning more about ImageReady, but I cannot find it. Where can I get a copy?

A ImageReady is not available as a stand-alone product anymore. It is installed automatically with Photoshop version 5.5 and upward.

21

Quiz

1. Which version of Photoshop features filters and plug-ins that are best supported in Fireworks?

    a. Photoshop 5

    b. Photoshop 6

    c. Photoshop 7

2. Fireworks supports how many alpha channels?

    a. 3

    b. 2

    c. 1

3. Which applications are designed mainly for creating Web graphics?

    a. Photoshop and Fireworks

    b. Fireworks and ImageReady

    c. Photoshop and ImageReady

Quiz Answers

1. a.—Photoshop version 5 and before are best supported by Fireworks. However, it is worth looking around on the Internet for third-party filters and plug-ins that will work in both applications regardless of the version.

2. c.—Fireworks supports only a single alpha channel. A Photoshop file may have multiple alpha channels, but only the first one will be supported in Fireworks.

3. b.—Fireworks and ImageReady have both been created and designed for the screen image industries rather than for creating printed media.

Exercises

Now that you have had a chance to look at PhotoShop and Fireworks, use the following exercises as an opportunity to develop your skills and understanding of how these applications can help with your Fireworks workflow.

1. Create an image file in Fireworks complete with layers, slices, and hotspots, and then export it to ImageReady. Develop an understanding of the functions that transfer well between applications and those that don't.

2. Repeatedly open a PSD file into Fireworks, changing the import settings a little each time you import it. Sometimes the best way to find the most appropriate import

settings is by trial and error. Don't assume that because the file does not import as you expect the first time that it is not possible to achieve success.

3. Use the help files in both Photoshop and ImageReady to learn more about their features. Combining at your fingertips the best parts of all the applications will help you get the most from your graphic creation tools.

Hour **22**

Macromedia FreeHand and Adobe Illustrator

Many people use either the FreeHand application or the Illustrator application with Fireworks, but it is not assumed in this hour that you have. Macromedia FreeHand 10 is a vector-based drawing application. It is a common misconception that FreeHand is designed only for the production of printed graphics or illustrations. In reality, while you can use FreeHand to produce documents for a printed environment, you can also turn FreeHand graphics into Flash animations and even preview your FreeHand files in a Flash player. The integrated workspace most closely matches those found in Dreamweaver, Fireworks, and Flash, giving you a working environment that is not too different from what you have in fact already experienced.

There are versions of FreeHand available for both Windows and Macintosh. You can download a free trial of the software from the Macromedia Web site. This will give you 30 days to try the software before deciding whether it's something you have an ongoing need for.

Adobe Illustrator is available in its 10th version. As with many products from the Adobe family, it's well respected within the graphics industry for producing print, illustration, and Web graphics. Although it is not the easiest application for an occasional user to learn, it is certainly a very powerful tool. Illustrator is available for both the Windows and Macintosh systems, and once you have registered with Adobe, you can download the trial or order it on CD. The download is 80MB, so if you have a slower connection, you may want to consider the CD option. The Illustrator trial has certain restrictions on saving and exporting but should allow you to explore the application's features.

All three applications—Fireworks, FreeHand, and Illustrator—are vector-based image programs. Vector objects can therefore be opened and transferred easily between them and as often as you wish. Using Fireworks with other vector-based applications is largely the same, regardless of whether you are using FreeHand or Illustrator.

In this hour you will

- Import vector graphics into Fireworks
- Export Fireworks files to FreeHand and Illustrator
- Optimize images and files to print
- Place a Fireworks file into Illustrator for PDF delivery

Importing Vector Graphics into Fireworks

Whether or not you have ever used illustration software, it is very rare to use Fireworks for long before someone asks you to work with a file created in Illustrator, FreeHand, or even CorelDRAW. All of these files can be opened directly into Fireworks or else pasted in via the Clipboard. Some native features from the original program, such as textures and blends, will likely be lost during this process. Providing a definitive list of unsupported features is not really possible, however, as the fate of the features will depend upon the settings used when the file was originally saved. When you open a vector file directly into Fireworks, a new document is created; when you import a vector file, it is placed in your currently open Fireworks document.

Task: Open FreeHand Files into Fireworks

To open or import a FreeHand file directly into Fireworks, follow these steps:

1. In Fireworks choose File, Open, to navigate to the desired folder.

2. Change the Files of Type menu to show FreeHand files, as shown in Figure 22.1. Select the file you wish to work with in Fireworks and click Open.

FIGURE 22.1

Select FreeHand from the file type drop-down menu to see only FreeHand files.

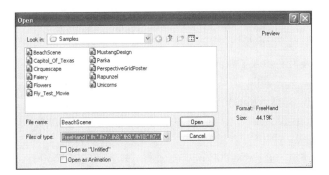

3. The Vector File Options dialog appears as shown in Figure 22.2. The options in the dialog are as follows:

Scale—You can scale the file by entering a value (percentage) in the scale box or by using the slider to change this value. When you reduce the scale this way, the width and height are adjusted.

Width and **Height**—If you know the exact dimensions you want for your imported image, type in these values in the Width and Height fields.

Resolution—If you want to change the image resolution, type a new value into the field.

Anti-Alias—You can choose to anti-alias Text, Paths, or both. By default Fireworks applies a Smooth Anti-Alias to your choice. To change this, use the drop-down menu at the end of the field. Crisp or Strong Anti-Alias modes are best for clearly defining areas of different colors.

> After importing the file, you can change objects to Anti-Alias or Hard Edge by selecting Modify, Alter, and then Hard Fill, Anti-Alias Fill, or Feather Fill.

File Conversion—If you are opening a multipage document, the File Conversion section allows you to choose how these are handled during the import, as follows:

> **Open a page**—Use this option to open a single page. By default the first page will open; use the Page drop-down menu to alter which page opens.

> **Open pages as frames**—This option imports and opens all pages from the document into a separate Fireworks frame within a single document.

> **Ignore layers**—This option imports all objects on a single layer.

> **Remember layers**—This option maintains the layer structure of the imported file.

Convert layers to frames—This option places each layer of the imported document into a separate frame.

Include Invisible Layers—By default invisible layers are not imported. To make sure that even invisible layers are imported, check this option.

Include Background Layers—By default background layers are ignored during import. To include background layers and have them imported to their own layers in Fireworks, check this option.

Render as images—This option is used to rasterize complex groups, blends, or tiled fills and place each as a bitmap object in Fireworks. When Fireworks encounters a group of more than 30 objects, it converts them to a bitmap that is treated as a single object. This single object will have the editability only associated with bitmaps. You can edit the number in the text box to change how many objects a group, blend, or tiled fill can contain before it is rasterized during import. To retain all objects without any rasterizing, deselect these options in the dialog.

FIGURE 22.2

The Vector File Options dialog allows you to control how Fireworks will deal with an imported file.

Be careful when choosing to preserve all objects. A complex document with many fills, blends, or tiled fills can create a huge file size.

4. Once you have made your selections, click OK to import the file into Fireworks.

Working with Adobe Illustrator Files

Adobe Illustrator files are saved in one of two formats: AI (Adobe Illustrator) or EPS (encapsulated post script). Opening or importing these files offers you many of the same choices outlined for FreeHand files in the previous section. The differences are now covered in the two following sections.

Task: Open or Import an EPS File into Fireworks

To open or import an EPS file, follow these steps:

1. From the File menu in Fireworks, choose either Open or Import. In the dialog choose EPS file and click Open.

2. In the EPS File Options dialog (shown in Figure 22.3), choose a new value for the width or height. The default setting constrains the image proportionately, so you need to enter only one value.

3. Choose the unit of measure that you prefer to work with in Fireworks. Typically, this will be pixels, but you can use the drop-down menu next to the width and height values to change this setting to suit your requirements.

4. If you require specific values for the image size, then deselect the Constrain Proportions check box.

> If you deselect the Constrain Proportions check box, then be careful to insert proportional width and height values. Otherwise, your file could easily look very squashed or stretched.

5. Choose whether Fireworks should apply anti-aliasing, the smoothing of the transition between pixels of different colors. The default is checked, so deselect the option for Fireworks not to anti-alias the file.

6. Click OK to complete the process.

FIGURE 22.3

Importing or opening an EPS file allows you to set size, resolution, and scaling options.

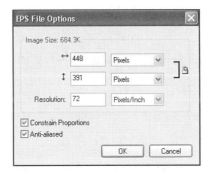

Task: Opening Adobe Illustrator Files

Opening AI files into Fireworks is a straightforward process. To open an AI file, simply choose File, Open; or File, Import. Then follow the steps outlined previously for importing a FreeHand file.

Exporting Fireworks Files to FreeHand and Illustrator

You have learned about opening nonnative Fireworks files into other applications, and the reverse process is just as simple. Just as you might need to work in Fireworks with a file that has been created in another application, it is possible that you will need to send a Fireworks file to someone who uses an alternate application.

Unsupported Fireworks Options

Although vector graphics created in Fireworks can be exported into FreeHand for further editing, some Fireworks features are not supported, so you will need to re-create certain effects within the destination application. This is true when exporting Fireworks graphics into any other vector-based application. These are the features that are not supported:

- Live Effects
- Blending modes
- Texture, pattern, Web dither fills, and gradient fills
- Slice objects and image maps
- Many text-formatting options
- Guides, grids, and Canvas color
- Bitmap images
- Some strokes

Task: Place a Fireworks Graphic into FreeHand

When exporting Fireworks images to FreeHand, you can either export vector paths or paste complete Fireworks graphics into FreeHand. Because FreeHand is also a Macromedia application, there is a quick export option available.

If you want to copy paths from Fireworks into FreeHand, use the following steps:

1. Click the QuickExport button and choose FreeHand, Copy Path Outlines.
2. Launch FreeHand and open a new or existing document.

3. Within FreeHand choose Edit, Paste, to paste the paths.

Exporting a complete Fireworks graphic involves a few more steps but is still a straight-forward process.

> Before following the next series of steps, refer to the unsupported options listed a little earlier in the chapter.

1. With the file that you wish to export open in Fireworks, you can either choose Export from the File menu or use the QuickExport button and choose FreeHand, Export to FreeHand.

2. When the dialog opens, type a name and location for the exported file.

3. In the Save as Type drop-down menu, choose Illustrator 7.

> Usually, the Save as Type dialog automatically defaults to Illustrator 7. This is a standard file type when exporting to another vector graphics application. Illustrator 7 is the most widely supported file type, regardless of where you're exporting your vector graphic.

4. Click the Options button to open the Illustrator Export Options dialog, as seen in Figure 22.4.

5. In the dialog select either Export Current Frame Only or Convert Frames to Layers.

6. Put a check in the FreeHand Compatible check box. This is required to export the file for use in FreeHand. Bitmaps within your Fireworks file will be ignored, and any gradient fills will be converted to solid fills.

7. Click OK and then click Save in the dialog. The image is now exported for use in FreeHand.

FIGURE 22.4

Choose which options best suit the file you're exporting.

Optimizing Bitmap Images and Files to Print

Fireworks is not often used to create printed images, and native Fireworks files are not well-suited for this medium, but that does not mean that it is impossible.

When creating printed graphics, quality is more important than file size, which in many ways is the opposite of creating graphics for the Web. The best solution, when using Fireworks to create print images, is to maintain the file as a vector image and export the file into FreeHand by using the steps outlined previously. This will automatically convert the file to the CMYK color model (used for printing) when the file is outputted to separations for printing.

Unfortunately, this is not a valid solution when you are working with bitmap images. Fireworks is based on the RGB (red, green, blue) color model, whereas the print industry uses CMYK (cyan, magenta, yellow, black), and there is no simple way within Fireworks to convert one to the other. If you have CMYK values that you want to use in Fireworks or, more likely, that a client has told you to use, it may look like an impossible task. However, there is a nifty shortcut for this.

Task: Convert Fireworks RGB Color to CMYK

In this task you will take an RGB color and create the correct CMYK values.

1. Open Fireworks and create a new blank document. Use the Drawing tools and create a simple shape fill of the shape in black.

2. From the Window menu choose Color Mixer to open the Color Mixer panel. Use the Options menu to make sure that RGB is selected, as shown in Figure 22.5. If the black fill is in place, then all values should be 0.

FIGURE 22.5

The Color Mixer shows you the values of your current fill. When black is the fill, then all RGB values are 0. The Options menu allows you to change color models.

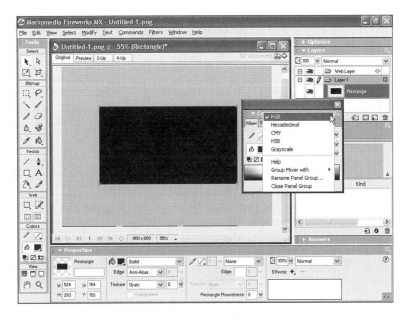

3. Now assume that a client has told you that he wants a particular burgundy color used, with CMYK values of 0, 76, 65, 38. With the Options menu in the Color Mixer, change to CMY. Notice that this does not change the color of your shape at all.

The term "CMY" might just seem to be a typo for "CMYK," but this points up another example of why Fireworks is not designed for creating print images. "K" stands for black, and to use CMYK values in Fireworks, you will first need to find the grayscale value of the black in the color you want to use.

4. For CMY values enter 0, 76, and 65, as shown in Figure 22.6. The color of your shape changes, but it is still not burgundy. It should be a fleshy pink color.

FIGURE 22.6

Inputting only three of the values for a CMYK color will change your fill but will not give you the correct results.

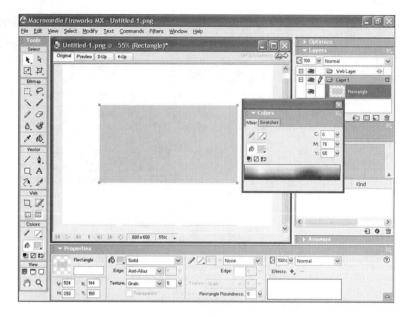

5. At the moment you have a color that is lacking black. To adjust for black, you have to enter equal amounts of C, M, and Y to produce the correct grayscale. You know from the client that the black value is 38. In this case the correct amount of black to add is three times the black value, so add 114 to each of the CMY values already in place. Notice that you now have a burgundy fill.

6. You can click the Options pop-up menu and switch the mode to RGB, retaining the correct color but using the color model that best suits Fireworks.

Image Resolution and Optimization

Whenever possible, you should consider the intended output of the file when creating it. Calculating the image resolution that should be set when printing a graphic is simple. The image resolution should be twice the printer's line screen. If you are unsure about this, check with the printer for their standard line screen. Then, when creating the file in Fireworks, set Resolution in the New Document dialog, as shown in Figure 22.7.

FIGURE 22.7

In the New Document dialog, set Resolution before creating an image to be printed. If in doubt about these settings, check with the printer.

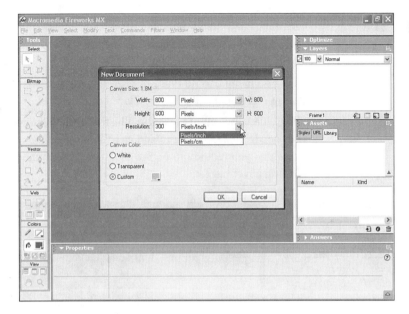

If you do not have access to FreeHand or another illustration application, you can still make the most of the tools that Fireworks offers to enhance image quality for printing. Once your image is finished and ready to go, start by saving it as a PNG file for future editing. Then open the Optimization panel, and from the Export File Format, choose TIFF 24 or 32. This setting will produce non-lossy compression for the file. As soon as you select this option, the rest of the Optimization panel grays out because there are no further options for this file type. Export the file, and it will be ready for use in almost any DTP application.

Task: Take a PNG File into Illustrator and then Export as a PDF

In this task you will take a native Fireworks PNG file, place it in Adobe Illustrator, and save it as a PDF file ready for delivery on the Internet or printed page. At the end of this task, you can see a complete layout created in Fireworks, with bitmaps, vectors, and effects. In fact, other than behaviors, most techniques available in Fireworks have been used somewhere in the layout.

1. From the File menu choose Export and then select Illustrator 7 from the File Type drop-down menu.

2. Name the file and select a location. Click the Options button and choose the best option for your file. As this will result in a single image, you would typically choose to export only the current frame. Make sure that if there are multiple frames in your file, you have first selected the appropriate frame in the Frames Panel.

3. Click Save to complete the export.

4. Open Illustrator and then the file in which you want to place the PNG file. You could also create a new document.

5. From the File menu choose Place to open the Place dialog. Locate the file that you saved from Fireworks and click the Place button.

6. Your PNG file is placed in the active Illustrator file. Complete the Illustrator file to suit your needs, remembering to add any file information and other document properties that you require. In Figure 22.8 you can see the Fireworks image forming part of a cover page.

FIGURE 22.8

The Fireworks document can be placed anywhere within your Illustrator file. Here it forms part of a cover.

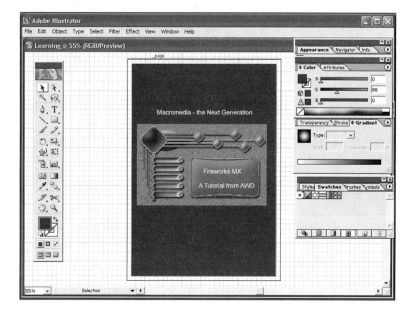

7. From the File menu choose Save As and then select Adobe PDF as the file format.

8. Name the file and click Save. Your PNG file is now within the Illustrator file, which has been saved as a PDF for delivery (see Figure 22.9).

FIGURE 22.9

Even seemingly complicated graphics can be used in Illustrator to form part of a PDF document.

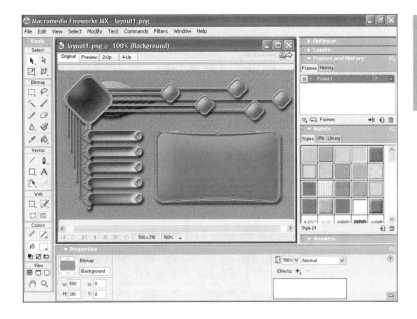

Summary

In this hour you have learned about using Fireworks with other vector graphics applications. Moving graphics files from one application to another is a common practice within the graphic design industry. In addition to the obvious benefits of making many different file types usable in Fireworks, this practice also opens up many opportunities either for working with graphics and converting them for the Web or for taking your Fireworks files and using them in a print environment. In the next two hours, "HTML Options and Editors" and "Microsoft Office," you will take integration one step further and look at using Fireworks in conjunction with other applications for creating your HTML files.

Workshop

In this hour you have looked at how Fireworks can work with other graphics applications, in this case applications aimed at creating printed media. The following section will help remind you of some of the key points. At the very end are some exercises for you to try. These are not outlined step by step for you like the tasks; completing them will require several of the skills you learned in this hour.

Q&A

Q **Why is my FreeHand file huge when I open it in Fireworks?**

A Try changing the Render as Image options: Restrict the number of objects that can be imported before Fireworks rasterizes the objects. Although this will reduce the editability (rasterizing flattens groups of objects), it will greatly reduce the size of the imported file.

Q **I exported my file from Fireworks but am having problems opening it elsewhere. What should I do?**

A Reopen the file in Fireworks and then reexport it. This time make sure that you choose Illustrator 7 as the file format. Other versions of AI files are not as well-supported in other applications.

Q **Why does my Fireworks file look awful when I print it?**

A Fireworks is intended for the creation of screen graphics. The application's default resolution is 72 pixels per inch, which is not sufficient for high-quality printed material. Try increasing the resolution of your graphic and then optimize it as a TIF file before printing.

Quiz

1. Which type of Illustrator file is most widely supported?

    a. Illustrator 7

    b. Illustrator 8

    c. Illustrator 9

2. What does *rasterize* mean?

    a. Flatten layers in a file

    b. Convert vector objects into bitmap format

    c. Remove unwanted formatting

3. Which applications are best suited to the creation of printed graphics?

    a. Fireworks and Photoshop

    b. Illustrator and Fireworks

    c. FreeHand and Illustrator

Quiz Answers

1. a.—Illustrator 7 is widely recognized by other vector graphics applications, making it the safest export option regardless of the intended destination.

22

2. b.—To rasterize is to convert images into raster (bitmap) form for display or printing. Vector graphics, as well as vector and outline fonts, must be rasterized for printing or display. All output of a display screen or printer is in raster format.

3. c.—FreeHand and Illustrator, but not Fireworks, are widely used for print jobs.

Exercises

1. Open a complex FreeHand file into Fireworks and convert it into a Web layout. Spend a little time working out the best way to overcome some of the unsupported features. Draw on the skills you have developed in these 22 hours to redraw or re-create effects that do not transfer.

2. In Fireworks create a cover page for a book or other document and then take the file into Illustrator. Use the native Illustrator tools to create your complete document. This will introduce you to several publishing techniques, especially for image placement and text flow, that are not normally considered when working only with Fireworks.

3. Learn a little more about color models and how they are used in different industries. The more you learn, the better your ability to achieve a color match between print and screen. When you develop Exercise 2, create a book or catalog of your skills. When you print this out, see how the print colors compare to the screen colors. Then experiment with color-matching adjustments.

Hour 23

HTML Options and Editors

In the two preceding hours, "Adobe Photoshop and ImageReady" and "Macromedia FreeHand and Adobe Illustrator," you saw how good Fireworks is at working with images and files from other graphics applications, whether they are from Macromedia or not. Hour 17, "Working with Dreamweaver MX," addressed roundtrip editing between Dreamweaver and Fireworks, which is the most common integration between Fireworks and any other application, but you may be wondering what other HTML options are open to you.

This hour will start by looking at the HTML setup options used for exporting Fireworks HTML and then will move on to look at other ways that Fireworks can use HTML. Did you know, for example, that you can use Fireworks HTML in almost any HTML editor, or that this latest version of Fireworks can open HTML content created in other applications, as long as it is table based? This means that you can now use nonnative Fireworks HTML created by someone else, even when you have not created the source code or images.

In this hour you will

- Learn about the HTML setup options in Fireworks
- Set the defaults for your exported HTML
- Set document-specific options
- Learn about using GoLive and Fireworks HTML
- Learn about importing HTML content

HTML Setup in Fireworks

You already know that Fireworks creates HTML when you export files containing rollovers, slices, or other behaviors. Fireworks generates a complete HTML file and all of the images and code you need. One of the best things about this is that you do not need to know any HTML to use the features offered by Fireworks. However, understanding the language will certainly not do you any harm!

Fireworks exports your slices as cells in an HTML table when you export your file. You have complete control over the way these cells are named and formatted during the export. In this hour you will look at how to make these settings and preferences suit your needs.

Setting General Preferences

Although you looked at Dreamweaver in Hour 17, you should spend some time becoming familiar with the HTML setup options that are built into Fireworks. These will be very useful if you need to work with other HTML editors.

The HTML Setup dialog specifies how you want your Fireworks HTML exported. Although you can change the settings for every document you make, you are also able to set defaults. This is handy for working on projects that require the same kind of HTML.

Task: Define HTML Export Options

Defining HTML export options is done using the following steps:

1. Once you have a file ready for exporting, select the Options button in the Export dialog or choose HTML Setup from the File menu. The HTML Setup dialog, shown in Figure 23.1, opens to the General tab.

2. Click the HTML Style drop-down menu to be presented with the options for exporting your HTML to the editor of your choice. The choices available are as follows:

   Dreamweaver HTML—Perfect for Macromedia Integration, this is probably the most commonly used HTML option.

   FrontPage HTML—Create HTML specifically designed to meet the quirks of

FrontPage HTML. For more about FrontPage HTML, check out Hour 24, "Microsoft Office."

GoLive HTML—To use with Adobe GoLive, this is discussed more later in this hour.

Generic HTML—This can be used in any other editor.

> Fireworks is now able to both import and export XHTML (Extensible Hypertext Markup Language). XHTML is a family of current and future document types and models that reproduce, subset, and extend HTML. It is becoming increasingly commonplace to come across XHTML documents on the Internet. If you aren't familiar with this development, you can find out more by reading *Sams Teach Yourself HTML and XHTML in 24 Hours* by Dick Oliver.

23

FIGURE 23.1

The HTML Setup dialog allows you to have control over the type of HTML that Fireworks generates.

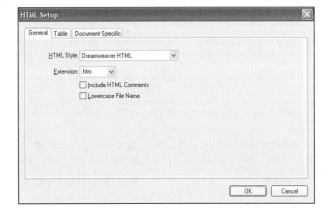

> Always choose to generate HTML specifically for the HTML editor that you intend to use. Choosing the wrong one may cause problems with scripts or interactions within your Fireworks file.

3. Choose a file extension for the exported file from the Extension drop-down menu.

4. Check the Include HTML Comments option, and Fireworks will annotate the code, telling you which parts you can copy and paste elsewhere.

5. Check the Lowercase Filename check box to export the file and all generated image files with lowercase filenames. This will not override the file extension that you chose in Step 3, so any uppercase file extension will be maintained regardless of your selection.

If you are working on a Macintosh machine, you also have the option to associate a File Creator to the exported File. This is handy to ensure that the correct application opens the file. Unlike a Windows-based computer, a Macintosh is not dependent upon the file extension.

6. Click the Table tab to see the options for the tables and cells that Fireworks generates. This tab is shown in Figure 23.2.

FIGURE 23.2

You can even control the format of generated tables and cells.

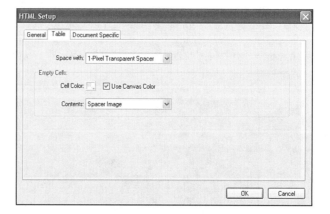

7. Spacing options are available for controlling the display of tables. Click the Space with drop-down menu to see the options. The default is to use a 1-Pixel Transparent Spacer. Fireworks creates this GIF image and then uses it as required. The alternatives are to use nested tables, which are created without the use of a spacer image, or to create a single table with no spacer GIF. This last option is the most likely to cause display problems. In most cases it is recommended that you stick to the default.

8. Choosing a cell color for HTML slices allows you to set a particular background for any HTML slice. The default is to use the Canvas color, but you can remove the check mark and select a different color through the color picker.

9. Leave Empty Cells as the default in order to use a spacer image. Otherwise, Fireworks will use a space tag ( ) in the cell, which can cause strange display effects.

Document Specific Settings

The previous section discussed how to set the options for your entire exported HTML. However, you can also input settings on a document-by-document basis by using the Document Specific tab of the HTML Setup dialog. This final tab of the dialog, shown in Figure 23.3, may look quite complicated, but it is very straightforward to use. You can set these preferences for each and every file you export or you can leave them as the default settings to let Fireworks decide.

FIGURE 23.3

Take care when changing the naming formats. Make sure that you are still able to identify which slice images are from which file.

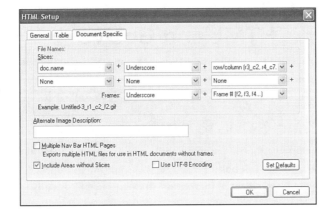

Task: Setting Document Specific HTML Options

In this task you will see just how simple and logical the Document Specific settings are to use.

1. Use the Slices drop-down menus to set the naming convention that you want for your slices. As you choose each option, the dialog shows you an example of the name that will be generated. The only thing to be careful of while setting these options is to avoid using the None options in the first menu. Choosing this would potentially cause Fireworks to create slice names that would overwrite existing files. Leaving the document name in the options somewhere will help to identify which image files are generated from which Fireworks exports.

2. Add any Alt text into the text box. This Alt text will appear as the image loads and in most browsers will be displayed when the mouse is over the image. It is a good idea to add Alt text when exporting a large image in slices, but it can be confusing to do so if you're working with a navigation bar that has buttons with their own Alt text.

3. If you want to place your Fireworks navigation bar on multiple pages and are not using templates, then check the Multiple Nav Bar HTML Pages box. This is a handy feature if Fireworks recognizes the number of buttons in your navigation bar and creates an HTML file for each of them.

4. Setting these options as defaults will store them in Fireworks and will make them the default settings for all exported files until you change them. Be careful not to click the Set Defaults button until you are sure that you are happy with the settings.

5. Click OK to close the dialog.

Fireworks HTML and GoLive

You have seen in the previous section that Fireworks can deliver content for HTML editors other than Dreamweaver. In Hour 24, "Microsoft Office," you will look at using Fireworks and FrontPage, but first you're going to look at using GoLive.

Exporting HTML to GoLive

With your Fireworks file prepared and ready to go, you have two options to get you started. The first is to click the QuickExport button and select Other, Export to GoLive. This will automatically tell the Export dialog to use GoLive HTML.

The other option is to do the following:

1. From the File menu choose Export and then click the Options button. Select GoLive HTML from the HTML Style menu.

2. Check the Include HTML Comments box. This makes it easier to identify Fireworks code in another application.

3. Name the file and choose a location for the images and slices that will be created. Click Save to continue.

4. Open GoLive. You now can open the Fireworks-generated page. All code should work as you intended (but see the following Caution).

GoLive doesn't support Fireworks' pop-up menu code. If you are creating a file that includes pop-up menus, you *must* choose Generic HTML in the Export options.

5. With the page open, click the Source tab in GoLive. Notice that the code is clearly marked as Fireworks MX/GoLive code, as in Figure 23.4.

FIGURE 23.4

The Fireworks-generated code is clearly marked within the exported file as being GoLive HTML.

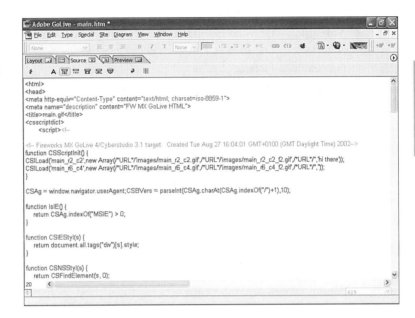

Importing HTML Tables

Fireworks MX can open or import HTML that is located within correctly built and formatted HTML tables. Any of the following file types should be supported: HTML, XHTML, SHTML, CFM(L), ASP, JSP, PHP, and DWT.

To import content successfully, the source code must be table based (using tables for layout). Because Fireworks exports HTML content in a table when the updated files are sent back to their location, it can only import content that is formatted the same way.

If the file that you want to open contains multiple tables, Fireworks will open all of them as separate documents.

Before you get too excited and think of all of the things that you can rush off and do, you need to be aware that there are some major importing limitations and restrictions, which are detailed in the following list:

Animation—Only the first frame of any animated GIF will be imported. Links to embedded media, such as Flash or QuickTime movies, will be retained, but they are not visible in Fireworks.

Behaviors—If the document you are importing contains behaviors that have been created in either Dreamweaver or Fireworks, you should be able to import them correctly, as long as they reside inside the <body> tags of the imported file and are behaviors that Fireworks can reexport.

Buttons and rollovers—Buttons will be imported with each state of the button on a separate frame. They will not import as button symbols, so they will need to be re-created. Rollovers also cause problems, so you often need to rearrange them after the import in order to get them back into the correct frame.

Hotspots and image maps—Hotspots and image maps will import but are prone to strange results, depending on how they were built. Overlapping slices or hotspots will cause problems.

Pop-up menus—Because Fireworks has full support for menus of this type, you will be able to import HTML pop-up menus successfully. If the file you are importing contains a graphic-based menu, it will be converted to HTML during the import process.

Nested tables—Nested tables are rebuilt as a single document in Fireworks. This often can create very strange results. The table will also be reexported as a single table unless you change the settings for nested tables in the HTML setup dialog.

Table cell properties—If a table cell contains text or code, it is imported as an HTML slice. Cells containing only images are imported as images. Because Fireworks exports HTML tables and cells that are content driven, there is no support for the width or height attributes.

Task: Open and Edit an HTML File in Fireworks

Start by locating the Hour 23 directory and the folder named Begin. In a Web browser open the file called topbar.htm. You should see the file shown in Figure 23.5. Notice that the file has buttons with hyperlinks attached. Obviously, those links will not work here, but the buttons are active and change when moused over.

FIGURE 23.5

Here is the correctly functioning HTML file in a browser, complete with buttons and links.

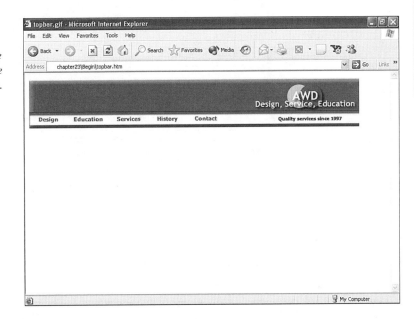

Now you will look at this file in Fireworks. To open an HTML file in Fireworks, do the following:

1. From the File menu choose Open.

2. Locate the Hour 23 directory and then the folder named Begin.

3. Choose the topbar.htm file and click Open. The file should open without a problem in Fireworks, as shown in Figure 23.6.

FIGURE 23.6

Fireworks opens the HTML file and displays the content in layers as slices and bitmap objects.

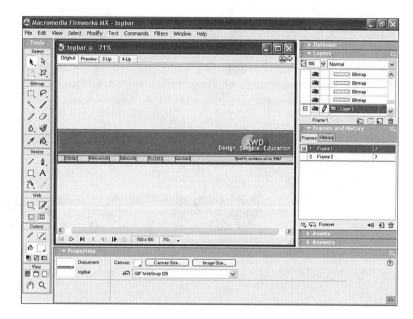

Even though you clicked to open an HTML file, Fireworks opens the file as a PNG for editing.

4. Check the Layers panel. Notice that slices are shown here with their original exported slice names. Other graphic elements are shown as bitmaps. Select a layer that contains a button and then look at the Behaviors panel, as shown in Figure 23.7. Even though the original file used a button symbol, the HTML imports complete with the behavior script intact for the Swap Image Restore.

FIGURE 23.7

The Behaviors panel shows the swap image attached to your buttons. This can be modified in Fireworks and reexported.

That is how easy Fireworks makes it to import HTML files. Once they're imported, you can make any changes, such as adding new buttons or interactions and then export the file back to its location with everything still working.

Summary

In this hour you looked at options for exporting Fireworks HTML, giving you maximum control over your exported code. You also had a quick look at importing HTML into Fireworks, which is a great new feature in Fireworks MX. This feature can be used to rebuild complete pages and update them without recourse to the original files. It is certainly something worth further investigation.

Workshop

The following questions will test your knowledge of HTML settings, export options, and other topics discussed in the hour. Answers are provided for your reference. The exercises will help you build experience with what you have learned in this hour.

Q&A

Q I exported my pop-up menu to GoLive, but it does not work. Why?

A Make sure that you select Generic HTML when exporting to GoLive a file that contains a pop-up menu script. Differences in the code mean that there will always be problems.

Q I get an error message when I try to import an HTML file. Is there a way around this?

A First make sure that the file that you're trying to open actually contains tables. Next see whether the file can be opened in an HTML editor. If so, you will need to check the code for any errors; Dreamweaver is a great tool for this.

Q Why do you recommend using a spacer GIF in exported tables?

A Using a transparent image that automatically resizes to the correct size will ensure that your tables display correctly when rebuilt in another editor or Web browser. Using spaces can cause problems in HTML Editors and older browser versions.

Quiz

1. The most common use of Fireworks HTML is in which program?

   a. Dreamweaver

   b. FrontPage

   c. GoLive

2. In imported HTML, where can you see the scripts for button behaviors?

   a. Layers panel

   b. Behaviors panel

   c. Not at all

3. How often does Fireworks allow you to set HTML options?

   a. Once

   b. As often as I like

   c. Never

Quiz Answers

1. a.—Dreamweaver is used most commonly for Fireworks HTML. This is mainly because Fireworks and Dreamweaver are still a very common partnership for designing, creating, and managing Web content.

2. b.—The Behaviors panel will show you mouseover effects, status bar text, and any other code that was attached to a button.

3. b.—You can change your HTML setup options as often as you want, using the Setup HTML dialog. There is no limit to the number of changes that you can make.

Exercises

The following exercises are purely optional but are designed to help you build on your existing skills and use them in a practical way.

1. Create a graphic in Fireworks that contains slices or other elements needing HTML when exported. Change the HTML settings and export the file two or three times. This will give you a better understanding of how the settings can affect the final outcome.

2. Practice importing HTML files that haven't been created in Fireworks. See how different elements are handled in a real environment. Then determine how you will need to either amend or re-create the elements that do not import or that import with errors.

3. Export files using HTML intended for different editors. Then check the code and see how many differences there are. Each available HTML editor that has its own quirks. Seeing the differences in the HTML styles is a good way to gain some understanding.

HOUR 24

Microsoft Office

Although not designed for creating Web applications and Web sites, with the obvious exception of FrontPage, Microsoft Office products are still used by the majority of computer users in their daily lives for office-related tasks. This means that many companies still have logos drawn in Word Art and charts created in Excel, not to mention complete Web sites that are designed and maintained within FrontPage.

This book is all about Fireworks and is not the place to discuss the merits of using Macromedia products for all Web applications. Nevertheless, despite the fact that the majority of users are integrating Fireworks with Dreamweaver, there are still many who use Fireworks as a graphics application with such Microsoft software as Word, Excel, or FrontPage.

For this reason Fireworks has the facility to let you use bitmaps from WordArt and Excel-created charts in Fireworks. Once there you can make some edits and additions before optimizing the images for use on the Web.

FrontPage is a different entity entirely. With this latest release of Fireworks, Macromedia has enhanced its integration with FrontPage, offering you the chance to create Fireworks images directly within a FrontPage or Web page.

In this hour you will

- Bring WordArt and Excel charts into Fireworks
- Export Fireworks HTML for use in FrontPage
- Work with Fireworks tables and behaviors in FrontPage
- Specify Fireworks as your external editor for images placed in FrontPage

Bringing WordArt and Excel Charts into Fireworks

Once in Fireworks you can redraw your WordArt or chart, using the techniques you have already learned in this book. In the case of charts, you can add additional information or even use them as part of a Web presentation or flowchart that you are creating within Fireworks.

Whatever your reason, the initial technique is the same—you paste the image into Fireworks and then make edits as needed, before using the optimization options offered by Fireworks to make the images as Web friendly as possible.

Bringing WordArt into Fireworks

Remember that even if you simply bring an image into Fireworks without wishing to change it, you can use the available optimization features to make this operation very worthwhile. As seen in Figure 24.1, text effects created in WordArt may not immediately look easily transferable into Fireworks, but it is not necessarily difficult. By this hour you have already looked at just about all of the techniques available in Fireworks, so re-creating anything from another application should not feel too daunting.

FIGURE 24.1

Even some simple WordArt may seem difficult to re-create, but in Fireworks you have the power.

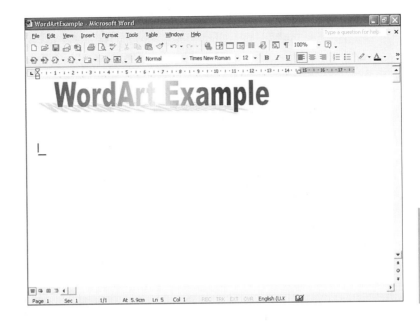

Task: Paste a WordArt Object into Fireworks

▲ TASK

To paste a WordArt object into Fireworks, follow these steps:

1. Start by opening the Word document or template that contains the WordArt you wish to use.

2. When the document is open, simply click the WordArt object once to select it. When selected, the object should have handles all around it. Click the Copy button on the Word toolbar, or use Edit, Copy, to place it in the Clipboard.

3. Launch Fireworks, if it is not already open, and create a new blank Canvas. Set the Canvas's color to white but do not worry too much about the size for now. Simply guess at an appropriate size for the copied WordArt, as you can adjust this later.

4. From the Edit menu in Fireworks, choose Paste to place the WordArt into your Fireworks document. You are now ready to make changes as required.

Although you have already learned that Fireworks can open many different image file types, a WordArt object is not an image in its own right. Therefore, you cannot open or import the file directly into Fireworks, which is why we use Paste for this.

24

After the image has been placed in Fireworks, you can adjust the Canvas size to suit your needs. From the Modify menu choose Canvas, Fit Canvas, to match the image size, or use the Canvas Size dialog to input values that you want. If the image does not display fully at 100%, use either the View menu or the Context menu to adjust the on-screen magnification. Choosing Fit Canvas will ensure that the pasted bitmap is fully visible.

Editing the Image

Because the image is in bitmap format, the options available to edit the image directly are limited. However, you can make edits and additions within these confines. In this section and the next, you will see two options for using Fireworks to enhance this image and make it more Web friendly.

Remember that when working with Web graphics, it is rare for them to need to be the same size as images prepared for printed matter.

Firstly, you can simply use Fireworks to edit the size of the image. From the Modify menu choose Canvas, Image Size, to open the Image Size dialog. In the dialog enter new dimensions for the image; make sure that you tick the Constrain Proportions check box to ensure that the aspect ratio is not compromised. Click OK when you are happy with the new dimensions. The newly sized image is displayed immediately, as shown in Figure 24.2.

FIGURE 24.2

Changing the size of a WordArt object within Fireworks is as simple as for any other bitmap object you work with.

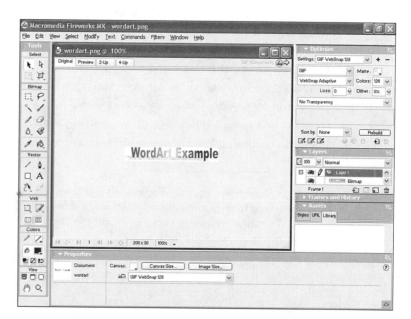

With the image resized, use the optimization techniques you learned in Hour 3, "Choosing Optimization Settings and Exporting Graphics," to export the image for use on your Web site. Using these techniques will ensure the best possible result for the file.

A WordArt object imported into Fireworks, edited, and optimized—what could be easier?

Re-creating the WordArt Text Object

The previous section showed exactly how simple it can be merely to edit and optimize an imported bitmap that happened to be a WordArt object. It is far more likely, however, that you will want to re-create the object so that it better fits your Web site. You may want to add a new or textured background or other image effects. Maybe you are simply attempting to be creative while retaining the basic image style.

As implied by its name, WordArt always involves the use of text, which lends itself particularly well to being re-created in Fireworks to the dimensions, quality, and colors you want for your Web site. Start by pasting the WordArt object into Fireworks as in the previous section, but instead of fitting the Canvas to the object, select Modify, Canvas, Canvas Size, and use the dialog to double the height of the Canvas. This will give you room to work with both the new object and the pasted one at the same time.

The steps required to re-create the example WordArt are as follows, although you will need to make amendments to suit the particular file you have:

1. Start by typing the text in the same font that was used in the Word document.
2. Edit the font size so that it matches the WordArt object as closely as possible, as shown in Figure 24.3.

If you intend the final result to be significantly smaller than the original, you can use an already resized copy of the WordArt to match your Fireworks image against. Creating your Fireworks object at the size you want is a better practice than waiting until later to resize.

FIGURE 24.3

Before attempting to add any effects, match the font and size as closely to the original as possible.

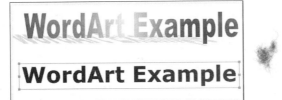

24

3. With the text selected, open the color picker and choose the Fill Options button at the bottom. See Figure 24.4.

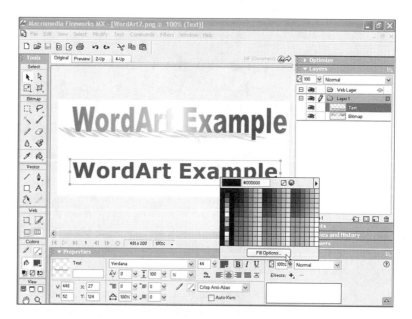

4. Choose the fill option that best suits your needs. Here a linear fill has been selected.

5. Click the Edit button for the fill, and add colors to match the required pattern. You should see something similar to Figure 24.5.

Remember that because the original is on-screen, you can use the eyedropper to match colors exactly in the two graphics.

6. Slide the color selections left and right until the newly created graphic matches the fill of the original.

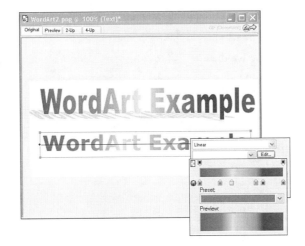

FIGURE 24.5

The Linear Fill dialog should look similar to this, as you add all the colors you need to match the original WordArt.

24

7. Save the file as a PNG before continuing. Then, with the text selected and the colors matching, choose Edit, Duplicate.

8. Modify the fill on the duplicated text so that it is a pale gray or silver, ready to act as a shadow. See Figure 24.6.

FIGURE 24.6

Select a pale gray or silver fill for the duplicated text object. This will be transformed to act as a shadow.

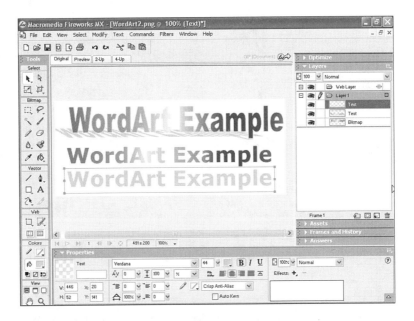

9. Select the linear gradient filled text and choose Text, Convert to Paths. Once it's converted, use the Context menu to modify the scale of the text to match the WordArt object.

10. Select the gray text and convert it to paths. With it still selected, choose Transform, Distort, from the Modify Menu.

11. Use each of the handles in turn to drag the gray object until it lies flat on the Canvas. You can continue to adjust the distortion, as shown in Figure 24.7, until it matches that of the original WordArt.

FIGURE 24.7

Use the handles to distort the gray text until it lies flat on the Canvas at an angle that matches the WordArt.

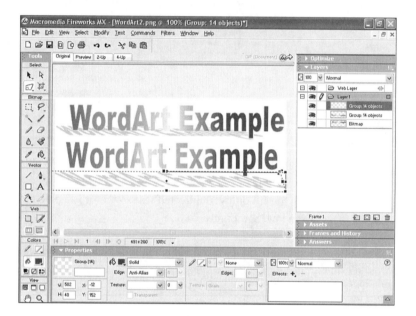

12. Finally, bring the colored text in front of the gray text and place as required. If necessary, adjust scales and skews until you are happy with the result. Figure 24.8 shows the re-created text below the pasted version.

FIGURE 24.8

The finished file should look the same as the original, ready for you to enhance or export to suit your Web site.

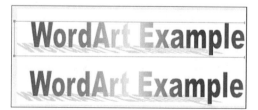

Now that you have seen the techniques available for re-creating the WordArt, you can resize the image, change the Canvas color to match your Web site without any strange outlines around the text, and make every other kind of edit that Fireworks offers for vector images over bitmaps.

Working with Excel Charts in Fireworks

This heading may suggest a strange combination. Indeed, in most cases it is best to use dynamic Web site technology to pull an Excel chart directly into your Web page so that its information is linked and automatically updated.

Nevertheless, if you do want to work with Excel in Fireworks, the most important thing to note is that to copy the chart from Excel into Fireworks successfully, you must have the chart placed in its own worksheet to start with. Although you can copy a chart that is part of a worksheet, you will find that the Paste option is not available within Fireworks.

Task: Bring an Excel Chart into Fireworks

▲ **TASK**

Open the Excel file that has the chart you wish to use. If the chart does not exist in its own page, you will need to move it. The process in Excel XP is as follows:

24

1. Select the chart. From the Context menu that opens, choose Location.

2. In the Chart Location dialog, choose the As new sheet radio button, as shown in Figure 24.9. The chart will be relocated to its own worksheet.

FIGURE 24.9

To copy your chart from Excel into Fireworks successfully, you should first place it in a new worksheet.

3. Select the chart, and then copy and paste it into Fireworks. Most likely you will be prompted to resample the image. When working with charts, it may be best to keep the original resolution, although this is a decision that you can base purely on your own needs.

4. When the chart is in Fireworks, set the Canvas size and on-screen magnification so that you can accurately work with it.

5. With the chart now in Fireworks, you can enhance it—adding pointers to important information or a further breakdown of the information—or merely use it as a template to create a more Web-friendly version. Because the chart is imported as a bitmap, the techniques and tools available are the same as those described in the previous section for working with WordArt.

Exporting Fireworks HTML for Use in FrontPage

By this time you are undoubtedly aware of the term *Roundtrip HTML*, referring to the integration facility within Fireworks that allows you to launch Fireworks for image editing from within both Dreamweaver and FrontPage. The Dreamweaver integration is well documented in many places; however, the move to FrontPage integration has taken longer.

Fireworks MX has improved this area quite dramatically, and in this section you will look at some of these options, starting with using Fireworks HTML in FrontPage. There are multiple ways of using Fireworks HTML in your FrontPage documents, and everyone has his or her favorite. You will look at the main techniques.

With any of the following options, the single most important thing to remember is that you must set FrontPage as the HTML type in the HTML setup dialog.

Copying Fireworks HTML to the Clipboard

The heading names what is far and away the fastest way to get your Fireworks HTML into FrontPage: You simply paste the generated code into the FrontPage document where you want it—nice, quick, and easy. However, there are certain restrictions in using this method when working with FrontPage. These restrictions will not always be a problem, but they are certainly worth mentioning. If you use Fireworks pop-up menus, your hyperlinks or other coded paths will point to a hard drive location, and you must save images into the same location as the HTML page.

Task: Copy Fireworks HTML and Paste into FrontPage

To copy and paste the Fireworks HTML, simply follow this procedure:

1. With your image file ready to export, choose Copy HTML Code from the Edit menu.

2. In the Copy HTML Code dialog, choose FrontPage from the HTML style drop-down menu, as shown in Figure 24.10.

3. Type in an appropriate base name for any slices created by the export. This helps keep them identified and separate from other image files.

FIGURE 24.10

Selecting FrontPage HTML from the Copy HTML Code dialog will ensure that the correct style of HTML is generated.

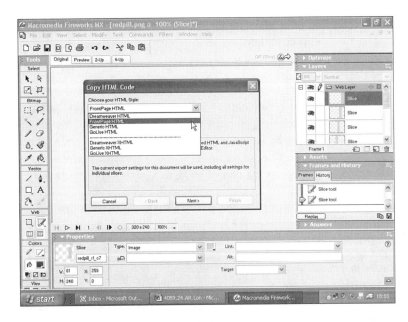

4. Click the HTML Setup button and choose FrontPage from the HTML style drop-down menu. Set any other options for your export as you would with other documents.

5. Choose a folder for the HTML. This needs to be the same folder that the HTML file exists in, or will exist in, if you are going to paste the code into a new page. Click Open to select the folder, as shown in Figure 24.11.

FIGURE 24.11

First choose a location for the HTML. You must be sure this is where a page already exists or where you intend to create a new page to hold the pasted code.

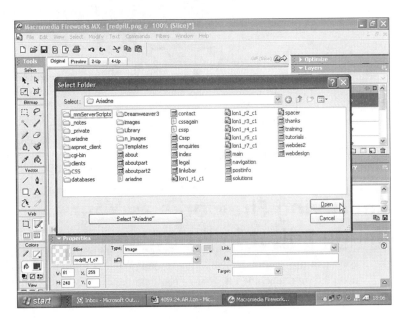

6. Choose a folder for the exported images. This must be the same folder that you specified earlier.

7. Click Finish to export the images to the specified location and copy the HTML to the Clipboard.

8. Once in FrontPage you can paste the HTML directly into the page in Code view. Alternatively, you can work in Normal view and choose Insert, Web Component, followed by Advanced Controls from the Component Type list, and then HTML from the Choose a Control list. Click Finish, and then in the HTML Markup dialog, paste the copied code, as shown in Figure 24.12.

FIGURE 24.12

Pasting the code directly into the HTML Markup dialog will ensure that the code remains unchanged by FrontPage and that you do not have to work in HTML view.

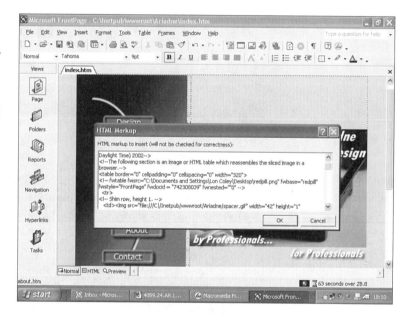

If you paste into the HTML Markup dialog, you will see the FrontPage Bot icon until you preview the page. Pasting the code directly into HTML view will show the image immediately.

Specifying Fireworks as Your Image Editor in FrontPage

Note that this section is applicable only to Windows users. When Fireworks MX is installed on a machine on which FrontPage is also installed, you are offered the chance to register FrontPage as an image editor. In most circumstances people simply say Yes to this, and the Edit and Launch button appears on the FrontPage toolbar.

Task: Designate Fireworks as Your Image Editor in FrontPage

▼ TASK

If you have recently installed FrontPage or chose No to the question at the point of installation, the following should help:

1. Open Microsoft FrontPage but do not open any files.
2. From the Tools menu choose Add-Ins. The COM Add-Ins dialog, shown in Figure 24.13, will open.

FIGURE 24.13

The COM Add-Ins dialog allows you to add the Fireworks Launch and Edit button to FrontPage.

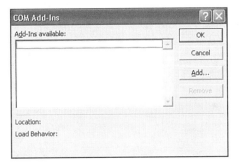

24

3. Click the Add button and then browse to your Fireworks MX directory. On a standard installation this will be `C:\Program Files\Macromedia\Fireworks MX`.
4. Select the `FP_Launch_FW.dll` file listed and click OK.
5. Click OK in the COM Add-Ins dialog.
6. Close and reopen Microsoft FrontPage. Although this is not necessary, it ensures that the button appears.

Make sure the standard toolbar is visible by choosing Toolbars from the View menu and selecting Standard. The Launch and Edit button is now visible and usable, as shown in Figure 24.14. You can now simply select any image in your FrontPage file, and then click the Launch and Edit button to open the image in Fireworks for editing.

The Fireworks Launch
and Edit button

FIGURE 24.14

Once installed, the Fireworks button appears on the standard FrontPage toolbar.

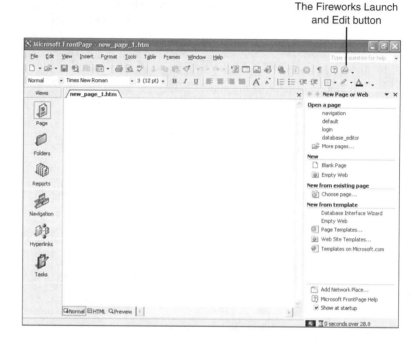

Fireworks Behaviors and FrontPage

Although support for Fireworks and FrontPage is still quite new, there is one area that seems to cause the most problems—using Fireworks behaviors in FrontPage. This section aims to address this problem by taking you through the process of exporting a Fireworks pop-up menu complete with behaviors and getting it to work in FrontPage.

Whenever you export a Fireworks PNG File into FrontPage, three things should be generated: an HTML file, a .js file, and the images created by the slicing. This can be any number, depending on your original image file.

You should export the Fireworks HTML to the same folder as the one where the HTML file exists or will exist in your FrontPage site. This is because the pop-up menus access an external JavaScript file that is linked to the HTML via a document relative path. If your Fireworks HTML was exported to any directory other than the location of the target FrontPage HTML, your pop-up menus will not work.

It is a good idea, before you do anything at all in FrontPage, to open the Fireworks-generated HTML directly into a browser. This will ensure that the file opens and performs correctly. Although not an essential step, it is a guaranteed way of identifying that any problems found after export to FrontPage are directly related to FrontPage and not caused by any kind of export error.

Start by opening the Fireworks HTML page in FrontPage, and then click the Preview tab to see whether everything works there. Click the HTML tab and notice the structure of the document. As you probably know by now, HTML documents have tags that are enclosed within < > characters. Assuming that your Fireworks file contains slices, there are two specific tags that you should locate in the file. These are the <JavaScript> and <Table> tags.

If you didn't use slices in Fireworks, it is quite possible that you will be dealing with another type of tag. However, because pop-up menus are generated by mouseEvents attached to buttons and slices, this is very unlikely.

Knowing what each tag is and what it does is pretty essential to getting things to work, so if you don't understand these, there are plenty of resources on the Web, such as http://www.htmlhelp.com, where you can learn what each tag is, what it means, and how it's to be used. Alternatively, if you have Dreamweaver, then you can use the built-in reference panel as a guide to tag information and syntax.

Fireworks exports FrontPage HTML with the JavaScript in the <body> tag. This is because FrontPage does not allow inserted code to write to the <head>, which is where JavaScript is normally to be found. To make sure that your pop-up menu works correctly, follow these steps:

1. Locate the code line that reads

   ```
   <script language="JavaScript1.2" src="mm_menu.js"></script>
   ```

   Select this single line of code, copy it, and then paste it into the target HTML file just after any Meta tags you have. If no Meta tags exist, just paste it between the <head> and </head> tags.

2. Find the code in the HTML that begins with <script language = javascript> and ends with the </script> tag. This should be found somewhere within the <head> and </head> tags in the Fireworks HTML. You may have more than one <script> ... </script> set of tags. When pop-up menus are involved, this is always the case.

   The first section has the <script language = javascript> tag, followed by a series of JavaScript functions and the </script> tag. These functions control all the JavaScript-enabled interactivity on your pages. Copy that code, including the `<script language = JavaScript>` tag, through to the `</script>` tag, and paste this code directly before the `</head>` tag in the FrontPage document's HTML tab.

3. The call to the external JavaScript file is also vital. It's usually this path that is incorrectly encoded, which causes files to work incorrectly. It looks like this:

```
<script language="JavaScript1.2">mmLoadMenus();</script>
```

This should appear just after the `<body>` tag in the Fireworks/FrontPage HTML; copy that line and paste it just after the `<body>` tag in the target HTML file.

4. Now you should be able to select your `<table>` through `</table>` content tags in the `<body>` and copy that code. Paste it in your FrontPage HTML after the call to the `mmLoadMenus` function shown in the previous step.

After you've successfully copied your code and pasted it into FrontPage, you should notice a Fireworks icon at the top left of the document window. Clicking this allows you to edit the Fireworks content in Fireworks and return it directly to FrontPage. Save your file; then preview it in a browser.

Place a Fireworks-Generated Image in FrontPage

For this task you will assume that you want to have a Fireworks-generated image in a FrontPage file. By following the steps shown here, you will be able to create the image in Fireworks and switch straight back to FrontPage. After it has been created, you will look at opening and editing it.

In the previous section you saw how to work with Fireworks HTML within FrontPage by taking the HTML and placing it in a FrontPage file. In this section you will look more closely at using Roundtrip HTML with Fireworks and FrontPage. The Macromedia description of this technique is "launch-and-edit-integration," which sums things up pretty well.

When using Launch and Edit, you can create and export only a single image with no slices or behaviors. After the file is created and inserted into FrontPage, you can edit it back in Fireworks to add interactive elements and slices.

Task: Use Launch and Edit to Create an Image

▲ TASK

Start by opening in FrontPage the file that you would like to contain the Fireworks image, if it is not already open. If working with an open file, make sure that it is saved before you start.

1. On the FrontPage toolbar click the Launch and Edit Selected Graphic in Fireworks button.

2. In the resulting message box, click Yes to indicate that you want to create a new image file, as shown in Figure 24.15.

FIGURE 24.15

Launch and Edit will prompt you to create a new graphic and launch Fireworks automatically.

24

3. Fireworks launches automatically for you to create a new document. Go ahead and create a new blank document ready to work with. The dimensions and Canvas color can be specified to suit your needs.

4. After creating your new image in Fireworks, save your PNG file for future editing. Then choose File, Export, to save the file into your FrontPage Web folder.

5. Back in FrontPage place the insertion point where you want your new image to appear. Then choose Insert, Picture, From File, from the File menu or click the Insert Picture From File button on the toolbar, as shown in Figure 24.16.

FIGURE 24.16

The Insert Picture From File button opens a simple dialog to allow you to select the picture you want to appear on your Web page.

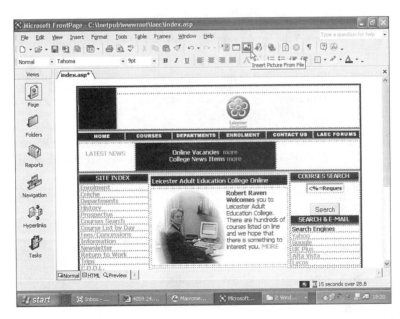

6. Locate the image file you just created and click Insert. The image is placed in your file, as shown in Figure 24.17.

FIGURE 24.17

Your newly created image is easily slotted into any FrontPage file.

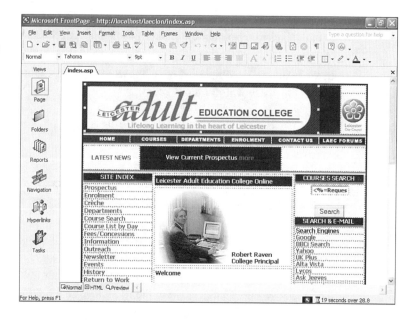

Task: Use Launch and Edit to Edit Your File

◄ TASK

Start by saving the FrontPage file containing the newly created image. Then follow the steps shown here to edit your image back in Fireworks:

1. Select the image on the screen so that its selection handles are visible.

2. Click the Launch and Edit Selected Graphic in Fireworks button. This will launch Fireworks if it is not already open.

3. Edit the image in Fireworks, adding any interactions, slices, or other features that you want on the image.

4. Click the Done button when you have finished working on the file.

5. If prompted, select the PNG file you saved when you created the image. This acts as the source file for the exported image.

6. The image is exported using the current settings, so you should make sure that the HTML setup is set to FrontPage if your image contains slices.

7. If you chose to work on a source file, this is also saved for any future editing that is required.

Switch back to FrontPage; your edited image should be immediately visible. If it's not, switch to the Folders view in FrontPage and click the Refresh button to update the page.

Summary

In this hour you have learned how to work with WordArt and Excel charts in Fireworks. Taking advantage of the Fireworks optimization techniques will make these exported images far more size and file type friendly in their intended Web or screen destination. Simply having them in Fireworks enables you to make changes and additions as required without taking up the challenge to re-create the images from scratch.

With many people still using FrontPage for their Web site design and development, the ability to switch to and from Fireworks for image creation and manipulation is a must-have skill. This hour took you through the options for using Fireworks and FrontPage together.

Workshop

Use this section to revisit the many topics covered in this hour. Realizing that you can even use files that are not actually graphic files can make life a lot easier. Exporting your HTML to FrontPage and getting it to work correctly can be time consuming if you do not follow the steps in this hour, so read the quiz and questions to make sure that you understand the techniques. Finally, use the optional exercises to practice some of the new techniques you have learned.

Q&A

Q Why do my pop-ups not work in FrontPage?

A Make sure that all the files are in the correct location. Exporting from Fireworks can cause problems if the images are not in the same location as the HTML file.

Q Why can't I just change the colors of my WordArt in Fireworks?

A To get your WordArt into Fireworks, you have to paste it in. The pasting action will import your WordArt as a bitmap image, meaning that you have no control over the editability of the file.

Q I said No to FrontPage support when I installed Fireworks. What can I do?

A You can add the required .dll file by using the instructions in this hour. If that fails, though, you can reinstall Fireworks and this time say Yes when prompted.

Quiz

1. You can use the Launch and Edit button in Fireworks to

   a. create a sliced image.

   b. create a simple image.

   c. create a pop-up menu.

2. WordArt is in what image format?

    a. GIF

    b. JPG

    c. Neither

3. What language is used for the scripts in pop-up menus?

    a. Visual Basic

    b. JavaScript

    c. HTML

Quiz Answers

1. b.—You can only create a simple image without slices or behaviors. After the image is created and inserted into FrontPage, you can use the same button to edit the image and add complex features.

2. c.—WordArt is not an image in its own right; it is merely an image creation within a Microsoft Office document.

3. b.—Fireworks generates JavaScript to control the functions and performance of pop-up menus. For pop-up menus to work correctly in FrontPage, the call to the JavaScript must be in the right place.

Exercises

1. Make a new WordArt object creating text that curves and has a gradient type fill. In the hour you looked only at straight text. Once you have the WordArt object, try re-creating it. You will need to remember how to attach text to a path, which was covered in earlier hours, as well as techniques from this hour.

2. Use the Launch and Edit technique to create a simple image in Fireworks, then Place it into FrontPage. Then move the image backward and forward between the two applications, adding slices and links, to see how well the system works.

3. In this hour you looked at using Excel charts as static images in Fireworks. Why not take the plunge and do some serious learning about data-driven Web sites and graphics in order to bring your chart or graph data up to date? Rather than having to keep re-creating and editing graphs and charts, you will need to create them only once.

GLOSSARY

A

action   The response when a Web page event takes place.

AI file   Adobe Illustrator file.

alt text   Short for alternative text, an attribute designed to provide an alternative source of information about elements. Alt text was originally used just for images in cases where the image was not visible. Today other elements also have alt text to support browsers that cannot display those elements.

animated GIF   Animation created by putting a number of images, to be displayed in sequence, into a single GIF file.

animated graphics   Moving images of any type. Often Flash graphics and animated GIFs are image types seen on the Web.

Answers panel   An updatable link to a central Macromedia Web location where you can find tutorials, TechNotes, and the most up-to-date information about Fireworks.

anti-aliasing   A method for smoothing edges in an image.

aspect ratio   The ratio of height to width. Like on a television or movie screen, an object retains the same shape, no matter its size.

attribute   An aspect of an element that defines how it differs from the basic definition of that element class. The size attribute, for instance, specifies how a font element varies from the default size. The color attribute shows the browser how to modify the color from the default color. In the HTML source code, attributes are placed in the start tag of an element.

B

background image   An image that fills the entire Web page by tiling (repeating copies of the same image).

batch processing   Processing a group of files automatically. In Fireworks this is a feature that lets you run automated find and replace searches or alter export settings for several files at once.

Behaviors panel   A panel used to set or modify JavaScript behaviors.

beveled edges   A Fireworks effect that forms a sort of frame for an object by creating the appearance of a slanting edge around it.

bitmapped graphics   Graphics in which each pixel in the image is individually editable. The combination of color and position of all the pixels in the image creates the picture. Bitmapped graphics become blocky when they are enlarged.

Blur   A Fireworks effect that makes an object look blurry or out of focus.

BMP file   Windows Bitmap file.

Brightness   A Fireworks effect that decreases the amount of black in an image.

Button Editor   In Fireworks the editor used to create rollover buttons.

button state   For rollover buttons a condition that causes the appearance of the button image to change. The Up state is the normal state of the button when nothing is being done with it. Over is the button's appearance when a mouse pointer is on it. Down is the state of a button that has been pressed. Over While Down determines the button's appearance when a mouse pointer passes over it while it is in a Down condition.

C

Canvas   In Fireworks the area in which you work on images. Unlike many image-editing programs, Fireworks does not start up with a default Canvas in place. You first need to create a Canvas as a new document.

CDR file   CorelDRAW file.

Color Mixer panel   In Fireworks the panel used to set the type of color model on which your images are based.

comments   In programming, items that are not run as code. Comments are generally used to provide information about the code itself, either for other programmers who will view the code or as a reminder to the original programmer. HTML comments are ignored by Web browsers.

Contrast   A Fireworks effect that increases the difference between shades in an image.

D

dithering   The process of putting different-colored pixels next to one another to fool the eye into seeing a third color. Dithering is used to mix available colors in an attempt to come as close as possible to a color that the system does not support.

Document window   The window that shows the Canvas, which contains the image.

Down state   A button state that occurs when the user clicks the button with the mouse.

DWT file   In Dreamweaver a template file.

E

editable region   In a Dreamweaver template the areas on the page that are not locked and can be changed. Editable regions are highlighted when you're creating or editing a template. When you're working on a Web page based on a template, the editable regions are the only parts not highlighted.

Effects menu   In Fireworks the menu used to add special effects—such as shadows, glows, and bevels—to images.

embossing   A Fireworks effect that appears to raise or lower the image's contents.

event   Something that takes place within a Web page. The first event, called the onLoad event, takes place when a page loads into a Web browser. Some events are triggered by the user, such as when the user clicks various objects (onClick events) or moves the mouse pointer over an object (the onMouseOver event).

export   To prepare a file or object from a Fireworks file for use on the Internet.

Export Wizard   A wizard that helps you export files. The Export Wizard analyzes your needs, creates optimized versions, and lets you make changes to further optimize the graphic for its target format.

Eye Candy   A group of plug-ins created by Alien Skin Software (see Web site at http://www.alienskin.com/). The LE version comes with Fireworks and provides three effects: Bevel Boss, Marble, and Motion Trail.

eyedropper   A mouse pointer used to pick up color from items in existing images or paths.

F

feathering   A method for softening edges in an image.

FH file   FreeHand file.

fill   The area within a path object. In Fireworks you can set various fill characteristics through the Fill panel.

FLA file   A native Flash file.

font face   The actual design of a font, as opposed to its style (such as bold or italic) and size. The three font faces that are commonly used on the World Wide Web are Helvetica, Times, and Courier.

font sizes   In HTML, sizes from 1 through 7. By convention, these are often thought of as corresponding to point sizes: 1 = 8 points, 2 = 10 points, 3 = 12 points, 4 = 14 points, 5 = 18 points, 6 = 24 points, 7 = 36 points.

font style   The style applied to the font, such as bold, italic, or strikethrough.

fps   Frames per second. In Dreamweaver the fps is the nominal rate of playback in frames per second. The actual rate of playback depends on the computer used.

frame-by-frame animation   Animation that uses a series of keyframes with no tweening, which creates a flipbook-like animation.

frame rate   The rate, stated in frames per second (fps), at which each frame in an animation is played back for the user.

G

GIF file   Graphics Interchange Format file, a standard graphics file format that is limited to a maximum of 256 colors. GIF is a lossless (non-lossy) compression format. GIFs can contain multiple images that can be displayed sequentially, like the frames in a movie. GIFs also support the use of transparency, which is the ability to let the Web page show through a portion of the image.

Glow   A Fireworks effect that makes an object look as though it were glowing. Glows are often described as halos.

H

History panel   The panel used to track actions and undo and redo actions.

hotspot   A portion of an image that leads to a particular link. In Dreamweaver and Fireworks, hotspots are used for multiple links in image maps.

HSL system A color-value system that uses hue, saturation, and luminance values.

HTML Hypertext Markup Language, the language used for constructing Web pages.

hue In the HSL system, this corresponds to the basic divisions of the rainbow (red, orange, yellow, green, blue, indigo, and violet). The hue value increases from left to right from 0 to 239, and at the far right side, the range returns to red. The degree of a particular base color—red, green, or blue—in a given hue changes as the hue's value increases.

I

image map An image that has multiple links. Each of the multiple links in an image map is referred to as a hotspot.

image slicing In Fireworks a technique for breaking a single image down into multiple files, each of which loads separately into a final composite table on a Web page. With image slicing, you can chop up a single graphic and export the pieces in different file formats as appropriate. Individual slices can also be exported as single files.

import To bring a file or object into a Fireworks document.

Index.html Typically, the name of the root page that is the starting point for visitors to your site.

Info panel The panel that displays information about the selected object's size and location and the actions of the mouse pointer.

instance The copy of a symbol that is created when that symbol is inserted into a document. When the original symbol is altered, each instance automatically reflects the changes. You can also release instances so that the copy becomes an independent object and will no longer be updated when the symbol is altered.

interlacing A technique that causes GIF files so that they begin their display as low-quality images, with the quality gradually improving as the download grows closer to completion. This effect is achieved by gradually filling in alternating bands of pixels.

J

JavaScript behavior A JavaScript program built into Fireworks. The combination of a Web page event and an action makes a behavior.

JPEG file Joint Photographic Experts Group file, a standard graphics file format that supports millions of colors. JPEG (or JPG) is known as a lossy compression format because the image suffers some degree of loss when you export the file.

JS file JavaScript file.

JSF file In Fireworks a batch process script file.

K

kerning   Spacing between characters.

keyframe   In Flash a point at which you specify the location of a layer. The other frames in between the keyframes are interpolated.

Knock Out   An effect that renders the object itself invisible, leaving only the shadow.

L

layer   A design element that allows you to position elements on top of each other and add animation.

Layers panel   The panel used to set levels on which you work with objects. Each different level, or layer, is like a transparency. You can stack several of them on top of each other. Objects drawn on one layer fall beneath or above objects drawn on other layers, depending on the relationship of the layers to each other.

LBI file   In Dreamweaver a library item file.

library item   An element that is shared among several different Web pages. The original library item is stored in a separate file. Any changes made to that file can be propagated to every Web page that contains that library item. A copy of the HTML code in the library item is placed on any Web page in which that item is inserted. Library items are suitable for smaller portions of Web pages that are identical.

Library panel   In Fireworks the panel used to store entire objects, such as buttons, to be easily reused later. The original object is known as a *symbol*.

low-res version   A version of an image that loads before the full-resolution version of the image. The low-res version is created in an image editor. It can be a grayscale version, with the smallest file size that still remotely represents the image, or it can be a color version that uses fewer colors than the original.

luminance   In the HSL system the brightness or amount of white in a color. The luminance value ranges from 0 to 240. A 0 value is the same as the color black, a value of 120 is a pure color of the original hue, and a value of 240 is the same as the color white.

M

Mailto URL   A URL for a link that triggers the user's e-mail program.

main toolbar   The toolbar that contains buttons for common tasks (such as opening files, saving files, copying, pasting, and printing) and for accessing Fireworks panels.

Modify toolbar   The toolbar that contains buttons for grouping, placing, and orienting objects within the Document window.

monospace font   A fixed-width font in which the amount of horizontal space taken up by every character is always the same. Courier is a monospace font.

Motion Trail   An Eye Candy effect that adds speed lines to the edge of an object.

N

navigation bar   A set of graphical buttons. Each button has a series of images assigned to it, and the image that is shown depends on the user's actions. A navigation bar (nav bar) automatically has its own set of JavaScript behaviors, including rollover effects and Go to URL commands. Usually, a navigation bar provides a graphical set of links that lead to other pages in the same Web site, but this is not a requirement. You can have your nav bar buttons link to any file anywhere on the Web.

nonbreaking space   A space that overrides the HTML rule that Web browsers ignore any spaces except those between words and collapse any extra spaces down to a single space. When you use a nonbreaking space, the white space will appear as it did when it was entered in the HTML source code.

O

Onion Skinning tools   Tools that enable you to edit a single keyframe while viewing (dimly) other frames before or after the current frame.

Optimize panel   The panel for setting and changing values for your images prior to saving or exporting, such as the file format, number of colors available, and transparency. The options on the Optimize panel depend on the type of file format you choose and what sort of color depth you set.

Over state   A button state that occurs when the user passes the mouse over a button.

P

path   In vector graphics the lines or curves that connect the points in a shape. An open path is a line, an arc, or a similar figure that has two ends that do not connect with one another. A closed path is an object whose space is fully bounded by a line, such as a rectangle, any other polygon, or a circle.

plug-in   A program that extends the functionality of an application into the browser. Common plug-ins are QuickTime, RealPlayer, Shockwave, and Acrobat. Photoshop-compatible filters are also often referred to as plug-ins.

PNG file   A Portable Network Graphics file, Fireworks' native file format. PNG is a lossless compression format. Like the JPEG format, it can handle millions of colors, but its file size is typically much larger than that of JPEG. PNG supports transparency better than GIF, but it doesn't support animation.

point On the Canvas an exact location that can be described by X and Y coordinates. A vector graphic file describes a series of points to be connected.

point size A measurement that equals 1/72 inch. For example, a 12-point font is 12/72, or 1/6, inch high, and an 18-point font is 1/4 inch high.

progressive display A technique used with JPEG files so that they begin their display as low-resolution images, with the quality gradually improving as the download grows closer to completion.

Property Inspector The panel that shows the current settings for the selected element's attributes (properties) and allows you to make changes to those settings.

proportional font A variable-width font in which the horizontal space given the characters varies.

PSD file A Photoshop file.

R

raster graphic An image file format that contains the color information for each pixel. Raster graphics' file sizes are relatively large.

regular expression An advanced find-and-replace operation that uses a variety of unique codes. Regular expressions are useful for advanced searches, such as finding every sentence that starts with a particular word or every word that contains several repeated characters.

relative URL A type of Web shorthand that refers to another file within the same Web site. A relative URL contains just the latter portion of the address. Also called a *partial URL*.

RGB color system A color-value system that uses red, green, and blue values.

rollover An event in which an image changes when a mouse pointer is placed over it or when it is clicked. Fireworks provides JavaScript behaviors associated with rollovers.

S

Saturation In the HSL system, a setting that corresponds to the purity of the color. Saturation decreases from top to bottom. The values range from 0 to 240, with 240 as the pure color. Saturation is reduced by mixing complementary colors (those that are opposites of one another), and the combination of complementary colors always tends toward gray.

shadows Effects that make objects look as though they have shadows, creating a three-dimensional appearance. In Fireworks the Drop Shadow setting applies a darkened effect, generally to the side and below an object (you can change the direction), making the object look raised. Inner Shadow, with darkness coming within the bounds of object, makes the object look recessed or hollow.

Sharpen   A Fireworks effect that makes an object look clearer.

storyboarding   Planning the action of an animation and breaking it down into its component parts. A storyboard should include all the elements that need to be in the animation and in the sequence necessary to achieve the desired effect.

stroke   The line formed when drawing a path object. In Fireworks you can set various stroke characteristics through the Stroke panel.

Styles panel   The panel used to apply predefined styles to existing objects. This gives you a way to create a standardized graphical appearance for your sites.

Swatches panel   The panel that shows the selection of colors that are currently available. The Swatches panel displays the palette of possible colors, not just the ones that are actually in use.

SWF file   An exported (Shockwave) Flash file.

symbol   An object stored for later use. A symbol can be exported for use in documents other than the one in which it was created. Symbols in different places can be changed simultaneously by altering the original base object.

T

template   In Dreamweaver a predesigned Web page where you essentially just fill in the blanks. Templates are useful when you need to create several virtually identical Web pages.

Text Editor   The Fireworks editor used to put text on the Canvas and edit that text.

TGA file   A Targa file.

thumbnail   An image link to a large image file. The thumbnail image is a smaller version of the large image.

TIF/TIFF file   Tagged Image File Format file.

tiling   A technique by which an image is repeated until it fills an entire row across the screen, a process that continues across the subsequent rows until the entire page is filled with copies of the image. Web page background images are created by tiling.

Tools panel   A set of tools for working with images.

tracing image   In Dreamweaver an image that is used as a mockup for a Web page. You can load the tracing image and make the Web page on top of it. A tracing image is similar to a background image except that it will not be visible on the actual Web page and it doesn't tile.

transparency   An effect that allows the Web page to show through a portion of an image.

tweening   An animation technique that automatically creates intermediate images between two or more original images.

U–Z

Up state   Normally, a button's default state, which occurs when the user has not clicked or passed over the button with the mouse.

vector graphic   A graphic in which the position of pixels depends on a series of mathematical calculations to determine its attributes, such as the shape and length of a line. The main advantages of vector graphics are that they scale smoothly and are usually smaller in file size than bitmap graphics.

W3C   The World Wide Web Consortium (`http://www.w3.org/`), which promulgates the HTML standard.

Websafe color palette   A palette that contains the colors that will appear the same regardless of the particular operating system platform and the number of colors the system is capable of displaying.

XML   Extensible Markup Language.

INDEX